For Donna,

With best
wishes for our
cooperation

2-19-14

Confronting Urban Legacy

Confronting Urban Legacy

Rediscovering Hartford and New England's Forgotten Cities

Edited by Xiangming Chen and
Nick Bacon

LEXINGTON BOOKS
Lanham • Boulder • New York • Toronto • Plymouth, UK

Published by Lexington Books
A wholly owned subsidiary of Rowman & Littlefield
4501 Forbes Boulevard, Suite 200, Lanham, Maryland 20706
www.rowman.com

10 Thornbury Road, Plymouth PL6 7PP, United Kingdom

British Library Cataloguing in Publication Information Available

Library of Congress Cataloging-in-Publication Data
Confronting urban legacy : rediscovering Hartford and New England's forgotten cities / edited by Xiangming Chen and Nick Bacon.
    pages cm
  Includes bibliographical references and index.
  ISBN 978-0-7391-4942-3 (cloth : alk. paper) — ISBN 978-0-7391-4944-7 (electronic)
  1. Urbanization—New England. 2. Urban policy—New England. 3. Regional planning—New England. 4. Hartford (Conn.) —Economic conditions—21st century. 5. New England—Economic conditions—21st century. I. Chen, Xiangming, 1955- II. Bacon, Nick, 1988-
  HT123.5.N45C66 2013
  307.760974—dc23
                                                                            2013020703

Printed in the United States of America

Contents

Illustrations

MAPS

FIGURES

TABLES

Acknowledgments

This volume is the second of the first pair of books developed and sponsored by the Center for Urban and Global Studies (CUGS) at Trinity College in Hartford, Connecticut. The book germinated from the research seminar titled "The Transformation of Hartford Through the Early 21st Century: Local, Regional, and Global Perspectives," sponsored by CUGS from 2008 to 2010. The purpose of this seminar was to widen and deepen Trinity's engagement with and contribution to its home city of Hartford by undertaking a comprehensive and multiscaled study of its transformation from a once strong manufacturing-insurance center to an economically challenged and ethnically diverse postindustrial city today, as well as of other dimensions of this fundamental transformation. This seminar involved a broad group of Trinity and non-Trinity faculty along with invited policy analysts and community representatives from Hartford, as well as interested Trinity students. The first stage (2008–2009) featured a series of open fora, extended discussions, and background research on a range of critical issues facing Hartford, while the second stage (2009–2012) was devoted to the research for and production of this book. In the process, we have brought in scholarly contributions on Springfield and Lawrence, Massachusetts, and Portland, Maine that add a comparative and New England regional flavor and insight to the book.

First of all, we would like to express deep gratitude to the Andrew Mellon Foundation for a major grant and the generous financial support from donors to the Trinity College Mellon Challenge for Urban and Global Studies that endowed CUGS and have supported its vibrant growth and accomplishments, as exemplified by the publication of this book. Second, we owe thanks to a variety of people at Trinity College including Paul E. Raether, Chairman of the Board of Trustees, President James F. Jones, Jr., former Dean of Faculty Rena Fraden, many faculty colleagues and friends, dedicated staff working at CUGS, and a growing number of students who have been contributors to CUGS as research assistants and in other capacities.

Two Trinity students from the Class of 2010, Nick Bacon and Ezra Moser, became a co-editor and critical contributor to the book, respectively. Nick Bacon was fully involved in this project as a Research Associate at CUGS since 2010. While starting out to create GIS maps, Nick became a co-author of one chapter, then a single author of another, and finally the co-editor of the book, helping edit and improve all the chapters. The book would not be possible without his passion for urban studies and his tremendous local knowledge of the Hartford region, especially his hometown of East Hartford. We are glad that the book has helped launch Nick onto his graduate career at City University of New York and become a budding urban scholar. As the first student doing a self-designed Urban Studies major after the launch of CUGS, Ezra Moser completed an excellent senior thesis with Professor Davarian Baldwin in American Studies that he has turned into a chapter for the book. Other Trinity students and recent graduates Tomas de'Medici '11, Henry Fitts '12, Brooke Grasberger '12, Michael Magdelinskas '12, Nicky Thai '15, Gaurav Toor '14, and Yuwei Xie '11 lent their hands in editing the various drafts of some chapters. Aalok Pandey '12 in particular played an important role in the final stages of putting the book together. We would like to acknowledge Jack Hale (Trinity Class of '71) for his assistance in reading three chapters; David Corrigan and Hyacinth Yennie for sharing their views on the Frog Hollow and Maple Ave Neighborhood Revitalization Zones (NRZs), respectively; Nancy Rossi for proofreading a couple of the chapters; and Teresita Romero for her skilled indexing of the book. We also thank Richard Frieder and Brenda Miller of the Hartford Public Library and Kate Steinway, Nancy Finlay, and Sierra Dixon of the Connecticut Historical Society for giving us the permission to include a number of precious historical photos of Hartford throughout the book. Thanks also go to Michael Sisson and Jana Hodges-Kluck, the former and current editor at Lexington Books, and Jana's assistant Jay Song, for their long-standing trust and unwavering support. Comments and suggestions from anonymous reviewers have helped improve the book.

We are grateful to the Mayor of Hartford Pedro Segarra, the President of Trinity College Dr. James F. Jones, Jr., Professor Sharon Zukin at the City University of New York Graduate Center, and Bruce Katz of the Brookings Institution for having endorsed the book.

Finally, we want to thank all the contributors for their wonderful spirit, cooperation, and patience. We would like to single out Clyde McKee, Professor Emeritus of Political Science at Trinity College, who contributed his encyclopedic knowledge of Hartford's political history to this book and wrote an insightful chapter that was later revised and finalized by Nick Bacon, but could not see the book in print after succumbing to brain cancer in May 2011. It is to his memory and the city of Hartford which he loved and supported that this book is dedicated.

Xiangming Chen
Hartford, Connecticut
Nick Bacon
New York, New York
March 2013

Prologue

James R. Gomes

When most people think about "urban issues" or "the problems of the cities," their minds likely turn to the globe's megalopolises, to Mumbai or Madrid, Shanghai or Sao Paulo, Los Angeles or Lagos. These familiar places with their huge concentrations of people and commerce are critical to our planet's and our species' future. Yet, as this volume makes clear, a fuller understanding of modern cities requires that attention also be paid to places that are less well known and much less well studied.

As is perhaps not surprising for someone born in Lowell, educated in Hartford and Cambridge, and working in Worcester, I have always found New England's smaller cities to be interesting places. They each have their own history and character. Many of them grew and prospered in the 19th century thanks to a blend of advantages such as ports or water power, plentiful cheap labor, and entrepreneurial ideas, human energy, and capital.

New England is home to a lot of these places. According to the 2010 census, the six-state region has more than two dozen cities of between 70,000 and 182,000 inhabitants, the great majority of which grew in population since the 2000 census. Boston is surely the region's hub, but at the other end of its many spokes are places that are worthy of examination as well.

The cities discussed in this book, and the many others like them just an hour or two down the road, exhibit many characteristics and tensions that will be familiar to students of our larger urban areas. One such characteristic is a level of poverty much higher than that of their neighboring areas or their states as a whole.

As Chen and Bacon note in the chapter that sets the stage for those that follow, there is an almost literal silver lining around Hartford's cloud, namely, that while the city proper is quite poor, its metropolitan region boasts the nation's sixth highest median income, making Hartford technically "the most economically polarized city-region in the country." As was the case across New England, early settlement led to the incorporation of cities and towns that covered the entire Hartford region. Hartford—and this is true of other cities as well—was thus never able to expand the city limits to grow its tax base and capture the economic benefits of growth and vitality on its outskirts.

Fixed municipal boundaries raise the issue of what it means for a city to have "home rule." Cities like those studied in this book are typically the economic engine for an area much larger than that contained within the legal boundaries of the cities themselves. Yet their governing authority stops where the first suburbs begin. Many of the services people look to government to provide have traditionally been the province of local government. These services tend to be labor-intensive and relatively expensive, even when provided as efficiently and honestly as possible. Most of our smaller cities, however, lack the real estate tax base to generate adequate revenues to support these services. Their only options, then, are to develop other non–real estate revenue sources, or to receive large amounts of aid from other levels of government, chiefly the state. Those that cannot do these things risk being caught in a downward spiral.

Related to the economic disparities between the core cities and their suburbs is the issue of regional government or the lack thereof. County governments, regional entities such as planning authorities or transit districts, municipal compacts, and so on can lead to more comprehensive decision-making and spread resources more evenly across municipal boundaries. But some governmental functions, most notably public education and land use planning and facilities siting, seem especially resistant to cross-boundary cooperation. Few suburban towns step forward voluntarily to merge their school districts with neighboring cities. And the cities, desperate for more tax revenues and jobs, tend to welcome almost any commercial or industrial development, even if it brings with it pollution, noise, traffic, or other undesirable side effects.

This suggests a number of questions, and not only for Hartford. Hartford the city has been in economic decline for decades—what have been the trends in its surrounding region over that time? How is prosperity sustained in the outlying areas if stagnation and decline have taken hold at the center? Do the people in the more prosperous suburbs still go to work in Hartford? Do they go there for recreation in the evenings and on weekends? Over time, is there a possibility for the wealth that remains in the region to resurrect the city? How does this occur? Or does the opposite happen, the problems of the core eventually dragging down the areas that ring the city?

Beyond the smaller cities and their nearby neighbors lies the wider world. *The New York Times'* Thomas Friedman has famously asserted that the world has become flat, as advances in education, communications, transportation, and a generally more open trading system have made economic competition as likely to come from around the globe as from around the block. The urbanist Richard Florida, noting the rise of megacities in all of the world's regions, counters that the world is actu-ally getting spikier, and that most of the innovation and dynamism of the early 21st century can be found in a relatively small number of huge metropolises. This volume takes a more nuanced position between the two, noting the persistence, numerousness, and importance of cities like Hartford, CT, Lawrence, MA, Springfield, MA, and Portland, ME.

Globalization has influenced many aspects of our lives, and the workings of our smaller cities are no exception. Globalization has resulted in the departure of many jobs from the smaller cities, such as electronics manufacturing and financial services, mirroring the earlier disappearance of textile and manufacturing jobs to the southern United States. Another obvious aspect of globalization's impact on smaller cities is immigration. These cities are sometimes referred to as "Gateway Cities," because they have frequently been points of entry for immigrants and become long-term settlements for ethnic communities, a role they continue to play in the present day. These new immigrants add to the local workforce, bring different languages and cultures, and over time change the politics of their new homes.

These smaller cities have a critical mass of population that typically supports a range of businesses, government services, and cultural institutions. Yet they are not so sprawling and populous as to have problems that appear intractable. They are large enough to provide efficiencies and synergies to private enterprises, and undertake sizable infrastructure projects, yet small enough to allow civic, political, and business leaders to know each other and to communicate face-to-face.

Several important questions also emerge as one examines these smaller cities. Here are just a few:

Are the economies and civic life of smaller cities more reliant than those of most municipalities on the *public and nonprofit sectors*? City government is usually a major employer in these cities, and Hartford in particular, which is a state capital, houses thousands of civil service jobs. Many of the smaller cities also host relatively large nonprofit institutions such as colleges and hospitals.

What do these smaller cities have to tell us about *sustainability*? Do their relatively high densities of population and convenient locations along interstates and waterways recommend them as places for future growth and investment in a world where resource challenges and limitations have increasingly been recognized and will increasingly constrain our choices?

And what about the role of *leadership and public policies*? Do strong mayors and city managers, an enlightened business community, creative and innovative policy choices, careful management, vision and prudence, and collaboration matter to the cities' health and well-being? Or is the fate of these places all about forces—globalization, deindustrialization, flight to the suburbs, even climate—that are much larger and thus beyond the control of these cities?

Poverty and inequality. Schools. Immigrants. Revenue shortfalls. Sustainability. Leadership. It should be clear by now that readers of this book will encounter many of the same issues that arise in the country's and the world's major metropolises. There may be eight million stories in the Naked City, but many of the stories recounted here about Hartford or Lawrence will be familiar to urban scholars and instructive in their own right. It may turn out that there are some advantages to studying urban phenomena in these somewhat smaller places, where the "background noise" is reduced simply because there are fewer things going on. In any event, I am confident that these smaller cities will play an increasingly important role in defining the United States of the 21st century.

I close on a personal note. Clyde McKee, who co-wrote "A Tragic Dialectic: Politics and the Transformation of Hartford" in this volume, and who was a leading scholar on Connecticut politics for decades, passed away before this book made it into print. I first sat in Clyde's Political Science classroom at Trinity 40 years ago, and that was the beginning of an association and friendship that have been truly transformative in my life and career. My own path of combining theory with practice has Clyde as its source, and thousands of other students, faculty, and practitioners have been touched by his work as well. We miss his energy and insight, we are inspired by his example, and we are warmed by his memory.

James R. Gomes, Director
Mosakowski Institute for Public Enterprise
Clark University
Worcester, Massachusetts
March 2013

1

Introduction: Once Prosperous and Now Challenged

Hartford's Transformation in Comparative and Global Perspectives

Nick Bacon and Xiangming Chen

> "On the eastern edge of town, looming over the broad brown waters of the Connecticut River, the old Colt firearms factory is losing its fight with history. Under its spangled blue onion dome, the 19th-century armory where Samuel Colt's inventions helped spawn the Industrial Revolution—and where his company made the guns that helped the United States conquer the West and win two world wars—now stands hollow, disintegrating into crumbling bricks and broken glass."
>
> ("Poverty in a Land of Plenty," *The New York Times*, August 26, 2002)

Though the above epigraph leaves unnamed the city upon which it laments, those who live or work in its sprawling metropolitan region would have no trouble attributing the passage to Hartford, Connecticut. The wealthiest city after the American Civil War in per capita terms, Hartford comprises 18 of the nation's most impoverished square miles, despite serving as the capital of one of the country's wealthiest states. What has happened to the city that invented the revolver, the pay telephone, the gas-pump counter, gold fillings, air-cooled airplane engines, and the first American dictionary? What is happening in the city that is still called the "Insurance Capital of the World"? While much has transpired over the last one and a half centuries, Hartford falling from peak to bottom is far more than an intriguing local story. Yet there is so little contemporary scholarship on Hartford that we continue to puzzle over this phenomenon's significant regional and global dimensions, and its generally unappreciated broader comparative implications for urban research and practice.

As global urban research brings more cities into its orbit, it continues to focus more heavily on "top-ranked" economic centers like New York and London or rapidly growing megacities such as Shanghai and Mumbai. While intentional, the literature tends to exclude an abundant supply of significant but severely understudied cities like Hartford in both developed and developing countries. The result is a

1

fundamentally incomplete discourse on global urbanism. The purpose of this book is to help fill this void by focusing on a particularly understudied American city: Hartford, Connecticut, along with several other small New England cities including Lawrence and Springfield, Massachusetts, and Portland, Maine. This introduction first positions the book properly within the urban field by identifying the salient features of Hartford in its various historical moments. Then it highlights the main themes of the book with cross-references to and between the chapters that make up its four parts. It wraps up with a summary discussion of the book's main contributions, while pointing out avenues for future research.

TAKING HARTFORD SERIOUSLY, FINALLY

Why study Hartford? After all, Hartford is a small, "sub-global," even provincial city. In fact, outside the United States the city is almost completely unknown. Nevertheless, we argue that Hartford can: (1) advance our understanding of a whole category of American cities—those that are small, old, postindustrial, and yet global(ized), and (2) help us better understand the complex regional or metropolitan dynamics that are shaping the local well-being of American cities. We identify a trio of reasons for subjecting the city to this badly needed in-depth study.

Figure 1.1.   Hartford: The Past in the Present. (William Moffett)

Hartford is:

1. *An Outcast City.* Hartford is one of a host of second-tier New England cities, and American cities more generally, that have been understudied, yet which, when taken individually or collectively, have significant economic, social, and political roles, both throughout history and today.
2. *A Misunderstood City.* Hartford occupies an important place in American urbanism, both today and in history, but is misinterpreted in much of its scant literature due to a lack of integrated research.
3. *A City Detached From Theory.* Hartford, along with other "small" or "non-research worthy" cities, has been excluded from urban theorizing, thus calling into question the generalizability of much contemporary urban theory, and offering lessons for better theorizing.

An Outcast City

With their disproportionate global significance, a few anomalous "global" cities understandably attract much of the attention from urban researchers. And yet it is impossible to generalize about the total urban or the total global, as well as their full interconnections, through studies of these cities alone. While the economic and cultural importance of global cities may be unsurpassed, they account for a relatively small share of the world's population. Most urban dwellers live not in significant global centers, but in smaller cities of peripheral importance (Bell and Jayne, 2009). This is particularly troubling because there are undoubtedly huge differences, both in general and specific terms, between larger and smaller cities. Even before the rise of global cities and megacities, Jane Jacobs was careful to differentiate between "great" and "non-great" American cities in her classic *The Death and Life of Great American Cities* ([1961] 1993), which, as she strictly stated, did not concern smaller cities like Hartford.[1] And yet, when small cities have been studied, they tend to either be compared to "great" cities, or analyzed using the same criteria. A silent but undesirable consequence of global city fetishism is that a large part of the urban world has yet to be studied, either for its own significance or for its broader potential insights for global urban scholarship.

For these reasons, in addition to producing new scholarship on Hartford, this volume accomplishes more by placing Hartford primarily, and three other small New England cities secondarily, into a broader regional framework (see Table 1.1, Map 1.1, and Map 1.2). This region[2] features cities, with the exceptions of Boston and (to a lesser extent) New Haven, that are almost completely absent from urban scholarship. As Table 1.1 shows, these cities are remarkably similar on several indicators and deserve a collective and comparative scrutiny. By including them as additional case studies alongside Hartford, we provide both differing evidence and complementary insights for improving our understanding of Hartford, other New England cities, and global urban processes more generally.

Table 1.1. Comparing Greater Hartford with Three New England City-Regions

Indicator	Hartford	Springfield	Lawrence	Portland
Year of Initial Settlement	1633–1636	1636	1655	1633
Municipal Population	124,775	153,060	76,377	66,194
Regional Population	1,212,381	692,242	422,228	514,098
Municipal Area	17.38	31.87	7.4	21.31
Regional Area	1,677	1182.5	462.2	553.1
Municipal % Non-white	70.8%	48.29%	57.2%	15.0%
Regional % Non-white	28.4%	25.5%	2.3%	6.5%
Municipal Poverty	32.9%	27.0%	28.64%	18.1%
Regional Poverty Rate (est.)	10.1%	15.8%	9.2%	10.3%

Source: Excepting the Lawrence PMSA (whose numbers are derived from 2004 American Community Survey), and the row on regional poverty (whose numbers, excluding those of Lawrence, are derived from the 2010 one year population estimate from the American Community Survey) all data is derived from the 2010 U.S. Census.

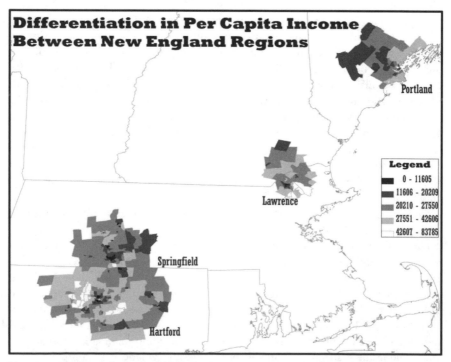

Map 1.1. Differentiation in Per Capita Income Between Hartford and Three New England City-Regions

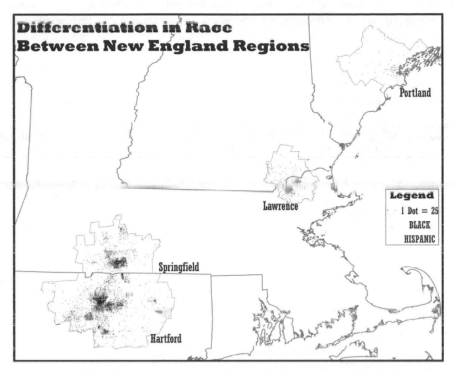

Map 1.2. Differentiation in Race Between Hartford and Three New England City-Regions

A Misunderstood City

Hartford is misunderstood. The fundamental reason for this is that, even more than other similarly sized cities, Hartford's *local, regional,* and *global* contours are far from clear cut, are highly contradictory and deeply intersected, and have been reshaped by continuous transformations throughout history. The bulk of publications[3] with some sort of focus on Hartford concentrate exclusively on the 18 square miles within the city's legal municipal boundaries. However, the fact that this area constitutes just 1 percent of the city's Metropolitan Statistical Area (MSA) highlights this unusual and problematic significance. While Hartford is a small city, it is not as small when understood within the context of its metropolitan region. Hartford is the 188th most populous city in the country, and yet the 43rd most populous metropolitan area. With a municipal population of 124,060 and a metro population of 1,188,241 spread throughout 57 municipalities, the population of Hartford makes up only 10 percent of its metropolitan area,[4] one of the lowest percentages for any American urban region. The small municipality of Hartford has consistently ranked as one of the absolute poorest cities in the United States, while the Hartford metropolitan region surprisingly took the top spot among the world's wealthiest regions, where a substantial upper middle class raises its per capita income above such well-established global cities as New York and Zurich (see Table 1.2).

A brief historical discussion may help us appreciate the reasons for, and consequences of, this phenomenon. At the beginning of its colonial history, Hartford was approximately 87 square miles, and included the current boundaries of West Hartford, East Hartford, and Manchester (see Map 1.3). Today, it contains only 1/5 of that area, even though metropolitan urbanization has extended far beyond even its larger initial bounds. Throughout the 18th and 19th centuries, as Hartford's residential population, economic productivity, cultural influence, and concentration of political power grew, its share of the region's space decreased dramatically. It was precisely at the moment when Hartford was becoming a prominent regional city and one of the wealthiest cities (in per capita terms) in the United States (at the end of the 19th century) that its municipal boundaries were finalized at 18 square miles. Only half a century later, Hartford saw a significant decentralization of its residential population, as well as of its production activities. By the 1970s, Hartford, along with most New England and Midwestern American cities, had become primarily suburban. In subsequent decades, Greater Hartford's population barely grew, and yet developed the worst case of "sprawl" by far, of any major city in New England.

Table 1.2.   World's Highest Per-Capita GDP Regions, 2011

Ranking	Metro Area	Region	Income ($)
1	Hartford	North America	75,086
2	Oslo	Western Europe	74,057
3	San Jose	North America	68,141
4	Abu Dhabi	Middle East and Africa	63,859
5	Bridgeport	North America	63,555
6	Zurich	Western Europe	63,236
7	Washington	North America	62,943
8	Stockholm	Western Europe	61,458
9	Boston	North America	60,074
10	San Francisco	North America	58,783
11	New York	North America	57,329
12	Seattle	North America	56,601
13	Houston	North America	56,050
14	Dublin	Western Europe	55,578
15	Des Moines	North America	55,335
16	Paris	Western Europe	54,430
17	Calgary	North America	54,080
18	Munich	Western Europe	54,978
19	Buffalo	North America	52,454
20	Los Angeles	North America	52,391

Source: Brookings Analysis of data from Oxford Economics, Moody's Analytics, and U.S. Census Bureau.

While the Hartford region had an 84.9 percent increase in land area growth between 1970 and 1990, Bridgeport only had an 8 percent increase, Providence 22.4 percent, and Springfield 27 percent. And yet, in the subsequent decade Hartford (the municipality) was the fastest shrinking major city in the country in terms of population (Rabinovitz, 1997). Meanwhile deindustrialization transformed about a third of Hartford's manufacturing land into brownfields (Bacon, 2010).

The urban geography of Hartford reveals a vast sprawl which is nevertheless highly differentiated and fragmented (see Map 1.3). While the core of Hartford has both a significant downtown area with an unmatched agglomeration of corporate employment centers (not to mention of state/federal government services), urban renewal projects, as well as the most significant concentrations of poor and minority populations, there is nevertheless an extraordinary corporate and retail presence throughout the region, particularly at sprawling but relatively coherent agglomerations in "edge cities," just north, southwest, and northeast of the municipality. Moreover, there are significant socioeconomic differences between neighborhoods throughout the city's "suburbs." In the past few years alone, Bloomfield has sported the region's lowest test scores and highest school-aged minority population; New Britain the lowest municipal bond rating; East Hartford the highest demographic instability ranking and the

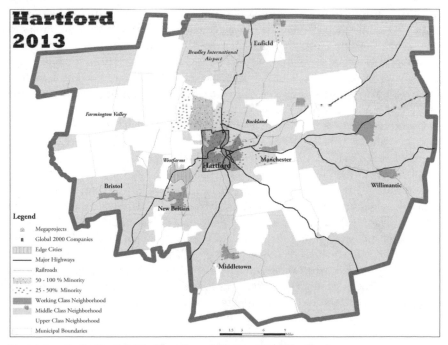

Map 1.3.   Socio-Spatial Configuration of Metropolitan Hartford

highest growth of urban poverty in the state; and all three of these municipalities' school districts are legally segregated by state standards (Bacon, 2010).

The urbanization of suburbia in Greater Hartford, with its increase in commercial and residential density, combined with the shrinking commercial presence and residential population of inner Hartford—a process which Edward Soja has called *density convergence* (2008)—has resulted in a centerless metropolitan form. Hartford was extremely polycentric (Bacon, 2010) for much of its history, but by the 21st century, Hartford was the most *dispersed* of all U.S. metropolitan regions (Lee, 2006), meaning that its polycentricism was submerged in and thus superseded by one giant sprawl. Hence, we describe the spatial form of Hartford as *polycentric dispersion*. The postwar process of "density convergence" has occurred not just in Hartford, but in/around satellite cities like East Hartford and New Britain. Density convergence does *not* mean that the urban and social forms of Hartford are now homogenous. Quite the contrary, the city is more complex than ever before. What the convergence implies is that what we call the Hartford region is actually in many ways one large and expansive urban entity. *Indeed, what we have hitherto called region is now the city.*

Hartford has several conflicting regional boundaries, all of which are used officially (see Map 12.1 in Rojas and Wray, this volume). The city itself makes up a very small portion of each regional definition. For the sake of consistency, when we speak of the metropolitan region, we are generally referring to the Metropolitan Statistical Area (MSA), although other contributors in this book have opted for Hartford County (which no longer exists officially), Capitol Region Council of Governments (CRCOG), and others. While this fact suggests that each regional definition has its own benefits, we should not assume that the authors who use a particular boundary necessarily regard it as the only legitimate one. Data availability alone often necessitates the use of one boundary over another, but we want to demonstrate here the overlapping nature of multiple boundaries to place the geographic focus of the chapters in a layered regional context.

One consequence of a generalized focus on the municipality alone is the production and saturation of extensive misinformation. For instance, in 2000, the U.S. Census revealed that Hartford had the second highest poverty rate of any American city. And yet in the same year Hartford's MSA had the nation's sixth highest median income. This unfairly represented Hartford as one of the most economically depressed cities and most socioeconomically polarized regions in the country. In actuality, Hartford's region is extremely differentiated. For instance, the city has the nation's most diverse "suburbs" in terms of resident income (Hall and Lee, 2009). Most of the municipalities of American cities either contain much larger shares of their urban area than what we see in Hartford, or at least have some sort of regional government, such as counties. Connecticut has the dubious distinction of being one of only two states without counties (the other being New Jersey).[5] Instead, the state employs a host of conflicting regional boundaries for a variety of purposes (e.g., watershed management and sewage). Without a solid and unitary definition of the city or the larger region(s) of which it is a part, and how their vectors may shift, both valid and reliable urban analysis is nearly impossible, and thus very few systematic studies have been produced.[6]

A City Detached From Theory

So far, we have demonstrated Hartford's wrongly perceived lack of relevance to the dominant urban discourse and its misunderstood city-regional spaces and boundaries. We now reveal Hartford's detachment from urban theorizing, partially through reconstructing its hidden "historicity" and true position in the general classification of urban places. Grafting a typology to a temporal template, we characterize Hartford as possessing certain superlative characteristics which are: prototypical, archetypical, and stereotypical (Beauregard, 2003; Brenner, 2003). Using a simple triadic chronology (*agrarian, industrial,* and *postindustrial*), we give an example of each type of superlative for each epoch. For Hartford, *Agrarian Society,* which is primarily concerned with agriculture and yet which eventually generates and coexists with mercantile cities, began in the 1630s and ended by the middle of the 19th century, followed by the emergence of *Industrial Society*, in which society leaves country life for cities and towns concerned primarily with production. This period ended by the mid-20th century with the emergence of a *Postindustrial Society*, in which industrial cities decline and see extensive suburbanization.

1. *Agrarian.*
    a. *Prototypical.* Hartford, first colonized in the early 1630s, was the first major inland settlement in the colonial U.S., which unleashed a wave of similar agrarian development throughout America's Northeast and Midwest and set the initial parameters for subsequent expansion and the eventual rise of the Industrial City.
    b. *Archetypical.* Most of the land in New England, with its rugged terrain, less fertile soil, and cold climate, was not particularly conducive to agriculture. The exception was the lower Connecticut River Valley, where Hartford, Windsor, and Wethersfield (and Springfield, MA) were sited. These lands were flat, cleared of brush, and largely made up of high quality soils. The area's agricultural advantages motivated its settlement, but also kept Hartford occupied with agriculture when the less fertile areas of New England were beginning to industrialize.
    c. *Stereotypical.* Until the 20th century, Hartford and the lower Connecticut River Valley was one of the country's most consistently agrarian regions. Though it became a regional economic and political hub early on, Hartford remained a rural village until well into the 18th century, maintaining the socio-spatial form which dominated most of America. This contrasts sharply with other early American urban settlements, such as Boston, New York, and Philadelphia, which urbanized very early in American history (see Walsh, this volume).

2. *Industrial.*

    a. *Prototypical.* Hartford was an early American experimenter and promoter of urban renewal in the 19th century. The city claims the first treatise on American city planning (Peterson, 2003: 342; see Bushnell, 1864: 314-341) and the country's first municipal park, Bushnell Park (1853–1867) (Clouette, 1976; Baldwin, 1997), both by Horace Bushnell. And his student, Frederick Law Olmsted, founded American Landscape Architecture and popularized the notion and construction of both urban and national parks.

    b. *Archetypical.* During the 19th century, Hartford earned the nickname "the insurance capital of the world," for its bustling insurance industry (see Chen and Shemo, this volume), a sector otherwise generally confined to large cities like New York.

    c. *Stereotypical.* Though often hailed as the richest (in per capita income) and most architecturally beautiful city throughout the late 19th and early 20th centuries, Hartford was also found by national housing expert Lawrence Veiller (1903) to have the "worst tenement conditions" of any city of its size. Meanwhile, the colloquialism "podunk," meaning an insignificant or out-of-the-way town, emerged to describe the land bordering Hartford to its east (see Bacon, this volume). Perhaps more than any city of its size, Hartford exemplified the conceptual dichotomies of rich/poor and urban/rural.

3. *Postindustrial.*

    a. *Prototypical.* Hartford saw an early transition to "Fordism," as exemplified both in economics (Norcliffe, 1996) and policy by the local character of Albert Pope, who produced the country's first bicycles in Hartford, using early mass-production assembly line techniques and supportive labor practices. Pope also exerted a powerful influence on public policy with consumption-privy activism for the "good roads movement," which initiated and popularized the construction of paved roads, prefiguring Fordist or motorist suburbanization.

    b. *Archetypical.* Hartford is sometimes cited as having the highest proportion of FIRE (Finance, Insurance, and Real Estate) employment in the country, largely because of its agglomeration of insurance firms (Immergluck, 2001). Yet Hartford's economic uncertainty is perhaps greater than that of any other region in the country. In 2008, the Center for International Competitiveness (CIC) named Greater Hartford the third most productive region in the world. Yet, that same year, other research (Owyang et al., 2008) declared Hartford to have the slowest growing economy of any region in the United States.

    c. *Stereotypical.* During the late 20th century, which generally saw significant disinvestment and stagnation in New England, Greater Hartford had the region's highest rate of suburbanization, a process which was proceeding with similar vigor throughout the country.

These superlative characteristics help demonstrate Hartford's under-valued importance, as well as its high potential for use in comparative urban research and theorizing. In the following section, we highlight what we can learn from small New England cities by distilling key themes from the chapters.

KEY THEMES

Part 1: The Rise and Fall of Hartford

Instead of examining every aspect of Hartford, the chapters in the book converge on a few substantive and analytical themes. A charting of Hartford's major historical transformations, its "rise and fall," is a logical starting point. As one of the oldest American cities, Hartford offers one of the longest possible temporal spans in which to identify and explain some of the major conjunctions and disjunctions in an American city's growth and urbanization. As Andrew Walsh (chapter 2) argues and demonstrates in his historical introduction, Hartford has experienced five main stages of development from the 1630s to the 21st century. Going beyond a simple chronological narrative, Walsh attributes these five stages, and the transition from one to the next, to particular sets of urban and global processes. These processes range from the particular roles of the city in 18th-century global mercantile trade to the explosive transformations of urban space resulting from massive waves of foreign migration, but they all established and have sustained, if only in part, the city's early urban legacy.

To get a better scope of Hartford's rise and fall, Nick Bacon (chapter 3) steps outside the city's undersized political boundaries and analyzes four hundred years of socio-spatial transformations in the hitherto unstudied adjacent municipality of East Hartford. Charting the town's evolution, Bacon uses and expands upon the locally inspired American colloqialism "podunk," to explain East Hartford's transition from a seasonal home of the nomadic Podunk indians, to an isolated and insignificant semi-agrarian podunk, to a center of the American military-industrial complex, to a declining postindustrial satellite in a state of dramatic socioeconomic flux. Finally, Bacon analyzes the economic, social, and spatial ramifications of this recent *urban podunkfication,* and analyzes the possibilities for renewal, or what he calls *depodunkification.*

Llana Barber (chapter 4) then provides us with a rich comparative study of Lawrence, Massachussetts. Like Walsh and Bacon, Barber uses a historical case-study approach to explain the postwar transformation of Lawrence, Massachussetts. While Barber details Lawrence's severe postindustrial decline, after which it became the poorest city in Massachussetts, she goes beyond the narrative of urban crisis and decay to reveal the positive socio-spatial transformation which accompanied the city's economic decline. As Barber illustrates, despite its deindustrialization, Lawrence avoided becoming a ghost town through the city's appropriation by what has become the largest Latino concentration in New England. The city's postindustrial Latinoization as described and analyzed by Barber paints a nuanced picture of a local transnational complex, and also serves as an interesting comparison case for Hartford, which also became a paragon of a city whose dramatic postindustrialization was followed by equally dramatic Lationoization (though Hartford's was Puerto Rican, and Lawrence's Dominican).

Part II: Social and Community Transformations

Following the preceding section on Hartford's rise and fall, Part II picks up on the social and communal transformations which have accompanied its postindustrialization, and on various political responses which have accompanied and followed these changes. Louise Simmons (chapter 5) delineates the concentration within Hartford since the 1970s of some of the United States' most overwhelming and racialized povety. As Simmons shows, however, Hartford's status as one of the nation's absolute poorest cities is made both morally disturbing but also politically potent in that the city is located in one of country's wealthiest metropolitan regions. Simmons emphasizes in particular the political dimensions of the gargantuan challange of addressing Hartford's concentrated poverty in a balkanized regional political structure, adopting a bottom-up perspective on the progress and limits of community-based movements and organizing that complements the analytical attention given to government and business. Finally Simmons stresses the need for solutions to Hartford's dramatic poverty to be designed, funded, and implemented at the scale of its metropolitan region.

Jack Dougherty (chapter 6) extends the theme of concentrated socioeconomic inequality into the educational domain of Greater Hartford. Drawing upon a large compilation of local scholarship conducted largely at Trinity College, he discusses the relationships between metropolitan residential location and school choice, and focuses on governmental and non-governmental approaches to closing the region's educational achievement gap, with an emphasis on consciously regional solutions.

Taking an explicit comparative approach and using comparable demographic data, Michael Sacks (chapter 7) has found systematic differences between the movement of Puerto Ricans and non-Hispanic Whites within and across the city-suburban divide in the Hartford and Springfield metro regions. Going a step further, Sacks has detected a broader negative effect of Puerto Rican concentration among Hispanics in 38 metro regions with varied levels of Puerto Rican dominance, which he frames in terms of specifically Puerto Rican racialization.

From another grounded community vantage point, Janet Bauer (chapter 8) gives us a rich profile of the diverse international immigrants and refugees who have recently settled in Hartford. Her analysis adds new insights to the heavily racialized residential landscape that has materialized since the eras addressed by the earlier historically oriented chapters. Drawing on her own rich ethnographic research on a variety of diverse immigrant communities in contemporary Hartford, Bauer emphasizes both the transnational networks which help make Hartford's various immigrant groups socio-culturally distinct, as well as the similarities that the diverse immigrants share as they construct new everyday lives, which reflect their unique experience of assimilating in a city that does not at all represent the American socio-demographic majority, but which in its unique domination by first-, second-, or third-generation Puerto Ricans and West Indians, instead resembles a sort of Carribean melting pot.

Ending the section and introducing Portland, Maine to our comparative mix of New England cities, Ezra Moser (chapter 9) adds new insights about the renewal of small New England cities in a complex transnational era. Specifically, Moser examines local reponses to the influx and formation of a Sudanese refugee community a geographically distant and more traditionally closed Maine city simultaenously undergoing a massive and widely hailed renewal tailored for its preexisting white middle class. Depsite the supposed success of its urban renaissance and a municipal government which is generally receptive to immigrant interests, Moser has identified significant problems with the integration of its increasingly socio-spatially signifiant population of Sudanese refugees. On the policy side, Moser addresses the problem of dwindling federal funding, while highlighting the positive effects that private local coalitions may have on the full integration of the city's refuges.

Part III: Renewing Hartford: Global and Regional Dynamics

If Part 1 of this volume has dealt with Hartford's history and urban legacy, and Part 11 has focused on the inheritance and contemporary ramifications of that legacy, our final section must logically examine how to renew Hartford or how to take charge of its future urban legacy in a complicated global era without losing sight of the city's unique spatial inheritance. Beginning this section, Xiangming Chen and John Shemo (chapter 10) have traced and located Hartford's evolving postion within the global economy. By looking at the city's unususually sequenced development of insurance and jet engine manufacturing since the mid-19th century and their complicated contemporary coexistence, Chen and Shemo have identified the resilient strengths and growing liabilities which typify Greater Hartford as it responds to the pressing economic challenges of the 21st century.

Clyde Mckee and Nick Bacon (chapter 11) probe the political countours of Greater Hartford during the final quarter of the 20th century. First, they delineate the flawed legal and political structure within which Hartford must respond to changing regional and global configurations. Then, they analyze several missed opportunities and failed public and private stategies, using the dramatic but short-lived case studies of (1) the Greater Hartford Process (GHP), a semi-private regional planing agency which came close to implenting what would have been the country's largest urban renewal project in the early 1970s; (2) the "Bishops," an elite political shadow group of downtown corporate interests which crumbled at the first sign of public scrutiny; and (3) Education Alternatives, Inc. (E.A.I.), a Minnesota based firm which was contracted by the City of Hartford to rescue its troubled public school system, but which ended in expensive failure. McKee and Bacon thus keep a sharp political lens on Hartford's persistent misses and mistakes to devise effective regional governance, a theme picked up by Rojas and Wray in the next chapter.

Meeting the new challenges of a changing global landscape, as Jason Rojas and Lyle Wray (chapter 12) argue, calls for more regional coordination and oversight across one of America's most politically balkanized regions whose governance is almost entirely performed by the region's dozens of municipalities. While lamenting the elimination of counties in 1960 as a main source for the emergence of uncoordinated middle-layer governance entities, Wray and Rojas point to a growing number of service sharing projects in the capital region as promising mechanisms for creating and strengthening regional governance that can not only improve an inefficient and fragmented system of everyday local service delivery, but which can also allow Hartford to surpass its balkanized political structure and move toward controlling its own urban legacy by producing imaginative and implementable solutions to otherwise insurmountable global problems.

To help bring the book to a close, local newspaper columnist Tom Condon (chapter 13) retraces Greater Hartford's recent history through a sharp journalistic lens that humanizes the ups and downs of the city and metropolitan region that he has covered up close and personal for about four decades by giving them a powerfully experiential dimension. Yet, more than offering a testimonial of Hartford's supposed postindustrial evisceration, Condon points also to the not-so-bad—qualitative—changes that Hartford has encountered, and extracts several practical lessons on how to positively confront the ever-changing urban legacy and global imprint of the region, pointing both to regionally tailored solutions such as those outlined by Wray and Rojas, as well as to privately implemented tactics like those advocated for Portland by Moser.

Following the final section in the chapter which concludes this volume, Xiangming Chen and Nick Bacon (chapter 14) distill the essential insights from the chapters for understanding the severe constraints of spatial inheritance and inertia on Hartford and implications for theorizing not just about this city and region, but on other New England cities, and on cities more generally. Then, reshifting its focus upon the region's potential for renewing itself and controlling its legacy, Chen and Bacon unveil Hartford's active and effective grassroots organizations like SINA and NRZs, while describing some of the more formal, but still promising new urban projects (e.g., iQuilt), in order to convey a sense of pragmatic hope and inspiration for remaking the city and region for the 21st century and taking control of Hartford's urban legacy.

MAIN CONTRIBUTIONS

This book makes two main contributions to the urban literature. First, the book's novel inclusion and juxtaposition of unique academic research on Hartford and other under-analyzed and unanalyzed New England cities and suburbs reveals some surprising continuities and discontinuities. The empirical richness of the cases in this book in itself provides ample food for thought about broader theorizing of how the urban and the global intersect in shaping our cities. Second, and most important, this book pioneers the closing of a massive lacuna in urban scholarship left by the lack of an integrated global and local probe into many second-tier cities in New England and beyond.

Nevertheless, in spite of our collective effort to complete a project that could be considered ground-breaking, the book admittedly falls short in that it cannot cover all major urban/global dimensions of small New England cities, or even of Hartford alone. This in turn limits what we have been able to theorize about the empirical discoveries reported in this volume. Still, we hope that other urban researchers can conduct future research and comparative analyses which build off our work. With the construction of a baseline of hitherto almost non-existent urban research on Hartford and a few other small New England cities (Lawrence, Portland, Springfield, and East Hartford), we hope that we have pioneered the formation of a new field in which, research questions regarding the distinctive transformations of small New England cities and the myriad of other underrepresented "outcast" cities across the globe, are formed, answered, and synthesized into the broader urban literature. Furthermore, we hope that the stressing in this book on practical solutions to urban problems extends beyond the realm of academia. In this overwhelmingly chaotic age which nevertheless offers new opportunities, we hope both academic and non-academic actors will draw inspiration to positively remake their cities. If only tangentially, we hope that this book inspires and informs cities to construct and implement imaginative strategies which allow them to take ownership over their urban legacies.

NOTES

1. In fact, Jacobs used the analogously sized and situated city of New Haven, Connecticut as the archetypical example of a city which was "not great," and which could thus not be analyzed in the *Death and Life of Great American Cities.*

2. The problem of the lack of one consistent definition of the Hartford metropolitan region by its residents parallels that of the lack of defining proper definition of the larger region of which Hartford is a part. In geography, a region is a "concentrated network of economic connections between producers, suppliers, distributions, and myriad ancillary activities, all located in specific urban or rural locations" (Smith, 1992: 73). While a region can certainly be metropolitan, it is usually larger, such as New England—the region with which this book is concerned. Between the early 19th and mid-20th centuries, New England served as a coherent mosaic of several local regions, but after World War II, the region saw its own "density convergence," and was submerged within a larger "Northeast" region, often called the "Bos-Wash" or North Corridor. To be sure, the contours of Hartford's region(s) have changed over time, and even before the postwar restructuring of regional scale, the city has not always neatly fit into the boundaries of New England. Along with other cities in Connecticut (New Haven, Bridgeport, and Waterbury) and southwestern Massachusetts (Springfield), Hartford has often

been grouped away from the New England economic region, and grouped with other cities, for instance, with the cities of New York and Northern New Jersey (Smith and Dennis, 1989). Moreover at a cultural level, Hartford's baseball fans are split just about evenly between the Boston Red Sox and the New York Yankees, perhaps signifying the postwar absorption of New England and New York into the larger "Northeast Region."

3. Andrews (1889) provides a detailed structural account of colonial settlement, land-use, and politics in Hartford, Windsor, and Wethersfield, but no text gives a comparable regional treatment of any other era. Peter Baldwin (1997) gives a detailed socio-spatial history of the municipality between 1850 and 1930, covering everything from industrial/urban growth, urban renewal, and parks to child labor, prostitution, and proletarian social dynamics, but neither this nor any other text discusses other parts of the region during this period. Most work on Hartford, and especially that which focuses on the city during modern times, collectively generates an urban discourse with an extremely reduced scope. While this unfortunately contributes to a myopic literature, it has nevertheless produced some very good work on economics (Forrant, 2002; Forrant and Wilkinson, 2003; Norcliffe, 1996); education (Eaton, 2007); architecture (Andrews and Randsom, 1988), urban form (Baird, 2008; McCahill and Garrick); urban poverty (Dickinson-Gomez, 2007, 2008, and 2009; Romero-Daza, 2003); homelessness (Glasser and Zywiak, 2003); community organizing (Close, 2002; Chambers, 2007; Simmons, 1998; Valocchi, 2010); housing (Donovan, 1994); and urban planning projects (Clavel, 1982; Krumholz and Clavel, 1994; Neubeck and Ratcliffe, 1988; Burns, 2002).

4. Cooke and Merchant (2006) describe Hartford as a paradigmatic case of analytical complication via political fragmentation, in opposition to Jacksonville, FL (a city almost completely encapsulated by one city boundary).

5. However, it should be noted that, throughout New England, municipal boundaries are similarly small and copious, and county and other regional jurisdictions tend to be very weak.

6. There are a few rare examples of regional literature on Hartford. Bacon (2010) provides a brief but comprehensive history and contemporary critique of urban space in Greater Hartford. Stave's (1979) edited volume too deals with Hartford at the extent of the region. This volume has valuable contributions from a motley crew ranging from Hartford mayor Nick Carbone to renowned historian of suburbia Kenneth Jackson, however it is not a thorough academic treatment. Older regionally aware texts include Burpee's (1928) extensive history of Hartford County and Andrews (1889) (discussed above). Though apart from these scarce regional treatments, very few scholarly pieces exist on Greater Hartford, almost every municipality in the region does have one or more published "local histories." While not exactly scholarly, these local histories are often rich sources of information.

REFERENCES

Andrews, Charles McLean. 1889. *The River Towns of Connecticut: A Study of Wethersfield, Hartford, and Windsor*. Baltimore: Johns Hopkins University.

Burns, Peter. 2002. "The Intergovernmental Regime and Public Policy in Hartford, Connecticut." *Journal of Urban Affairs* 24 (1): 55–73.

Andrews, Gregory, and David F. Ransom. 1988. *Structures and Styles: Guided Tours of Hartford Architecture*. Hartford: Connecticut Historical Society.

Bacon, Nicholas. 2010. "Lost in Dialectic: A Critical Introduction to Urban Space in Greater Hartford." Hartford, CT: Trinity College Undergraduate Honors Thesis.

Baird, Jim, et al. 2008. "Immigration Settlement Patterns: The Role of Metropolitan Characteristics." *Sociological Inquiry,* 78 (3). 310–334.

Baird, Brian A., and Norman W. Garrick. 2004. "Decentralization in the Hartford, Connecticut Metropolitan Region, 1900–2000." *Transportation Research Record* 1986 (1): 157–164.

Baldwin, Peter C. 1997. *Domesticating the Street: The Reform of Public Space in Hartford: 1850–1930.* Columbus, OH: Ohio State University Press.

Beauregard, Robert A. 2003. "City of Superlatives." *City & Community* 2 (3): 183–199.

Bell, David, and Mark Jayne. 2009. "Small Cities? Towards a Research Agenda" *International Journal of Urban and Regional Research* 33 (3): 683–699.

Brenner, Neil. 2003. "Stereotypes, Archetypes, and Prototypes: Three Uses of Superlatives in Contemporary Urban Studies." *City & Community* 2 (3): 205–216.

Burpee, Charles W. 2009. *History of Hartford County, Connecticut 1633–1928. Three Volumes.* Chicago: S. J. Clarke Publishing Company, 1928.

Bushnell, Horace. 1864. *Work and play; or. Literary varieties.* New York: C. Scribner.

Center For International Competitiveness. 2008. "The World Knowledge Competitiveness Index."

Chambers, Stefanie. 2007. "Minority Empowerment and Environmental Justice." *Urban Affair Review* 43 (1): 28–54.

Clavel, Pierre. 1986. *The Progressive City: Planning and Participation, 1969–1984.* New Brunswick: Rutgers University Press.

Close, Stacey. 2001. "Fire in the Bones: Hartford's NAACP, Civil Rights and Militancy, 1943–1969." *The Journal of Negro History* 86 (3): 228–263.

Clouette, Bruce Alan. 1976. "Antebellum Urban Renewal; Hartford's Bushnell Park." *Connecticut History,* November. 1–21.

Cooke, Thomas, and Sarah Merchant. 2006. "The Changing Intrametropolitan Location of High-poverty Neighborhoods in the U.S., 1990–2000." *Urban Studies* 43 (11): 1971–1989.

DeVol, Ross, et al. 2009. "Best Performing Cities 2009." *Miliken Institute.*

Dickinson-Gomez, Julia, et al. 2009. "Hustling and Housing: Drug Users' Strategies to Obtain Shelter and Income in Hartford, Connecticut." *Human Organization* 68 (3): 269–279.

Dickinson-Gomez, Julia, et al. 2007. "Unofficial Policy: Access to Housing, Housing Information, and Social Services Among Homeless Drug Users in Hartford, Connecticut." *Substance Abuse Treatment, Prevention and Policy* 2 (8): 1–12.

Dickinson-Gomez, Julia, et al. 2008. "Structural and Personal Factors Related to Access to Housing and Housing Stability Among Urban Drug Users in Hartford, Connecticut." *Contemporary Drug Problems* 35: 115–152.

Donovan, Shaun. 1994. *Moving to the Suburbs: Section 8 Portability and Mobility in Hartford,* Cambridge, MA: Harvard University Press.

Eaton, Susan. 2006. *The Children in Room E4: American Education on Trial.* Chapel Hill NC: Algonquin Books of Chapel Hill.

Forrant, Robert. 2002. "The International Association of Machinists, Pratt & Whitney, and the Struggle for a Blue-Collar Future in Connecticut." *IRSH* 47: 113–136.

Forrant, Robert, and Frank Wilkinson. 2003. "Globalisation and Degenerative Productive Systems: the Case of the Connecticut River Valley." Paper presented at the Conference on Clusters, Industrial Districts and Firms, September 12–13, in Modena, Italy.

Glasser, Irene, and William H. Zywiak. 2003. "Homelessness and Substance Misuse: A Tale of Two Cities." *Substance Use & Misuse* 38 (3–6): 551–576.

Hall, M., and Lee, B. 2009. "How Diverse Are US Suburbs?" *Urban Studies Online.*

Immergluck, Daniel. 2003. "The Financial Services Sector and Cities: Restructuring, Decen-
  tralization, and Declining Urban Employment. *Economic Development Quarterly* 15 (3):
  1274–288.
Jacobs, Jane. 1993. *The Death and Life of Great American Cities.* New York: Modern Library.
Krumholz, Norman, and Pierre Clavel. 1994. "Hartford: Snapshot 1992." in *Reinventing
  Cities: Equity Planners Tell Their Stories:* 169–186. Philadelphia: Temple University Press.
Lee, Bumsoo. 2006. "Urban Spatial Structure, Commuting, and Growth in US Metropolitan
  Areas." PhD diss., University of Southern California: 29–30.
McCahill, Christopher T., and Norman W. Garrick. 2010. "Losing Hartford: Transportation
  Policy and the Decline of an American City." *Congress for New Urbanism* 18: 1–8.
Neubeck, Kenneth J., and Richard E. Ratcliff. 1988. "Urban Democracy and the Power of
  Corporate Capital: Struggles Over Downtown Growth and Neighborhood Stagnation in
  Hartford, Connecticut." In *Business Elites and Urban Development,* edited by Scott Cum-
  mings, 299–332. Albany, NY: SUNY Press.
Norcliffe, Glenn. 1996. "Popeism and Fordism: Examing the Roots of Mass Production."
  Regional Studies 31 (3): 267–280.
Owyang, Michael T., et al. 2008. "The Economic Performance of Cities: A Markov-Switching
  Approach." *Journal of Urban Economics* 64: 538–550.
Peterson, Jon A. 2003. *The Birth of City Planning in the United States, 1840–1917.* Baltimore:
  The Johns Hopkins University Press.
Romero-Daza, Nancy, Margaret Weeks, and Merrill Singer. 2003. "Nobody Gives a Damn if I
  Live or Die": Violence and Street-Level Prostitution in Inner-City Hartford, Connecticut."
  Medical Anthropology 22: 233–259.
Smith, Neil. 1992. "Contours of a Spatialized Politics: Homeless Vehicles and the Production
  of Geographical Scale" *Social Text* 33: 54–81.
Smith, Neil, and Ward Dennis. 1989. "The Restructuring of Geographical Scale, Coalescence,
  and Fragmentation of the Northern Core Region" *Economic Geography* 63 (2): 160–182.
Soja, Edward J. 2008. "Regional Urbanization and the Crisis of Governance." Paper presented
  at the Workshop on the Diversity and Dynamics of Global City-Region: Asian and Euro-
  pean Cases Compared, 31 May–1 June, Fudan University, Shanghai.
Stave, Sondra Astor. 1979. *Hartford, the City and the Region: Past, Present, Future: A Collection
  of Essays.* Hartford: University of Hartford.
Rabinovitz, Jonathan. 1997. "A Very Personal Investment in a Blighted Hartford Street." *New
  York Times,* August 27.
Simmons, Louise B. 1998. "A New Urban Conservatism: The Case of Hartford,
  Connecticut."*Journal of Urban Affairs* 20 (2): 175–198.
Valocchi, Stephen. 2010. *Social Movements and Activism in the USA.* New York: Routledge.
Veiller, Lawrence. 1903. "Housing Conditions and Tenement Laws in Leading American Cities."
  In *The Tenement House Problem.* De Forest, Robert W. and Lawrence Veiller (eds.): 129–170.
Zeilbauer, Paul. 2002. "Poverty in a Land of Plenty." *The New York Times.* August 26.

I

URBAN PAST AND PRESENT IN NEW ENGLAND

2

Hartford: A Global History

Andrew Walsh

Over the course of almost four centuries, Hartford's cultural identity, its economy, and its population have been shaped and reshaped by shifting global flows of people, capital, and knowledge. The city is one of the oldest "American" settlements and just about every significant event or trend in the nation's history has left its mark here, from the frontier experience to postindustrial malaise and suburban sprawl.

This brief account of the city's history will focus on "global" Hartford, on the pattern of changes in economy and population that have produced the most significant transitions in its history. It will argue that Hartford has moved through a sequence of five major stages of development, each fundamentally shaped by a new set of global circumstances. At each of these stages, changes in the local economy and its connections to the prevailing global economy produced dramatic change in the region's population, both in total size and demographic composition. There have been, in other words, a series of five quite different Hartfords. Repeatedly in the course of the region's long history, middle-aged people have complained that rapid and extensive change has rendered their hometown barely recognizable.

These discontinuities have made it difficult for many of the region's contemporary residents to identify much with residents of preceding eras, or with the city's past. Nevertheless, much of Hartford's past is forgotten but not gone. The legacies of previous choices and structures persist, giving the region much of its character, but also making it challenging for the region to respond effectively to changing circumstances. The most notable contemporary example of this is the persistence of the colonial system of decentralized local government in what is now an interdependent, urbanized region.

The Hartfords this paper will outline have not all enjoyed equivalent salience. The manifestation with the greatest impact, both positive and negative, was the third Hartford, an industrial hub and financial services center that developed in the mid-19th century. Hartford became, in the words of urbanist Joel Kotkin (2005), a prototypical "Anglo-American industrial city" (also see Bacon and Chen, this volume). Hartford grew, rather quickly, into a small, dense, manufacturing city. It was pragmatic, unglamorous, and utilitarian, but nevertheless a substantial magnet for immigration.

Hartford has rarely been regarded, here or elsewhere, as "Fun City." Lovers of the town relish Mark Twain's oft-repeated (in Hartford, at least) comment that the town was "the best-built and handsomest" he had ever seen. Charles Dickens was less impressed, writing in his 1842 *American Notes* that "too much of the old Puritan spirit exists in these parts to the present hour; but its influence has not tended, that I know, to make the people less hard in their bargains, or more equal in their dealings." Dan Shaughnessy of the *Boston Globe* put Hartford firmly in its place in 1997, when it appeared for a nanosecond that Hartford might steal away the New England Patriots, calling the city "America's filing cabinet." But, as that epithet faintly suggests, Hartford has usually been regarded as an above-average place to make a living. Since the 1630s, the region has moved in its own orbit and its long-term self-image is accurately captured in the text of a bumper sticker distributed by Real Art Ways, a local arts organization, in the early 1990s: "Hartford: You Could Do Worse."

The City of Hartford, as the municipality now stands, was largely built from 1870 to 1930 as a manufacturing city where factory workers lived in tight-packed neighborhoods within walking distance of their jobs. The rapid erosion of manufacturing between 1950 and 1980 left the old manufacturing core of Hartford to deal—largely alone—with immense economic problems and an increasingly impoverished population. This was in sharp contrast to the larger, far more prosperous metropolitan region that then was developing on the foundations of the old industrial city (see Map 2.1). But the point to be emphasized here is that each in the succession of Hartfords responded to changing global flows and circumstances, and each era has left legacies.[1]

HARTFORD ONE: THE EARLY
COLONIAL ERA (1630s TO 1740s)

Hartford was established in 1635 as part of the transatlantic and global military and commercial expansion of Europeans. Its founders were English Puritans who were extending the reach of the just-established English colony in Massachusetts Bay. There were several economic and political motives for English expansion into the Connecticut River Valley: colonists wanted access to trade in beaver pelts, furs, and, eventually, forest products; they wanted to block Dutch expansion from the Hudson River Valley eastward into New England; and, most ardently, they wanted access to better farmland than was available in the Boston area. The broad valley of the Connecticut River, with its annual floods and wide river meadows, offered the best potential agricultural land in New England. The English moved here in the mid-1630s, to the newly planted "River Towns" of Windsor, Wethersfield, and Hartford, with the encouragement of local Indians (see Bacon, this volume), who were seeking allies against the locally dominant and recently arrived Pequot Indians,

Population Density in Hartford County, 1800-2010

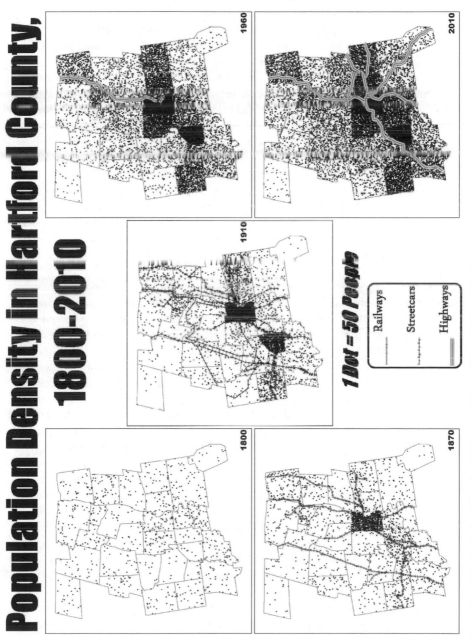

1960

2010

1910

1 Dot = 50 People

Railways

Streetcars

Highways

1800

1870

Map 2.1.   Five Periods of Hartford's History, Selected Years during 1800–2010

who had moved into the region from the Hudson Valley. The anti-Pequot alliance and the arrival of English colonists precipitated war almost immediately; the Pequots were then exterminated in a brutal campaign during 1637.

The colonists who settled New England in the 1630s stood out among the Europeans who seized the Americas in the 15th and 16th century. Their prime motive for settlement in North America was religious and not commercial, although they were keenly interested in making a living. The New England Puritans sought to establish a distinctively Protestant society and culture in this region, one that aimed to serve as a "city on a hill," to inspire English society to launch a more thorough version of the Reformation. The subsequent history of the region was profoundly shaped by this religious commitment. Connecticut and New England stood not only out but apart from the other English Atlantic colonies for the entire colonial period. Non-Puritans avoided the place. New England was also largely settled by a single wave of newcomers during the 1630s, a wave which ended abruptly in the early 1640s when the English Civil War began. In the region's interior, large-scale in-migration did not resume until the 1840s. This odd pattern of population movement produced a strong, quite homogeneous, and very isolated English subculture, one driven by very rapid natural population growth. This subculture, eventually called Yankee, evolved largely on its own terms for two hundred years.

There was intense effort here during the 17th century to transform the region's landscape to support English modes of agriculture, focused on raising grain and feeding cattle and pigs for meat production. This often involved conflict with Indians who struggled to live on the same land in their traditional ways.[2] In interior New England, subsistence agriculture was the dominant form of economic life throughout the 17th century. Hartford and the other Connecticut Valley towns settled in the mid-17th century were highly communal settlements shaped by English feudal patterns of land tenure and agriculture. Hartford was one of America's first planned settlements, and land here was allocated by the town government to individuals who were admitted to citizenship and then given scattered parcels of meadow, field and woodlot land in quantities that reflected their social status.[3] From the first days of the settlement, the Connecticut colony had important military functions in the larger world of English America, especially after 1660, when the Stuart monarchy was restored in Britain, and New Englanders worried that their "errand into the wilderness" would be suppressed by the restored monarchy. But New England preserved its peculiar local religious and political autonomy, to a considerable degree because it was willing to mobilize repeatedly to assert or defend English interests against the French and Indians. New England's prime imperial function in the late 17th and early 18th centuries was to protect the economically more valuable colonies in the Middle Atlantic and Chesapeake regions from the French.

In this slowly evolving setting, Hartford served mostly as a governmental and market center for a growing and dispersing, very rural society. The town grew slowly, from a few hundred inhabitants, to about 4,000 by 1780. The overwhelming majority of its inhabitants were direct descendants of the English immigrants of the 1630s, although there existed small, increasingly interrelated, communities of African Americans and Indians living on the margins of Puritan society.

HARTFORD TWO:
MERCANTILE CENTER (1740 TO 1830)

During the middle decades of the 18th century, Hartford and the region suddenly developed new and dynamic connections to the British imperial Atlantic economy, which, in turn, generated a dramatic increase in commerce and wealth, which was then concentrated mostly in the hands of the local gentry. The entrenched slave economies of the Caribbean and the American Southern colonies powered a sharp increase in transatlantic commerce by mid-century. While 18th-century New England remained a deferential, patriarchal society, the communal dimension of New England society relaxed somewhat in Hartford's second century—property was bought and sold by individuals, newly established towns no longer enforced residence in a village centers, and farming families assembled consolidated farm parcels, rather than the dispersed strips within communal fields that had marked New England farming practice in the 17th century.[4]

These changes accelerated as new forms of commercial agriculture replaced subsistence agriculture—notably in the form of a cattle farming industry that raised and shipped cattle and pickled beef to feed slaves in the Caribbean (Farrow et al., 2005). Money, hitherto a scarce commodity in interior New England, began to circulate, and trading partnerships and shipbuilding became features of the local economy, strung along the length of the Connecticut Valley. Products of the Caribbean slave plantations, chiefly sugar and molasses, also began to be imported, providing raw materials for distilleries and for further trade (see Chen and Shemo, this volume).

At mid-century, for the first time, a cluster of several dozen shops and small-scale manufacturing enterprises appeared in the central settlement of Hartford. These served a far-flung regional population. Profits from commercial agriculture also produced a building boom—many of the region's surviving 18th-century farmhouses and churches were direct products of the new trading economy based on participation in the slave economy. Chattel slavery itself became more visible in Hartford and Connecticut, with about 1 to 3 percent of the population in many towns held in bondage. One suggestive measure of Hartford's slowly rising status as an urban space in the 1770s was that it was one of 20 localities in the American colonies where a newspaper was published.

There were, however, challenges for this very sharply defined regional subculture. A century of very high rates of natural population growth was causing land shortages and forcing the settlement of increasingly marginal land in northern New England. Grievances over imperial restrictions on the settlement of colonists west of the Allegheny Mountains contributed significantly to local grievances about British rule that eventually led to the American Revolution. During the war itself, the Hartford region's cattle farms proved to be important sources of supply for the Continental Army and of considerable profit to the local gentry.

After 1780, and the American victory in the Revolution, rapid change began in the region. The local elite reinvested the capital it had reaped from cattle export into banking and insurance mostly, at first, outside the region, and then in land speculation in the Ohio Valley. In the late 1790s and the first decade of the 19th century, profits from these investments were re-invested in the region, producing the first banks and insurance companies based in Hartford. Usually, these were established and run by overlapping groups of kin, who shared capital and management experience. Despite this economic stimulus, the most striking feature of regional life in this period was massive internal migration to the West, which drained the population of much of the New England countryside, although Hartford itself continued to grow slowly. By 1820, when the city's population was about 9,000, New England's continuing economic vitality was in question as young New Englanders, mostly farmers, poured westward and out of the region. Colonial New England was dissolving itself.

HARTFORD THREE: THE RISE OF MANUFACTURING (1830–1890)

Early-19th-century Hartford was a fairly sleepy place. While new "financial service" companies were getting off the ground, the region's agriculture was in eclipse and Hartford, as a "flat water" town, missed the first phase of the Industrial Revolution in New England. The most dramatic change in New England's economic life during this period followed the rise of the region's maritime power. New England-based maritime traders became a global force after the War of 1812, dramatically expanding commerce with Europe, introducing trade with Asia, and establishing whaling on a global scale (see Figure 2.1). These changes put New England into direct commercial contact with a much larger slice of the world, but the impact in interior New England was far less dramatic than in coastal areas.

Figure 2.1.   Early View of Hartford, 1827. (Connecticut Historical Society)

The region's first factories all depended on water power, which required falling water. New Englanders were deeply involved in the process of pirating the first generation of manufacturing technology from English and Scottish sources. The pioneering mills, however, depended on water power, which Hartford largely lacked, although Hartford investors began to build small manufacturing operations in outlying parts of Hartford County and in Eastern Connecticut, where falling water could be harnessed.

Hartford County became a net importer of food in the mid-1820s, which suggested that an industrial economy was nevertheless developing in the region. More of the workforce was moving into manufacturing and population growth was returning. Throughout the 1840s, however, manufacturing was concentrated in small villages on the slopes of the walls of the Connecticut River Valley. It was only with the perfection of steam technology, and especially the construction of the first railroads, that the Hartford region leapt into industrial transformation. In the region, there was a long-standing elite class with surplus capital to invest, there were unusually literate and numerate workers to put to work, and a vigorous local culture which valorized savings, investment, and tinkering. In the Connecticut Valley there was a strong tradition of craft-manufacture of firearms. What the region lacked in natural resources, it made up for, at least potentially, in human capital.

The railroad arrived in Hartford in 1839, triggering rapid economic development. The railroad revolutionized transport, and made it possible to import coal and raw materials relatively cheaply and then to distribute new manufactured goods widely. But the economic and technological logic of steam-driven power favored very dense concentrations of population and enterprise. Hartford, along with a number of other New England cities, was suddenly well-positioned for economic take-off.[5] Economic development was driven for the next several decades by local investors and entrepreneurs, the most famous of whom was Samuel Colt, who learned through trial and error how to manufacture technically demanding products like firearms. In the early years of industrialization, Hartford also became a center of steam-powered printing, and of publication, especially of textbooks for the evolving educational market. There was a substantial contrast between Hartford's early manufacturing efforts and those of other parts of New England. Rather than mass-market products like textiles or shoes, which required relatively modest skills to produce, Hartford focused on very high skill metalwork—guns, printing, machine tools, boilermaking, and industrial infrastructure such as the production of the leather belts to transmit power from steam-driven mechanisms to production machinery. During the 1850s and 1860s, Colt Firearms proved to be a critical incubator for industrial talent, with Colt workers spinning off into separate enterprises, especially in machine tools, creating companies like Pratt & Whitney, Atlantic Machine Screw, and Hartford Machine Screw, which would all play a national role in their industries for many decades. Talented machine designers like Elisha Root, Francis Pratt, Amos Whitney, Christopher Spencer, George Fairfield, and George Capewell were drawn to Hartford during the middle decades of the century to work at Colt and other pioneer mills.

During this period of initial industrialization, Hartford investors were also creating new mill enclaves in the larger region—papermaking in Windsor Locks, silk in Manchester, carpet-weaving in Thompsonville, hardware in New Britain, hand tools in Collinsville, and textile production in Willimantic, Rockville, Stafford Springs and Broad Brook. Many of these companies were administered from Hartford and so the new industrial hub surrounded itself with satellite industrial communities. During the same period, Hartford's young banks and insurance companies were also expanding, forging global economic ties, and establishing a reputation for paying when customers filed claims—often because their interlocking, interrelated directorates loaned one another money when problems arose. Hartford companies were also writing new forms of insurance: life insurance and travel insurance, and not simply property and casualty insurance (Chen and Shemo, this volume). All of these required skilled workers, who began to concentrate in the region.

During the 1840s and early 1850s the major obstacle to industrialization in the Hartford area was a shortage of workers, mostly the result of the Great Migration to the west of the preceding generation. This shortage would be addressed by an epochal global development, the re-opening of massive migration from Europe. Overpopulation and famine produced an enormous exodus from Ireland in the 1850s, and this migration transformed New England over the next few decades. Between 1850 and 1890, immigration into New England was overwhelmingly Irish (an average of about 70 percent of Hartford's foreign-born were Irish throughout this period). Hartford's population, which had grown only by a few hundred between 1840 and 1850, more than doubled between 1850 and 1860, reaching about 30,000. In a city which had been almost entirely native-born in 1850, Irish immigrants and their children suddenly made up a third of the population.[6]

The social frictions that developed in the 1850s were very substantial, with public struggles over religion (the Irish were overwhelmingly and actively Roman Catholic and the native-born were militantly Protestant), public education, the social habits of the Irish, and the extreme poverty of their circumstances. The immigrant population clustered in the city's oldest neighborhoods on the west bank of the Connecticut River, close to where the new factories were concentrated. More prosperous Yankees withdrew to the city's first "suburbs" to the north, west, and south of the downtown area, although still well within municipal boundaries. This introduced, for the first time in Hartford's history, very clear segmentation of residential areas by income level and "ethnicity." (There were other immigrant groups arriving, but they were dramatically smaller in size. In 1860, Germans, many of whom were Jewish, composed the only other numerically significant group, at about one sixth the size of the Irish community.)

The downtown also emerged in the 1860s as a distinctive commercial and administrative zone. With the Yankees and the Irish withdrawing into distinctive neighborhoods, local culture moved toward bifurcation. The Yankees controlled the resources, but knew they needed Irish labor to prosper and the Irish, in turn, sought to control as many aspects of their community's life as they could. In the larger civic arena, they were chiefly interested in access to jobs and access to democratic politics. One result of this substantially bifurcated society was that Hartford's Irish immigrants made very slow economic progress between 1850 and 1890. The overwhelming majority of skilled workers remained Yankees and most male immigrants of the first generation remained unskilled laborers throughout their lives. Some of their sons rose to become skilled workers, but most did not.

Industrialization, therefore, brought a very uneven sort of prosperity to the region (the working class, who made up the majority of the population, remained desperately poor well into the 20th century). There were, nevertheless, substantial investments, including in a new civic infrastructure, an expanding public school system, colleges like Trinity, libraries, and a variety of nascent social-service organizations, many of which still exist.

Hartford's role as Connecticut's capital also shifted in this period, with the city becoming Connecticut's sole capital in 1874, a transition marked by the construction of a large new capitol overlooking Bushnell Park. State-government-related employment remained quite modest, however, with all three branches of the state government adequately housed in the new capitol. The state's government was growing, but its employees were largely dispersed around the state, staffing jails, the prison, normal schools and new institutions designed to care for mentally ill people, dependent Civil War veterans, neglected children, and the developmentally disabled.

HARTFORD FOUR:
INDUSTRIAL POWERHOUSE (1890–1970)

A new stage of dramatic change took hold of the local economy at the end of the 19th century, with Hartford developing into a substantial magnet for external investment. These investments were driven by the maturation of corporate manufacturing enterprise, the creation of larger manufacturing firms taking advantage of new economies of scale, surging foreign investment in the United States, and the development of national economic actors in the United States concentrated on "Wall Street." Hitherto, Hartford's economic development had been driven mostly by local actors and entrepreneurs who worked with local sources of capital and homegrown technological and commercial ideas. The first firms to tap into this global economic transformation were local insurance companies, which were already developing national and international sales networks in the mid-19th century. But the most visible change accompanied the arrival of new and large-scale manufacturing corporations whose managers chose to locate in Hartford because its workforce demonstrated strengths in high skill manufacturing. During the 1890s and 1900s a series of new factories—all financed from outside the region—opened in the city. These included the Pope Manufacturing complex devoted to automobile manufacturing—a complex of five, closely related factories—and two major typewriter makers, Royal and Underwood (see Figure 2.2). These enterprises located their factories along the railroad lines running west of downtown Hartford, forming the backbone of a new industrial corridor stretching to the southwest. This concentration of new work stimulated the transformation of Frog Hollow and Parkville into working-class factory districts.

Figure 2.2.   Underwood Typewriter Company. (CT Historical Society)

The most important example of this trend of external investment was the arrival of a group of Midwestern investors and engineers in 1925 to begin production of a lightweight engine for airplanes in surplus space at the Pratt & Whitney Machine Tool Company on Capitol Avenue in Frog Hollow. Led by Frederick Rentschler and George Mead, the new company shared the Pratt & Whitney name, but soon out-grew the old machine tool factory in Frog Hollow. In 1929, Rentschler spun the new company off, making it a key player in the newly formed conglomerate called United Aircraft and Transportation that included the Boeing Company and what would become United Airlines. At about the same time, Rentschler's new company bought 1,000 acres of land in East Hartford and built a new factory complex there—the first major factory complex outside the city limits and a massive economic force that would become the major driver for metropolitan expansion east of the Connecticut River. By World War II, the new Pratt & Whitney complex employed more than 25,000 workers. Total Pratt employment in Connecticut exceeded 40,000 by the 1970s (also see Chen and Shemo, this volume).

The arrival of so much new industry and the continued expansion of local insur-ance and banking companies created massive demand for new labor, which was met largely by increased and much more diverse immigration. The city's population in 1890 was 53,230. It had almost doubled by 1910 and, after the boom years of World War I, the city's population would reach 138,036 (see Map 2.1). During the 1920s, for the first time, there was large-scale suburban population growth in the towns bordering Hartford, a harbinger of the main trend of the 20th century—toward the creation of a sizeable metropolitan region.

But the changes in population went far beyond mere growth in size. During the 1890s, the region's population, which previously had been divided between Yankees and Irish immigrants and their children, was profoundly reshaped by immigration from Eastern and Southern Europe. While the largest single group of immigrants continued to be Irish in the 1890s and 1900, substantial numbers of Italians, Swedes, and Danes began moving to the city, along with thousands of immigrants from the Russian, Austro-Hungarian, and German Empires, many of whom were Jews. By 1920, Italians and Russian Jews outnumbered the Irish-born, and there were surging communities of Poles, Lithuanians, Greeks, Armenians, and French Canadians. Many of these groups clustered in neighborhoods around the periphery of the downtown.

The East Side, Hartford's main "port of entry" neighborhood, was transformed in the 1890s into a remarkable polyglot neighborhood, filled with boardinghouses, stores, bars, ethnic clubs, sweatshops, and religious institutions that catered to new immigrants. After 1910, Hartford was a city of immigrants and their children and the most important local marker of identity became religious affiliation. In the middle decades of the 20th century, the population of the city was about 10 percent Protestant (mostly Yankee, but also African American), 80 percent Catholic, and 10 percent Jewish. The new suburban areas outside the city remained mostly Yankee, with a growing Catholic population.

After decades in which local politics was dominated by positional struggles between Yankees and the Irish, the new and massive wave of migration finally broke the Yankee hold on local politics. A new city charter was adopted in 1897 abolishing the old dual form of government in which there were overlapping city and town governments, with a new form that gave much more representation to the crowded immigrant wards on the city's east and south sides. The first Irish American mayor, Ignatius Sullivan, was elected in 1903. The Irish were the most obvious beneficiaries of the great economic expansion, partly because of their acculturation over the preceding decades and partly because they spoke English. After several decades at the bottom, in the 1890s and 1910s, Irish Americans surged up the local socioeconomic ladder, dominating the ranks of skilled blue-collar workers and acquiring middle-class jobs in new fields like public school teaching, nursing, municipal employment, beginning to move into the professions, and even dominating property ownership on the East Side as slum lords. The Irish Americans then began to follow the Yankees out of the old core city neighborhoods into new settlements north, south, and west of downtown.[7]

The period of massive migration from Europe came to an abrupt halt in 1914 and did not really resume after the end of World War I. New laws that set sharp quotas on immigration, especially from Eastern and Southern Europe, took effect in 1924 and 1925, largely foreclosing the possibility of continuing immigration from the places most likely to send emigrants to the United States.

In compensation, the city's small, but deeply rooted, African American community began to grow and change during this period. After 1925, the most important source of migration into the Hartford region would come to be the American South, and later the Caribbean. Until the early 20th century, most local African Americans were New England–born, but a small migration from the South, especially from Virginia, opened in the 1870s. African Americans faced considerable economic competition from white European immigrants for service jobs and were not hired in local factories. Indeed, the African American population, which hovered at around the 1 percent level throughout the 19th century, began to fall slightly after 1910. That changed dramatically during World War I, when combat prevented continuing migration of Europeans across the Atlantic and local employers faced a very tight labor market because of the superheated demand of the war years. One sector of Hartford employers—the operators of commercial tobacco farms in the Connecticut Valley towns outside Hartford—faced particularly dire labor shortages because their workers were being hired by Hartford factories. Tobacco farmers responded by tapping an underutilized labor pool—African Americans in the segregated South, most particularly in Georgia. In 1915 alone Hartford's African American population tripled to 3 percent. The attractions of Hartford were clear—wages that were often triple those available in Georgia, the promise of voting rights for African-American males, and access to a public education system that was not segregated by race. The challenges were equally clear: functional segregation in the city's factories that limited African Americans to unskilled work, difficulties in obtaining housing, some de facto segregation of public accommodations, and considerable racial friction, especially with European immigrants in the city's poorest neighborhoods.[8]

By the 1930s—even after very modest growth in the city's African American population during the 1920s—it was becoming clear that de facto forms of racial segregation were taking hold in Hartford, where, for the first time, clear African American neighborhoods were developing. A 1934 municipal report on slum housing admitted

> that it cannot be truthfully denied that as a racial group [African Americans] have been shown discrimination in matters of houses available to them. In Hartford, as well as in cities like New York, Newark, Boston, Cleveland, Chicago, Milwaukee, etc., the Negroes due to their low position in the social and economic groups have been forced to live in whatever tenements were abandoned and no longer desired by the white families. (Hartford [Conn.]. Slum Clearing Society, 1934)

By 1940, when the city's minority population was still less than 5 percent, the first African American majority Census Tract was recorded, at the northern edge of the East Side stretching into the South Arsenal neighborhood.

By the late 1920s, it was clear that the entire Connecticut Valley around Hartford was being reshaped by population growth and movement (Map 2.1). Yankees led the movement out of the old core city, especially into Hartford's western neighborhoods, and then on to adjacent suburban towns like West Hartford, Windsor, and Wethersfield. Rising middle-class incomes, the new electricity grid, and the increasing ownership of automobiles made it possible for thousands of families to aspire to a life lived in single-family housing in new residential neighborhoods far removed from Hartford's factories and social tensions (but also from the region's social amenities). The children and grandchildren of European immigrants, led by the Irish Americans, were following the Yankees into city neighborhoods and eventually into suburbs, often creating very distinctive neighborhoods build around Catholic parish complexes or the religious and commercial infrastructure required by Jewish life.

As early as 1911, many in the city's elite appreciated that the city's form was changing significantly. The decentralizing impact of electrification, the internal combustion engine, the change in industrial architecture required to accommodate the assembly line, and the ideal of the single-family house all pointed toward urban expansion that would overrun the border of the old city. John LaCarrere, the New York architect and city planner who produced the city's first master plan in 1912, took it for granted that the municipal borders would expand to encompass the new urban reality, "the Greater Hartford to be." Quoting City Park Superintendent George Parker's preliminary report on the region's economic prospects, LaCarrere predicted that Hartford is the

> municipal unit that is bound sooner or later to include all of this beautiful valley from Bissell's Ferry to Rocky Hill, a valley full of delightful promises. The special blessing of a great opportunity seems to have rested upon all who have lived here in the past, and greater promises to those who are to follow. Half way between its northern and southern extremities, between its eastern and western hills, is the Hartford of the present, the nucleus of what the Hartford of the future will be. (Carrere and Hastings, 1912)

LaCarrere, in other words, envisioned an enlarged municipality stretching from Rocky Hill in the south to the northern border of Windsor, an area that would eventually include hundreds of thousands of residents. While LaCarrere's prophecy made considerable economic sense, it failed to take into account the force of local custom, including the sanctity of town borders in New England. Over the course of its history, the original Hartford has been subdivided into four towns (Hartford, East Hartford, Manchester, and West Hartford), but no Connecticut town has ever been incorporated into another. Carrere's plan would have called for the merger of up to a dozen towns into a new metropolitan municipality.

The city's economic elite wrestled with such problems and was open to sweeping municipal expansion, which after all, would not have affected its power much, if at all. Carrere's study, for example, was commissioned by the Hartford Board of Trade, and not the city government, which was an accurate predictor of the source of most pressure for change and "redevelopment" during the 20th century. It turned out, however, that the region's historic municipalities and most voters weren't and aren't open to regional consolidation (see Rojas and Wray, this volume). The region's most important missed opportunity for a fundamental rebalancing of municipal government that would take account of the changing scope of the city came in 1929, when a new quasi-governmental commission to provide modern water and sewer service to the region's core city and emerging suburbs was created. The legislative charter granted to the Metropolitan District Commission (MDC) empowered it to perform planning and zoning functions and to lay taxes in Hartford and five surrounding towns.[9] But the section of the MDC charter authorizing regional planning never took effect because of opposition from suburban towns. Had a new, regional municipal authority with power to plan and tax taken hold in the 1930s, the subsequent history of Hartford and the region might have looked very different.

While the economic news was not all good during this period (the fledgling automobile industry, for example, failed to compete effectively with low-cost Midwestern automakers, and the Great Depression was as difficult here as in most American cities), in retrospect, the middle decades of the 20th century represent a kind of local golden age. The region's economy was dominated by very sizeable, very stable manufacturing and insurance companies, which were among the most innovative and successful in their fields. In these decades, jobs at Aetna, Travelers, or Pratt & Whitney turned out to be safe for most workers and rising incomes secured by both white-collar expansion and the unionization of skilled workers made Hartford's economy the most complex, technologically sophisticated, and profitable in New England.

The city itself reached peak population during the manufacturing boom caused by World War II, surging from 164,072 to 177,397 between 1940 and 1950. The actual peak was probably reached in 1944 or 1945, just before substantial movement to new suburban developments began in the late 1940s. In 1950, the Census reported a metropolitan population of just over 300,000.

Local business leaders had begun to warn as early as the 1930s that the city's 19th-century factory districts were obsolescent and the factory neighborhoods around them faded as newer housing provided a much higher standard of living (toilets inside apartments rather than in the hall, and central heating, for example). During the 1940s and 1950s major manufacturers began to follow Pratt & Whitney to the suburbs. Pratt & Whitney's vast manufacturing and assembly plant in East Hartford was eventually joined by large satellite plants in Middletown, Southington, and North Haven. In the early 1940s, Colt Firearms and Pratt & Whitney Machine Tools left the old urban core for the new industrial zone along New Park Avenue in West Hartford, where the company constructed sprawling new single-story buildings that provided modern manufacturing space. Thereafter, manufacturing withered away almost completely in the city's oldest industrial zone, along the Connecticut River to the east and south of downtown. As early as the late 1930s, population began falling on the East Side and in the old downtown.

These trends were dramatically amplified by increasing federal intervention and investment in local economies and infrastructures that began in the 1930s but mushroomed in the 1950s. New Deal reforms to the industries providing finance for homeownership drastically shifted incentives away from rental housing toward single-family ownership, triggering a massive boom in suburban house construction that began after World War II and extended into the 1970s. The reforms associated with the Federal Housing Act of 1934 created an ingenious system of federal guarantees of qualifying mortgages which created a supply of inexpensive, stable home mortgages that had never existed before and which helped move most of the middle and working class into homeownership. Between 1940 and 1960, the percentage of Hartford County families living in a home they owned shot up from about 32 percent to 60 percent. In 1940, about 25 percent of families in the City of Hartford lived in housing they owned. At that point, rental housing was the norm in American society and not the indicator of economic weakness that it would become. Hartford's municipal boundaries were almost full by 1940, however, and the city had little space for new subdivisions of single-family houses. Because of its fixed boundaries, the great housing boom of the middle and late 20th century drained Hartford, rather than building it up. During the 1950s, for example, the populations of nearby Enfield, Bloomfield, East Hartford, Windsor, Simsbury, Glastonbury, Manchester, and Newington all doubled. By contrast, Hartford's population fell for the first time, from its peak of 177,397 to 162,178 in 1960. One study included in the 1960 Census estimated that more than 90,000 of the city's residents had moved to the new suburbs during the 1950s. Homeownership rates inside the city haven't budged since 1940 and are among the lowest in the nation.

The urbanized landscape was further transformed by three other federally-funded efforts that all accelerated during the 1950s, the construction of a new and expansive interstate highway network that linked Hartford to bedroom suburbs, the launching of "urban renewal" focused on creating a new regional downtown, and the construction of new, government subsidized housing projects to house the poor, almost all of which were located in Hartford (see Condon, this volume).

Several of these programs had the effect of raising racial barriers, just as Hartford was beginning to attract a significant stream of minority migrants and eventually immigrants. The mortgage reforms of the 1930s indirectly created a set of mortgage practices that made it very difficult for urban neighborhoods with African American populations to qualify for the new, federally guaranteed mortgage products, a process popularly called "red-lining." Red-lining drastically accelerated white flight from urban to suburban neighborhoods in the 1950s and 1960s and largely blocked minority population movement to the suburbs. Meanwhile, urban renewal and the construction of public housing projects leveled the old East Side and North Main Street in the North End became a public housing corridor with a concentration of very low-income residents, increasingly cut off from access to jobs or to local retail. Similar things happened in most American cities during this period, but because of the Hartford area's fundamental prosperity in the 1950s and 1960s, the local situation became unusually skewed, very quickly.

After 1950, the City of Hartford underwent dramatic demographic transformation. In that year, its population was more than 90 percent white. In the 1950s, it remained an industrial center that provided more than 30,000 manufacturing jobs within its city limits. But by the early 1970s, the city was about half white and home to only about 20,000 manufacturing jobs. It lost half of those manufacturing jobs by 1975, and most of the rest by 1990. By 2010, fewer than 20 percent of the city's residents were white, about 37 percent were African American, and 41 percent Latino. The Latino surge in population reflected the city's largest immigration trend of the late 20th century, movement into the region by immigrants from the Caribbean, most notably from Puerto Rico and Jamaica (see Bauer, this volume). Once again, work in the suburban tobacco industry opened major migration vectors to the region.

Those arriving in Hartford after World War II entered an economic market where the traditional first jobs of newcomers in manufacturing were beginning to dry up. For the first time in its history, Hartford drew a continuing migration or poor people who settled despite shrinking economic opportunities. By the 1970s, Hartford began to appear on national statistical summaries as one of the very poorest cities in the nation, although its much larger metropolitan area remained one of the most prosperous. By 2010, the city's poverty rate had exceeded 32 percent, with 46 percent of its children living below the federally defined poverty line (see Simmons, this volume).

As suggested above, much of this had to do with the rapid erosion of the industrial base that had made Hartford a good place to make a living for more than a century. After a long stretch in which it was in the right place at the right time, national and global economic factors began to shift against it as a relatively high-cost center of manufacturing. In the late 1960s and especially the early 1970s, the city lost factory after factory, some to the suburbs, but more to national and global competitors. The city's machine tool factories shrank and then closed, unable to compete with Japanese manufacturers, Fuller Brush moved away, and both of the city's large type-writer factories closed, as the office typewriter machines business went first to IBM and then to computers. The spaces occupied by former factories emptied and the adjacent neighborhoods of working-class housing slipped further and further into poverty. The general outline of this story is shared with many other cities in New England and the Northeast.

Meanwhile, the region's white-collar boom continued, although by this time most white-collar employees now lived outside the city. Few American cities experienced such a schizoid fate—simultaneous and massive blue-collar job loss and white-collar expansion in the same place at the same time. And until the late 1980s, there was little movement of the city's new minority population into the more prosperous suburbs. So, in the late 20th century, Hartford presented a double face to the world: as an increasingly poor core city and as a fundamentally prosperous metropolitan region.

One important contributor to white-collar growth was the state government, which began a long period of expansion in the 1930s as it took on new regulatory and service commitments. The first office state office building opened in the 1930s, with many more following on. By the 1990s, state executive, judicial and legislative branch offices created a new "government district" surrounding the capitol and stretching along Capitol Avenue from Main Street to Sigourney Street. In November 2012, the state labor department counted 79,000 state and municipal employees in the Hartford labor market, by far the largest concentration of government employees in the state.[10] Public higher education also became a significant employer after World War II. The Hartford region is now the site of five community colleges, Central Connecticut State University, and a satellite undergraduate campus of the University of Connecticut, along with several of its professional schools.

The city government and the local business elite struggled to find solutions to Hartford's accelerating industrial decline, but most of these involved building up white-collar employment in the financial services, professions, and government sectors, which did not provide much work for the city's own changing population. In the late 1950s and 1960s, the city government and the business leadership struggled to address white flight and attempted to preserve racial balance in Hartford's public schools, enlisting the aid of the Harvard Graduate School of Education to design a new school structure that would balance school populations despite the rapid changes in the city's population, then mostly concentrated in the northern third of the city. The full implementation of the plan was blocked, however, by opposition concentrated in the white, working-class neighborhoods of the South End. Racial change accelerated to the point that, by the 1980s, Hartford's public school population was more than 90 percent African American and Latino.

There were some efforts to reshape local governance to reflect the complex, metropolitan reality that was then developing. In 1958, the Capitol Region Planning Authority (CRPA) was established to promote regional planning. But by the mid-1960s it was already clear that suburban interests—now a well-established majority of the region's population—resisted the idea of surrendering town powers to plan, zone, and tax to a new regional structure. Roger W. Conant of MIT reported in 1964 that the representatives sent by local towns to serve on the planning authority were deeply ambivalent about its goals.

> Our interviews among them reveal a reserved support, skepticism, and outright opposition to what they perceive as the objectives of the CRPA. Those who count themselves as supporters believe vaguely in planning and have learned that the Agency is harmless. The skeptics look for reassurances that the Agency is not power seeking and they wonder about the feasibility of planning. The opposition worry about super government and regional control by "the boys in Hartford." (Conant, 1964)

As a result, regional conferences of governments have served only a weak, advisory role in the region.

The city's business leadership, on the other hand, grew more assertive during the 1950s and 1960s. The city's Chamber of Commerce, led by Arthur Lumsden, provided key support for the downtown urban renewal projects of the mid-20th century, mobilizing the city's insurance companies, banks, and major industries to modernize the downtown and make it the center of regional white-collar employment. These priorities became urgent in the mid-1950s, when both the Connecticut General Insurance Company and the newly organized University of Hartford purchased large suburban campuses and moved out of town. In the mid-1950s, it appeared that Hartford was losing its population and its factories to the suburbs, the prospect of losing white-collar and retail employment downtown seemed too much to bear.

The result was substantial "slum clearance" downtown, which reduced the area's resident population from 10,000 to a few hundred, the construction of the Constitution Plaza Project on the site of the old East Side, and the refitting of the downtown for automobile commuters. Led by Lumsden, the region's business leaders even dreamed of a private-sector-led effort to reshape the region in the late 1960s and 1970s. "Greater Hartford Process" dreamed of using real estate development, first in the suburbs and then in declining city neighborhoods, to reshape and stabilize the whole region. The key was a set of plans to create satellite "new towns" and then to reinvest profits in urban renewal in the city itself, focused on the declining North End. Since they viewed this venture as, in essence, a real estate development project, the leaders of Greater Hartford Process and its corporate development arm called the Development Company or DevCo, proceeded largely in secret. The group's first project called for the construction of a new town in the northern part of Coventry, a rural town east of Hartford. DevCo secretly purchased options for 1,800 acres of land there. When, unsurprisingly, residents of Coventry began to ask who was buying up land so avidly in their town, speculation centered on a "corporate plot" to dump poor, minority people on underpopulated, eastern Connecticut and redevelop the land they lived on in Hartford. DevCo's actual plan was to build a mixed-income town, with enough high-priced real estate to generate profits that could be used to fund redevelopment in Hartford itself. But as the Coventry plan sank into public controversy, Greater Hartford Process fell apart in steps in the early 1970s. Its managers were unable to reconcile themselves to the public's need for full disclosure, and the prospects of actually building the new town faded away (see McKee and Bacon, this volume).

Failures like these contributed to a sense that overwhelming problems were building up in Hartford, and by the late 1960s the city was racked by a series of riots that were among the most serious suffered by American cities in that tumultuous decade. The riots, culminating in 1969, expressed African American rage at racial isolation, housing and job segregation, overcrowding in slum neighborhoods, and troubled relations with police and the city government. Their chief immediate impact, however, was to accelerate white flight from the city and to damage the neighborhoods where the rioters lived.

HARTFORD FIVE: TROUBLED METROPOLIS, 1970 TO THE PRESENT

During the 1970s, the Hartford region turned a new corner. The long white-collar expansion that had begun in the 1940s slowed and eventually stopped in the mid-1980s. For the first time since the 1830s, the region became a place of slow, sometimes negligible, growth in economy and population. This was the direct result of Hartford's changing place in the national and global economy (see Chen and Shemo, this volume). As with many other parts of both the Northeast and the United States as whole, new global competition has put immense strain on both the industrial and white-collar economies. There are two plausible ways to read the results in the Hartford area. The first is that deindustrialization and then white-collar corporate downsizing have caused immense and continuing damage to local life and prospects. The second is that the metropolitan region has nursed its residual strengths so that catastrophic economic challenges have, so far, been largely fended off. Under this second scenario, the region has achieved a kind of stagnation at a comparatively high level that must be seen, because of the magnitude of the forces acting against it, as a revelation of its continuing strengths.

In the early 1960s, optimistic regional planners projected that the region would grow to about 1 million in 1980 and 2 million by 2000. In fact, the region, which is now home to about 1.2 million people, hit the 1980 target, but then growth pretty much stopped. Despite this population plateau, suburban expansion continued, pushed by the construction of larger houses on larger plots of land in ever more distant suburbs.

During the 1970s, industrial decline spread beyond the city's borders and throughout the region. By that point, most of Hartford's major industrial concerns had either closed or weakened, so most of this contraction occurred in the new manufacturing zones developed outside the city since 1940. Around the region, historic mill complexes in Enfield, Windsor Locks, New Britain, Bristol, and other industrial towns were also abandoned. A recession in the early 1970s drastically reduced non-

Figure 2.3. The End of an Era: IAM Machinists Vote on Pratt & Whitney Contract, 1974. (Hartford Public Library)

defense-related manufacturing. Defense–related manufacturing, and in particular, the massive Pratt & Whitney complex in the state, began to downsize dramatically in the mid-1980s (Chen and Shemo, Bacon, this volume).

While the region's white-collar boom had persisted into the 1980s, in that decade major local financial service institutions began to experience competition in national and global financial service markets with deregulated marketplaces. In Hartford, banking and insurance firms began to restructure their workforces, and especially to move less-skilled white-collar workers into the new suburban office facilities. But as the decade passed, more and more "pink collar" work was affected by changing technology, and particularly by computerization, which began to eliminate many routine, white-collar jobs. The City of Hartford reached peak employment in 1988, when it had 160,000 jobs, about 50,000 of which were in the so-called Finance, Insurance, and Real Estate Sector, and about 46,000 in the service and nonprofit agency sectors. Employment in the state government had also become an increasingly important local source of work. (As the region grew in size, the city's share of the region's total employment sank in turn. In 1966, half of the region's jobs were located in Hartford. In 2011, the city's share was closer to 20 percent. And since the 1960s new job creation has taken place almost exclusively in the suburbs.)

Between 1985 and 1995, the high end of the local economy followed the industrial sector into crisis. Deregulation and global competition brought profound new competition to the financial services sector. As patterns of bank regulation shifted,

Hartford's major commercial banks all merged with larger regional entities. The region's insurance companies also encountered the most severe turbulence in their history. Connecticut General, Connecticut Mutual, and the Travelers were all absorbed into larger holding companies. Aetna, the biggest of the insurance companies, repositioned itself as a provider of health insurance, rather than a multi-line company offering property, casualty, and life insurance. One positive result was that by the mid-1990s Hartford had emerged as a major national center of the health insurance industry, but along the way companies shed thousands of employees in waves of contraction. Similar things were happening in what was left of the manufacturing sector. Pratt & Whitney struggled to maintain its competitive edge against other aircraft engine manufacturers and began to relocate much of its manufacturing first outside Connecticut and then outside the United States. Pressed hard to stay in business, the leadership of Hartford's big-business sector paid ever less attention to the region's problems and to invest less in redevelopment. One measure of this decline is the long pause in downtown development that took place in Hartford. From 1960 until the mid-1980s, Hartford was one of the fastest growing office markets in the nation. But recession in the late 1980s stopped three major office tower projects in their tracks and for almost 20 years there were no new downtown office building developed.

Meanwhile, demographic change continued in the region. After 1970, the major source for immigration into the region was the Caribbean. After several decades of strong migration by African Americans, after 1980 there was a surge of migration of Latinos, who became the most important group in city's population (see Sacks, this volume). The city's politics slowly tracked these changes. In 1980, the first year with a majority-minority population, Thirman Milner was elected the city's first African American mayor. He was succeeded by another African American, Carrie Saxon-Perry, who lost a reelection bid in the middle of the severe economic downturn of the early 1990s. The last two majors of Hartford have been representatives of the surging Latino population, Eddie Perez and Pedro Segarra, both produced by the city's Puerto Rican community. For most of the 1990s and 2000s, politics as practiced in Hartford was a matter of balancing delicately between Latinos, African Americans, Afro-Caribbeans and a small group of whites. The 1990s brought further immigration to the region, but at a slower rate than in other American regions where the economy was growing faster. The population influx included more Central and South Americans, South Asians, and Southeast Asians, some Africans, and more than a trickle from Eastern Europe and the Balkans (see Bauer, this volume). Increasingly, however, the region's immigrants moved directly to the suburbs.

For the city itself, the period between 1985 and 1995 brought new lows. National survey after national survey placed it among the poorest of all American municipalities, the population was shrinking quickly, crime and poverty—complicated by wars between competing drug gangs—were growing, redevelopment stalled, the city's schools were in extended crisis, along with police and other public services, and, quite suddenly, middle-class minority residents were leaving for the suburbs themselves. The city engaged in desperate measures between 1994 and 1997. It contracted out the school system to a corporation (see McKee and Bacon, this volume), before the state government finally took over the schools in 1997.

The situation deteriorated so far that it seemed like the bottom might be falling out. Urbanist David Rusk (2000) identified Hartford as one of a handful of American cities too poor to solve its own problems. In the absence of meaningful metropolitan governance, that left the state government as the main hope for reinvestment in the city. Large scale state spending began to come in measurable forms in the 1990s, when the state government briefly took over management of the school system and took control of downtown redevelopment. State funds were poured into the school system and many of the city's schools were replaced or rebuilt. A major school desegregation case, *Sheff v. O'Neill*, originally filed in 1989, also moved the region toward more concerted action to end the racial isolation of Hartford and suburban schoolchildren. The suit challenged the constitutionality of basing public school districts on municipal units when that produced racially unbalanced school districts. After losing the first round of the case in 1992, the state Supreme Court upheld the plaintiffs in 1996. The decision did not lead to massive school reorganization, but rather toward a complex system of more open enrollments and magnet schools, with the target of moving at least 30 percent of Hartford's minority schoolchildren into enrollment in integrated settings. Despite the reconfiguration of Hartford's own schools and the construction of many new magnet schools funded by the state, those targets remain unrealized (see Dougherty, this volume).

In the late 1990s, Gov. John Rowland's "Six Pillars" program, built around a series of major state-funded projects, channeled new investment into Hartford a new convention center, the transformation of the city's oldest department store into a community college campus, the refurbishment of the Old State House, and public support for a number of large residential and mixed-use projects downtown. During the same period, the city's public housing authority began a sweeping deconstruction of the city's housing projects, replacing them with smaller and more suburban-style units designed for mixed use. While other cities in the region—notably Boston, Providence, and New Haven—staged substantial recoveries in the late 1990s and 2000s, Hartford made a more modest and tentative recovery. By 2010, a wave of building renovations and some new construction downtown had created hundreds of new market-rate apartments that were fully occupied. Some signs of urban revival were becoming visible. Crime rates also subsided after peaking in the early 1990s, and Hartford's schools showed some signs of improvement.

Despite all of this, during the 1990s the City of Hartford was no longer the main zone of change in the region. The total population of the region remained quite stable, but the demographic composition of the population shifted away from white, European roots. The extreme polarization between Hartford and at least some of its suburbs began to soften quite dramatically. The most obvious change was a rapid shift of large numbers of minority residents to the suburbs. When the *Sheff v. O'Neill* lawsuit was filed, only three of Hartford County's 29 school systems had majority African American and Latino student populations (Hartford, New Britain,

Andrew Walsh

and Bloomfield). By 2010 public school systems in East Hartford, Manchester, and Windsor had joined the group and several others had very significant minority student populations. For many suburban towns, most notably East Hartford (see Bacon, this volume), the shifts brought falling incomes. This raised the sharp question of whether Hartford's poverty was spreading to the suburbs. In other places, notably in Windsor, the growth in African American and Afro-Caribbean population had little impact on economic status. Windsor became one of a handful of American communities in which average African American income is higher than average white income. And in other northern suburbs, incomes generally fell in the 1990s and 2000s, without large-scale demographic change. So, by 2010, the metropolitan region had moved far beyond the mere polarization of a poverty-stricken old core and its prosperous suburbs. Metropolitan Hartford was a complex patchwork of competing municipalities with widely varying assets and strengths.

At the economic level, the Hartford region functioned like an integrated unit, with the vast majority of residents living and working in sprawling, low-density "suburbs." A grid of highways bound the region together. There were retail centers around the suburban shopping malls in West Hartford, Manchester, and Enfield, and major centers of office parks in Windsor, Farmington, and Rock Hill. A mixed-use "Uptown" focused on upscale retail and restaurants had developed in the 1990s in West Hartford Center, serving the entire region. It was augmented substantially in the late 2000s by the ambitious Blue Back Square mixed-use complex.

And while the period from the late 1990s to 2008 was definitely better for the region than the proceeding decade had been, signs of trouble weren't hard to find. The urbanists who produced the *Connecticut Metropatterns* study in 2003 argued that the Connecticut pattern of uncoordinated, competitive development was hurting all of the state's communities at every income level, pitting municipalities against one another, sprawling unnecessarily into rural space, and ignoring developing economic problems in the state's oldest urban centers. The study argued, for example, that in an era when global economic trends were not arranged in Connecticut's favor, "59 percent of Connecticut's residents live in municipalities that either show clear signs of current fiscal and social stress or are at-risk of such difficulties in the near future." A belt of old manufacturing towns running from Bristol in the west through New Britain and onto East Hartford and Manchester were already seriously stressed and several others—including a clump of five towns north of Hartford—were judged "at risk."

But at the political level, the region remained disconnected and unwilling to engage energetically in the effort to address its collective challenges. The very sharp recession that began in 2008 showed the limits of the state government's capacity or willingness to stabilize or rebalance the region's governance. Less can probably be expected from the state government in the next decade.

Those inclined to see the glass as half full can take reasonable comfort from the way that the region absorbed the heavy blow of deindustrialization. Compared with many other former industrial centers, the Hartford region has not done so badly, considering the magnitude of the global forces acting on it. It retains considerable residual strength, perhaps even to a surprising degree, after decades of major change and diminishment in its white-collar economy. But, at best, its prospects seem stagnant in an era of continuing global challenge. The problem with this view is that it overlooks the severe and spreading problems of poverty and underemployment spreading out from Hartford.

Those who see the glass as half empty can point with concern to the region's maladaptive responses to the fundamental shift of local life to a metropolitan scale and the region's consequent failures to adapt to meet difficult challenges. The drastic decline of manufacturing created a deep crisis here, one that made coping with rapid demographic change even harder. The slower subsidence of the white-collar economy could bring even more pain. But this view probably undervalues the progress of many low-income people into more economically stable lives in the region's suburbs since the late 1980s. The region's more diverse population brings with it new strengths as well as new problems and more newcomers are tasting the benefits of American life than in the polarized years that preceded it.

And yet, in the current era, the region faces very serious challenges without any obvious new engines of economic growth. As its population grows poorer, the comparative skills of its workforce erode as well. As suburban communities come under greater stress, their educational systems move toward crisis and then produce more graduates who have trouble finding a productive place in the economy.

But whether one inclines to an optimistic or pessimistic reading of the region's responses to the challenges it faces, Hartford remains what it has been for most of its history, a region of rapid change whose experience illuminates the main channels of American life. Whether, and to what degree, the region embraces its metropolitan identity will make a big difference in the American future. Its diffidence about metropolitan reality is far from unique. I am disinclined to count Hartford out, but it must be admitted that the region hasn't been trying very hard to get its house in order.

NOTES

1. There are several histories of the city and region. The most scholarly is Glenn Weaver and Michael Swift's *Hartford: Connecticut's Capital: An Illustrated History* (Sun Valley, CA: American Historical Press, 2003); Ellsworth and Marion Hepburn Grant, *The City of Hartford, 1784-1984: An Illustrated History* (Hartford: Connecticut Historical Society, 1986) is also useful.

2. For an account of the drastic transformation of New England's landscape, see William Cronon's *Changes in the Land: Indians, Colonists and the Ecology of New England* (New York: Hill & Wang: 1983).

3. See George McLean Andrews, *The River Towns of Connecticut: A Study of Wethersfield, Hartford and Windsor* (Baltimore: Johns Hopkins University, 1889). This is one of the first pieces of professional historical scholarship on an American topic.

4. See Bruce C. Daniels, *The Connecticut Town, 1635–1790* (Middletown, CT: Wesleyan University Press, 1979); Bruce C. Daniels, *The Fragmentation of New England: Comparative Perspectives on Economic, Political, and Social Divisions in the Eighteenth Century* (New York: Greenwood Press, 1988); Jackson Turner Main, *Society and Economy in Colonial Connecticut* (Princeton, NJ: Princeton University Press, 1985); William DeLoss Love, *The Colonial History of Hartford: Gathered from Original Sources* (Hartford: Case, Lockwood & Brainard Co.: 1935).

5. For an account of New England urbanization that illuminates Hartford's experiences as well as New Haven's, see Douglas Rae, *City: The End of Urbanism* (New Haven: Yale University Press, 2004).

6. Bruce Clouette, *"Getting Their Share:" Irish and Italian Immigrants to Hartford, Connecticut, 1850–1940* (UConn PhD Diss.). is the best source on the Irish migration of mid-century. David Dalin and Jonathan Rosenbaum, *Making a Life, Building a Community: The History of the Jews of Hartford* (New York: Holmes and Meier, 1997) is the best account of the development of the local Jewish community.

7. For an account of the transformation of the East Side during the 1890s, see Gergely Baics, *Port of Entry Neighborhood in an American Industrial Town: Hartford's East Side, 1870–1920*, Trinity College undergraduate thesis, 2001.

8. See Charles Sheldon Johnson's masterful sociological study, *The Negro Population of Hartford* (New York: National Urban League, 1921). For a sophisticated study of African American residential patterns see Kurt Schlichting, Peter Tuckel, and Richard Maisel. 2006. "Residential Segregation and the Beginning of the Great Migration of African Americans to Hartford, Connecticut: A GIS-Based Analysis." *Historical Methods* 39 (3): 132–143.

9. The MDC was established after ratification by town votes in November 1929 in Hartford, Wethersfield, Windsor, Bloomfield, and Newington after two years of preliminary planning and enabling legislation passed by the Connecticut General Assembly in 1927. West Hartford voted against the MDC, but its opposition failed to throw the MDC off track. Writing in 1930, political scientist Lane Lancaster observed that West Hartford "next to Hartford itself, is the largest and wealthiest of any in the proposed district, being a choice residential suburb of the metropolis. The residents of the town seem to have feared that the proposed plan would lead to eventual annexation, and had a not unnatural desire to prevent their affairs from falling into the hands of Hartford politicians." See: Lane W. Lancaster, "Hartford Adopts a Metropolitan Charter," *American Political Science Review*, Vol. 24, No. 3 (Aug., 1930), pp. 693–698.

10. The slightly different statistics reported by the Connecticut Employment Resource Center suggest the continuing importance of government employment in the Hartford region. CERC reported that 9.6 percent of Hartford County's 438,071 total labor force worked in government. The comparable figures for Fairfield and New Haven counties, the only other Connecticut counties with comparably large labor forces, were 3.1 percent and 5.4 percent, respectively. See the country and town profiles at http://www.cerc.org/.

REFERENCES

Andrews, George McLean. 1889. *The River Towns of Connecticut: A Study of Wethersfield, Hartford and Windsor.* Johns Hopkins University.

Baics, Gegerly. 2001. *Port of Entry Neighborhood in an American Industrial Town: Hartford's East Side, 1870–1920.* Trinity College undergraduate thesis.

Carrere and Hastings. *1912. A Plan for the City of Hartford, Preliminary Report Advisory Architects, to the Commission on the City Plan of the City of Hartford, Connecticut.* Hartford: Case Lockwood, and Brainard.

Clouette, Bruce. *"Getting Their Share:" Irish and Italian Immigrants to Hartford, Connecticut, 1850–1940.* UConn PhD Dissertation.

Conant, Roger W. 1964. "The Politics of Regional Planning in Greater Hartford." Greater Hartford Chamber of Commerce.

Cronon, William. 1983. *Changes in the Land: Indians, Colonists and the Ecology of New England*. Hill & Wang.

Dalin, David G., and Jonathan Rosenbaum. 1997. *Making a Life, Building a Community: The History of the Jews of Hartford*. Holmes and Meier.

Daniels, Bruce C. 1979. *The Connecticut Town, 1635–1790*. Wesleyan University Press.

Daniels, Bruce C. 1988. *The Fragmentation of New England: Comparative Perspectives on Economic, Political, and Social Divisions in the Eighteenth Century.* Greenwood Press.

Dickens, Charles. 1842. *American Notes for General Circulation*. London: Chapman & Hall.

Ellsworth and Marion Hepburn Grant. 1986. *The City of Hartford, 1784-1984: An Illustrated History.* Hartford: Connecticut Historical Society.

Farrow, Anne, Joel Lang, and Jenifer Frank. 2005. *Complicity: How the North Promoted, Prolonged, and Profited from Slavery*. New York: Ballantine Books.

Hartford (Conn.). Slum Clearance Study Committee. 1934. *Report of the Slum Clearance Study Committee in the Preliminary Survey of Housing Conditions in Slum Areas for the Purpose of Laying Out a Slum Clearance and Rehousing program in Hartford, Connecticut.* June 1934.

Johnson, Charles Sheldon. 1921. *The Negro Population of Hartford*. National Urban League.

Kotkin, Joel. 2005. *The City: A Global History*. New York: Random House.

Lancaster, Lane W. "Hartford Adopts a Metropolitan Charter," *American Political Science Review* Vol. 24, No. 3, Aug. 1930, pp. 693–698.

Love, William DeLoss. *The Colonial History of Hartford: Gathered from Original Sources.* Case, Lockwood, and Brainard Co.: 1935.

Main, Jackson Turner. 1985. *Society and Economy in Colonial Connecticut*. Princeton University Press.

Orfield, Myron, and Thomas Luce. 2003. *Connecticut Metropatterns: A Regional Agenda for Community and Prosperity in Connecticut*. Connecticut: Ameregis.

Rusk, David. 2000. *Cities without Suburbs: A Census 2000 Update*. Washington, D.C.: Woodrow Wilson Center Press.

Schlichting, Kurt, Peter Tuckel, and Richard Maisel. 2006. "Residential Segregation and the Beginning of the Great Migration of African Americans to Hartford, Connecticut: A GIS-Based Analysis." *Historical Methods* 39 (3): 132–143.

Shaughnessy, Dan. 2009. "This Was a Killer Win for the Former Whalers." *Boston Globe*, May 24.

Weaver, Glenn, and Michael Swift. 2003. *Hartford: Connecticut's Capital: An Illustrated History.* Sun Valley, CA: American Historical Press.

3

Podunk after Pratt

Place and Placelessness in East Hartford, Connecticut

Nick Bacon

Urban spaces located outside the technical boundaries of most American cities are substantially underrepresented in urban theory. This is particularly true for Hartford, Connecticut, where the city's legal boundaries contain a smaller proportion of its actual urban area than any other major U.S. metropolis (see Bacon and Chen, introduction, this book). In this chapter, I explore the transformations of a dynamic, but hitherto completely unexamined,[1] portion of Hartford's urban area: the adjacent municipality of East Hartford, Connecticut. East Hartford is particularly ripe for analysis because:

1. Before the town's colonization in the 17th century, it was the primary residence of the Podunks, the first Connecticut Indian tribe to make contact with Europeans and among the first to disappear. This fact, as joined with the town's long subsequent agrarian history, inspired the American colloquialism "podunk," denoting an insignificant, out-of-the-way, or fictitious town.
2. It was one of the most important American military-industrial centers during the 20th century, serving as the headquarters of aerospace giant Pratt & Whitney, one of the primary producers of fighter jets for 20th-century American wars and military projects.
3. It is now undergoing massive deindustrialization, disinvestment, and urban renewal to a degree unprecedented in the rest of the Hartford region, while its new demographic transformations are the result of the dispossession of the inner city for the poor.

In order to explain theoretically East Hartford's unique history, this chapter is organized around the town's curious claim to "podunk." After excavating the hidden history behind the word's production (see below), I have created a somewhat rhetorical term to understand "podunk" diachronically, i.e., to describe the word's actual materialization in space and consciousness. *Podunkification* refers to the process whereby the place of an unrecognized "other" is annihilated to make way for a place which is itself insignificant, out of the way, or fictitious not only to the dispossessed, but also to the general population of colonists.

With this conceptual apparatus in hand, I delineate East Hartford's history as it transforms over time from the lands of the semi-nomadic Podunk Indians, to a colonized agrarian podunk, to its apparent antipode an industrial center and city. Then, I excavate the town's contemporary moment as a disoriented urban periphery undergoing deindustrialization and perpetual demographic flux. As I show, the politics of space in East Hartford today indicates that the town is not recognized as a place at all. And this perception that East Hartford is an urban podunk, I argue, is actually intensifying its podunkification, as the municipality embraces an urban strategy of place negation: demolishing what's left of its local fabric while actively constructing destructively alien megaprojects. With tentative optimism, I close the chapter with a critical discussion on alternative tactics which may lead to place (re)making—or what I call *depodunkification*—in post-urban East Hartford.

FROM PODUNKS TO PODUNK

Before its European colonization, the lands contained in what is now known as East Hartford were "home" to the Podunks, a semi-nomadic Algonquin Indian tribe. Like many northeastern Indians (Cronon, 1984), the Podunks moved from place to place according to ecological rhythms. They primarily alternated between summer sites along the Connecticut River, where they subsisted on fish and deer, and winter sites further inland, where they escaped floods and kept warm with the plentiful furs of local beaver, deer, and bear (Goodwin, 1879). In 1631, after being dispossessed of part of their land by the Pequots (Spiess, 1933), a Podunk representative journeyed to Massachusetts to attract the English to their territory for protection. The English, in turn, came two years later, but not for this purpose. Rather, they sought to escape their own overpopulated and over-farmed colony after hearing favorable reports on the region's ecology from the Dutch. Though the colonists did successfully (and brutally) put down the Pequots, by the 1650s the former had merely replaced the latter as a far more formidable threat to Podunk livelihood (Spiess, 1933). Around this time, historians documented an event in which a dwindling band of Podunks passionately resisted a group of Puritan missionaries attempting to convert them to Christianity. As they put it, they had already lost their land and weren't looking to become slaves as well. Because the Podunk way of life depended on perpetual and organic movement over what was then an accessible and variegated ecosystem, the tribe's demise was assured the moment that the colonists began transforming the landscape into an agrarian patchwork of private lots. Sure enough, by 1760, the Podunks had permanently dissolved (Spiess, 1933).

Interestingly, the Podunks are conspicuously absent from their namesake, which emerged not in reference to the vanquished tribe that first attracted inland colonization in the United States, but to the irrelevant social spaces which replaced them. For more than a century after its colonization, East Hartford was merely a minor agrarian extension of Hartford. At a time when industry was an entirely peripheral affair confined to falling-water sites on the most rugged and inaccessible terrain (Stilgoe, 1983), the town was the state's most "industrious" (Daniels, 1980: 442), signifying (perhaps ironically) its inherent peripherality. "Podunk" came into use about a century after the tribe's demise as a name for a particularly peripheral corner of the town near an integral part of former Podunk human ecology (the Podunk River). To be sure, the term's distinctly American colonial connotations derive from the fact that it comes from a tribe completely unknown, not just to Europeans, but to Americans. Thus, while the term's origins *must* come from East Hartford, its very success is rooted in its dissociated later uses describing other small and insignificant places with no relation to either East Hartford or the Podunk Indians (Read, 1939). In a way, the word is successful because it demonstrates its meaning; with a lack of place in English linguistic structure, othered (Indian) roots, and dissociated application, it is insignificant, out of the way, and essentially fictitious.

PAVING OVER PODUNK: THE CONNECTICUT YANKEE IN KING CAPITAL'S COURT

It will be useful to describe the late-19th-century "depodunkification" of East Hartford in reference to another American colloquialism with East Hartford roots: the "Connecticut Yankee," a term popularized by Mark Twain in his classic novel, *A Connecticut Yankee in King Arthur's Court* (1889). This archetype has almost the opposite attributes of a podunk. As portrayed by Twain, the Yankee is a pragmatic, industrious, character who is driven to invent, produce, and develop. We know that Twain thought East Hartford to be something of a podunk, once (in 1878) commenting: "Rome interests me as much as East Hartford could, and no more." Yet, Twain glorifies the virtues of his book's Yankee, Hank Morgan, an East Hartford industrialist. As Allen (1966) suggests, Morgan is the epitome of a 19th-century Yankee. He is industrious, skilled mentally and technically, can build machines to do virtually anything, and believes fundamentally in democracy and industrial development. Twain's Yankee prides himself as having made "guns, revolvers, cannon, boilers, engines, all sorts of labor saving machinery" (Twain, 1889: 5), all of which were staples in the burgeoning manufacturing sector of late-19th-century Hartford.

While Twain portrayed the "Connecticut Yankee" as an enviable hero, the story of his hometown is ultimately Faustian.[2] Though the Yankees may have meant well, they annihilated their entire way of life to make way for dubious industrial/urban spaces that only brought jobs and development temporarily, while permanently urbanizing their land, thus creating the horrifying possible future of a fully built-up place becoming a modern ghost town. Yankees transformed East Hartford into one of America's most important manufacturing centers. First, landowning family farmers who survived on subsistence agriculture were deposed as properties were increasingly centralized into the hands of a few capitalists and dedicated to the production of tobacco (largely by young or black seasonal employees from as far away as the American South) (Harrison, 2010). Starting in 1881, when the New York & New England railroad built its freight yard in East Hartford's north end (at that time called "Podunk"), the town gradually began to industrialize. Just a few years after its arrival, the railroad built tracks over a road which (1) long pre-dated the company; and (2) served as the only connection from a neighborhood to the rest of the town. A court ruled that the railroad had the right to shut the road down, and shut it down they did (Paquette, 1976, 142–143). Not long after, the company moved to Hartford to cut costs.

This early case only served as a prelude for what was to come. Depodunkification would culminate with the emergence of the headquarters of one of the country's largest aerospace giants. Given that Mark Twain was a vehement critic of imperialism (Hawkins, 1993; Rowe, 2000), this final event is particularly Faustian. Pratt & Whitney (which developed out of the very Hartford arms industry in which Twain's Hank Morgan worked) gained a vital role in military aircraft design and production during the various wars of the 20th century.

PODUNK LOST: THE ETERNAL URBANIZATION OF PRATT CITY

In 1919, the *American Enterprise* published an article titled "East Hartford: the ideal place for a home or industry: come live, grow, prosper here." It promoted East Hartford as a "thriving town of 11,000 inhabitants offering exceptional opportunities for industrial growth and development [where] all modern city facilities are enjoyed by its people." It went on to call out: "Come with us. Let us build up our town together, until that day when it shall stand as one of the *big cities* of the state" (my emphasis). Many in East Hartford wanted their town to be more than a podunk; they wanted to transform it into a true urban-industrial center.

However, East Hartford faced significant hurdles to development. Influential Hartford landowners were opposed to the development of East Hartford's west side, which was a short ferry ride, bridge walk, or trolley trip away from the city's highly profitable downtown. Moreover, frequent, and sometimes disastrous flooding from the Connecticut River made building there nearly impossible. Rather than modern manufacturers or corporate edifices, East Hartford was built up with informal, heavily polluting factories, and low-cost housing for poor foreign immigrants. In 1937, the Home Owners Loan Corporation's (HOLC) red-lining maps of the Hartford region ensured that much of East Hartford would never be profitably developed (see Map 3.1). Because of its tendency to flood, its haphazard industrial development, and its populations of poor immigrants, East Hartford had more of its geographic area red-lined than any other municipality in Greater Hartford. However, what is most important to note here is that unlike the more urbanized municipalities of Hartford and West Hartford, most of East Hartford isn't graded at all (due to its agricultural character). Yet, this relative underdevelopment would help pave the way for drastic suburban overproduction in mere decades.

Partly because of its thirst for urbanity and partly because it was so poorly positioned for urban development, East Hartford sported some of the region's most lax land-use regulations. The lack of oversight paid off. In 1929, Pratt & Whitney built its massive headquarters on a vast stretch of tobacco fields in the town's south end. Greater Hartford was forever changed. Perhaps fulfilling its goal to become a "big city," Pratt & Whitney made East Hartford the "aerospace capital of the world." Depodunkification seemed complete. But metropolitan politicians were worried. East Hartford's massive de-centered industrialization implied extensive future suburban development, for which no management system was in place. Therefore, an attempt was made to create a regional government in the Metropolitan District Commission (MDC), but it failed to receive the necessary levels of municipal support (Tondro, 1999; see also Rojas and Wray, this volume; Walsh, this volume).

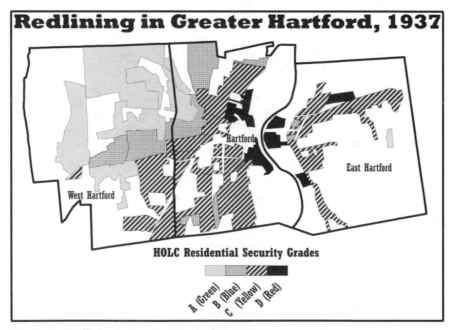

Map 3.1.   Redlining in Greater Hartford, 1937
Base GIS data from CT MAGIC. In the 1930s, HOLC began hierarchically ranking neighborhood districts by "residential security." Higher scores (blue and green) made it easy to obtain mortgage loans; lower scores made it impossible (red) or nearly so (yellow). Despite its suburban character, East Hartford had the highest proportion of low grade neighborhoods in Greater Hartford.

Regardless of whether or not Greater Hartford had regional oversight in place, the region was going to grow dramatically in the decades to come, and East Hartford would serve as its epicenter. Between 1940 and 1943, East Hartford saw the construction of eleven separate mass-produced, high-density, low-income housing projects totaling 2,500 dwelling units. This represented—in but a four-year period—a 70 percent increase in the town's total housing stock: 3,400 units (Hausmann, 1995). Indeed, during World War II, Pratt became so important that by 1949, East Hartford was the fastest growing town east of the Mississippi River in terms of population (Johnson, 2009: 9) and had the largest geographical range of commuters of any town in Connecticut (McKain, 1949).

The population influx of mostly poor French Canadians from northern New England did not occur without local complications. Given the sudden monopoly of rental housing in the housing shortage, landlords were often cruel. They unpredictably raised rents, banned children, and exposed tenants to public health risks. Moreover, there was next to no social infrastructure in place. The overwhelmingly disproportionate male population was so isolated that some protested for a municipal dating center. With dwellings crunched together and Pratt employees forced to work odd hours, it was difficult for people to adapt. In general, animosities ran high between old-time residents and new factory workers. *Harper's Magazine* ran an article attacking the town for deriding the military workers and their families with the epithet "trailer trash." The poor social conditions in East Hartford during its most productive years calls into question the tendency to associate industrial growth with development. If anything, the town went through the grueling stage of industrialization, only to see development skip it in favor of newer suburbs later.

We might caution that East Hartford was not so much the epitome of the American Dream, so much as its co-creator and rough draft. In general, East Hartford was built up with lower-end suburban housing, not the large houses and verdant lots typically associated with our more idyllic images of suburbia. Their quality often exceeded that of temporary public housing, but they quickly became outmoded. With this in mind, it is important to here remember that East Hartford, as the headquarters of Pratt & Whitney, produced a bewildering portion of the U.S. air force during the 20th century (Chen and Shemo, this volume). By playing an essential role in the U.S.'s winning of wars like World War II, and in its more hegemonic projects such as the war in Vietnam, East Hartford was an integral co-producer of America's postwar economic boom and its heavily interlinked suburban expansion. Thus, without places like East Hartford, there could not have been the massive wave of suburbanization which depopulated not just the inner cities like Hartford, but also makeshift pre-Levittown suburbs like East Hartford, whose pioneering but too-quickly produced housing stock and infrastructure—so necessary for the country's survival and development—were no longer desirable as "better" suburbs emerged on the periphery.[3] Thus, by successfully fulfilling its role, East Hartford ironically created the conditions for its own subsequent podunkification.

A PODUNK WITHOUT A COUNTRYSIDE

In 1957, Founders Bridge was erected between East Hartford and Hartford. At this point, private development began to efface the town's vague identity. A massive suburban shopping center opened on a former tobacco field at the town's geographic center, while its political and cultural center—Main Street—saw the exodus and downsizing of both government and retail functions. Meanwhile, single-family homes continued to abound in a haphazard dispersion of piecemeal subdivisions. However, the tipping point for East Hartford's road to urban podunkification came in 1961, when the state routed two interstate highways through the town. Meant to foster the growth of new suburbs to the east and south, the new highways would obliterate the town's already fractured landscape by splitting it in two. East Hartford's mayor and state representatives proposed an alternative highway plan in support of which they produced more than 10,000 resident signatures. But, it was all for naught. Today, the massive interchange at East Hartford's western edge is roughly the same size as Downtown Hartford.[4]

By the 1970s, East Hartford was almost completely urban. Yet in subsequent decades, it saw sizeable reductions in population, productivity, and property values. Without regaining its forests or pastures, East Hartford once again became a podunk, but this time an urban one. How can an urban place be or become a "podunk?" While the word "podunk" has both rural origins and connotations, it is undeniable that certain contemporary urban places (e.g., Detroit, Flint, and Youngstown) have a certain "podunkness" about them. Podunkification needs to be understood in the context of uneven development, which, as Henri Lefebvre ([1961] 2008: 3) asserted, is "the prime law of the modern world." Neil Smith describes uneven development as the "seesaw of capital," under which "capital attempts to seesaw from a developed to an underdeveloped area, then at a latter point back to the first area which is by now underdeveloped, and so forth" (Smith, 1984b: 198). Simply put, *urban* podunkification is a textbook manifestation of the disinvested side of the seesaw at the scale of an entire place or locality. Implicit in this term is that a formerly significant place stays *physically* urban (i.e., the built environment has already semi-permanently replaced the former natural or agrarian environment), but loses the economic and social forces necessary for its reproduction.

East Hartford's transformation must be understood in context. Since the late 20th century, the United States has seen a wave of deindustrialization that is unlikely to be fully superseded (Smith, 1984c: 121). Concurrently, metropolitan restructuring has led to the devaluation of certain types of urban spaces and the revaluation of others. While many outer suburban areas and downtown cores have seen investment or reinvestment, many traditionally valuable areas have been significantly devalued (Hackworth, 2007; Smith, et al., 2001). By the year 2005, suburban areas had a higher share of people below the poverty line than inner cities across all American metropolitan regions (Kneebone, 2006; Hall and Lee, 2009; Holliday and Dwyer, 2000). Because inner-ring suburbs like East Hartford, which were rapidly built up with mass-produced ranch houses and strip developments during the mid-20th century, have become increasingly unappetizing to contemporary homebuyers (Short, et al., 2007), it is primarily in these areas that the "negative" socioeconomic transformations have been concentrated.

THE POLITICAL CONTEXT FOR
DEPODUNKIFICATION STRATEGIES

Contemporary urban politics can be characterized as having two essential and contradictory themes: *human mobility* on the one hand and *local management* on the other. On one side, we see a general increase in human mobilization caused by increasing work-related relocations, with people in their twenties, for instance, now moving once a year (Census, 2010). This perpetual movement of people between jurisdictions clearly limits how well local governments can perform democratically (especially since many towns require inhabitants to wait more than a year to obtain residency), and indeed there is an increasing divide between residents and their representative governments. Yet, a newfound reliance on municipal debt and a cataclysmic reduction of federal aid has forced cities to become more entrepreneurial in governance. "Entrepreneurial Urbanism" refers to a broad set of late-20th-century urban strategies and tactics whereby local governments, usually in conjunction with other private entities, compete with other cities to increase the economic vitality and perceived cultural importance of their territories, by focusing on investment and speculative development rather than by dealing with social problems (Harvey, 1989). This strategy is exemplified by what Neil Smith (2002) calls a "geo-bribe." Smith uses the term to denote the actual transfer of cash from a government to a company already located in its territory, though I might extend the term to include subtler and less direct bribes which sway companies to relocate to their territories using methods like special enterprise/empowerment zones (which limit or even do away with taxes for certain businesses). The second strategy involves more expressly government planned/run projects, and incorporates both destruction (including demolition and gentrification) and new construction. While there's nothing new about government funded/planned urban renewal, contemporary practice is distinguishable from the immediate post–World War II variety in that (1) economic obsolescence has superseded "blight" as the new rationale for the creative destruction of urban space (Weber, 2002), meaning that even the most socially desirable spaces have become ripe for the taking in cases for which a governmental body thinks that such dispossession will create jobs or tax revenue; (2) a state taking of a property for redevelopment often ends with the property still undeveloped; (3) those projects which do get built may have little to no use value absent revenue generation, at least at the local scale; and (4) despite the neoliberal rhetoric of "locally run" urbanism, the reality is that many local governments have very little say in the production/management of urban space, with private interests increasingly dominating urban/economic development projects, either by themselves, or in quasi-public "urban regimes" (Hackworth, 2007: 61–78). Furthermore, these regimes are often not spearheaded by local governments at all, but rather by detached state agencies (Burns, 2002).

PRIVATE MOBILIZATIONS: OUT WITH THE GOODS, IN WITH THE HOODS

New England's economy experienced a particularly dramatic transformation after the end of the postwar boom. By the 1980s, the region's exodus of jobs in textiles, shoes, paper, electronics, metalworking, and aerospace was masked by a simultaneous infusion of unstable and low-paying jobs in the service sector (Harrison, 1982). As paychecks got smaller, the cost of living stayed the highest in the United States, giving New England the lowest real wages in the country. Skilled workers laid off from declining industries were unable to find similar wage jobs both in and outside the region. Like many other small New England regions, Hartford's economy was severely battered, though the effects were uneven: the FIRE (Finance, Insurance, and Real Estate) Sector saw dramatic mergers and dislocations of central operations to global cities, but essentially stayed intact; but the manufacturing sector (especially aerospace) all but disappeared (Forrant and Wilkinson, 2004). A small class of people in higher-end and managerial jobs remain, but the middle class, which was so central to East Hartford's identity, began to seriously decline, resulting in an ever-increasing gulf between the region's wealthy and ordinary residents, and the complete transformation—indeed, Podunkification—of formerly working-class areas such as East Hartford.

By the 1970s and 1980s, East Hartford was experiencing significant stress. Pratt & Whitney had begun shifting its operations outside Connecticut (Forrant, 2002; Rayman and Bluestone, 1982). Starting in the 1980s and early 1990s massive strikes followed layoffs and forced concessions. In 1993, East Hartford's bond rating was downgraded from AA to A1, due to concerns from the bond-rating agency Moody's Investment Service, over the declining local presence of aerospace. Relative quiet reemerged until 2001, when Pratt laid off thousands of workers across the country, and threatened both the State of Connecticut and the International Association of Machinists that they would leave the state unless they got a combined $60,000,000 in geo-bribes. Connecticut was skeptical, but it had no choice but to pay up. Simultaneously, competing states with smaller plants offered Pratt enticing development packages. During this time, the company signed contracts promising East Hartford more employment, but actually moved scores of jobs to other states (e.g., Georgia) and countries (e.g., Singapore, Turkey, and China) and decreased local wages. When Pratt failed to tell the union that it planned to relocate much of its operations to Oklahoma without even attempting to work things out locally (Forrant, 2002:129–131), a court held that Pratt must agree to produce a new engine in Connecticut.[5] However, as the working-class jobs continue to diminish at a more or less gradual rate, Pratt's apocalyptic relocation threats continue. Recently, for instance, they stated publically their "need" to move production to "any place outside of Connecticut" in order to cut costs (Haar, 2010).[6]

By 1990, the once economically vital railroad tracks had become little more than escape routes for criminals (Miller, 1990) and un-policed living spaces for the homeless. Distribution plants, fast-food joints, and strip clubs sprouted along main traffic arteries, especially around the shrinking headquarters of Pratt & Whitney. While good jobs were generally leaving the town, there was some re-industrialization, albeit of a lower quality. In 1984 Coca-Cola placed a manufacturing plant on Roberts Street, offering jobs which, while less desirable than those which had previously existed at Pratt, were still better than most other new employment opportunities in the low-end service sector. Sixteen years later, ignoring resident protests, Coke expanded their East Hartford presence by building a massive bottling plant just across the street from Pratt. Meanwhile, big boxes and strip developments were being abandoned or downgraded. Indeed, while the service sector has generally risen in economic importance since the mid-20th century, East Hartford has, in a manner similar to that of central cities (e.g., Hartford), seen a massive decline in both the quality and quantity of its locally relevant service establishments. In the past decade alone, East Hartford has lost its sole movie theater (see Figure 3.1) and one of two major grocery stores. Truly an urban podunk, despite being almost entirely built up, East Hartford has the greatest proportion of undeveloped space of any municipality in its region, including rural towns on the metropolitan fringe and the brownfield-burdened city of Hartford.

Figure 3.1. The abandoned Showcase Cinemas lot, alongside Silver Lane and I-84, is just one of a plethora of retail spaces that have shut down in the past several years. (William Moffett)

Beginning in the 1980s, this amorphous physical landscape came to underlie an equally incoherent social landscape. As industrial jobs from firms like Pratt & Whitney left, skilled workers followed suit in overwhelmingly vain searches for new opportunities. Simultaneously, in 1987, the law changed to allow Section 8 recipients to use housing vouchers outside their MSA jurisdictions. Thus, housing projects have been almost unilaterally demolished in Greater Hartford, while a select number of residents have been put into a privatized system that breaks apart their former communities. Like all other types of neoliberal policy, Section 8 masquerades as a sort of newfound "choice" for the impoverished, but functions largely as a means of disrupting their social reproduction, while fostering a disturbing ideology in which those who make the (easy) mistake of "choosing wrong" must live with the consequences (Maskovsky, 2000). Indeed, those few people who did receive vouchers after losing public housing did not move wherever they wanted, but rather to suburban working-class neighborhoods, many of which were undergoing deindustrialization-led population exodus, and all of which presented impoverished migrants with the added burden of hidden costs like automobile dependence.

By the 1990s, East Hartford was by far the largest recipient of Section 8 relocations in Greater Hartford (Donovan, 1994). However, because many laws were formulated upon the "spatial mismatch" theory (Weicher, 1991), which is based on the pre–Section 8 premise that all poverty is contained in central cities and jobs are in suburbs that are generally rich and white, the town was denied much-needed funds. East Hartford lacked the services or revenue to accommodate its new inhabitants. In the early and mid-1990s, the decade in which East Hartford saw the highest growth in poverty of any town in the state, an explosion of poor minority students flooded unprepared municipal schools. One elementary school, built without walls in the experimental 60s, became so loud and overcrowded that many classes were temporarily relocated to trailers parked on its basketball court. Meanwhile, East Hartford's only public high school saw a rapid and dramatic demographic transformation, along with bouts of restructuring-related turbulence for which administrators were unprepared. Indeed, in 1988, East Hartford's school district was 23 percent minority, and by 2006, that number had grown to 76 percent. Today, East Hartford is a racially isolated school district by state standards (Dougherty et al., 2007). Further still, at 79.6 percent retention of students, it is the region's least stable, meaning that the town's youth is more transient than that of any other school district in the region. This exceptional transience is partially a function of the town's lack of clear sense of place, as illustrated by East Hartford's unique demographic configuration. Unlike in all other cities and towns throughout the region, East Hartford's ethnic groups don't cluster in their own particular neighborhoods, but instead in a socially and spatially indistinguishable sprawl. The only common denominator is relative poverty.

Without justifying some of the more or less blatantly racist and classist politics practiced by some pre–Section 8 East Hartford residents after their town began to change (which I discuss in the next section), it is important to understand the effects of the town's dramatic socioeconomic transformation on the largely white, lower-middle-class populations who had not yet left. Almost overnight, these already economically stressed populations saw their taxes increase, property values fall, and entire social landscapes dissolve. As much of this population—both in East Hartford and in similar locations throughout the country—was driven to move to more expensive housing at the precise time that their resources were dwindling, it is likely that Section 8 helped induce the international mortgage crisis, especially when we also account for the decisions of many of the nearly 50 percent of poor blacks and Hispanics who lost their public housing and never received a voucher (Hackworth, 2007) to buy the housing of such outward white middle-class migrants. With few affordable housing options, many of the former had little reason not to get sub-prime mortgages, particularly because they were highly publicized by commercial and government entities alike. Unsurprisingly, particularly in its heavily minority areas, East Hartford has among the highest rates of sub-prime mortgages in the state (State of Connecticut, 2007).[7]

DESTRUCTION WITHOUT CREATION: PODUNKIFICATION IN THE NAME OF DEPODUNKIFICATION

If the real and perceived consequences of specifically urban podunkification galvanize empowered stakeholders to work toward reversing the process, it should be no surprise that East Hartford is something of an archetype when it comes to eminent domain, having made a national ranking of the country's 20 worst failures (Castle Coalition, 2006), for demolishing a nearly 100-year-old landmark restaurant on Main Street to make way for a mall that ended up jumping ship just after the restaurant, along with two other adjacent businesses (including a live-in motel), was demolished. Later, East Hartford demolished three large private apartment complexes at a central point of "underclass" migration, leaving many people homeless (Ohlemacher, 1998). Over a decade later all three sites are still vacant. In the end, East Hartford paid 4.7 million dollars out of pocket to demolish the structures, lost more than a decade of tax revenue on valuable properties, relocated an enormous consumer base from an area with several businesses to isolated residential areas, and put a gaping hole in one of its most important urban thoroughfares. Here, antipodunkification strategies not only failed but actually exacerbated the process.

East Hartford's most prominent example of actual urban *production* via antipodunkification is Rentschler Field: two massive mega-projects built on 75 acres of land donated by Pratt in a move which took two million dollars off the town's grand list (and thus forced East Hartford to quickly make up the lost revenue). Given its massive size and location in what could be described as an inner-ring suburb, Rentschler Field is a very rare and important case of urban renewal. Rentschler Field became the center of East Hartford's "enterprise zone," a space with particularly business-friendly regulations designed to attract additional private development. As of 2013, the space has only two (albeit massive) complexes, both of which are alien to East Hartford's residents: a state-run and mandated stadium, and a destination retail outlet which caters largely to rural whites (see Map 3.2).

Rentschler Stadium, with 40,000 seats, was dropped onto East Hartford by the state after the latter failed to bring the New England Patriots to Hartford (Condon, this volume). Subsequently, the state all but forced a compromise project onto East Hartford: the construction of a football stadium for the University of Connecticut (UConn), based in Storrs (though placing the rural university's stadium on a barren industrial field more than a half hour away from campus was certainly an end result few wanted). What is immediately troubling about Rentschler Field is that, despite technically being a public space, it is an inaccessible one that "customers" must pay to enter and experience. Surrounded by barbed wire at all times and patrolled by state troopers during events, the space is inherently not public, even if it was developed for and by the state. However, Rentschler Field is even more problematic because to East Hartford residents it is simply a NIMBY that was forced on them by the state. Most East Hartford residents have not attended any college, let alone UConn, and have no reason to attend the games. Instead, they must simply live with drastically increased levels of noise and traffic, and coexist with a massive space designed explicitly for others.

Similarly, East Hartford got Cabela's, a massive destination store for hunting/camping supplies, at a time when its population of increasingly urban-born poor minorities had absolutely no use for it. The fact that East Hartford intentionally packaged itself to receive it is thus of special importance. Even though Cabela's has no effect on regional labor markets (Hicks, 2007), it requires incentive packages for every new development. In this case, public funds were used for $120 million in area infrastructure development and $9.9 million in direct investment. Given that Cabela's is itself an investment meant to at the very least produce multiplier effects, one should note that there is no incentive for visitors at the East Hartford location to go anywhere but Cabela's. The store, which is most quickly reached by a route bereft of other businesses, is equipped with everything from a restaurant to a child entertainment center.

To add insult to injury, the Rentschler developments have placed new burdens on the town and its residents. After traffic levels far exceeded initial estimates, East Hartford asked the State of Connecticut for $10.3 million to cover costs. Despite the fact that this congestion was caused by the state's own football team, East Hartford found itself begging for what it needed just to break even. Even with these problems, government funds continue to pour into East Hartford in hopes of transforming edge city dreams into physical realities. Seven million dollars in state bonds were recently approved to build a road linking East Hartford's south end (and its highway on-ramps) to the site (Gosselin, 2009). While the road may be crucial to create a truly functional edge city, it may also create more visitor indifference for local arterial roads and businesses and completely separate the area into a non-revenue-generating consumption zone for outsiders.

In a final irony, the means employed to counter podunkification have not only failed; but, by wasting millions of public dollars, destroying huge chunks of the town's urban landscape, displacing scores of its residents, and producing nothing but costly and conspicuously out-of-place mega-projects, they have simply intensified the process. The silence of this colonization, demonstrated by the lack of protest over any of the projects here described, comes from the materialization of East Hartford as a podunk to its own residents, who, devoid of any sense of place, lack consciousness not only of their dispossession, but that there is even anything to possess, repossess, or appropriate.

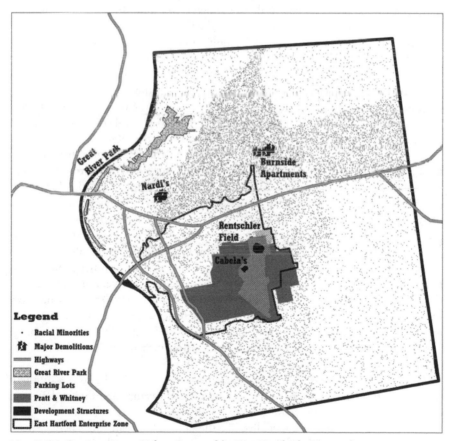

Map 3.2. Contemporary Urban Renewal in East Hartford, Connecticut
Data from CRCOG and Census 2010. While the projects take up relatively little space, the surrounding parking lot makes up more than ¼ of the Pratt complex.

CONCLUSION: APPROPRIATING PODUNK

Perhaps, this chapter has unfairly given "podunkification" a bad rap. Assuredly, for the "original" inhabitants of a location undergoing the process, it is overwhelmingly destructive: jobs are lost, property values plummet, and communities disappear. Similarly, many of the urban strategies used to combat the process produce results ranging from the dubious to the detestable. Yet podunkification also has a positive side. When an entire place is devalued, it offers new opportunities for place making. "Depodunkification" goes beyond the more vulgar economistic ideas of "reinvestment" and "urban renewal," to describe an organic and socially meaningful process that transcends the sorts of self-exploitative, out-of-place projects of local insignificance à la Rentschler Field, and produces not just a few dissociated pockets of reinvestment, but rather a rich social place which is continuously *lived* by inhabitants as both significant, non-fictitious, and "in-the-way." In this section, I will briefly discuss a few examples of "depodunkification" attempts in East Hartford.

Governmental organizations have only played a partial role in most of the urban strategies initiated within East Hartford. Small groups have silently appropriated certain spaces, some more formally than others. For instance, beginning in the 1980s, a private nonprofit called "Riverfront Recapture" spearheaded and oversaw the design and construction of two closely linked riverfront parks in East Hartford and Hartford (see Marfuggi and Porth, 1999). While management authority over the park was granted to Riverfront Recapture, funding was obtained extraneously from private and public sources, and the actual construction labor was performed by Connecticut prisoners. While East Hartford must provide funding to keep the park open, it is located too far away from the homes of the town's residents (minus a lone riverfront luxury condominium) to foster local place making. Still, once a year, the riverfront park becomes the most important space in Greater Hartford by hosting the region's most widely attended event: Riverfest, a massive and consciously regional Fourth of July spectacle with fireworks, concerts, and huge concentrations of people and vendors. Thus, even though the river park was essentially created by/for non-residents and has very little impact on local everyday life, its distinctly regional production and function may help serve a different need. Unlike Rentschler Field, Riverfront Recapture has the potential to foster long-overdue consciousness for a region which has outgrown the local scale (see Rojas and Wray, this volume).

There is also a quite different riverfront project of note. In the town's southern stretches, "homeless" populations dwell in unmapped swamps and forests that seem detached from the modern world (Dempsey, 2009). To avoid the constant wrath of river floods, the homeless campers live like the nomadic Indian tribes before them, alternating between summer/fall sites (East Hartford's forest) and winter/spring sites (motels in suburban Newington). Fueled with kerosene, their temporary dwellings conceal material possessions: stereos, bicycles, and electric scooters purchased with bank cards and Social Security funds. However profound South Meadows may seem, it is a flimsy appropriation of unwanted metropolitan space, and is unlikely to develop into anything more than a small, temporary camp. A leftover fluke of the mid-20th century, South Meadows cannot be developed due to environmental laws, and most of its parcels' owners are either absent or unknown. However, the space is no frontier—the town's government has expressly allowed a small number of select individuals to camp there (the municipality would certainly never allow these numbers to grow to anything substantial). Moreover, if the space could be converted into a park, or if property owners were to take a tougher stance on trespassing, or if the last vestiges of social welfare were eliminated, it would become impossible for the "new urban podunks" to reproduce themselves, leaving them to face the same silent fate as their Indian predecessors.

Even if both of these examples represent very different groups working at distinct scales, they nevertheless share the implicit aim of depodunkification. Certainly, my two examples represent problematic and perhaps unsuccessful attempts of this process. However, "purer" examples of recent depodunkification are out there. Even in this book, Llana Barber has illustrated how Lawrence, Massachusetts, was transformed from a shrinking postindustrial city into a vibrant community of Dominican migrants. Without the city's devaluation, Lawrence could not have been renewed in this socially meaningful way. However, unlike Lawrence (which effectively became a Dominican city in the 1980s), East Hartford's relatively low-density suburban form and lack of any dominant ethnic or social group means that most onlookers are probably more likely to identify the town with the incongruous mega-projects that have colonized its center than with the people who call the town home. While a few local and regional projects suggest the possibility that East Hartford may one day undergo depodunkification, the town's future is uncertain. Yet, even if the amorphousness of present-day East Hartford makes the very act of conceiving a "non-podunk" future difficult, it is precisely this contemporary "urban podunkness" that demands for East Hartford a politics and production of meaningful place.

NOTES

I should like to thank those people who provided me with helpful comments on earlier drafts of this paper: Monica Barra, Llana Barber, Dana Cohen, Xiangming Chen, Ray Johnson, Elliot Liu, Setha Low, Mary McCombie, William Moffett, Jason Rojas, Terry Romero, Neil Smith, Guarav Toor, and Andrew Walsh.

1. While East Hartford has been completely unexamined in the literature of urban studies, there are a few books and articles on the town. For an early but thorough local history, see Goodwin (1879). For a more recent, but less detailed update, see Paquette (1976). For a rare article examining the town's recent economic and social transformations, see Forrant (2002).

2. *Faust* was integrated into urban theory by Marshall Berman in the aptly titled opening chapter of *All That is Solid Melts Into Air: The Experience of Modernity* (1982), "Goethe's *Faust*:

The Tragedy of Development." In the story, an initially well-meaning intellectual is bewitched by the drive for development, and begins a mission to transform his medieval world. In the process, he grows mad and destroys everything in his path, supplanting the very world he loves with dubious industrial-urban spaces.

3. A notable exception to (or local example of) this phenomenon of "superior" suburb creation can be found in parts of the southeast of East Hartford. In the 1960s, this area was zoned to accommodate larger lot sizes and higher quality (post-Levittown) suburban housing. It has remained a relatively middle-class neighborhood, insomuch as it is attractive to higher-income minorities and some Pratt engineers. Aesthetically, the neighborhood looks more like adjacent sections of the more affluent town of Glastonbury than the rest of East Hartford. The neighborhood's relative survival may stem from the fact that its housing (like Glastonbury's) was built for and is still attractive to engineers (who *are* still employed in great numbers at Pratt), while the rest of East Hartford was built for machinists and other lower level workers. Not only have these latter sorts of jobs drastically shrunk in recent years, but the housing built for them in the 1940s and 1950s has significantly devalued and is now essentially unattractive to contemporary middle-class workers. The Southeast neighborhood may survive to some extent as a more socially diverse version of its 1960s self, but may suffer as East Hartford in general is devalued. As Jack Dougherty (this volume) has shown, the perceived quality of public education is a particularly powerful indicator of home prices and sales. While the area's elementary schools (e.g., Pitkin and O'Connell) have scored much better than other area schools, they have still declined relative to schools in neighborhoods with analogous housing and densities throughout the region. Moreover, all East Hartford residents go to the same (town-wide) schools from 6th grade on. While current residents may adapt by sending children to private schools or (lottery-based) magnet schools, future residents may opt to move to neighborhoods in towns with better public schools.

4. East Hartford is certainly not the only municipality which was torn apart by highways. The disastrous impact of highway construction on Hartford is commonly cited as one of the worst blows to the city (see Condon, this volume). Yet, despite the fact that East Hartford is covered by more highways and interchanges than any other town in the region, the town's story is largely unknown.

5. It should be noted that Pratt & Whitney has recently added 500 new engineers to its East Hartford plant to work on a new engine (Saporito, 2011). While this number is not insubstantial, and is certainly a good thing for the Hartford Region as a whole, it is inconsequential to East Hartford, because (1) it does nothing to address the thousands of jobs which have been lost in the past several decades; and, perhaps more important, (2) because all of these jobs are for skilled workers, they will not go to East Hartford residents, not even to its few remaining blue-collar veterans. Much like Downtown Hartford's insurance companies, Pratt & Whitney no longer creates jobs for its local population, but for commuters from wealthier suburbs such as Glastonbury and South Windsor.

6. Not all of Pratt's spatial expansion is directly attributable to cutting costs, however. For instance, new offices in Shanghai and Chengdu, China, are designed to tap their large new emerging markets (see Chen and Shemo, this volume).

7. For comparison, in West Hartford, a Puerto Rican neighborhood has emerged called Elmwood, which sees almost 100 percent of the town's Section 8 vouchers. However, perhaps because West Hartford's population has stayed steady over the past several decades, and because its housing prices have skyrocketed, there are very few subprime mortgages in Elmwood, especially when compared with East Hartford.

REFERENCES

Allen, Gerald. 1966. "Mark Twain's Yankee." *The New England Quarterly* 36(3): 288–297.

Berman, Marshall. 1982. *All That is Solid Melts Into Air: The Experience of Modernity.* New York: Penguin.

Burns, Peter. 2002. "The Intergovernmental Regime and Public Policy in Hartford, Connecticut." *Journal of Urban Affairs* 24(1): 55–73.

Castle Coalition. 2006. "Redevelopment Wreckers: 20 Failed Projects Involving Eminent Domain Abuse." See at http://www.castlecoalition.org.

Cronon, William. 1983. *Changes in the Land.* New York: Hill & Wang.

Daniels, Bruce C. 1980. "Economic Development in Colonial and Revolutionary Connecticut: An Overview." *The William and Mary Quarterly,* 37(3): 429–450.

Dempsey, Christine. 2009. "River Life: Peace, Pain." *Hartford Courant,* Sep 23.

Donovan, Shaun. 1994. "Moving to the Suburbs: Section 8 Mobility and Portability in Hartford." In *Joint Center for Housing Studies Working Paper Series.* Cambridge: Harvard University.

Dougherty, Jack, et al. 2007. "Missing the Goal: A Visual Guide to *Sheff vs. O'Neill* School Desegregation." Hartford: Trinity College Cities Suburbs and Schools Research Project.

Forrant, Robert. 2002. "The International Association of Machinists, Pratt & Whitney, and the Struggle for a Blue Collar Future in Connecticut." *IRSH* 47: 113–136.

Forrant, Robert, and Frank Wilkinson. 2004. "Globalization and degenerative productive systems: the case of the Connecticut River Valley" presented at *Clusters, Industrial Districts and Firms: The Challenge of Globalization* (Modena, Italy).

Goodwin, Joseph. 1879. *East Hartford: Its History and Traditions.* Hartford: Lockwood & Brainard.

Gosselin, Kenneth. 2009. "Rentschler Road Project Advances," *Hartford Courant,* Dec 8: A14.

Haar, Dan. 2010 "UTC's Trash-Talking; A Savvy, Planned Assault Offers a Chance for Healthy Dialogue" *Hartford Courant,* Mar 19: A10.

Hackworth, Jason. 2007. *The Neoliberal City: Governance, Ideology, and Development in American Urbanism.* Ithaca: Cornell University Press.

Hall, Matthew, and Barrett Lee. 2009. "How Diverse Are U.S. Suburbs?" *Urban Studies* 47: 3–28.

Harrison, Brian. 1982. "The Tendency Toward Instability and Inequality Underlying the 'Revival' of New England." *Papers of the Regional Science Association,* 50: 41–65.

Harrison, Brian. 2010. "Mobility, Farmworkers, and Connecticut's Tobacco Valley, 1900–1950" *Journal of Historical Geography* 36: 157–168.

Harvey, David. 1989. "From Managerialism to Entrepreneurialism: The Transformation of Governance in Late Capitalism." *Geogriska Annaler* 71(1): 3–17.

Hausmann, Norm. 1995. "Wartime Housing in East Hartford: 1940–43 and its impact on the Town." *Hartford Studies Project.* Hartford: Trinity College.

Hawkins, Hunt. 1993. "Mark Twain's Anti-Imperialism," *American Literary Realism: 1870–1910* 25(2): 31–45.

Hicks, Michael J. 2007. "A Quasi-Experimental Test of Large Retail Store Impacts on Regional Labor Markets: The Case of Cabela's Retail Outlets," *Journal of Regional Analysis & Policy,* 37(2): 116–122.

Holliday, Amy L., and Rachel E. Dwyer. 2009. "Suburban Neighborhood Poverty in U.S. Metropolitan Areas in 2000." *City* 8(2): 155–76.

Johnson, Raymond. 2009. *East Hartford.* San Francisco: Arcadia Publishing.

Kneebone, Elizabeth. 2006. "Two Steps Back: City and Suburban Poverty Trends 1999–2005." Brookings Institution.

Lefebvre, Henri. 2008[1961]. *Critique of Everyday Life, Volume 2.* New York: Verso.

Marfuggi, John, and Rick Porth. 1999. "A Riverfront Runs Through it." *Parks & Recreation* 48.

Maskovsky, Jeff. 2000. "Managing" the Poor: Neoliberalism, Medicaid HMOs and the Triumph of Consumerism Among the Poor. *Medical Anthropology* 19(2):121–46.

McKain, Walter. 1949. "Occupational and Industrial Diversity in Rural Connecticut." *Storrs Agricultural Experiment Station*, 263.

Miller, Steve. 1990. "East Hartford Officers are Pedaling the Beat." *New York Times,* May 27.

Ohlemacher, Stephen. 1998. "Holdout Tenant Slows Redevelopment Woman Says She and Son Can't Afford to Move" *Hartford Courant,* December 8: B6.

Paquette, Lee. 1976. *Only More So: The History of East Hartford 1783–1976.* East Hartford: Raymond Library Company.

Rayman, Paula, and Barry Bluestone. 1982. *Out of Work: The Consequences of Unemployment in the Hartford Aircraft Industry.* Boston: Social Welfare Research Institute.

Read, Allen. 1939. "The Rationale of Podunk." *American Speech* 14(2): 99–108.

Rowe, John Carlos. 2000. "On Twain's Anti-Imperialism." Pp. 67–70 in Howard Bloom (ed.) *Mark Twain.* Philadelphia: Chelsea House Publishers.

Saporito, Bill. 2011. "How to Build a Job Engine." *Time Magazine Business,* May 19.

Short, John Rennie, et al. 2007. "The Decline of Inner Suburbs: The New Suburban Gothic in the United States." *Geography Compass* 1/3: 641–56.

Smith, Neil. 1984a. "Deindustrialization and Regionalization: Class Alliance and Class Struggle." *Papers of the Regional Science Association* 54: 113–128.

Smith, Neil. 1984b. *Uneven Development.* New York: Blackwell.

Smith, Neil. 2002. "New Globalism, New Urbanism: Gentrification as Global Urban Strategy." *Antipode* 34(3): 427–450.

Smith, Neil, et al. 2001. "The 'Camden Syndrome' and the Menace of Suburban Decline." *Urban Affairs Review* 36: 497–531.

Spiess, Mathias. 1933. *The Indians of Connecticut.* New Haven: Yale University Press.

State of Connecticut. 2007. *Sub-Prime Mortgage Task Force Final Report.*

Stilgoe, John. 1983. *Common Landscape of America, 1580–1845.* New Haven: Yale University Press.

Tondro, Terry J. 1999. "Fragments of Regionalism: State and Regional Planning in Connecticut At Century's End." *St. John's Law Review* 73(4): 1123–1158.

Twain, Mark. 1878. "Letter to J.H. Twichell, in Hartford" in *Mark Twain's Letters.* New York: Harper & Brothers Publishers, 1919.

Twain, Mark. 1889. *Connecticut Yankee in King Arthur's Court.* New York: Harper & Brothers Publishers.

Weber, Rachel. 2002. "Extracting Value from the City: Neoliberalism and Urban Redevelopment." *Antipode* 34(3): 519–540.

Weicher, John C. 1991. "Policy Implications of the Spatial Mismatch Hypothesis: Comment on 'Deconcentrating the Inner City Poor,' *Kent Law Review* 67: 855–870.

4

"If We Would . . . Leave the City, This Would Be a Ghost Town"

Urban Crisis and Latino Migration in Lawrence, Massachusetts, 1945–2000

Llana Barber

There are two very different ways to tell the story of how Lawrence, Massachusetts, came to be the city it is today. The first version explains how the textile industry, the backbone of Lawrence's economy, left the city after World War II, provoking an economic collapse. The city's population, mainly hardworking mill operatives with an array of European-immigrant origins, declined dramatically after the mills closed. This version of the story claims that the struggling city came to be populated by a motley cast of drug dealers, gang members, and welfare cheats. The huge brick mills that had formerly attracted international attention for the scale of their industrial output began to crumble with decay, becoming the haunt only of addicts and arsonists. Nearby residents drove in an arc around the city, rather than driving through to get to the other side. Lawrence earned the moniker the "armpit of the Northeast," and was widely derided throughout the region.

The second version tells how Puerto Rican and Cuban immigrants were drawn to Lawrence in the early 1960s to work in the few low-wage manufacturing jobs that still remained in the city. Migrant networks beckoned others to Lawrence, and family and friends of the original Latino settlers joined their kin in the city. This version of the story explains how the diverse Latino population of the city swelled, with Dominicans coming to predominate, and by 2000, the U.S. census reported that the majority of Lawrencians were Latino. An array of Latino-owned businesses sprung up in New England's first Latino-majority city, those that provided transnational services like shipping, travel, and money transfers, and those that provided bilingual/bicultural services and products for local Latinos: the sale of Latin American foods (either in groceries or in restaurants); local taxi services and van services to Latino neighborhoods in New York City; bilingual/bicultural health and legal services; assistance obtaining a home or access to government social services; Spanish-language and bilingual media; and leisure sites, such as bars and nightclubs that catered to a

Latino clientele. Latinos came to the forefront of Lawrence's public culture, as Spanish became the main language of commerce and conviviality in the city, as *bachata*, *merengue*, and *reggaeton* regularly floated through the summer air, and as the streets and parks of the city became the site for public celebrations of Latin American and Latino cultures.

These two versions of Lawrence's recent history, the one emphasizing Lawrence's crisis and the other its Latinization, are both true in most respects (although the story of Lawrence's descent into criminality and decay has often been wildly exaggerated.) Lawrence is both a shocking example of the extreme impact of deindustrialization and an unparalleled illustration of the extent to which Latinos have transformed U.S. cities in recent decades. Two questions remain, however. The first is how do these two versions of Lawrence's history relate? In other words, what does Lawrence's crisis have to do with Latino settlement in the city? And the second is why should anyone care? Lawrence is a tiny, seven-square-mile city with fewer than 100,000 residents on the border between Massachusetts and New Hampshire; should anyone be invested in learning its history? This chapter will attempt to answer both these questions, exploring the relationship between urban crisis and Latino settlement, and also proposing, along with many of the chapters in this book, that the history of such small cities is emblematic of larger changes in globalized urbanism.[1]

As Lawrence's economy and social infrastructure decayed alongside its physical infrastructure, many longtime Lawrence residents blamed Latinos for the city's decline. Some white residents believed that Latinos had brought with them the poverty, crime, and deterioration that plagued Lawrence. To those who scapegoated Latinos for the city's problems, the connection between the city's crisis and its new Latino population seemed obvious. Yet this facile explanation for the city's decline obscures far more than it reveals. In fact, the city's economic decline began decades before Latino settlement gained momentum in the late 1970s and early 1980s. Not only were Latinos innocent of the charge that their presence ruined a once-great city, the truth was quite the opposite: Latinos *reinvigorated* a city that was in a state of extreme neglect after decades of white flight and deindustrialization. As the title of this chapter suggests, without Latino settlement in Lawrence, many speculated that the city was on its way to becoming a "ghost town" (Eduardo Crespo, quoted in Hernandez and Walker, 1991).

SUBURBANIZATION AND URBAN CRISIS

The invisible thread that connects the city's economic decline with Latino settlement is the national history of suburbanization and urban disinvestment. The decades after World War II saw a massive public and private investment in suburban homeownership and development throughout the United States. Former industrial cities in the Northeast and Midwest experienced a massive exodus of their white residents, as Federal Housing Authority loans, the GI bill, and government-constructed highways facilitated homeownership in the new suburban developments that were springing up like mushrooms after the rain across the American landscape. A range of legal and extra-legal practices restricted these new suburbs almost exclusively to white residents, while communities of color were concentrated within the deteriorating urban centers that white residents were leaving behind en masse.

The late 1940s and 1950s, a peak period of suburbanization across the nation, saw a dramatic decline in Lawrence's population as well as unprecedented growth in the population of Lawrence's surrounding suburbs, with nearby Salem, New Hampshire, almost doubling in population in a single decade. Historians have extensively chronicled "white flight" from large urban centers like New York, Chicago, Oakland, and Detroit (Self, 2003; Sugrue, 1996; Avila, 2006; Cohen, 2003; Seligman, 2005; Kruse, 2005), but this process remains somewhat understudied for small cities. Lawrence, like many small cities in the 1950s, was nearly 99 percent white, and had never developed a sizable African American community. The traditional history of white flight from large cities generally chronicled white residents leaving the city as a means to avoid racial integration, when people of color, particularly African Americans, moved into previously all-white neighborhoods. But this simply does not apply to Lawrence in the decades after World War II, as there was no substantial community of color in Lawrence. Yet, Lawrence still lost 12 percent of its population between 1950 and 1960. Indeed, between the 1940 and 1980 census, Lawrence lost a total of nearly 40 percent of its white residents, before substantial Latino migration to the city was even underway.[2] In this sense, Lawrence encourages us to look at the "pull factors" of white flight, to explore what *drew* white urban residents out into the suburbs, not what *"pushed"* them from the city. Across the nation, rising wages and federally guaranteed mortgages brought the cost of single-family suburban homes into range for many middle- and working-class white families, while federally sponsored highway development kept the city accessible. At the same time, tax incentives and ample space for parking increasingly brought industry and retail establishments out to the suburbs, cutting the commute to work and shopping. Suburban growth in turn swelled suburban tax bases, enabling strong infrastructures and effectively segregated public schools flush with resources, as well as significant state and national political power relative to urban neighbors. The draw of Lawrence's suburbs in these early decades was not that they offered an escape from the racial tension of the city, because there wasn't really any racial tension yet. Rather the pull of the suburbs related to changes in the metropolitan political economy that developed the suburbs at Lawrence's expense and enabled the suburbs to limit economic diversity through exclusionary zoning practices, such as restricting multifamily housing and apartments.

Lawrence is completely surrounded by three suburbs: Andover, North Andover, and Methuen. I also include Salem, New Hampshire, directly over the New Hampshire border from Methuen, in this analysis. Lying just north of Greater Lawrence, Salem would come to be the closest major retail center in tax-free New Hampshire and a heavy retail competitor with Lawrence. As a result, it was often considered part of "Greater Lawrence," (i.e., Lawrence and its suburbs). The four suburbs had somewhat different trajectories; Andover and North Andover, lying to the south-west and southeast of Lawrence, respectively (in other words, on the Boston side of Lawrence), were significantly more prosperous than Methuen and Salem (lying to the north). Yet they all shared a development path between 1950 and 1980 that was substantially different than that of Lawrence. Between 1950 and 1960, the number of people living in the Greater Lawrence metropolitan region remained relatively stable. This stability, however, obscured substantial shifts in urban and suburban populations. While Lawrence lost 12 percent of its population, or almost 10,000 residents, Andover's population increased by 28 percent, Methuen's by 15 percent, and North Andover's by 29 percent. The increase was even more dramatic just over the New Hampshire border, where Salem (soon to grow into a commercial hub) al-most doubled in population during the 1950s, with a whopping 92 percent increase.

The decline in Lawrence's population continued over the next few decades, as the suburbs continued to develop. New highway construction in the 1950s and 1960s facilitated easy access between the suburbs and to the city, and the suburbs had ample open space for development. Housing development was largely restricted, however, to single-family homes, with federally guaranteed mortgage programs and expanded credit opportunities making these homes affordable for purchase and thus promot-ing high owner-occupancy rates. Homes in the suburbs were also often newer and in better condition than Lawrence's housing, much of which had been built at the turn of the century or earlier to house immigrant workers in Lawrence's textile mills dur-ing its industrial heyday. Federal funds were also far easier to obtain for new home purchases than for renovations.

In 1950, at the beginning of this suburban swell, median home values and house-hold incomes were similar in Lawrence and its suburbs. Across the Lawrence met-ropolitan area, urban and suburban residents shared quite similar demographics. As a result, suburban homeownership was in reach for even average-earning Lawrence residents. In 1950, the median value of a single-family home in the city of Lawrence was $8,989 ($72,844 adjusted to 2005 dollars, to give a sense of the change between decades),[3] quite near the median home value for the Greater Lawrence area as a whole, which was $9,210 ($74,635 adjusted). Those Lawrencians who could afford to buy a home in this era most likely had a good deal of choice over whether they purchased in the city or the suburbs. Indeed, considering that much of the federal support for homeownership was geared toward new construction, it may even have been easier for Lawrencians in 1950 to buy a home in the suburbs than in the city. This is significant in the study of suburban development, because at this time, when the *economics* of suburban homeownership were so egalitarian, the *racial politics* of suburban homeownership were their most exclusionary. This very federal processes that enabled homeownership for so many white families often explicitly excluded families of color from suburban homeownership opportunities in the pre–Civil Rights era. Although restrictive covenants were made legally unenforceable in 1948, and explicit references to race were removed from the Federal Housing Authority materials in the 1950s, discriminatory practices continued, such as the federally established bank policies of red-lining (refusing to provide mortgages within an entire non-white or integrated neighborhood) and denying mortgages to non-white applicants based on the perceived risk of the loan. Housing discrimination by Realtors continued as well. By the time an (imperfect) enforcement mechanism existed in the 1970s to try to ensure equal opportunity lending and prevent housing discrimination, a chasm had opened up between urban income and suburban housing prices.

As mentioned above, the median home value in Greater Lawrence in 1950 was $9,210 ($74,635 adjusted,) just over three times the median annual household income of Lawrence residents. Suburban housing was economically accessible to a large number of white urban families looking to buy their own single-family homes in this era that celebrated domesticity and the nuclear family. By 1980, however, the difference between urban wages and suburban housing prices had become dramatic. In Andover, in 1980, the median housing value had grown to $80,684 ($191,234 adjusted), nearly six times the median household income in Lawrence, and by 2000, at $344,895 ($391,161 adjusted), the median home value in Andover was nearly twelve times the median household income in Lawrence! Even in a less wealthy suburb such as Methuen this process occurred. By 1980, the median home value had only grown to $50,004 ($118,517 adjusted), just three and a half times the median household income in Lawrence. But by 2000, it was $159,000 ($180,329 adjusted), or five and a half times the median household income in Lawrence. Average household incomes in Lawrence declined slightly over these decades, but the true responsibility for this major gap lays in the virtually exponential growth of suburban housing prices. As Robert Self has noted in his study of Oakland and suburban Alameda County, at the same time that explicitly racial barriers to suburban living were being eradicated in the 1960s, "property value differentials hardened across space" (Self, 2003: 269). As the decades advanced, discrimination was no longer necessary to ensure that the suburbs remained racially and economically homogenous, as low-income, urban workers (as most Latinos in Lawrence were), had been effectively priced out of the market to buy suburban homes.

Unable to *buy* homes in the suburbs by 1980, could working-class Lawrencians at least obtain *rental* housing in the suburbs? This was also quite difficult. Zoning standards and public opposition had dramatically limited the quantity of both multifamily rental housing and subsidized (or "public") housing in the suburbs. By 1980, between 87 and 94 percent of houses in Andover, Methuen, and North Andover were only in single-family dwellings (Chamber of Commerce, 1980). Families looking to rent an apartment would be hard-pressed to find one in the suburbs. Those reliant on subsidized housing were even more constrained to the city. Although Massachusetts had passed landmark legislation in 1969 to encourage the development of subsidized housing in its suburbs, such development remained slow and the suburban units that were built were most often for the elderly, not for low-income families (Schuetz, 2008). In 1976, Andover had 232 units of subsidized housing, North Andover had 154, and Methuen with 308 units. All of these units combined, however, do not even come close to Lawrence's 2,203 units of subsidized housing!

Not only did the suburbs have dramatically less subsidized housing than Lawrence, but the majority of units that were located in the suburbs were reserved for the elderly: 76 percent of Andover's subsidized units, 87 percent of North Andover's, and 81 percent of Methuen's. By contrast, only a quarter of Lawrence's subsidized units were for the elderly; the rest were for low-income families (Merrimack Valley Planning Commission, 1976).

By 1980, subsidized and even private multifamily rental housing was overwhelmingly concentrated in the central city, dramatically constraining renters' choices. Median home prices in most suburbs were beyond the means of the average Lawrence worker, particularly beyond the range of the average Latino worker, whose wages were substantially lower than the Lawrence median. The overwhelming majority of Latinos who settled in the Greater Lawrence region had little opportunity to find a home outside Lawrence. Not only did this residential divergence constrain the settlement choices of Latino migrants, it also had a dramatic impact on the quality of public services. The skyrocketing property values in the suburbs contributed to their expanded tax bases, supporting more solid school systems and more effective government services in other realms as well, such as public safety.

Residential property values were not the only rapidly growing source of suburban prosperity in the decades after World War II. Suburban industry also experienced a dramatic acceleration. The new highways and ample parking space in the suburbs drew formerly urban manufacturers to relocate in the suburbs throughout the nation, particularly in the Northeast and Midwest. The security priorities of government defense contracts, which emphasized decentralization in Cold War weapons production, also drew production out of central cities. Some suburbs offered substantial financial incentives for industries to relocate, as well, including tax breaks that many struggling cities could not afford. Suburban competition for industry dramatically accelerated urban deindustrialization. Although many manufacturers moved to the South and eventually off-shore, many others remained tantalizingly near—within the metropolitan region, but outside municipal boundaries, outside the urban tax base, and beyond the reach of many urban workers.

Lawrence's deindustrialization began as early as the 1920s and 1930s, as the textile industry moved to the non-unionized South from a city that was famous (or infamous) for its militant labor activity since the 1912 "Bread and Roses" strike (and the less well-known strike of 1919). Although the mills were brought back to life by the textile demands of World War II, within a few years of the war ending, Lawrence was facing massive layoffs. The collapse of New England's textile industry was not limited to Lawrence. Particularly in Massachusetts, the textile mills that had clothed the nation and provided the backbone of the region's economy shut down soon after World War II, some heading south and others folding completely in the face of competition from southern industries and synthetic fabrics. As textile production was in decline, however, electronics production in New England was ascending, aided by government support for education and for defense development. Along Rt. 128, outside Boston, a high-tech electronics industry corridor began to develop, changing the industrial base of the state from textile manufacturing to electronics, which were in high demand in the post–World War II consumption-based economy and the Cold War–based defense industry. In the decades after World War II, the backbone of New England's manufacturing economy shifted from textiles to electronics. This change occurred slowly throughout the state, but in Lawrence, the change was seismic. As the *Boston Globe* reported, "New England adjusted gradually to the changed economic world, but nowhere was the transition more dramatic, the extremes of prosperity and adversity so marked, as in Lawrence." As Lawrence had been at the center of the textile industry, it would also come to demonstrate the most significant drawback to New England's industrial transition. Whereas textile manufacturing had been largely an urban mill town phenomenon, electronics development and manufacturing would come to be largely a suburban process. As New England's industrial base shifted to electronics, it also shifted to its suburbs, and this shift from urban textile production to suburban electronics manufacturing left former mill towns grasping for a new economic base (Dudley, 1960).

In the decades after World War II, the largest and most profitable manufacturers in the Greater Lawrence area were located in, or had relocated to, the suburbs. Two of the most notable suburban manufacturers in Greater Lawrence were Raytheon and Western Electric (which would become AT&T and then Lucent Technologies). Raytheon was located in Andover and was flush with Cold War defense contracts throughout this era, constructing high-end machinery. Western Electric, however, demonstrates cleanly the arch of intrametropolitan (urban/suburban) competition for industry in the postwar era. During World War II, Western Electric produced communications equipment for both consumer and defense uses. In the postwar era, the company expanded into Lawrence, beginning to manufacture and warehouse in the former Monomac Spinning Mill in 1951. Yet, just two years later, Western Electric broke ground on a larger, more modern plant in North Andover. By 1960, the plant in North Andover covered over 150 acres, compared to the six acres of the Lawrence plant, and had enough room for 1,500 parking spaces. By 1978, after years of rumors and decades of gradually transferring its operations and its workers to North Andover, Western Electric closed the Lawrence plant. Meanwhile, the North Andover plant was thriving, having expanded seven times in the intervening years. Western Electric continued to provide employment for a substantial number of Lawrence residents, including Lawrence Latinos, for almost two more decades. Yet, after its Lawrence plant closed in 1978, Western Electric (like many other Greater Lawrence manufacturers) no longer contributed directly to Lawrence's tax base, to the maintenance of any of its old mill buildings, or to Lawrence's rapidly declining reputation (Western Electric archives).

Suburban competition for manufacturing was perhaps less ruinous for urban economies than suburban competition for the region's retail establishments. The postwar boom in suburban malls and shopping plazas devastated urban downtowns across the nation, and Lawrence was no exception. The decline of the city's retail sector began in the mid-1950s as Methuen and Salem gradually became the consumer hubs of the region. Already in 1957, a report commissioned by the city leadership pointed out, "The people of the Greater Lawrence Area are doing business outside [downtown]." The report acknowledged that the economic impact of this was currently small, but made the dire prediction that "this point will be the most serious problem faced by [Lawrence's downtown] within the next three years." They speculated that, if Lawrence's downtown "could remain isolated from competition for the next ten years, as it has in the past," the city's retail sector could recover. This isolation, however, was impossible, as suburban shopping centers sprang up across the region (with ample free parking), and the new highways made them easily accessible to all Greater Lawrence residents (Liebke, 1957).

Retail establishments came to line Route 28 in Salem in the 1960s, and the town's growing importance as a consumer site was aided by Massachusetts' decision to introduce a sales tax in 1966, which made the quick drive over the New Hampshire border (to one of the few states left in the country without a sales tax) quite appealing. The *Journal of Greater Lawrence* called the commercial sector along Route 28 in Salem, "a sizzling strip of neon and a motorist's nightmare," yet stores like K-Mart still drew shoppers. The final blow to Lawrence's established retail sector was dealt in the early 1970s with the construction of the Methuen Mall. In late November, 1973, *Journal of Greater Lawrence* reporter, Andrew Coburn, wrote, "Excuse the messy metaphor, but one hell of a heavyweight is flexing its muscles for the biggest money battle this area has known . . . the Methuen Mall versus every other shopping scene (particularly plazas) from here to Newburyport." At the time, the mall, what Coburn called "one huge consumer circus with something for everybody," was only partially open, with less than half of its projected 75 stores up and running, but Coburn reported that it "already [was] doing damage in downtown Lawrence." The Methuen Mall would be the biggest of its kind in the region, posing an immediate threat to retail centers throughout Greater Lawrence. Most troubling for the city itself, Coburn predicted that the mall "will touch the core of communities whose downtown districts have little to offer as it is" (Coburn, 1973).

Coburn detailed the suburban mall's advantages, "A concrete ballfield for free and easy parking, with no chance of a ticket on the windshield." This was particularly important to those fed up with parking tickets in downtown Lawrence. The Methuen Mall also had "huge stores like Sears and Howland's, with all the latest gimmicks, advertising money, and promotional fanfare to draw crowds from far and wide." Sears had just left its longtime location on Essex Street in downtown Lawrence and so its relocation to the Methuen Mall must have caused some Lawrencians particular chagrin. Whatever hope Lawrencians may have had for returning downtown to its prior prominence suddenly became unrealistic, as the Methuen Mall laid Essex Street down for the count (Coburn, 1973). Even the local paper, the *Lawrence Eagle-Tribune*, had moved from its downtown Lawrence location to suburban North Andover in 1968 (and in 1987, at a high point in the city's crisis, the paper even removed the word "Lawrence" from its name).

By 1980, the shared demographics of the Greater Lawrence region after World War II had given way to dramatic inequality between the city and its suburbs. The suburbs had effectively won the battle for Greater Lawrence's middle-class residents, its major industry, and its retail sector. The income gap between the city and its suburbs was pronounced, with Lawrence households only earning an average of 57 cents to Andover residents' dollar, and the city was in the throes of severe economic crisis.

LATINO SETTLEMENT

Onto this stage of suburban prosperity and urban decline stepped Latino migrants, beginning with a trickle of Cuban refugees and Puerto Rican migrants in the late 1950s and early 1960s. The Latino population in Lawrence grew steadily over the next few decades, from dozens in the 1950s, to hundreds in the 1960s, to thousands in the 1970s. By 1980, census figures reported that over ten thousand Latinos lived in Lawrence, and unsurprisingly, members of the community estimated that the real population was substantially higher. By 1990, the census indicated that the Latino population in Lawrence had tripled to nearly 30,000, and most districts in North Lawrence had already developed Latino majorities. As the local paper noted in the early 1990s, "The most dramatic increase in Lawrence's Latino population came in the 1980s, when Dominicans drawn by family ties and the lure of a smaller, safer city streamed in from New York City and other East Coast locales" (Hartnett, 1992b). It

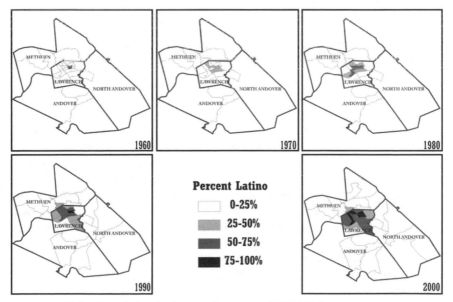

Map 4.1.   Latino Population in Greater Lawrence, 1960–2000

is significant that the 1980s were the time in Lawrence when racial tension was at its height, when the remaining industries in the city were leaving and unemployment was growing, and yet it was also the time when the Latino population grew the most substantially. By 2000, with the further addition of more than ten thousand Latinos in the 1990s (a portion of which probably occurred through natural increase), the census indicated that Lawrence had developed a substantial Latino majority (59.7 percent) in the city as a whole. Current census estimates place the proportion of Latinos in the city as high as 71.1 percent.

According to census figures, the majority of Latinos who arrived before 1980 were Puerto Rican. Dominicans did not dominate numerically until the 1990s, although many Dominican migrants arrived during the earlier period as well, and by 1980 they were already a close second to Puerto Ricans. Many community leaders, however, argued as early as the 1970s that the Dominican population had overtaken the Puerto Rican population numerically. Undocumented Dominicans may have been reluctant to announce themselves to census takers, and there is evidence that some undocumented Dominicans successfully claimed that they were Puerto Rican in order to stay and work in the United States without fear of deportation (Huard, 1973). Together, Dominicans and Puerto Ricans made up the vast majority of Latinos in the city, but more than 20 other national-origin groups were present in Lawrence as well. Although some Latinos came straight to Lawrence from their home countries, the bulk of Latino settlement in Lawrence before the 1980s was made up of internal migrants, mostly from New York City (Borges-Méndez, 1994; Andors, 1999). As longtime Lawrence resident and community organizer Isabel Meléndez described, in the 1970s, "Lawrence filled-up with New York" (Isabel Meléndez, quoted in Borges-Méndez, 1994). Direct migration from Latin America increased in later decades, but ties and movement between Lawrence and New York remained strong.

In 1992, the director of Lawrence's Minority Business Council, Jose Zaiter, told his family's migration story to the local paper, explaining that it was typical of how many Latinos ended up in Lawrence. His family had moved from the Dominican Republic to New York City in 1965, and a year later, his uncle left New York for Lawrence and got a job in the city's garment industry. While living in Lawrence, his uncle returned for frequent visits to New York, and he described Lawrence to his relatives as a safe city where jobs were plentiful. In the context of Lawrence's crisis in the early 1990s (when Zaiter was telling his story to the newspaper), as well as the city's reputation for crime, Zaiter found the fact that safety motivated Latino migration to Lawrence "ironic." Yet in comparison with New York City's notorious struggles with crime and drugs in the decades after World War II, Lawrence seemed a safer, more manageable alternative. The presence of jobs in Lawrence must have seemed no less ironic to Zaiter in the early 1990s, as Lawrence in 1990 had a 25 percent Latino unemployment rate. Decades earlier, however, when his family first came to the city, he remembered not only that "there were many jobs available" in the city's declining manufacturing sector, but added that companies even used to pay $50 bonuses to people who recruited new workers (Zaiter quoted in Hartnett, 1992a).

Zaiter's migration narrative demonstrates many of the "ironies" or apparent contradictions of Latino settlement in Lawrence, Massachusetts. Unless one has been to or lived in Lawrence, the idea of a tiny, seven-square mile city on the border of New Hampshire, over a thousand miles away from the nearest Latin American country, becoming home to one of the highest proportions of Latinos in the nation seems preposterous. Lawrence is certainly not a major urban center with obvious name recognition or the home of a long-standing Latino community, like New York City. Further, throughout Lawrence's history, many city officials and white residents worked hard to make the city unappealing as a Latino settlement site, both through official policy and through quotidian harassment and exclusion. Finally, when one considers the dramatic economic crisis facing the city as a result of suburbanization and deindustrialization, the pull of the city for Latino migrants seems puzzling indeed! Why would tens of thousands of Latinos settle in a small, obscure city, with a resistant white population and a troubled economy? Why would they choose a deteriorating, often bigoted, New England city, over New York, with its longstanding Latino neighborhoods, businesses, and communities and its reputation for racial tolerance? As Ramón Borges-Méndez has aptly phrased it, "Who in their right mind, looking for a job and looking for better economic opportunity . . . would move to Lawrence?" (Borges-Méndez, 2004).

The answer to the question of "Why Lawrence?" is threefold, and all three parts are related to the development of urban crisis in U.S. cities in the second half of the twentieth century. First, racialized patterns of urban disinvestment in New York City led many Latinos to believe that New York City was not a suitable place to make a life for themselves and their families. New York had been the major East Coast settlement site for Latinos for generations, but the national postwar process of suburbanization and urban disinvestment left the city, particularly Latino neighborhoods, in crisis. Although slums were certainly not unique to the post–World War II urban landscape, these decades oversaw the development of racialized patterns of concentrated poverty in bleak, barren public housing sites, combined with the flight or demolition of formerly vibrant retail areas, the shift to a two-tier, low-wage service economy with little chance for upward mobility, growing joblessness, and the erosion of basic educational and public safety services. The perceived hazards of postwar New York City were partially responsible for the dramatic drop in the proportion of stateside Puerto Ricans living in New York. In 1940, an incredible 88 percent of stateside Puerto Ricans lived in New York City. By 1970, New York City's share had declined to only 59 percent, a smaller proportion, but one that still left New York City as home to the majority of stateside Puerto Ricans. By 2000, however, less than a quarter of stateside Puerto Ricans lived in New York City (Whalen and Víctor Vázquez-Hernández, 2005). This dispersion from New York City was true of Dominicans as well by 2000. Many scholars have looked at factors that determine Latino settlement sites (Whalen and Vázquez-Hernández, 2005; Sánchez Korrol, 1983; Sagás and Molina, 2004; Grasmuck and Pessar, 1991; Dávila, 2004; Georges, 1990; Hernández, 2002; Levitt, 2001; Pérez, 2004; Whalen, 2001). Particular attention has been paid to the "pull" factors that caused this decline in New York's share of stateside Puerto Ricans and Dominicans; yet these accounts demonstrate that New York's urban crisis created a "push" from the city, as well, and that "push" was largely responsible for the growth in Lawrence's Latino population.

Oral history interviews with Latino Lawrencians confirm that Latino settlement in Lawrence was due partially to a "push" from New York City. A young Dominican man explained, "We had a tough life in New York. . . . Lawrence has a lot more to offer" (quoted in Urban Studies Institute, 1986). A Dominican woman explained, "I moved to Lawrence because New York is, I don't consider [it] a nice place for a child to be raised in. You know, I was thinking about my kids to be raised in a nice city, not gangs, stuff like that, bad things" (DeJesus, 1995). A young Dominican man explained to the *Eagle-Tribune* why his mother chose Lawrence, and the paper reported, "[she] first went to New York for a year and then she found Lawrence. To her . . . the city was like a church—quiet and peaceful. It was a much safer place to send her children to school" (quoted in *Eagle-Tribune*, 1979) One Dominican woman explained, "One of the reasons so many Dominicans have immigrated to Lawrence is the peace and quiet. You know that Lawrence is small and outside of the large urban centers . . . the children can play in the streets, they can be outside until late (above all in the summer); this wouldn't be possible in other cities. The tranquility is what attracts us to come here" (quoted in Andors, 1999: 96). Another Dominican woman who came to Lawrence as a child in 1970, believed that her parents came to Lawrence because, "It was quieter than New York" (Garcia, 2009). Although Lawrence today contains some migrants from large Latin American cities, like Santo Domingo, many early migrants came from much smaller towns, like Tenares in the Dominican Republic and Juana Diaz in Puerto Rico. The relative *tranquilidad* of Lawrence resembled the life many Latinos lived before migration, "*Se parece más a nuestros barrios, a nuestro pueblo.*" [It more closely resembles our neighborhoods, our towns] (quoted in Andors, 1999: 32). Latino settlers in Lawrence believed that this small-town life provided a safer environment in which to raise children. One Latina explained that she came to Lawrence from New York City in 1981 not because she had been told about jobs in the area, but because she had been told that "it would be more peaceful for my children" (Stein, 1988). Many Latinos chose Lawrence because they were specifically trying to escape the urban experience of congestion and crime that they had found in New York City.

Yet, if *tranquilidad* was the goal, why not settle in the suburbs or a small town? This brings us to the second part of the answer to "Why Lawrence?" The racialized suburbanization that had taken place across the nation after World War II constrained the settlement options of most Latinos, making the question of where to settle really a question of in which *city* to settle for all but the wealthiest and luckiest Latinos.[4] Not only had uneven metropolitan development transformed Lawrence from a bustling, working-class city into a sparsely populated, impoverished city, it also dramatically constrained the settlement options of incoming Latinos, as decades of protected suburbanization had created the huge differential in the cost of urban and suburban housing discussed above.

Although Lawrence would come to be known, at least regionally, for its economic problems and its crime and poverty, many of the Latinos who chose to move there were looking for the closest thing they could get to small-town life in the United States. Constrained by the exclusionary practices of suburbanization, Latinos looked for a small city, where they could build community, raise children and start businesses in safety, and escape the perceived danger and anonymity of life in New York. The "push" from New York City and the limiting factors of suburbanization were essential to the development of a Latino community in Lawrence; the development of such a substantial Latino community in Lawrence was not overdetermined by these processes alone, however, as there existed countless other cities throughout the United States that did not develop such an ethnic profile. Rather, the final critical factor in the rise of Lawrence's Latino community was the impact of urban disinvestment on the city. The process of urban decline in Lawrence opened the city's job market and housing to Latinos. As much of New England transitioned to high-tech manufacturing, Lawrence's remaining non-durable goods manufacturers welcomed and even recruited Latinos to Lawrence in the 1960s and 1970s as a means of remaining competitive with Southern and overseas manufacturers. This initial migration (demonstrated in the recruitment Zaiter described) formed the basis of a Latino community in the city that was then fed through kinship networks, even after the employment incentive to settle in Lawrence receded after the late 1970s. In addition, white flight made rental housing available in the city, although it was not necessarily "cheap" relative to Latino wages.

Perhaps most critically, urban disinvestment was so thorough in Lawrence that the Latino community was allowed to grow relatively undisturbed by gentrification or large-scale urban renewal. The absence of gentrification in the city enabled long-term community and small-business development, relatively uninterrupted by the displacement suffered by many Latino communities in larger cities. Unimpeded by gentrification, the Latino community grew, Latinos developed an unmistakable public presence in the city, and Latino businesses and organizations proliferated, all of which in turn became factors that drew more Latinos to the city. Latinos came to Lawrence because of what previous settlers were able to build and create there. The *Boston Globe* reported in 1988 that "In a typical week several dozen new families show up in Lawrence, drawn by reports from relatives and friends who have come before. The city's huge Hispanic population—estimated at 20,000 to 30,000—seems to be the biggest attraction. Hispanics can find grocery stores, dry-cleaning shops and plumbing businesses run by other Hispanics." Jorge Santiago added, "The weather is different and the architecture is different but otherwise you could be walking around in your home town" (Stein, 1988).

In 1992, the *Eagle-Tribune* profiled a young Latino couple, a machinist at Lawrence Pumps Inc. and a nursing aide, who had just married and bought a two-family house in Lawrence, where the husband's brother would live upstairs. "They have read the stories about Lawrence that have made headlines nationwide this year, stories of stolen cars, fires, teen-aged pregnancy, insurance scams and welfare schemes. They know the city is home to all of those problems and more. But it is also home to their families and friends, their memories and their hopes." The husband was Dominican, and had moved to Lawrence ten years ago with his parents and seven siblings, all of whom live in the area. The wife was Puerto Rican, but born in Lawrence, and considered herself, "more Lawrencian than Latina." The paper described the couple, as "among many people in the city's Latino community who view Lawrence's problems as its shadow, not its substance." The profile argued that family ties and the potential for homeownership was not the city's only draw; Lawrence had elected its first Latino official, two hundred Latino-owned businesses operated in the city, and community resources were abundant, including parents' groups that gathered in homes "sharing information about schools, city government, health and other neighborhood concerns." The article continued, "Latino churches are thriving, from storefront ministries to established parishes." Perhaps most shocking to city leaders who had spent decades unsuccessfully trying to revitalize downtown's Essex Street was Lawrence's fresh development. "Downtown Lawrence has developed a decidedly Caribbean flavor. Clothes boutiques, restaurants and nightclubs catering to a Latin crowd are attracting people from Boston, Lowell, Worcester and New Hampshire" (Hartnett, 1992a). The city was experiencing a renaissance, but it looked nothing like what Lawrence's old elites had envisioned.

Latino migration had brought life to the city, and that life was responsible for drawing more Latinos. Lawrence Garcia was a Lawrence-born Dominican whose parents had named him after the city. He drove a cab for Borinquen Taxi, and insisted that Lawrence was a prime settlement spot for Latinos, in spite of its struggles. "Outsiders don't come in to see what it's all about," he observed. "There's a lot of bad, but there's a lot of good, especially for the Hispanics. That's why there are so many Hispanics here. It's the best town in the world for me" (Hartnett, 1992c). By the 1990s, Lawrence was unabashedly a Latino city in most aspects of its public culture, and that in turn attracted more Latinos to the city.

For the long-term residents of the city who had viewed the growing Latino population as the *cause* of Lawrence's problems, rather than the *solution*, the increasing Latinization of Lawrence was just another mark of how far the city had fallen. Indeed, many white residents and city officials had resisted Latino settlement for decades, creating a degree of racial animosity in the city that drew international attention when white and Latino Lawrencians battled each other in the streets in 1984. In the context of the brutal economic devastation of the 1990s, however, the perception of Latinos began to shift, as many Latino Lawrencians argued that empowering the Latino community was the best (if not the only) hope for revitalizing Lawrence. By 1990, the city had lost more than half of its white population, and had experienced massive industrial and retail flight. The city's economy had become reliant on Latino-owned businesses and businesses oriented toward serving the Latino community, as well as industries that specifically hired poor Latinos in order to reduce labor costs. Also crucial to the city's economy was the bilingual and bicultural social-service industry that was coalescing to provide health, education, and other services to Latino families, and to serve as a bridge between the Latino community and the city, state, and federal governments.

By the 1990s, it had become obvious that Latinos were consumers, workers, tenants, and, most important, Lawrencians—above all else, the city was reliant on the vitality and public presence that Latinos brought to the city, filling the streets and parks of Lawrence during public festivals and daily activities, public spaces that might otherwise have been deserted. As Latino community leader Eduardo Crespo argued, "Hispanics are bringing Lawrence back to life . . . If we would, hypotheti-cally, leave the city, this would be a ghost town" (quoted in Hernandez and Walker, 1991). In addition, Crespo tied the growth of Latino-owned businesses explicitly to earlier urban flight, saying "Hispanics are replacing traditional establishments that no longer believe in the city" (quoted in *Philadelphia Inquirer*, 1991).

As Lawrence became an increasingly Latino city, it took on a prominent role in Latin American economies and politics. This is particularly evident in Lawrence's relationship with the Dominican Republic. Lawrence's small size was no barrier to it becoming one of the most influential U.S. cities in Dominican politics, arguably playing a more important role than its nearest big-city neighbor, Boston. Ramón Borges Méndez noted that his interaction with high-level Dominican politicians did not occur in the Dominican Republic or even in Boston; "as a matter of fact, I've met two of the former presidents of the Dominican Republic and the acting President of the Dominican Republic in *Lawrence*" (Borges-Méndez, 2004). When current Dominican president Leonel Fernández was first elected in 1996, he named Lawrence-resident Julio César Correa as Dominican Consul in Boston. Although the post may have been in Boston, it was a Lawrencian who filled it (Rozemberg, 1996). A Dominican barber from Essex Street, Carlos Jose Cepeda, won a seat in the Do-minican congress in 1995. He had joined the Partido de la Liberación Dominicana (PLD) in 1980 and had been a member of the Lawrence chapter since he arrived in the city nine years earlier. While working as a barber in downtown Lawrence, he was simultaneously building his political career in the Dominican Republic. Cepeda had been elected in the Salceda Province (now called the Hermanas Mirabal province), near Santiago, which contained the villages of Salceda, Tenares, and Villa Tapia. His remarkable success in the Dominican election was directly attributable to transnationalism, as the *Eagle-Tribune* claimed that 60 percent of Greater Lawrence Dominicans came from that province, particularly Tenares. He noted that Lawrence support had been key to his success and he planned to work on behalf of both his Dominican constituents on the island, as well as his Lawrence supporters. He ex-plained that people in Lawrence "now have a representative and even if they are here, they can come to me for any problems or needs in their towns back home which I can help solve there" (quoted in *Eagle-Tribune*, 1995).

This transnational activity was not confined to politics. Latinos in Lawrence had been writing and calling their home countries, sending money and gifts to friends and family, traveling (and even moving) back and forth, since migration to Lawrence began. Although many white Lawrencians stereotyped Latinos as welfare recipients, from a transnational perspective, it was the complete opposite: Lawrence Latinos were *philanthropists*, sending money and other aid to their home countries, particularly in times of crisis, like when hurricanes struck. This aid was not only for crises, however, but contributed substantially to island economies. When asked whether Lawrence was important and well-known in the Dominican Republic, Dominican Consul Julio César Correa replied, "The city of Lawrence is widely recognized all throughout the island, but especially so in the region of El Cibao, from where most emigrate. Most important is the economic connection—most Dominicans here left family back in the island and constantly send money back to support them. This money is money that contributes to the economy of the island" (quoted in Rozemberg, 1996). It was not only the Dominican Republic that benefited from this transnationalism; transnational economic activities were central to the growth of many local Latino-owned businesses, as well. Many Latino-owned businesses in Lawrence were based on moving money, goods, or people between Lawrence and the Caribbean. Money transfer companies, travel agencies, and shipping companies were important not just to island economies, but to *Lawrence's* economy, as well, in the context of the devastation of Lawrence's retail sector that had occurred in the previous decades. *In spite* of its small size, Lawrence played an important role in transnational politics and economics; *because* of Lawrence's small size, this transnational activity played a disproportionately important role in shaping the local economy and public culture of the city.

The history of the relationship between Lawrence's urban crisis and Latino settlement in the city is complex, and much remains to be explored. Yet, at the very least, it is quite clear that Lawrence's struggles have deep roots in the postwar decades, and thus cannot be laid at the feet of the city's most recent immigrants. On the contrary, Latino settlement brought crucial labor, investment, energy, and vision to a city that had been deeply undermined by disinvestment; Latino Lawrencians indeed brought new life to a "ghost town."

NOTES

1. For a more detailed account of Lawrence's history, including more detailed citations on the material included here, see Llana Barber, "Latino Migration and the New Global Cities: Transnationalism, Race, and Urban Crisis in Lawrence, Massachusetts, 1945–2000," (Unpublished PhD Dissertation, Boston College, 2010).

2. All statistics are from the United States Census, unless otherwise noted. Census data accessed either in published form, through the website census.gov, or through the U.S. Department of Housing and Urban Development, State of the Cities online database, http://socds.huduser.org/.

3. 2005 numbers are used rather than 2010 numbers because many of the statistics from 1970 and after are from the State of the Cities database, which gives figures consistently in 2005 dollars. U.S. Department of Housing and Urban Development, State of the Cities online database, http://socds.huduser.org/ accessed throughout 2009 and 2010. Conversions

were done using an online calculator from the Bureau of Labor Statistics, http://data.bls.gov/ cgi-bin/cpicalc.pl, accessed throughout 2009 and 2010.

4. This is less true on the West Coast and Southwest, where Latino agricultural labor and longstanding Mexican American communities complicate this postwar paradigm of racialized metropolitan development.

REFERENCES

Andors, Jessica. 1999. "City and Island: Dominicans in Lawrence: Transnational Community Formation in a Globalizing World." Master's thesis, MIT.

Avila, Eric. 2006. *Popular Culture in the Age of White Flight: Fear and Fantasy in Suburban Los Angeles.* Berkeley, CA: University of California Press.

Borges-Méndez, Ramón. 1994. "Urban and Regional Restructuring and *Barrio* Formation in Massachusetts: The Cases of Lowell, Lawrence and Holyoke." PhD dissertation, MIT.

Borges-Méndez, Ramón. 2004. Presentation at the "Forgotten Cities" seminar series on October 27, hosted by the Department of Urban Studies and Planning at the MIT. Transcript archived with the Department of Urban Studies and Planning, and quote used with permission from the speaker.

Chamber of Commerce of Greater Lawrence. 1980. "Greater Lawrence Economic Profile." (John F. Buckley papers, at the Lawrence History Center).

Coburn, Andrew. 1973. "Battle of the Buck: Methuen Mall flexes its muscles and downtown and others flinch." *Journal of Greater Lawrence*, November 29.

Cohen, Lizabeth. 2003. *A Consumers' Republic: The Politics of Mass Consumption in Postwar America.* New York: Random House.

Dávila, Arlene. 2004. *Barrio Dreams: Puerto Ricans, Latinos, and the Neoliberal City.* Berkeley: University of California Press.

DeJesus, Carolina. 1995. Interviewed by Joan Kelley (Lawrence History Center).

Dudley, Uncle. 1960. "City that wouldn't die," *Boston Globe*, December 11 (reprint Lawrence Public Library Archives).

Eagle-Tribune. 1979. "Dominican student unhappy with education, food, weather." April 30.

Eagle-Tribune. 1995. "Barber helps relatives help family back home." March 11.

Garcia, Ingrid. 2009. Interviewed by author, November 10.

Georges, Eugenia. 1990. *The Making of a Transnational Community: Migration, Development, and Cultural Change in the Dominican Republic.* New York: Columbia University Press.

Grasmuck, Sherri and Patricia R. Pessar. 1991. *Between Two Islands: Dominican International Migration.* Berkeley: University of California Press.

Hartnett, Hilda. 1992a. "For Latinos, a dynamic time." *Eagle-Tribune*, September 20.

Hartnett, Hilda. 1992b. "Lawrence's Latino history diverse, complex." *Eagle-Tribune*, September 20.

Hartnett, Hilda. 1992c. "Should it be called Latino or Hispanic?" *Eagle-Tribune*, September 20.

Hernandez Jr., Efrain, and Adrian Walker. 1991. "Hispanic gains don't translate into power." *Boston Globe*, March 24.

Hernández, Ramona. 2002. *The Mobility of Labor Under Advanced Capitalism: Dominican Migration to the United States.* New York: Columbia University Press.

Huard, Ray. 1973. "Ex-revo." *Eagle-Tribune*, June 5.

Kruse, Kevin Michael. 2007. *White Flight: Atlanta and the Making of Modern Conservatism.* Princeton: Princeton University Press.

Levitt, Peggy.2001. *The Transnational Villagers.* Berkeley: University of California Press.

Liebke, James F. & Associates. 1957. "An Analysis and Recommended Program for the Central Business District: Lawrence Massachusetts."

Merrimack Valley Planning Commission [MVPC]. 1976. "Chapter 774 (the anti-snob zoning law): its impact on the MVPC region."

Pérez, Gina M. 2004. *The Near Northwest Side Story: Migration, Displacement, & Puerto Rican Families.* Berkeley: University of California Press.

Philadelphia Inquirer. 1991. "In New England, Hispanics have an increasing impact." April 21.

Rozemberg, Hernán. 1996. "Consul knows politics of 2 lands." *Eagle-Tribune.* November 18.

Sagás, Ernesto, and Sintia E. Molina, Eds. 2004. *Dominican Migration: Transnational Perspectives.* Gainesville: University Press of Florida.

Sánchez Korrol, Virginia E. 1983. *From Colonia to Community: The History of Puerto Ricans in New York City, 1917–1948.* Westport, CT: Greenwood Press

Schuetz, Jenny. 2008. "Guarding the Town Walls: Mechanisms and Motives for Restricting Multifamily Housing in Massachusetts." *Real Estate Economics* 36.3. Retrieved January 4, 2010 (http://dx.doi.org.proxy.bc.edu/10.1111/j.1540-6229.2008.00222.x).

Self, Robert O. 2003. *American Babylon: Race and the Struggle for Postwar Oakland.* Princeton, NJ: Princeton University Press.

Seligman, Amanda I. 2005. *Block by Block: Neighborhoods and Public Policy on Chicago's West Side.* Chicago: University of Chicago Press.

Stein, Charles. 1988. "Lawrence case study: A struggle of the poor." *Boston Globe,* June 24.

Sugrue, Thomas J. 1996. *The Origins of the Urban Crisis: Race and Inequality in Postwar Detroit.* Princeton, NY: Princeton University Press.

Urban Studies Institute (Lawrence High School/Phillips Academy). 1986. "Growing Up Hispanic in Lawrence."

Western Electric Company. Merrimack Valley Works documents (courtesy of AT&T Archives and History Center).

Whalen, Carmen Teresa. 2001. *From Puerto Rico to Philadelphia: Puerto Rican Workers and Postwar Economies.* Philadelphia: Temple University Press.

Whalen, Carmen Teresa, and Víctor Vázquez-Hernández, Eds. 2005. *The Puerto Rican Diaspora: Historical Perspectives.* Philadelphia: Temple University Press.

II

SOCIAL AND COMMUNITY TRANSFORMATIONS

5

Poverty, Inequality, Politics, and Social Activism in Hartford

Louise Simmons

The persistence of poverty in Hartford is arguably the most deeply rooted social issue that has confounded city leaders and residents for decades. This chapter focuses on various aspects of poverty and the responses generated in the community by actors in different settings. First, specific features of poverty and other indicators are reviewed to paint the picture of stark contrasts between Hartford and some of the affluence that surrounds it. Then, community responses, the urban movements that attempt to address Hartford's dire situation, as well as several responses from elites in different time periods, are chronicled. Finally, suggestions for shaping a future where residents might see change and more opportunity are offered.

POVERTY AMID PLENTY

To put it succinctly, Hartford's population is exceedingly poor. Multiple indicators and multiple dimensions of life in poverty exist. Data from the 2005–2009 American Community Survey (ACS) conducted by the Census Bureau indicate that 31.6 percent of Hartford's 123,925 residents, or some 39,160 people, lived below the federal poverty level in the 2005–09 period (U.S. Census Bureau, 2011). Contrast this to the state of Connecticut's population of 3.57 million people, of whom 9.3 percent live under the poverty level. But what is worse is that child poverty in Hartford is at much higher levels. A startling 42.8 percent of children under 18 in Hartford live under the poverty level. In addition, 48.4 percent of all children under 5 years old live under poverty, and among those who live in single parent households headed by women, 60.3 percent of children under age 5 live in poverty (U.S. Census Bureau, 2011). According to the Annie E. Casey Foundation's KIDS COUNT Data Center (2008), in 2008 Hartford was tied with Detroit for the highest child poverty rates in the continental U.S. at 46 percent, compared to the national average of 18 percent. So many children in the Hartford public schools qualify for free and reduced cost lunch that the school district has made free lunches available to all students rather than deal with a costly administrative apparatus to determine eligibility.

Hartford is in the center of several rings of municipalities that shoulder much less poverty. Its 18 square miles are surrounded by a number of very affluent communities and the state of Connecticut is consistently one of the highest income states in the United States. Exceptions are the Town of East Hartford and the City of New Britain—not really a suburb of Hartford, but a small city in its own right. East Hartford's child poverty level has risen substantially in recent years to 24.0 percent, but it still has a much higher median family income than Hartford in the ACS of 2005–2009: $58,980 compared to Hartford's $32,512. New Britain's child poverty rate in this period was 30.6 percent and median family income was $50,085 (U.S. Census Bureau, 2011). Both of these municipalities have suffered from de-industrialization, particularly New Britain, while East Hartford remains the home of Pratt & Whitney Aircraft, a division of United Technologies, a company that has also downsized in recent decades. Consider the following data comparing the city of Hartford, Hartford County, which consists of 29 municipalities, the state of Connecticut, and the United States (see Table 5.1).

High child poverty rates imply tremendous family stress, including intermittent employment for wage earners, high rates of underemployment or unemployment. Lack of transportation and/or child care hinder opportunities to obtain work. Besides low incomes, services such as healthcare are often inadequate for poor families. Educational achievement often lags in comparison to more affluent families: Connecticut has the highest "achievement gap" in the United States, that is, the largest difference in educational achievement between affluent students and students in poverty (*Hartford Courant*, 2010), and Hartford's students figure prominently in that equation. Moreover, since the advent of welfare reform in 1995[1] and 1996, there is a weaker social safety net to rely on in times of need. These issues all combine to maintain high levels of poverty in the city.

Table 5.1. Population Indicators: Hartford, Hartford County, Connecticut (2005–2009)

Measure	City of Hartford	County of Hartford	State of Connecticut	United States
Percent of Individuals Living Below Poverty Level	31.6	10.1	9.3	13.5
Median Family Income	$32,512	$78,826	$83,797	$62,363
Per Capita Income	$17,094	$32,779	$36,468	$27,041
Percent of Children Under 18 Living Below Poverty Level	42.8	14.5	11.7	18.6

Sources: U.S. Census Bureau American Fact Finder, 2011.

Poverty researcher Mark Rank (2004) presents a compelling argument for moving away from individual, moral, and behavioral explanations of poverty toward a more expansive structural explanation. Poverty, he asserts, is a result of structural failings: lack of opportunities to escape poverty and a society that has come to rely on low-wage work. He sees the interplay between lack of education or human capital, in combination with a very weak social welfare system, and these larger structures and processes:

> (T)here are simply not enough viable opportunities for all Americans. Individual deficiencies, such as the lack of human capital, help to explain who is more likely to be left out in the competition to locate and secure such opportunities, but it cannot explain why there is a shortage of opportunities in the first place. In order to answer that question, we must turn to the inability of the economic, political, and social structures to provide the supports and opportunities necessary to lift all Americans out of poverty (176).

He characterizes poverty for individuals and families as a "conditional state" that people move in and out of during different periods of their lives. Therefore, he argues that we should be refocusing efforts from poor *people* to the *condition of poverty* as we look for solutions. These are important insights to bear in mind in considering Hartford's poverty.

RACIAL AND ECONOMIC SEGREGATION IN THE HARTFORD REGION

Hartford began to experience population decline during the mid twentieth century and has lost residents every decade since the 1950s. Even if modest population gains are reported in the 2010 Census, the city is unlikely to recover much of this loss in the foreseeable future. Besides the familiar phenomenon of "white flight," Hartford lost professional and middle-income families of color who have sought more effective education systems than that available in Hartford. Although populations in several suburban towns have become more diverse in the past 10 to 15 years, Hartford still is home to the *poorest* segments of the communities of color, and among its population, as well as the students in the school system, the majority are Latino, African American, and West Indian. Figure 1 charts population for the city since 1950, revealing that during the second half of the twentieth century, Hartford lost more than 50,000 people. The total net loss would have been more, but for the migration/immigration of people from the Caribbean.

Hartford County had a population in 2009 of 874,409 while the City of Hartford's 123,925 people constituted only 14 percent of the county's population. Yet, Hartford is home to significant pluralities of African Americans, other blacks, and Latinos in the region. Hartford has 43 percent of Hartford County's black population and 42 percent of its Latino population. Given the concentration of the region's poverty in Hartford, it is logical to conclude that Hartford's communities of color are

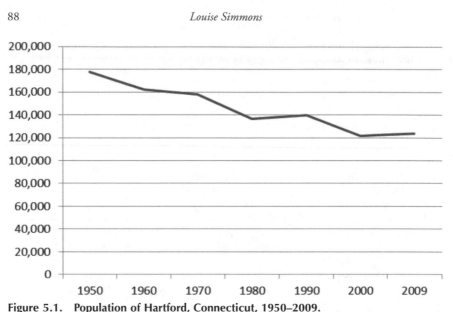

Figure 5.1.   Population of Hartford, Connecticut, 1950–2009.

Source: Historical Abstract of the United States, U.S. Census Bureau, Connecticut Economic Resource Center (CERC).

among the poorest in the area. Table 5.2 illustrates the disparities between Hartford and its first-ring suburbs in terms of population groups, median household income and poverty rates. More remote suburbs have even greater disparities.

This 2009 demographic snapshot reflects population shifts that developed and now persist over decades. In the 1980s school integration advocates filed a lawsuit on behalf of Hartford students, *Sheff v. O'Neill* (Sheff, the lead plaintiff, and O'Neill, then the Governor), alleging that the deep racial and economic isolation of Hartford's students deprives them of equal educational opportunity, a right guaranteed in the Connecticut state constitution. Twenty years later, achievement gaps endure and Hartford's students remain the poorest in the region, and the suit's original goal of integrating the schools still has not been fully met (Dougherty, this volume). Some progress has been made by initiating new magnet schools and making more suburban school seats available to Hartford students, yet the city's school system is chronically under-funded. Issues of education reform in Hartford require their own detailed analysis, but one can argue that educational equity for Hartford's children remains a difficult goal and contributes to the income gaps and life chances of the city's people.

THE LABOR MARKET AND LOW-WAGE JOBS

In July, 2010, Hartford had an unemployment rate of 16.9 percent, while the rate for the entire state was 9.4 percent. Hartford's unemployment rate has always been greater than that of its region or the state and has usually been the highest in Connecticut. According to *The State of Working Connecticut 2009*, a report published an-

Table 5.2. Selected Population Characteristics of Towns in Hartford County: Black and Latino Populations, Median Household Income, Poverty Rates (2005–2009)

City or Town	Population	Number of Black Residents	% of County Black Population (N=108,417)	Number of Latino Residents	% of County Latino Population (N=118,714)	Town/City Median HH Income	% All People % Blacks % Latinos in Town in Poverty
Hartford	123,925	46,375	43%	50,413	42%	$32,512	31.6% 27.8% 40.7%
West Hartford	60,573	3,074	3%	5,319	4%	$74,499	5.9% 10.4% 9.8%
Bloomfield	20,468	11,372	10%	1,861	2%	$68,875	5.2% 3.2% 1.9%
Windsor	28,747	8,766	8%	2,262	2%	$79,294	3.4% 3.2% 3.7%
East Hartford	48,627	11,207	10%	10,929	9%	$43,747	14.0% 16.5% 25.8%
Wethersfield	25,788	560	>1%	2,034	2%	$70,525	3.4% 6.4% 10.3%
Newington	29,530	1,083	1%	1,879	2%	$69,221	5.1% 14.0% 10.8%

Source: U.S. Census Bureau, American Community Survey 2005–2009.

nually by Connecticut Voices for Children (Hero and Kramer, 2009) unemployment and underemployment are higher among African Americans and Latinos than whites in Connecticut. The African American unemployment rate was three times that of whites, and for Latinos, two and a half times greater than whites. Also in 2008, people with less than a high school education had unemployment rates of over 15 percent in Connecticut, while those with college educations had rates below 3 percent. Rates of underemployment, "discouraged" workers who have given up searching for work, and involuntary part-time workers who seek full-time jobs are also much higher among Africans Americans (21 percent) and Latinos (20 percent) than whites (8 percent) (Hero and Kramer, 2009). These problems are quite evident in Hartford.

Shifts in the local labor market in recent decades conform to the larger trends in the United States, with a huge loss in manufacturing and some growth in service-sector jobs. Table 5.3, compiled by Connecticut Voices for Children and the Economic Policy Institute, illustrates growth and loss among various sectors of the economy in Connecticut in the second column, with the notable loss between 1990 and 2008 of 113,300 jobs in manufacturing, once the bedrock of the state's economy. The third column shows employment numbers in Connecticut by sector as of July 2009, and the fourth column shows the net changes between March 2008 and July 2009 in each sector. Connecticut took longer than most states in the nation to recover from the recession of the early 2000s, and its recovery was less robust

Table 5.3. Changes in Connecticut Non-farm Employment, Selected Sectors, in Recent Period

Employment Sector	Changes in Jobs (1990–2008)	Total Jobs in Sector (July 2009)	Percent Change in Recession (March 2008–July 2009)
Information	−4,500	35,100	−7.6%
Construction	+3,000	50,700	−25.9%
Transportation & Utilities	+3,700	52,800	+0.6%
Other Services	+6,100	62,600	−1.7%
Wholesale Trade	−3,000	66,800	−4.3%
Leisure & Hospitality	+30,300	139,300	+1.2%
Financial Activities	−10,000	139,100	−3.9%
Manufacturing	−113,300	172,100	−8.5%
Retail Trade	−8,800	178,000	−6.6%
Professional and Business Services	+36,200	189,700	−8.8%
Government (includes Casino Workers)	+41,900	247,100	−2.3%
Education and Health Services	+98,700	299,400	+1.5%

Sources: Connecticut Department of Labor, Labor Market Information Data, and Bureau of Labor Statistics, August 2009, published in *The State of Working Connecticut* (2009) by Hero and Kramer of Connecticut Voices for Children.

than those of other states and seems to be following a similar pattern following the 2008 recession.

Additional labor market dynamics in the area that impact the extent of local poverty include whether or not Hartford's residents fit within the areas of projected job growth, and the proliferation of low-wage jobs. Table 5.4 is based on Connecticut Department of Labor data which indicate the projected top ten occupations for job openings between 2006 and 2016 and their average annual wages. These data were devised before the start of the 2008 recession.

Given that the Federal Poverty Level for a family of three was $18,310 in 2010 (U.S. Department of Health and Human Services, 2010), it is obvious that several of these occupations would barely support a family of three. Only four of the occupations pay above 175 percent of the poverty rate for a family of three (2010 levels). As one might expect, occupations on the list with higher salaries require college education, an education level that is elusive for many impoverished Hartford residents.

One final piece of the picture is the manner in which wages have changed in the past decade in Connecticut. Data in the Connecticut Voices for Children's *State of Working Connecticut 2009* details the patterns of wage changes by various income percentiles of workers. It reveals a growing divide among high-wage and low wage workers, with high-wage workers' hourly wages showing growth at the end of the eight-year period (after various ups and downs), but low- and very-low-wage workers losing ground in the same period. These trends illustrate Connecticut's high measures of income inequality (Hero and Kramer, 2009). In a separate report on inequality by Connecticut Voices on the Gini coefficient, a measure of income inequality in which 0 would equal perfect equality and 1 indicates perfect inequality, Connecticut's Gini coefficient of 0.481 was second only to the state of New York's of 0.500 as a measure of inequality. When future analysis on the impact of the 2008 recession is undertaken, it is likely that this pattern will persist or worsen.

THE WEAK SOCIAL SAFETY NET

With the advent of "welfare reform" in the 1990s, in combination with retrenchment of government programs and erosion of public commitment to ameliorating poverty (particularly for poor women and their children), people in cities like Hartford bear a heavy toll. Connecticut has some of the most restrictive provisions in the country in its Temporary Assistance to Needy Families (TANF) Program, particularly its 21-month time limit for assistance. Early in the welfare reform era, Connecticut adopted a "Work First" approach for clients, an emphasis on rapid employment and few options for education and training, as well as a sanctioning regimen and other strict provisions. Thus TANF recipients in Connecticut have been pushed into the low-wage workforce and also cope with a cumbersome bureaucratic apparatus. Hartford is consistently the city with the state's largest caseload (Connecticut Department of Social Services [DSS], 2010).

Table 5.4. Top Ten Occupational Openings Projected among North Central Connecticut Occupations, 2006–2016, and 2009 Average Annual Salaries

Occupation	2006 Employment Level	2016 Employment (Projected)	Total Annual Openings Due to Growth & Labor Market Churning	Annual Openings Due Solely to Labor Market Growth	Annual Growth Rate based on 2006 Employment	Education & Training Requirements	Statewide Average Annual Salary 2009
Retail Salespersons	15,502	17,658	679	216	13.9%	Short term OJT	$27,249
Cashiers	13,972	14,089	668	12	0.8%	Short term OJT	$20,473
Customer Service Reps	12,378	14,682	579	230	18.6%	Moderate Term OJT	$37,889
Waiters & Waitresses	8,050	9,006	534	96	11.9%	Short term OJT	$21,485
Registered Nurses	10,472	12,228	354	176	16.8%	Associates Degree	$71,699
Office Clerks	11,104	11,966	290	86	7.8%	Short term OJT	$31,600
Janitors & Cleaners (except maids & housekeepers)	9,850	10,879	288	103	10.5%	Short term OJT	$28,617
Accountants & Auditors	7,416	8,527	237	111	15.0%	Bachelors	$73,820
Food Preparation workers	4,259	4,947	216	69	16.2%	Short term OJT	$23,516
Bookkeeping, Accounting & Auditing Clerks	8,769	9,710	228	94	10.7%	Moderate Term OJT	$40,550

Source: Connecticut Department of Labor Market Information website; Connecticut Department of Labor, *Connecticut Occupational Employment and Wages Statewide 2009.*

At the end of each fiscal year, the DSS calculates an Annual Monthly Average for the previous year for several programs, including the Temporary Family Assistance (TFA) Program [Connecticut's TANF program], Supplemental Nutrition Assistance Program [(SNAP), formerly Food Stamps], Medicaid, and State Administered General Assistance [(SAGA), a state program serving mainly single adults with Medicaid benefits and limited cash assistance]. For Fiscal Year 2010 (July 1, 2009 through June 30, 2010) the number of Hartford residents in various assistance programs included the following: for TFA, 3004 assistance units (generally families) or 6822 total recipients; for SNAP, 23,998 assistance units or 44,299 recipients; for Medicaid, 25,908 assistance units or 47,045 recipients; and for SAGA, Cash assistance, 672 recipients; and Medicaid only, 6838 recipients (Connecticut DSS, 2010).

Note the lower numbers of both "assistance units" and total recipients involved with TANF as compared to SNAP or Medicaid. Typically TANF is geared toward lone mothers with children, while SNAP and Medicaid are available to many individuals in poverty or at a threshold that is somewhat above the Federal Poverty Level. TFA recipients are subject to time limits, work requirements, and sanctions. Therefore it is conceivable that there are numbers of families in Hartford who may not be eligible for the program, or have "timed out" of TFA, or opt not to participate in TFA due to the "hassle factors" (intrusions into one's life, multiple appointments, unrealistic expectations, and/or discouragement by eligibility personnel). This pattern is consistent with national trends, as documented in a report by the Institute for Women's Policy Research (IWPR) (Henrici et al., 2010), which states that "(n)ationally, only 12 percent of impoverished adult women with dependent children reported receiving TANF cash assistance in 2008." In Connecticut, 78.8 percent of impoverished adult women with dependent children did not receive cash benefits. Moreover, the phenomenon of people with no cash income and "Living on Nothing but Food Stamps" (DeParle and Gebeloff, 2010) is increasing across the United States: at least six million people in the United States have no other income than food stamps, and the trend is upward since the beginning of the 2008 recession. Undoubtedly, there are individuals in this situation within Hartford.

RESPONSES TO HARTFORD'S POVERTY AND INEQUALITY

These conditions generate diverse responses, by both community forces and local elites. Reponses have translated into community demands on both political structures and the legislative bodies whose policies impact Hartford's population, as well as demands within the economic arena. One response has been in electoral politics, with the election of more black and Latino office holders and also activities of various third parties. Achieving greater representation for communities of color is regarded as an equity issue in a city where they are the majority, and these communities maintain that their own members will best represent their needs.

Other popular responses include community organizing on issues such as education, public safety, services to neighborhoods, and equitable distribution of city resources. Issue and advocacy organizations also raise concerns in Hartford in specific areas such as housing and fair housing, homelessness, AIDS services, assistance to previously incarcerated persons, and other issues. Economic issues are addressed through union organizing, community-labor coalitions' activities, living wage campaigns, community development activity, small business and minority-owned business assistance, creation of intermediary organizations to facilitate local hiring on development projects, and more. Elites and downtown business interests have also been active in different ways, depending on the business environment and individual firms' ties to Hartford as a home base.

Due to space constraint, a detailed historical account of all the varied responses to Hartford's poverty will not be provided. Rather, some well-known (even controversial) responses are portrayed as are some less well-known, but still interesting examples.

Political Responses

Given the size of the city's population and its small geographic area, organizing to increase black and Latino political representation in the city council, the mayor's office, and the Connecticut Legislature often unfolds on a very personal scale, producing many hard-fought battles, very close elections, and a variety of "firsts." African American and Puerto Rican representation on the city council (a nine-member body elected at large) and in the Connecticut General Assembly began in the mid to late 1960s. There are currently six legislative districts in Hartford and two state senatorial districts. In recent years some of the boundaries have shifted to include parts of suburbs to the north and south of Hartford. Most of the city's legislative delegation is African American or Latino.

In 1981, Hartford elected its first African American mayor, Thirman Milner. Previously a state representative, he was also the first popularly elected black mayor in New England. His election was a difficult contest that brought a sense of triumph and pride to the city's black community, signaling the beginning of a political power shift within the city. However, until a revision to the city's charter in 2004 which modified city government, the office of the mayor was considered a "weak mayor" in a council-manager system. The mayor was highly visible, but not vested with much institutional power via the city charter then in effect. The deputy mayor, the leader of the city council elected by the majority caucus, had the most power in city hall, particularly during the 1970s under the tenure of Nicholas Carbone. Carbone, a Democrat, amassed a great deal of power both within the Democratic Party structure and city government. Although celebrated in Pierre Clavel's *The Progressive City* (1986) as a progressive policy leader, as a politician he eventually came under fire for his rigid control of Democratic politics in Hartford. Given that the vast majority of registered voters are Democrats, control of nominations and primaries within the local Democratic Party are the arena for most locally significant political contests.

After several terms in office, frustrated with the limitations of the office, Milner declined to run for re-election and urged his legislative colleague, Carrie Saxon Perry, to run for mayor. She won the office in 1987 and became the first African American woman elected mayor of a major city in the United States. She was well aware of the office's limitations and during her first two terms relations with a city council that minimized her role and influence in policy-making were particularly contentious.

The structure of Hartford's city council creates space for formation and activism of third parties in local politics. The council has nine seats, all elected at large, with three seats reserved, per state statute, for a minority party or independents. Voters may vote for up to six candidates. Since registered Democrats outnumber registered Republicans by well over ten to one, Democrats routinely win six seats and, when no other individuals or parties are on the ballot besides Republicans, Republicans take the other three seats.[2] Winning a minority party seat requires less than half the amount of votes Democrats receive. In 1987, a coalition of community, labor, and civil rights organizations formed a local third party, People for Change (PFC), and began to run candidates for the three seats reserved for a minority party. In both 1987 and 1989, two of the three-person slates won seats and in 1991, all three PFC candidates, including this author, won their bids. Thus no Republicans served on the council during 1991–1993. In the 1991 election, PFC worked with Mayor Perry and a slate of insurgent Democrats who won a Democratic primary and ousted all incumbent Democrats and Republicans. Space does not permit a full discussion of the PFC experience, but other accounts are available for those interested (Simmons, 1994, 1996a, 1996b, 1998). After a tumultuous two-year term from 1991 to 1993, all of the PFC candidates lost to Republicans and Mayor Perry lost her reelection bid.[3] Several of her Democratic slate allies returned to office but others lost. During subsequent years, Green Party candidates have won council seats and another regional third party, the Working Families Party, has won spots both on the city council and the board of education.

Puerto Rican political activism as detailed by Cruz (1998) has also been an important political factor in the city, particularly during the 1980s through the development of the Puerto Rican Political Action Committee (PRPAC) (see also Glasser, 2005), which played a significant role in PFC. Although the PRPAC waned, Puerto Rican and Latino political activism did not. In 2001 Eddie Perez was elected Mayor and during his tenure, in 2004, the city charter was revised in a referendum that created a "strong mayor" system. His victory was heralded by the Puerto Rican and Latino community in Hartford and beyond: the election of the first Puerto Rican mayor in New England and of a state capital city in the United States. Unfortunately, after eight and a half years in office, he resigned in June, 2010, plagued by a scandal involving free renovations performed at his house by a city contractor and other matters. He was succeeded by another Puerto Rican, Pedro Segarra, a social worker and attorney, who serves as mayor as of this writing.

These particulars concerning electoral activism over the past several decades are presented to illustrate that one aspect of the quest to improve conditions for community residents is expressed by electing leaders who are from the communities most in need—leaders who face huge expectations to address these needs. Yet the challenges facing local elected officials of color are staggering since even strong mayors in major cities lack the juridical power to overcome trends within the larger economic order (Reed, 1988). This is even more severe in a city of Hartford's geographic size and relatively small population, centered in a region with tremendous wealth in suburban towns that have not been forthcoming in alleviating poverty-related problems of Hartford. In recessionary periods, the challenges are ever more daunting. And while regionalism is often advanced as an important way to solve Hartford's problems, it seems to remain more a slogan than a reality, and poverty now extends beyond the city limits.

Community Organizing

During the 1980s and into the 1990s, Hartford was often described as one of the most organized cities in the United States. Local Alinsky-style groups (see Fisher, 1984) existed in three key areas of the city and during their hey-day frequently brought hundreds of people to city hall or the legislature to protest, advocate, and lobby for issues. The three organizations, Hartford Areas Rally Together (HART), Asylum Hill Organizing Project (AHOP) and Organized North-Easterners/Clay Hill and North End (ONE/CHANE), operated locally through block clubs and raised grassroots concerns around traffic, policing, jobs, and local taxes. They sometimes worked together on citywide issues, such as a campaign to have the city enact a "linkage" policy that would tax downtown development in order to address neighborhood concerns for housing and employment. Annual neighborhood congresses held by each group would draw hundreds of people to define priorities for each area. On occasion these groups would join in larger coalitions, but most of the time formulated agendas around their very immediate concerns (Simmons, 1994; Radcliffe, 1998). The fortunes of AHOP and ONE/CHANE dwindled in the 1990s amid leadership and funding problems, however HART remains in existence.

Besides these groups, other organizations exist with modus operandi typical of traditional neighborhood associations. The Blue Hills Civic Association, the West End Civic Association, long-standing organizations in their respective areas of the city, and other groups pursue their work, raising issues at City Hall or the state legislature, yet are usually less confrontational than were the neo-Alinsky groups.

At their strongest, these organizations provide or provided a voice for disenfranchised residents. However, the limitations of an almost completely "localist" approach and their aversion to engage in systemic or ideological critiques involving poverty, power, racism, and other fundamental issues meant that their organizing rarely took on large targets in the private sector such as the large insurance companies either headquartered or substantially present in Hartford (see Fisher, 1984; DeFilippis, Fisher, and Shragge, 2010).

During the 2000s Hartford had a local chapter of the Association for Community Organization for Reform Now (ACORN). This once nationwide organization did take on corporate interests and framed issues of inequality in campaigns that revealed how poor communities are targeted by practices such as predatory lending, payday loan operations that gouge low-wage workers and immigrants, and other processes that prey on the poor and unbanked. ACORN engaged in living wage campaigns, unionization drives and other methods to actually raise wages for low-income residents, as well as voter registration drives and election turn-out efforts. For this they became a national target of the right wing and a concerted campaign to destroy ACORN by the right forced them to liquidate (Fisher, 2009; DeFilippis et al., 2010; Atlas, 2010). ACORN in Hartford did not reach the prominence of chapters with large stalls in large cities, but it had begun organizing disenfranchised residents before the organization's national demise.

Hartford's community organizing has had its ebbs and flows. One aspect of its legacy is that a number of local political leaders have come through the ranks of HART, AHOP, ONE/CHANE, and other local organizations, including mayors, councilmembers, and state representatives, many of whom are African American or Puerto Rican. Another, perhaps even more important legacy, is that residents learned how to go to city hall and raise demands. Local policy-making is demystified and now, even without the presence of as many neighborhood organizing groups, people in Hartford do know how to fight city hall. Yet one might expect a stronger local anti-poverty agenda as a central theme in Hartford's contemporary political discourse.

Labor and Labor-Community Coalitions

The desire of people to raise their wages and improve working conditions has historically translated into drives for unionization of workplaces. Yet, as is widely known, union membership in the private sector is in serious decline, although the public sector is much more highly unionized. However, Connecticut has a relatively high percentage of its workforce in unions: the United States Bureau of Labor Statistics (BLS) (2010) annual report on unionization showed that 18.4 percent of Connecticut's workers were represented by a union in 2009, some 282,000 people, the 10th highest union representation rate of all U.S. states. Unionization makes substantive financial differences in people's lives. Consider the difference in median weekly earnings for unionized workers of various backgrounds in comparison to their non-union counterparts: median weekly earnings of all workers in the United States who are union members is $908 while non-union members' median weekly earnings are $710; for African American men, the differences are $780 to $599; for African American women, $717 to $560; for Latinos, $824 to $535 and for Latinas $683 versus $493 (BLS, 2010).

For almost all groups of workers (Asian men being the one exception), on average, union membership means appreciably higher median weekly earnings that translate into thousands of dollars more in annual incomes. Although one might expect that tens of thousands of workers would be trying to unionize, the reality is that it is an incredibly difficult process to organize a workplace and employers fiercely resist unions. Illegal firings, captive audience meetings, and intimidation by employers are the norm in organizing drives.[4] In Hartford, for those workers who have successfully organized, particularly in historically low-wage service sectors, the payoffs have been considerable. Yet there have been setbacks as employers resist unions and the large insurance companies remain unorganized.

The differences in median weekly earnings between unionized workers and non-unionized workers for service and low-wage job categories are considerable. These are the jobs that many individuals in cities like Hartford take if they lack the education required for higher paid jobs. Consider the difference unionization translates into for these workers: nationally, union members in healthcare support occupations had median weekly earnings of $518, while non-union workers made $464; food preparation workers in unions made $463 while non-union workers made $395; building, grounds, and maintenance workers in unions had median weekly earnings of $597 while non-union workers made $418 (BLS, 2010).

Although it is not possible to disaggregate Bureau of Labor Statistics data regarding union wages versus non-union wages on a town-by-town basis, information ascertained from two unions in Hartford illustrates the differences in their respective industries that having a union provides. Both unions are affiliated nationally with the Service Employees International Union (SEIU). The buildings services union 32BJ of SEIU nationally represents more than 120,000 workers and in Hartford County represents more than 2,000 workers. Within the City of Hartford, some 1,500 workers are covered by its contracts, and approximately 700–800 of these members are Hartford residents. The union has achieved a pattern for wages with area contractors whose employees work as janitors and building services workers in local and suburban businesses. According to Kurt Westby, the Area Director of the Connecticut District of 32BJ, wage levels in their collective bargaining agreements for janitorial services in buildings over 100,000 square feet are $14.10 per hour for heavy duty and $13.10 per hour for light duty. Benefits for 32BJ members include free family health insurance, modest pension provisions, paid vacation, sick days, and paid holidays for full-time employees (over 30 hours of work per week). The union has a Training Fund which offers classes for English-language learners and course in technical areas. There is also a legal fund that offers free or low-cost legal services for issues involving citizenship, legalization, and family issues. For non-union janitors and building services workers, wages are in the range of $8.50 to $10 per hour and there are no benefits to speak of. Moreover, before 32BJ began to organize the industry in the area, most workers were part-time workers and worked less than 30 hours per week, thus having to cobble together several jobs in order to sustain themselves and their families (personal communication with Kurt Westby, August 27, 2012).

In the healthcare industry, a dominant union in Connecticut is SEIU District 1199 New England (1199NE) which represents more than 29,000 workers in Connecticut and Rhode Island. Their membership includes nurses, direct care workers, certified nursing assistants (CNAs), cooks, case managers, therapists, doctors, maintenance staff, home care workers, and others. This union has thousands of State of Connecticut employees in its ranks as well as thousands of nursing home workers. For nursing home workers in Hartford-area facilities, many of whom are Hartford residents, union membership translates into better wages and benefits than their non-unionized counterparts. Deborah Chernoff, Communications Director for 1199NE, provided information on wage rates (email communication, August 29, 2012). She developed a chart with starting wages in five Hartford/West Hartford nursing homes and compared these wages to starting wages for Hartford-area nursing home workers that are listed on salary.com. She notes that workers who have been employed for more than 15 years in unionized facilities make at least $5 more per hour and that the benefit levels at unionized nursing homes are far superior to non-unionized facilities. As with the janitorial union, 1199NE has a training fund and provides a range of other services to members.

What also is significant is that these unionized salaries are factored into the salary .com salary levels and thus, it could be anticipated that if union salaries were excluded from these calculations, the salaries on that website would be even lower than what is reported. Another important aspect of these jobs is that hundreds of nursing home workers live in the City of Hartford and are women of color.

Locally, unionized workers periodically resort to strikes to defend their interests. A four-year strike in the 1980s by UAW members at the manufacturer, Colt Firearms resulted in a multimillion-dollar back-pay award ordered by the National Labor Relations Board, as did a three-year strike at a local nursing home by workers in the Service Employees International Union District 1199 from 1999 into the early 2000s. These strikes were extremely difficult to sustain and unions turned to community groups and religious organizations for both material and moral support. Labor-community coalitions have been important for unions and workers to get their stories out to a broader public and to build understanding within the community as to what unions stand for and how they work. Rallies, vigils, civil disobedience actions, and political strategies accompanied the strikes (as well as union organizing drives). Important relationships between community, advocacy, religious, and labor organizations developed in the 1980s that continue to the present, and community-labor coalitions now assert significant presence in Hartford, other communities, and the state capital on public policy matters.

One outcome of labor-community efforts is Hartford's Living Wage Ordinance. As in over 150 cities, Hartford's city council adopted a Living Wage Ordinance in 1999. Unions and community groups advocated for this measure so that city contracts would not contribute to creating poverty-wage jobs. Living Wage ordinances vary, but generally mandate that businesses who contract with local governments in areas such as janitorial services, transportation, or food services or who receive development incentives pay higher wages than minimum wage (generally by at least 40 percent) and offer health benefits to their workers (Brenner and Luce, 2005). The original Hartford ordinance was narrow in scope compared to those of other cities, and was amended in 2011 to cover more categories of workers and different types of contractual arrangements with the city. For those workers who are covered, these ordinances raise incomes.

A broader effect of labor and coalition efforts is in redefining public policy debates and redefining what is acceptable private corporate behavior. Within the network of unions and community organizations, viewpoints are not monolithic, but on important issues like healthcare reform and workers' rights, these organizations impact policy and raise incomes of many local workers.

Elite Responses

Due to Hartford's relatively small size, elites within the corporate and civic activist sectors occasionally come up with grandiose plans to socially engineer the problems that are deemed "bad for business" or pressure City Hall to adopt local policies to facilitate business goals. More so in the 1970s and 1980s than of late, several controversial and notorious plans were introduced to the public by think tanks that acted on behalf of elite interests in Hartford. These are briefly described below, but a more recent retreat from grand plans and exerting power in local affairs by corporate leaders seems symptomatic of a new era of corporations being less involved in home communities (if they even think of Hartford in such terms), given the global environment in which they now operate.

In the 1970s, the heads of the large local banks and the insurance companies came to be known as "the Bishops." As noted in Neubeck and Ratcliff (1988), despite being competitors, these individuals were also a cohesive social grouping:

> The small size of Hartford also facilitates close personal ties among the Bishops. As the long-time head of the local Chamber of Commerce observed in regard to the "unusually high degree of cooperation" in Hartford among the Bishops:
>
> > They bump into each other at cocktail parties, luncheons, dinners, civic affairs. . . . God, they might as well be roommates. These guys see each other daily, someplace. (Martin 1983)
>
> While most of their investments in Hartford have been guided by clear profit motives, Hartford's Bishops have also pursued certain goals . . . seemingly guided by elements of an "enlightened self-interest" beyond short-run profit maximization. . . . A series of racial riots in the late 1960s reinforced the threats (of urban decline and a city in crisis). The growth of the insurance companies posed the question of whether they would continue to expand and build new facilities within the city, or move elsewhere. (306–307)

In the 1970s these corporate leaders, with support from the Chamber of Commerce and key politicians, formed a think tank, the Greater Hartford Process, to help chart the future of Hartford (see also Pawlowski, 2005). Similar corporate backed think tanks in other cities were functioning in analogous fashion. Greater Hartford Process (which became known simply as "Process") was particularly bold and controversial in its proposals. One of their first plans to rebuild Hartford included a proposal to build a new community in rural Coventry, Connecticut, near the University of Connecticut. Among other, mixed-income, populations, the new town would be home to displaced people from impoverished areas of Hartford whose neighborhoods would be redeveloped. The effort was to disperse poverty and offer new "opportunities" in the ex-urbs. Resistance was strong in Hartford's African American community who viewed this as a means to dilute their emerging political power, as well as in the rural town of Coventry whose residents were fearful of urban African Americans and Latinos being transplanted to their community. After a great deal of public controversy and resistance, Process dropped the proposal. However, a later foray into urban redevelopment produced a new round of turmoil.

After the Coventry debacle, Process decided to focus on a "geopolitical or demographic strategy" (as quoted in Neubeck and Ratcliff, 1988: 323). Planning focused on strategies for specific neighborhoods and protecting the downtown areas where corporations functioned. When a "confidential memo" drafted by a Process staff person appeared in the local press in the mid 1970's,[5] another uproar ensued. The memo particularly offended Puerto Ricans. The text of the infamous Process memo follows:

> The attached memorandum is predicated on an unstated but implied "geopolitical" or demographic strategy for the city. The question is, what neighborhoods shall be "saved" and who shall live where. My proposition is as follows:
>
> 1. The ghetto will remain. Low income areas must be assumed and planned for. They should include Clay Hill and the eastern edge of Upper Albany, North Arsenal, Garden Clark, Charter Oak (Dutch Point public housing and Martin Luther King housing), and Charter Oak Terrace/Rice Heights.
> 2. Over time, however, the ghetto should be moved away from Downtown—at least one (bus) stop away. Bellevue Square (a public housing development) should come down and SAND (South Arsenal Neighborhood Development) and points south (Ann-High, and the strip of Main Street from I-84 to Albany Avenue) consolidated for other than low-income housing uses. Cleared and land banked if necessary. The Southern Gateway should be recycled as a mixed to upper-income residential area building around enclave developments that start on Congress Street and Buckingham Street. State office and public development should be encouraged in this area (east side of Washington Street). This buffers Downtown.
> 3. The key neighborhood preservation and rehabilitation areas are western Upper Albany, Sargeant-Ashley in Asylum Hill, the near South End, the southern and western edges of Frog Hollow, and Parkville. We must manage the population mix in those areas, including by selective relocation to keep welfare populations below 15–20 percent.
> 4. Puerto Rican in-migration must be reduced. Efforts should be made to consolidate the welfare dependent elements of this population in Clay Hill and eastern Frog Hollow, using Section 8 rehab to provide relocation resources in these areas and in the suburbs.

5. The single family areas—far Southeast and Southwest, the West End, and Blue Hills—must be stabilized and enhanced. Try to create a backfire of suburban relocation into these areas. Immediate spot rehab where blight begins to show. Watch out for tax revaluation impact in these areas where people tend to have the financial ability to pull out. Concentrate school resources here.

(Copy in possession of author; also partially quoted in Pawlowksi, 2005)

Upon its release another huge outcry erupted, led by the Puerto Rican community, and a large demonstration took place at the dedication ceremony for the newly built Hartford Civic Center. At the grand opening of this Center, a symbol of corporate urban renewal, a largely suburban crowd attending an entertainment event had to enter through a human chain of protesters surrounding the entire square block building, demonstrating in opposition to the memo (Pawlowski, 2005).

Many in Hartford believe that despite disavowal by corporate and civic leaders, a great deal of the plan did indeed unfold. Ultimately Process's role shrank and its remaining staff was absorbed into the Chamber of Commerce. Two other examples of responses to community problems briefly illustrate additional instances of controversy over plans for altering the city. One is also from the 1970s and one from the 1980s.

Another controversial plan in 1974 by a now defunct organization, the Hartford Institute of Criminal and Social Justice, proposed to fence off high-crime areas (Ingrassia, 1974) in a peculiar form of gating communities. The areas were proposed to be fenced off from automobile and pedestrian traffic to reduce "stranger-to-stranger" crimes. The rationale was to prevent opportunities to *commit* crimes by fencing off residential areas, thereby preventing criminals from entering, and blocking or closing street intersections to inhibit traffic and deter criminals from quick access and exit. Funding came from Law Enforcement Assistance Administration (LEAA), then a federal government agency. Neighborhood activists were incensed at the proposal, organized against it, and ultimately few suggestions were actually implemented. However, several intersections in the Asylum Hill neighborhood near the large St. Francis Hospital complex are permanently blocked and still inconvenience motorists.

Some ten years after the Process memo brouhaha, in 1985, a coalition of neighborhood groups and unions worked together to craft a "linkage" policy proposal for the city that would tax downtown development, then in full swing of a reinvestment cycle. Proceeds would go to housing and job training for low-income residents of Hartford, especially those who would suffer displacement. An attorney for Aetna Life & Casualty drafted yet another memo directed to colleagues in other large companies with headquarters in Hartford's downtown, warning them about what was transpiring. Excerpts from the March 5, 1985 memo as published in the *Hartford Courant* (Pazniokas, 1985) include:

None of us have been paying any serious attention to a developing debacle—the potential call for a "linkage fee" or "lease tax" to help pay for low and moderate income housing in Hartford.

. . .

They are actually toying with a "linkage fee" from $5 per square foot (neighborhood caucus proposal) to a "lease tax" of 25¢ per square foot. All of this is quite controversial, and is based on studies of similar efforts in Boston, San Francisco and (the Peoples Republic of) Santa Monica. None of these cities closely resembles the situation in Hartford.

. . .

I gather that (a Chamber of Commerce staff member) has convinced (two developers) that the business community should acquiesce in some form of linkage fee or lease task. That kind of talk concerns me, particularly in light of the lack of *real* business community representation.

When this appeared in the local press, many seasoned activists called it "Process 2," referring to the earlier memo that offended so many. This time, the linkage proponents continued their work, presented the proposal to the city council, and watched as it was defeated before a packed audience at city hall in 1986. Cries of "we'll be back in November" were realized with the formation of People for Change, detailed above.

For balance, it is important to note that there is and has been significant corporate philanthropy in Hartford in support of the arts and various human service programs. Some large corporations have established local foundations; others sponsor local sporting events where proceeds are donated to philanthropy. Internships for students are also offered. However, in the early 21st century there does seem to be a smaller role assumed by the large corporations in Hartford in local planning and local politics, unless they feel directly impacted by proposals being considered at city hall. In a globally competitive economy and in a recessionary climate, Hartford's issues are small by comparison to what these companies feel are their true current challenges.

WHERE DOES THIS ALL LEAVE
HARTFORD AND WHAT CAN BE DONE?

All of the aforementioned issues beg the question: who is doing what to try to address Hartford's staggering social and economic problems? Some may yearn for a 21st-century set of "Bishops" to craft a local agenda. Some in the region may close their eyes to the challenges of this central city and remain content to let the problems fester. Yet, many forces *do* respond to the poverty, unemployment, and educational obstacles that people in Hartford face and have endured for decades. However, sometimes these efforts are duplicative or the problem of uncoordinated "silos" of activity comes into play. Nonetheless, as for other similarly poor and medium-sized central cities, there are strategies to suggest that can alleviate some of the worst aspects of poverty for Hartford residents. This chapter concludes by offering suggestions in several strategic areas that may begin providing solutions for Hartford.

Harness All Possible Government Resources

In a period where "big government" has become a target of derision by politicians, media personalities, and segments of the U.S. populace, Hartford should still be aggressively pursuing any and all federal and state funding that address poverty. Outreach to inform and enroll individuals who may be eligible for programs such as SNAP, other nutrition programs, disability benefits, fuel assistance, housing assistance, tax credits, or any other assistance needs to take place. The city government in collaboration with the regional Workforce Investment Board and other partners should leverage the maximum available funding for job training and placement, particularly in the "green jobs" arena. The Hartford Delegation at the State Legislature should push the state government to maximize funds for healthcare programs, Medicare, Medicaid and any other entitlements that have previously not been fully pursued. Working with community-based organizations, the city government should promote collaborations that overcome unnecessary duplication of efforts and should target funding for services that have high impact. The city government should also track and apply in a timely manner for any federal funding for which it is eligible.

Corporate involvement in urban issues should have a transparency such that confidential memos and private plans are not developed in secret that engender negative community responses upon their release. Input from the local community is essential.

End TANF As We Know It

Community organizations, welfare rights advocates, and local public officials should urge the state legislators, U.S. congresspeople, senators, and the president to amend Temporary Assistance to Needy Families (TANF) such that time limits and work requirements are relaxed or eliminated, particularly in times of recession. Emphasis should be placed on education and training opportunities, in concert with supportive services (child care, transportation, and other supports), that develop the potential of recipients to fully participate in the labor market or pursue educational options. Rather than pushing TANF recipients into low-wage jobs with weak or non-existent benefits, individuals should be provided opportunities to train for higher skilled and better paying employment. Connecticut should reconsider its restrictive 21-month time limit. A stronger safety net should be devised to protect vulnerable populations who end up using central city social services within Hartford. TANF recipients and other low-income individuals would be helped by a 21st-century version of the WPA or other public works programs that would address an aging infrastructure and the necessity to transition to an environmentally sustainable economy.

Emphasize Income Raising Strategies

Modern poverty is a product of many social processes, but the best way out of poverty is employment that pays decent wages. Job development should encourage living-wage-level remuneration and decent benefits. Parents and caregivers should be allowed paid sick days and family leave to tend to illnesses and other needs of family members. Rather than using the outmoded Federal Poverty Level as a standard of need, more realistic indices of poverty should be utilized when determining who actually would benefit from public programs and what those programs' benchmarks should be. Especially in the creation of public-sector jobs and for those private-sector firms that receive public subsidies of any form, living-wage jobs should be the standard, rather than minimum wage or poverty level wages. Unionization should not be resisted when workers want it.

Promote Regionally Equitable Solutions to Urban Problems

With emphases on metropolitan and regional approaches to economic development being promoted by policy experts and the Obama administration (Katz, 2010), federal and state governments should provide incentives for regionalism and sharing regional assets. Within these processes, the preeminent needs of Hartford's population should not be eclipsed by the affluent segments of the regional population. Planning that makes sensible use of existing physical infrastructure and assets, thoughtful use of natural resources, and social inclusivity needs to be emphasized. In order to accomplish regional solutions for Hartford or other major cities in Connecticut, leadership and courage will be required by policy leaders. There is recognition by many policy leaders and public officials that regional solutions offer promise, but there is also a fear that constituents will punish legislators electorally if too much local power is ceded to regional entities. Successful regional entities exist such as the water and sewer system for the Hartford area, the Metropolitan District Commission, but regionalism that entails education, housing, and complex social issues are much more difficult to accomplish. Regional solutions have to be presented in "win-win" terms to wary suburbanites and there is often resistance. This is one of the greatest challenges in addressing the concentrated poverty of Hartford (see Condon, Rojas and Wray, this volume).

IN SUM

Poverty in Hartford is a historic reality. It existed as previous groups of immigrants and migrating populations within the United States made their way to Hartford and similar cities of the Northeast. Patterns are deeply entrenched, even as more recent newcomers have taken the place of previous immigrant groups. However, Hartford's residents find ways to take action, elect leaders from their communities, and struggle together to overcome obstacles and make their community more livable. Twenty-first-century issues of poverty have much in common with 19th- and 20th-century poverty. Hartford could be and should be among the cities that create new solutions.

NOTES

The author wishes to acknowledge University of Connecticut Hartford Regional Campus Librarian Jan Lambert, Connecticut Department of Labor Analyst Jonathan Hand, and Connecticut Department of Social Services Analyst Alex Koskinas for their invaluable assistance in compiling and interpreting information that was used in this chapter. Additionally, Kurt Westby of SEIU 32BJ and Deborah Chernoff of SEIU 1199NE were extremely helpful and resourceful in providing information that informs this chapter.

1. Connecticut began to implement "welfare reform" in 1995 under a waiver to Aid to Families with Dependent Children (AFDC) regulations before passage of Temporary Assistance to Needy Families (TANF).

2. If Republicans run more than three people, they essentially run against themselves to see who comes in seventh, eighth, and ninth in total votes.

3. Mayor Perry won the Democratic Primary but lost to a "fusion slate" of Democrats and Republicans in the General Election, when Michael Peters, a white South End political activist and firefighter, was elected mayor.

4. See the website www.americanrightsatwork.org for ongoing discussion of these issues.

5. Neubeck and Ratcliff have the date as January, 1975, while Pawlowski cites 1973. A *Hartford Courant* article (Papirno and Grava 1975) dated January 18, 1975, described community and Process leadership reaction. Therefore, we will assume that 1975 is the correct date.

REFERENCES

Annie E. Casey Foundation Kids Count Data Center. "Children in poverty (Percent)—2008." Accessed August 13, 2010, http://datacenter.kidscount.org/data/acrossstates/Rankings.aspx?loct=3&by=a&order=a&ind=43&dtm=322&tf=35.

Atlas, John. 2010. *Seeds of Change: The Story of ACORN, America's Most Controversial Antipoverty Community Organizing Group*. Nashville: Vanderbilt University Press.

Brenner, Mark, and Stephanie Luce. 2005. *Living Wage Laws in Practice: The Boston, New Haven and Hartford Experiences*. Amherst: University of Massachusetts Political Economy Research Institute.

Clavel, Pierre. 1986. *The Progressive City: Planning and Participation, 1969–1984*. New Brunswick: Rutgers University Press.

Connecticut Department of Labor. "North Central Occupations Ranked by Opening: 2006–1016." Accessed August 25, 2010, http://www1.ctdol.state.ct.us/lmi/forecast2006–2016/ncforecast.asp.

Connecticut Department of Labor. 2010. *At-A-Squint Jobs First Employment Services Participants Served by CTWorks June 2010*. Brochure. Wethersfield: Connecticut Department of Labor.

Connecticut Department of Labor. 2009. *Connecticut Occupational Employment & Wages Statewide 2009.* Wethersfield, CT: Connecticut Department of Labor Office of Research. Accessed August 25, 2010, http://www.ctdol.stae.ct.us/lmi.

Connecticut Department of Social Services. 2010. "Department of Social Services Average Monthly Assistance Units and Recipients by Town State Fiscal Year 2010 (July 2009–June 2010)." Report.

Connecticut Economic Resource Center. "Hartford, Connecticut CERC Town Profile 2010." Accessed May 31, 2011, http://www.cerc.com.

Connecticut Economic Resource Center. "Hartford County CERC Region Profile 2010." Accessed My 31, 2011, http://www.cerc.com.

Connecticut Voices for Children. 2009. "Family Well-Being Indicators for Larger Connecticut Cities and Towns, 2006–2008." Accessed August 13, 2010, http://www.ctkidslink.org/publications/well09largecitydata.pdf .

Cruz, José E. 1998. *Identity & Power: Puerto Rican Politics & the Challenge of Ethnicity.* Philadelphia: Temple University Press.

DeFilippis, James, Robert Fisher, and Eric Shragge. 2010. *Contesting Community: The Limits and Potential of Local Organizing.* New Brunswick: Rutgers University Press.

Deparle, Jason, and Robert Gebeloff. 2010. "Living on Nothing but Food Stamps." *New York Times.* January 3.

Fisher, Robert, ed., 2009. *The People Shall Rule: ACORN, Community Organizing, and the Struggle for Economic Justice.* Nashville: Vanderbilt University Press.

Fisher, Robert. 1984. *Let the People Decide: Neighborhood Organizing in America.* Boston: Twayne Publishers.

Glasser, Ruth. 2005. "From 'Rich Port' to Bridgeport: Puerto Ricans in Connecticut." In *The Puerto Rican Diaspora: Historical Perspectives,* edited by Carmen Teresa Whalen and Víctor Vázquez-Hernández, 174-199. Philadelphia: Temple University Press.

Hartford Courant Editorial. 2010. "Losers Again, this Time on School Aid; Race to the Top Connecticut's heart just wasn't in it." August 8.

Henrici, Jane, Allison Suppan Helmuth, Frances Zlotnick and Jeff Hayes. 2010. "Women in Poverty During the Great Recession: Public Benefits Do Not Always Respond to Rising Need, Variation Across States is Substantial." Briefing Paper, IWPR #D493. Washington, DC: Institute for Women's Policy Research.

Hero, Joachim, and Tamara Kramer. 2009. *State of Working Connecticut 2009.* New Haven: Connecticut Voices for Children. Accessed August 13, 2010, http://www.ctkidslink.org/publications/econ09sowctfull.pdf.

Historical Statistics of the United States Millennial Edition Online. Table Aa832-1033—Population of cities with at least 100,000 population in 1990: 1790–1990 Aa 965 Hartford, Connecticut. Accessed August 18, 2010, http://hsus.cambridge.org/HSUSWeb/table/expandtable.do?id=Aa832-1033.

Ingrassia, Michele. 1974. "Plan Offered to 'Fence Off' Crime." *Hartford Times.* October 2.

Katz, Bruce. 2010. "Obama's Metro Presidency." *City & Community* 9, no. 1: 23–31.

Martin, Antoinette. 1983. "The Powerful in Hartford: 'Bishops' of the Board Rooms Set City's Course." *Hartford Courant.* January 23.

Neubeck, Kenneth, and Richard Ratcliff. 1988. "Urban Democracy and the Power of Corporate Capital: Struggles over Downtown Growth and Neighborhood Stagnation in Hartford, Connecticut" in *Business Elites and Urban Development,* edited by Scott Cummings, 299–332. Albany: State University of New York Press.

Papirno, Elissa, and Bill Grava. 1975. "Process Head Rejects Puerto Rican 'Cutback.'" *Hartford Courant*. January 18.

Pawlowski, Robert. 2005. *Something in Common: Hartford 1970–1995 A Personal Memoir*. Essex VT: Argo Books.

Pazniokas, Mark. 1985. "Memo Casts Doubt on Commitment to City Residents' Needs." *Hartford Courant*. May 22.

Radcliffe, David. 1998. *Charter Oak Terrace: Life, Death, and Rebirth of a Public Housing Project*. Hartford: Southside Media.

Rank, Mark. 2004. *One Nation, Underprivileged: Why American Poverty Affects Us All*. New York: Oxford University Press.

Reed, Adolph. 1988. "The Black Urban Regime: Structural Origins & Constraints." in *Power, Community and The City*, edited by Michael Peter Smith, 138–189. New Brunswick: Transaction Books.

Simmons, Louise. 1994. *Organizing in Hard Times: Labor and Neighborhoods in Hartford*. Philadelphia: Temple University Press.

Simmons, Louise. 1996b. "Dilemmas of Progressives in Government: Playing Solomon in an Age of Austerity." *Economic Development Quarterly* 10, no. 2: 159–171.

Simmons, Louise. 1996a. "The Battle for City Hall: What Is It We Fight Over." *New England Journal of Public Policy* 12, no. 1: 97–116.

Simmons, Louise. 1998. "A New Urban Conservatism: The Case of Hartford, Connecticut." *Journal of Urban Affairs* 20, no. 2: 175–198.

U.S. Bureau of Labor Statistics. 2010. "Union Members—2009", Report. January 22. Accessed June 23, 2011, http://www.bls.gov/news.release/archives/union2_01222010.pdf.

U.S. Census Bureau American FactFinder. "Bloomfield town, Hartford County, Connecticut 2005–2009 American Community Survey 5-Year Estimates Data Profile Highlights." Accessed June 23, 2011, http://www.factfinder.census.gov.

U.S. Census Bureau American FactFinder. "Connecticut 2005–2009 American Community Survey 5-Year Estimates Data Profile Highlights." Accessed June 23, 2011, http://www.factfinder.census.gov.

U.S. Census Bureau American FactFinder. "East Hartford CDP, Connecticut 2005–2009 American Community Survey 5-Year Estimates Data Profile Highlights." Accessed June 23, 2011, http://www.factfinder.census.gov.

U.S. Census Bureau American FactFinder. "Hartford County, Connecticut 2005–2009 American Community Survey 5-Year Estimates Data Profile Highlights." Accessed June 23, 2011, http://www.factfinder.census.gov.

U.S. Census Bureau American FactFinder. "Hartford Town, Hartford County, Connecticut 2005–2009 American Community Survey 5-Year Estimates Data Profile Highlights." Accessed June 23, 2011, http://www.factfinder.census.gov.

U.S. Census Bureau American FactFinder. "New Britain city, Connecticut 2005–2009 American Community Survey 5-Year Estimates Data Profile Highlights." Accessed June 23, 2011, http://www.factfinder.census.gov.

U.S. Census Bureau American FactFinder. "Newington town, Hartford County, Connecticut 2005–2009 American Community Survey 5-Year Estimates Data Profile Highlights." Accessed June 23, 2011, http://www.factfinder.census.gov.

U.S. Census Bureau American FactFinder. "West Hartford CDP, Connecticut 2005–2009 American Community Survey 5-Year Estimates Data Profile Highlights." Accessed June 23, 2011, http://www.factfinder.census.gov.

U.S. Census Bureau American FactFinder. "Wethersfield CDP, Connecticut 2005–2009 American Community Survey 5-Year Estimates Data Profile Highlights." Accessed June 23, 2011, http://www.factfinder.census.gov.

U.S. Census Bureau American FactFinder. "Windsor Town, Hartford County, Connecticut 2005–2009 American Community Survey 5-Year Estimates Data Profile Highlights." Accessed June 23, 2011, http://www.factfinder.census.gov.

U.S. Census Bureau. "Poverty Thresholds 2008." Accessed August 25, 2010, http://www.census.gov/hhes/www/poverty/data/threshld/thresh08.html.

U.S. Department of Health and Human Services, Administration for Children and Families, LIHEAP Clearing House. "2009/2010 HHS Poverty Guidelines." Accessed August 25, 2010, http://liheap.ncat.org/profiles/povertytables/FY2010/popstate.htm.

6

Investigating Spatial Inequality with the Cities, Suburbs, and Schools Project

Jack Dougherty

For nearly a decade, Trinity College students, colleagues, and I have worked together on the Cities, Suburbs, and Schools Project to better understand the past and present relationship between public education and private housing in metropolitan Hartford, Connecticut. The CSS Project refers to the collective work done by undergraduates in the interdisciplinary seminar I teach, as well as independent studies, summer research assistantships, and other presentations and papers. Together, we formulate research questions from provocative readings from literature in history and the social sciences, and design studies using historical, qualitative, and/or quantitative methods to test these ideas in the Hartford region. Several leading scholars have kindly provided guidance and critical feedback via conference calls and professional meetings. We also have designed several studies in collaboration with local partner organizations who help us to frame questions, identify sources, and interpret our findings.

In its broadest sense, our work explores spatial inequalities arising from the increasingly tightening bonds between schooling and housing in the city-suburban Hartford region over the last century. Looking back, our past has been shaped by the lines we have drawn to separate ourselves. Real estate agents maintained the color line. Mortgage lenders engaged in discriminatory redlining. Locally elected officials drew exclusionary residential zoning lines. Suburban homebuyers shopped for better opportunities on the other side of public school attendance lines. As these boundaries became more powerful over time, civil rights activists fought to cross over, redraw, or erase these lines.

The story of schooling and racial inequality in Greater Hartford has attracted many scholars and journalists, most notably Christopher Collier's encyclopedic history, *Connecticut's Public Schools* (2009), and Susan Eaton's close examination of one classroom amid the *Sheff v. O'Neill* segregation case in *The Children in Room E4* (2007). The work of the CSS Project expands upon this literature by analyzing how the relationship between schooling and housing became more influential from the late 19th century to the present, generating the contemporary policy challenges of voluntary desegregation remedies and public school choice. Specifically, this chapter highlights and synthesizes research conducted by Trinity students who have worked with me to answer two questions. First, when and how did the most desirable schools shift from the city to selected suburbs, and what role did the real estate industry play in this transformation? Second, under growing pressure from civil rights activists, state and local governments have implemented voluntary desegregation remedies and public school choice. Whose interests have been served by these policies—and whose have not? To answer those questions, we need to understand the historical evolution of the marketplace commonly known today as "shopping for schools," and recent policy reforms that have attempted to decouple public education and private housing. Readers may wish to consult a more extended presentation of this argument in a web-book, *On the Line: How Schooling, Housing, and Civil Rights Shaped Hartford and its Suburbs* (Dougherty and colleagues, 2011), with links to interactive maps, online archives, and ongoing research with undergraduates.

FOLLOW THE MONEY FROM CITY TO SUBURBS

Trinity students encountering this topic for the first time are astounded to learn about the stark economic disparity surrounding their campus. According to the most recent estimates from the US Census Bureau (2010), Hartford ranks as the 4th poorest city among those with populations over 100,000 in the continental United States, with an average family income of only $42,775 in 2009. Nearly three out of ten families in Hartford live below the current federal poverty line, currently around $22,000 for a family of four. But what is most striking is that this impoverished city is located inside the 13th richest metropolitan statistical area, ranked by more than 350 such areas across the United States. In the Hartford metropolitan region (currently defined by the Census as Hartford, Middlesex, and Tolland counties), the average family income reached $99,597 in 2009. When comparing the two columns in table 1, an income gap of over $56,000 separates the average family living inside the Hartford city boundary from those residing in the Hartford metropolitan area.

But the region did not always look this way. In the late 19th century, national headlines declared Hartford to be "the richest city in the United States," relative to its number of inhabitants (Clark, 1876). When tabulating the value of all bank deposits, insurance company assets, and taxable property of homes and businesses, Connecticut's capital city outperformed more famous competitors such as New York and Chicago. To be clear, this claim defined "richest" based on corporate (rather than individual) wealth. In later years, scholars such as Hartford Seminary sociologist Alexander Merriam (1903) pointed out that local wealth varied widely in Hartford, between residences of "wealthier citizens . . . scattered in different parts of the city" and "a slum of almost the first magnitude" along the Connecticut river. Nevertheless,

Table 6.1. Income in Hartford's City and Metropolitan Region, 2009

Lowest Average Family Income in 2009, by US Cities Over 100,000 Population

1	Flint city, Michigan	$40,368
2	Cleveland city, Ohio	$40,600
3	Detroit city, Michigan	$41,443
4	**Hartford city, Connecticut**	**$42,775**
5	Dayton city, Ohio	$43,406
6	Hialeah city, Florida	$45,010
7	East Los Angeles CDP, California	$45,320
8	Brownsville city, Texas	$45,507
9	Paterson city, New Jersey	$46,954
10	Toledo city, Ohio	$48,846
11	Rochester city, New York	$49,072
12	South Bend city, Indiana	$49,691
13	Allentown city, Pennsylvania	$50,105
14	Syracuse city, New York	$50,220
15	Laredo city, Texas	$51,152

Highest Average Family Income in 2009, by US Metropolitan Statistical Areas

1	Bridgeport-Stamford-Norwalk, CT Metro Area	$150,336
2	Washington-Arlington-Alexandria, DC-VA-MD-WV Metro Area	$127,167
3	San Jose-Sunnyvale-Santa Clara, CA Metro Area	$120,407
4	Trenton-Ewing, NJ Metro Area	$119,590
5	San Francisco-Oakland-Fremont, CA Metro Area	$118,713
6	Boston-Cambridge-Quincy, MA-NH Metro Area	$113,192
7	Boulder, CO Metro Area	$110,988
8	Napa, CA Metro Area	$106,579
9	NY-Northern NJ-Long Island, NY-NJ-PA Metro Area	$105,680
10	Baltimore-Towson, MD Metro Area	$101,836
11	Oxnard-Thousand Oaks-Ventura, CA Metro Area	$100,854
12	Naples-Marco Island, FL Metro Area	$100,466
13	**Hartford-West Hartford-East Hartford, CT Metro Area**	**$99,597**
14	Santa Cruz-Watsonville, CA Metro Area	$98,712
15	Anchorage, AK Metro Area	$98,290

Source: American Community Survey 2009, US Census Bureau, in Social Explorer table T59
Note: Excludes three urban zones in Puerto Rico, and one micropolitan area (Torrington CT)

the central city of Hartford served as an economic engine for the capital region well into the first few decades of the twentieth century.

Where did the money go? One way to visualize this spatial economic shift is to compare data maps from two points in time. While we lack income data for the entire region prior to the 1960 Census, one proxy for personal wealth from archival records is the average home value by town in Hartford County. Figure 1 depicts the values of the average residential dwelling in 1910, as reported by town tax assessors (Connecticut Tax Commissioner, 1911) with equalization adjustments, and the average market sale price for single-family homes in each town nearly a century later in 2007 (Capitol

Region Council of Governments 2007). To allow for comparison across time, home values have been indexed to the regional average for each year (designated as 1.00), and towns with home values higher than the regional average have been shaded darker. Indeed, there are limitations to comparing historical data on home values from two different sources, and neither considers rental values. But when comparing the two maps side by side, the suburbanization of housing wealth is clearly visible. In 1910, the assessed home value in the city of Hartford (and neighboring West Hartford) stood far above the outlying rural towns. But a century later, the region has experienced a near-reversal of fortunes, as single-family home values have fallen in Hartford, and risen to their highest levels in today's elite suburbs, such as Avon.

In some eyes, the once-powerful city-based economic region now resembles a "doughnut," with a fiscally depressed center surrounded by a yeasty suburban ring. But a closer look at recent data reveals wider variation across suburbs than most assume. The *Connecticut Metropatterns* report (Orfield & Luce, 2003) dispelled "the myth of the affluent suburban monolith" by illustrating how some suburbs face high levels of fiscal stress, based on the cost of educating their population of needy children relative to their local capacity to raise tax revenues.

THE RISE OF "SHOPPING FOR SCHOOLS" IN SUBURBIA

The status of Hartford's city and suburban school districts also reversed trajectories during this same period. A century ago, Hartford Public High School offered what nearly all agreed to be the best secondary education in the entire region, attracting students into the city. According to HPHS student records (1882), one out of five students resided outside Hartford, many in bordering towns, and paid tuition to

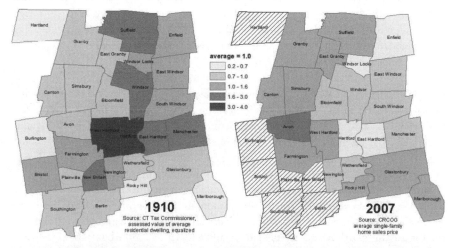

Map 6.1.   Home Value Index in Hartford County, 1910 and 2007 (Jack Dougherty)

enroll. Emerging suburbs typically had no high school or one that some viewed as substandard. In nearby Wethersfield, parents strongly objected to plans to eliminate Latin in their fledgling high school, while four members of the local school board sent their children to Hartford city schools (*Hartford Courant*, 1917). Two decades later, a prominent survey by Columbia University Teachers College (1937) praised Hartford's public high schools for "maintaining the 'gold standard' of its college preparatory students," with a reputation "widely and favorably known through eastern collegiate circles." As late as 1958, surveys of Hartford teachers reported it to be "common knowledge in education circles that the city of Hartford and its school system have enjoyed an excellent reputation as a good place in which to live and work over the past 20 years," according to Trinity researcher Eric Lawrence (2002). At the same time, ten miles west of the city, the rural town of Avon ceased busing its older students to a neighboring district and began constructing their own high school building. By the late 1990s, after decades of urban decline nearly resulted in Hartford Public High School losing its accreditation, Avon High School claimed title to the most prestigious public secondary education in the Hartford region.

What attracted white middle-class families to move from the cities to the suburbs? Ken Jackson's *Crabgrass Frontier*, which paved a way of thinking for a generation of suburban historians, boiled down the causes of postwar mass suburbanization to "two necessary conditions . . . the suburban ideal and population growth—and two fundamental causes—racial prejudice and cheap housing" (1985, p. 287). Indeed, there is supporting evidence for Jackson's thesis in the Hartford region, particularly the influence of discriminatory public policy decisions on private housing markets. For instance, my colleagues at the University of Connecticut Libraries MAGIC Center (2010) and I reconstructed Hartford-area maps, originally created by the federal Home Owners' Loan Corporation and private lenders in 1937 to assess mortgage risks by neighborhoods (see Map 3.1 in Bacon, this volume). Officials coded the best investments in green, and the worst in red, which led them to be known in later years as "redlining" maps. But, rather than evaluating only the physical property conditions, field agents were instructed to record the racial, ethnic, and social composition of current residents, based on the prevailing white standards of the time. The reports discouraged lenders from offering mortgages to neighborhoods with an "infiltration" of "Negro," "Foreign-born," and "Relief families," thereby favoring mortgage lending to white middle-class areas. Similarly, during the early 1940s, suburban West Hartford officials blocked African Americans from moving into federally subsidized wartime public housing (Winterbottom, 1998). Around the same time, some West Hartford real estate developers wrote racially restrictive covenants into deeds that prohibited residents "other than the white race" from renting or buying property, which remained legally enforceable until 1948, as Trinity alumna Tracey Wilson (2010) and student researcher Katie Campbell discovered.

But Jackson does not explain how public schools fit into his equation, because their role shifted over time. During the immediate postwar years, doubts about the quality of schools in new suburbs meant that they did not serve as a primary motivator for leaving Hartford. Yet by the late 1950s and 1960s, suburban schools became powerful magnets that, on their own, began to attract white middle-class families. How do we explain this shift? The story of postwar metropolitan history needs to address how real estate interests, suburban homebuyers, and government officials contributed to the rise of a relatively new practice known as "shopping for schools" (Dougherty, 2012).

Migration out of Hartford was not driven by a perception of higher-quality suburban schools in the late 1940s and early 1950s. In several oral history interviews that Trinity researcher Jacqueline Katz (2004) conducted with former Hartford residents who moved to suburbs in the immediate postwar era, none mentioned educational quality as a deciding factor. Clifford Floyd, a Hartford insurance accountant who moved to Avon in 1952 with his spouse and three young children, gave a typical response. "We didn't come to Avon because of the schools," he explained. "We just thought it would be better to have a lot more land for the kids to play around in." Even in West Hartford, where suburbanization began decades before the war, local newspaper editor Bice Clemow found low standards in school facilities, curriculum, and teacher salaries when using a survey drawn from *Life* magazine. "If we lived in a mill town, where the income level was modest, it would not be startling to find that we could not afford the best in public education," wrote Clemow (1951). "To document that we have grade B-secondary education available in West Hartford is a shock of another order."

The rise of suburban schools can be attributed partly to the actions of real estate firms, which promoted selected private suburban homes by marketing their access to more desirable public schools. In West Hartford, as school enrollments grew with the postwar baby boom, a heated controversy arose at a 1954 school board meeting over a proposal to address overcrowding by redistricting neighborhoods to less crowded schools. Parents who objected based their views on the real estate market. "Whenever real estate men sell property, they tell their clients that they are in the Sedgwick, Webster Hill, or Bugbee areas," attendance zones on the newly constructed western side of town. Superintendent Edmund Thorne responded by blaming real estate agents for creating "social class consciousness" in the suburb, and asked, "Doesn't it boil down to some people thinking there is more prestige to going to one school than another?" (*Hartford Times* 1954). But what Thorne perceived as an imaginary distinction was becoming very real for suburban homebuyers.

Newspaper advertisements reflect the rise of "branding" marketing by real estate firms during the 1950s and 1960s. Trinity researcher Kelli Perkins and other students compiled a sample of real estate ads in the *Hartford Courant* Sunday edition from 1920 to 1990. We tabulated the proportion of ads that mentioned a specific school by name, rather than a generic description such as "near school." Compared to other suburbs, West Hartford had the highest proportion of school-specific ads, peaking at 38 percent of all residential ads in the town in 1965 (Dougherty, 2012). Through marketing, real estate firms sought to increase the dollar value of a private home by signaling its location within what homebuyers perceived as a more desirable public school attendance zone. Simply moving into the suburb of West Hartford was no longer sufficient: success also entailed buying into the "right" neighborhood" to attend a "good" public school.

But real estate firms did not treat all suburbs equally. Most agents refused to sell homes to blacks in any suburb in the region during the 1950s, but they eventually shifted their stance on one town, Bloomfield, located on the northern border of Hartford and West Hartford. Middle-class African Americans such as Spencer Shaw (2003), a librarian from the city of Hartford, reported having had "several refusals before from real estate people," yet finally succeeded in purchasing a home through an agent in the early 1960s, from a Greek couple in Bloomfield. The sale sparked a racial transition. "I think within about two months, four or five of the other families moved out," Shaw told Trinity interviewer Jacqueline Katz.

Real estate firms engaged in two discriminatory practices—block-busting and racial steering—that shaped the composition of Bloomfield and neighboring suburbs during the late 1960s and 1970s. In block-busting, a real estate agent introduced black homebuyers into a white neighborhood to scare owners into selling their homes below market value to the agent, who immediately resold them above market value to black buyers. This sales technique played on white racial fears to make a quick profit. Trinity researcher Aleesha Young (2005) compared city directory listings for selected streets where block-busting occurred in Bloomfield, and found some, such as Alexander Road, experienced a residential turnover rate of 41 percent from 1970 to 1975. In the related practice of racial steering, real estate firms diverted black buyers to home sales in areas such as Bloomfield, while redirecting white buyers to places such as Avon and West Hartford. According to witnesses such as John Keever, a white homebuyer who asked to view homes in Bloomfield, real estate agents "made innuendos about the school system" there and warned about racial attacks against his daughter, but spoke about white suburban school districts in "glowing terms" (Ross, 1973). Together, busting and steering contributed to the racial population of the Bloomfield school district changing at a much faster rate than the town at large, illustrating a strengthening bond between public schools and private real estate, in the opposite direction.

Local organizations, with assistance from National Neighbors, a multiracial advocacy group, led different challenges against real estate firms in the Hartford region. Adelle Wright (2005), chairwoman of Bloomfield's Human Relations Committee, recalled the "snowstorm of signs" on streets visited by block-busting real estate agents. The signs "reminded the people going into that neighborhood, every day of their lives [that], 'My neighborhood is turning. I might be the last one here,'" she recalled in an interview with Trinity researchers. In 1973, Wright's committee persuaded the Bloomfield town council to pass an ordinance against door-to-door and telephone solicitation by real estate agents, and a ban against "for sale" and "sold" signs being posted in front of private homes.

Meanwhile, a Hartford-based organization known as Education/Instrucción, led by a trio of activists—Ben Dixon, Boyd Hinds, and Julia Ramos—mounted a broader challenge against discriminatory practices across the entire real estate and lending industry. In 1973, they organized teams of testers to visit real estate firms and pose as buyers to document racial steering, which was a violation of the 1968 Fair Housing Act. As Ramos explained in an oral history interview with Trinity researcher Jasmin Agosto (2010), she and a Hispanic male "posed as a couple that barely spoke English, you know, our English was supposedly very minimal to a West Hartford real estate company. We walked in and basically made known through gestures and a little bit of English that we wanted to buy a house in West Hartford." After some back and forth with the real estate office staff, "we were steered to the North End of Hartford and the South End of Hartford, shown houses and given listings in these two locations. All of this we taped." With dozens of detailed accounts like this, activists built a legal case against eight large real estate firms in the Hartford area, and persuaded the US Justice Department to prosecute them for racial steering. In addition, Education/Instrucción (1974) published a series of reports, *Fair Housing at its Worst*, which extended charges of discrimination to mortgage lenders, downtown insurance corporations, and complicit government regulators. Although the court case resulted in a settlement against the real estate firms, they denied all wrongdoing and received a relatively mild penalty: monitoring and mandatory training on fair housing law.

The only large realty firm not to be charged with discriminatory practices was The R. W. Barrows Company. Former co-owner Larry Barrows (2007) spoke about real estate sales during this period during oral history interviews with Trinity researcher Cintli Sanchez. Barrows never used racial scare tactics nor had firsthand knowledge of those who did, but he conceded that, "We said some stuff we couldn't say now." He openly discussed racial, religious, and other qualities of neighborhoods and schools with clients. "I'm an old time liberal Democrat, so I would tell them, 'Mixed neighborhood, mixed schools,' and so forth," Barrows explained, to help his clients identify the social composition of the neighborhood they desired. Sometimes he had candid discussions with Jewish homebuyers, to help them break into neighborhoods that had previously excluded them. Barrows acknowledged that when real estate agents talked about schools, "we were making judgments on the teachers and principals, which we had no business doing." Still, Barrows emphasized that agents needed to be responsive to the needs of clients, especially Hartford's large insurance corporation employees, who transferred into the region and "were brainwashed before they even looked at houses," by co-workers who coached them to buy into a particular neighborhood." As he remembered, "People used to call an agent, and they would say, 'I want to be in a certain school district' . . . They wanted somebody who really knew quite a bit about the schools and the districts and so forth. So that was how you got business."

By the late 1980s, real estate firms had discovered how to respond to clients' requests about neighborhood school quality without violating fair housing laws. Rather than voicing their opinions, agents began distributing packets of school data, which became more widely available after Connecticut passed a 1985 law to create standardized student achievement tests (such as the Connecticut Mastery Test [CMT]

and the Connecticut Academic Performance Test [CAPT], and subsequent requirements for uniform reporting of district data [the Strategic School Profiles]. "Agents
get so many questions from buyers about schools, and they are very conscious and
concerned about giving out misleading information," Lynda Wilson, President of the
Greater Hartford Association of Realtors, told a reporter in 1993. "They are afraid
if they give wrong information, they can be accused of steering." Margaret O'Keefe,
who had previously served as PTO president of two West Hartford schools, added
that she understood new federal restrictions to mean it was permissible to share
objective education data with clients, but not her own subjective judgments about
the quality of individual schools. "You're treading on very dangerous ground," she
concluded, "unless you have facts" (Hathaway, 1993).

The politics of the school accountability movement, combined with growing access
to the Internet, fueled this data-driven wave of "shopping for schools" in the suburban
housing market. In 1995, the Prudential Connecticut Realty Company opened its
first experimental "computerized library," located at their West Hartford office, for
potential buyers to browse photographs of homes and "information on communities' demographics and school systems." The Connecticut Department of Education
launched its own website in 1996, and began to include test score data for individual
schools for the first generation of Web surfers in 1997 (Dougherty, 2012). By the year
2000, homebuyers with computer access could easily and instantly view details about
local schools, whether located around the corner or across the country. Part of the
data revolution was driven by state education agencies, to comply with the federal No
Child Left Behind Act of 2001. But private real estate firms and nonprofit education
advocates also harnessed the Web to deliver school-level test scores and demographics
to millions of families who eagerly consumed it.

How much money were families willing to pay to purchase a private home on
the more desirable side of a public school boundary line? Trinity Professor Diane
Zannoni and her team of econometrics students collaborated with me to answer
this question (Dougherty et al., 2009). We compiled public records for single-family
home sales in the West Hartford Public School district (to avoid differences between
suburbs), and mapped them inside the eleven elementary school attendance zones,
which varied by test scores and racial composition. We limited our study to a ten-year
period (1996 to 2005) where test formats and attendance zones remained relatively
stable, which we split into two halves to gauge the growing influence of school data
available via the Internet. Furthermore, we controlled for characteristics of the house
(such as interior square footage and lot size) and also the neighborhood, by identifying sales within a very close distance of boundary lines that were drawn through the
middle of residential areas, rather than along major roads or parks. Overall, we found
that the test-price relationship was positive and significant: a one standard deviation
in elementary school test scores produced a 2 percent increase (about $3,800) in the
price of an average home during this decade. But we also discovered the increasing
significance of race in this predominantly white suburb. During the latter half of our
time period (2002–2005), the racial composition of the school became much more

influential: a one standard deviation in the percentage of minority students led to a 4 percent decrease (about $7,500) in the cost of an average home. In other words, as homebuyers in this predominantly white suburb make decisions about where to live, the sales data suggest that they are becoming more sensitive to the racial composition of their children's future classmates than their test scores.

In this suburb, how do we explain why test scores mattered, but the school's racial composition became more influential on single-family home prices over time? Part of the answer comes from a parallel qualitative study conducted by Trinity researcher Christina Ramsay and co-authors in the CSS seminar (2006), based on door-to-door interviews conducted with 89 recent homebuyers in West Hartford. Fewer than 35 percent of those homeowners with (or expecting) children reported directly "researching" schools by searching for school information online or visiting schools in person. By contrast, over 50 percent found information about school quality through indirect means: their social networks of family, friends, and co-workers. Another part of the answer appears in a Washington DC study (Buckley and Schneider, 2007), which monitored how users actually conduct searches with an online school information site. They found that users were strongly biased toward checking demographic data on schools, and when making comparisons, tended to reject those with higher percentages of black students. Together, these three studies suggest that while not all homebuyers directly access school information online, the expansion of the Internet may amplify the power of racial and test data as it travels through their social networks.

THE CHALLENGES OF VOLUNTARY DESEGREGATION AND PUBLIC SCHOOL CHOICE

For nearly half a century, school desegregation advocates have pushed for a metropolitan Hartford solution to lift urban minority students up to the same quality of education as white suburban students. Advocates lobbied for voluntary interdistrict busing in the 1960s, then pressed for stronger desegregation mandates across the entire metropolitan region in the 1989 *Sheff v. O'Neill* lawsuit. Victory finally arrived for the Sheff plaintiffs in the Connecticut supreme court's 1996 decision, by a 4–3 vote, that racial and socioeconomic isolation deprived Hartford schoolchildren of their state constitutional right to an equal education opportunity. Yet the court did not specify any remedy or timetable to address this injustice, handing the responsibility over to the executive and legislative branches, where neither the Republican Governor nor the Democrat-led General Assembly desired to alter the boundary lines that divided city and suburban districts. Although Sheff allies proposed a metropolitan school district to unite students across the Hartford region, this bold plan never gained sufficient political traction among local education officials in the suburbs, nor the city, as Trinity researcher Jennifer Williams (2006) documented in her interviews with key actors. At present, the limited school desegregation remedies that exist in the Hartford region are based primarily on voluntary measures, under the popular slogan of "choice," that effectively serve the interests of privileged suburban families more than the intended urban beneficiaries.

In 1966, when representatives of the Project Concern interdistrict busing program attempted to persuade suburban districts to enroll small numbers of Hartford minority students in their districts, they encountered intense resistance from white residents determined to defend their boundary lines. Trinity researcher Grace Beckett (2004) discovered that even in West Hartford, one of the few districts that eventually agreed to start up Project Concern, the controversy generated the largest crowd (estimated at 1,200) at a board of education meeting, including many residents who booed religious leaders speaking in support of the plan. After the initial controversy faded, more suburban districts agreed to participate in Project Concern and accept the state subsidy that came with it. In its peak year in 1979, the program enabled approximately 1,175 Hartford students to enroll in suburban districts. Based on 24 interviews that students conducted with Project Concern alumni, Trinity researcher Dana Banks and I found a mix of support and ambivalence about the program. More than half suggested that daily bus rides of an hour (or more) represented a "forced choice," with less autonomy than the suburbs that voluntarily decided to accept them (Banks & Dougherty, 2004; see also Gutmann, 2003).

A second wave of voluntary metropolitan desegregation arose with interdistrict magnet schools, designed to attract families from city and suburban towns with specialized curricula. While three magnets emerged in Hartford during the 1980s (Reynolds, 1994), the largest expansion occurred in the aftermath of the Sheff ruling, when the state legislature agreed to fund most construction costs for selected proposals. Magnet schools became a politically popular response to segregation because they allowed individual suburban districts and families to "choose" whether or not to participate in a policy solution.

Magnet schools also served multiple interests, and not exclusively those of Hartford students. In the early 1990s, Trinity College faced increasing urban poverty and declining admissions statistics, and its Board of Trustees "even began to explore the feasibility of moving the College out of the city," according to a former vice president (Sullivan & Trostle, 2004). Incoming Trinity President Evan Dobelle leveraged private endowment funds to gain state support for the Learning Corridor, a $110 million magnet school complex built on an abandoned field adjacent to the campus in 2000. But Trinity researcher Nivia Nieves (2006) and I found that Sheff magnet school funding diverted earlier plans for a Hartford neighborhood school, and reduced the number of seats available to city youth from the Latino community around campus. Although interdistrict magnets were more racially diverse than most city or suburban schools, the relatively low percentage of Hartford students able to attend them led Trinity researcher Sarah Kaminski (2002) to question their effectiveness in addressing overall segregation levels.

Years after the Sheff ruling, plaintiffs and state officials finally agreed to a legal settlement in 2003, with a four-year goal of placing 30 percent of Hartford minority students in "reduced isolation" settings, generally defined as schools with under 75 percent minority students. Together with Trinity researchers Jesse Wanzer and Christina Ramsay, our *Missing the Goal* report illustrated the limited success of voluntary remedies in meeting that objective, followed by a more detailed analysis of overlapping policy obstacles (Dougherty, Wanzer, & Ramsay, 2007; 2009). We also detected spatial inequalities in how desegregation was implemented. For instance, suburban districts enrolling the highest proportion of Hartford minority students through the Open Choice transfer program (previously known as Project Concern) were more likely to be located farther away from the city, requiring longer bus rides. Also, suburban districts with the highest magnet school participation rates were more likely to have fewer White students (such as Bloomfield), making racial balance more difficult than desegregation planners had anticipated. In 2008, plaintiffs and state officials agreed to a second Sheff settlement, featuring a more comprehensive management plan and a more ambitious desegregation goal to be reached by 2013.

Public school choice became more prevalent in the Hartford area in 2008, as the new Regional School Choice Office recruited suburban applicants for interdistrict desegregation, and the Hartford Public Schools launched its own district-wide choice initiative to increase school accountability. For many Hartford parents, the opportunity to go "shopping for schools" as suburban parents had done felt empowering, yet the confusion caused by competing choice programs (with similar names but separate application processes) was overwhelming. To address this concern, Trinity students and community partners and I collaborated with Academic Computing staff Jean-Pierre Haeberly and David Tatem, and Social Science Center Coordinator Rachael Barlow. In January 2009, we launched SmartChoices, a parent-friendly digital guide that lists all eligible public school options across the metropolitan region, with an interactive map and tools to sort schools by distance, racial balance, and student achievement (Hughes, 2009). With funding from a local education foundation, Trinity students conducted parent outreach workshops with hands-on guidance on using the tool, while interviewing parents in English or Spanish about their decision-making process. Based on our sample of 93 workshop participants, we found that providing richer information makes a difference: two-thirds either changed or clarified their top-ranked school after the hands-on workshop, and many found options with higher test scores or greater racial balance located closer to their neighborhood. But we also observed some black and Latino parents using the tool to avoid schools with high concentrations of students from racial groups other than their own (Dougherty et al., 2013).

To better understand this secondary "shopping for schools" market, the next phase of our research is to analyze which Hartford families do (and do not) participate in public school choice programs, and the types of schools they desire. Working with Professor Diane Zannoni and another team of econometrics students, we are comparing choice applicant data to thousands of records from the broader school population, to search for characteristics that may be associated with individual students, their classmates, and their neighborhoods (Del Conte et al., 2012). Our spatial analysis builds upon prior work by Trinity researchers who used geographic information system (GIS) tools to analyze magnet school application data, or conducted door-to-door interviews with parents in selected Hartford neighborhoods with very high or low application rates (Estevez, 2006; Wanzer, Moore, & Dougherty, 2008). Displaying our results through data maps also enables us to study how different stakeholders interpret their meaning (Price, 2009).

Figure 6.1. Trinity Researcher Ada Avila and Colleagues Conducted a SmartChoices Workshop while Interviewing Parents at a Hartford School, 2009. (Jack Dougherty)

More research remains to be done in several related areas that Trinity students and faculty have begun to study. Our understanding of magnet schools would improve with further examination of student-to-student relationships and attitudes toward other races (Schofield, 2002; Blacklaw, 2002; Reuman, 2003). We also would benefit from more cultural comparisons between suburban school districts (DePina, 2003), and analysis of achievement gaps within suburban districts (Wetzler, 2006). The role played by Catholic and private schools in educational markets deserves closer study (Green, 2004; Moore, 2005), as does the legislative history of funding school districts (Pennington, Steele, & Dougherty, 2007) and interdistrict programs (MacDonald, 2005). Of course, fruitful ideas for researching schooling and housing in metropolitan Hartford can be found in publications by scholars at other institutions, and in works on other regions. (See additional references in *On the Line* by Dougherty and colleagues, 2011.)

CONCLUSION

While our society preaches the ideal of equal educational opportunity, our CSS Project research has challenged my students to recognize the powerful role that real estate values play in determining access to this public good, and raising (or lowering) its market value. Although we call them "public" schools, we buy and sell access to most as "private" commodities, based on the underlying real estate and governmental boundary lines that restrict entry. Access to more desirable elementary and secondary schooling became more valuable in the post–World War II labor market, with rising economic returns for students attaining higher education degrees, which fueled the practice of "shopping for schools" in suburbs today. As civil rights activists have battled against barriers to equal access over the years, state lawmakers have gradually begun to decouple housing and schooling by offering interdistrict transfers and magnet schools, which do not require families to rent or buy a home in a suburban district. In essence, Connecticut's voluntary desegregation policy has created a second "shopping" marketplace, called public school choice, in our attempt to remedy the ills of the existing market based on private housing.

Yet desirable public school options remain scarce. Moreover, this second government-run choice market relies on individual families (with varying levels of literacy) to sort through glossy brochures and competing advertising campaigns to identify the "best" schools for their children, without fully considering the aggregated effects of these decisions on who gets ahead, and who is left behind.

By itself, research will not eliminate the disparities that divide us. But it is an essential step in the process. Uncovering the underlying causes of inequalities, and understanding the success and limitations of past reform efforts, helps us come to terms with the depth and scope of the real issues facing us. Learning about the evolution of cities, suburbs, and schools—particularly in the company of reflective community partners, with perspectives broader than our own—can teach us important lessons about privilege and power, and strengthen our collective capacity. Reconstructing a road map of how we arrived at our present-day policy dilemmas does not provide us with a detailed reform agenda. But the process can suggest possible avenues and future directions for moving all of us a few steps forward.

REFERENCES

Agosto, Jasmin. 2010. "Fighting Segregation, Teaching Multiculturalism: The Beginning of the Education/Instrucción Narrative of the 1970s Hartford Civil Rights Movement." Educational Studies, Trinity College, Hartford, CT. http://digitalrepository.trincoll.edu.

Banks, Dana and Jack Dougherty. 2004. "City-Suburban Desegregation and Forced Choices: Review essay of Susan Eaton's *The Other Boston Busing Story.*" *Teachers College Record.* 106:985–996. http://digitalrepository.trincoll.edu.

Barrows, Larry. 2007. Oral history interviews with Cintli Sanchez, June 27 and July 5. West Hartford Real Estate Agent Oral History Collection, Hartford Studies Project, Trinity College. http://digitalrepository.trincoll.edu.

Beckett, Grace. 2004. "Suburban Participation in Hartford's Project Concern School Desegregation Program, 1966–1998." Educational Studies senior research project, Trinity College. http://digitalrepository.trincoll.edu.

Blacklaw, Nicola. 2002. "The Presence of Contact Conditions in a Magnet School." Educational Studies senior research project, Trinity College, Hartford, CT. http://digitalrepository.trincoll.edu/cssp_papers/10.

Buckley, Jack, and Mark Schneider. 2007. *Charter Schools: Hope or Hype.* Princeton, NJ: Princeton University Press.

Capitol Region Council of Governments. 2007. *Connecticut Capitol Region Home Sales Price Report, July 2006–June 2007.* Hartford: CRCOG.

Clark, Charles H. 1876. "The Charter Oak City." *Scribner's Monthly.* 13 (1):1–21.

Clemow, Bice. 1951. *A Layman Looks at Schools in West Hartford: a series reprinted from the West Hartford News from January 25 through February 15, 1951, based on the Life magazine questionnaire.* West Hartford, CT: West Hartford News.

Collier, Christopher. 2009. *Connecticut's Public Schools: A History, 1650–2000.* Orange, CT: Clearwater Press.

Columbia University, Teachers College. 1937. Institute of Educational Research. Division of Field Studies. *The Hartford Public Schools in 1936–37: A Comprehensive Report of the Survey of the Public Schools of Hartford, Connecticut.* New York: Columbia University, pamphlet X, page 13.

Connecticut Tax Commissioner. 1911. *Information Relative to the Assessment and Collection of Taxes as Given to the Connecticut Tax Commissioner by Town Officials*: Hartford: State of Connecticut.

DelConte, Matthew, Sushil Trivedi, Diane Zannoni, and Jack Dougherty. 2012. "Who Chooses? A Preliminary Analysis of Hartford Public Schools." http://digitalrepository.trincoll.edu.

DePina, Antonio. 2003. "Comparing Suburban School Culture in Metropolitan Hartford: How Does the Formal and Hidden Curriculum Vary Across Two High Schools?" Educational Studies senior research project, Trinity College, Hartford, CT. http://digitalrepository .trincoll.edu/cssp_papers/15.

Dougherty, Jack. 2012. "Shopping for Schools: How Public Education and Private Housing Shaped Suburban Connecticut." *Journal of Urban History* 38 (2):205–24.

Dougherty, Jack, Diane Zannoni, Maham Chowhan, Courteney Coyne, Benjamin Dawson, Tehani Guruge, and Begaeta Nukic. 2013. "School Information, Parental Decisions, and the Digital Divide: The SmartChoices Project in Hartford, Connecticut." in *Educational Delusions? Why Choice Can Deepen Inequality and How to Make Schools Fair*, edited by Gary Orfield and Erica Frankenberg. Berkeley, CA: University of California Press.

Dougherty, Jack, and colleagues. 2011. *On the Line: How Schooling, Housing, and Civil Rights Shaped Hartford and its Suburbs.* Trinity College: Hartford: CT. <http://OnTheLine.trincoll .edu>.

Dougherty, Jack, Jeffrey Harrelson, Laura Maloney, Drew Murphy, Russell Smith, Michael Snow, and Diane Zannoni. 2009. "School Choice in Suburbia: Test Scores, Race, and Housing Markets." *American Journal of Education.* 115 (4):523–548.

Dougherty, Jack, Jesse Wanzer, and Christina Ramsay. 2009. "Sheff v O'Neill: Weak Desegregation Remedies and Strong Disincentives in Connecticut, 1996–2008." Pp. 103–127 in *From the Courtroom to the Classroom: The Shifting Landscape of School Desegregation*, edited by Claire Smrekar and Ellen Goldring. Cambridge, MA: Harvard Education Press.

Dougherty, Jack, Jesse Wanzer, and Christina Ramsay. 2007. *Missing the Goal: A Visual Guide to Sheff vs. O'Neill School Desegregation.* Hartford, CT: Cities, Suburbs, and Schools Research Project at Trinity College. http://digitalrepository.trincoll.edu/cssp_papers/6.

Eaton, Susan. 2007. *The Children in Room E4: American Education on Trial.* Chapel Hill, NC: Algonquin Books.

Education/Instruccion. 1974. *Fair Housing At Its Worst: The Flagrant Violation of Title VIII of the 1968 Civil Rights Act in Greater Hartford, Connecticut (reports 1–8).* Hartford, CT. http:// digitalrepository.trincoll.edu/cssp_archive.

Estevez, Naralys. 2006. "Do Magnet Schools Attract All Families Equally? A GIS Mapping Analysis of Latinos." Conference paper presented at American Education Research As-

sociation, Cities, Suburbs, and Schools Project at Trinity College. http://digitalrepository
.trincoll.edu/cssp_papers/16.

Green, Carmen. 2004. "Catholic Schools, Racial Change, and Suburbanization, 1930–2000."
Conference paper presented at the History of Education Society, Cities, Suburbs, and
Schools Project at Trinity College, Hartford, CT. http://digitalrepository.trincoll.edu/cssp_
papers/13.

Gutmann, Laurie. 2003. "Whose Concern Matters? Student Support and Project Concern."
Educational Studies senior research project, Trinity College, Hartford CT. http://digital
repository.trincoll.edu/cssp papers/17.

Hartford Courant. 1917. "Kicks on Schools in Wethersfield: Dissatisfaction Expressed at Parents' Meeting: City Gets Sons of Board Members." April 11. Page 11.

Hartford Public High School. 1882. Student records. Hartford Public High School Museum
and Archive.

Hartford Times. 1954. "New School Lines Offered by Thorne." April 8.

Hathaway, William. 1993. "How Are the Schools? Now It's Easy to Find Out," *The Hartford
Courant*, September 26, page J1.

Hughes, Devlin. 2009. *Designing Effective Google Maps for Social Change: A Case Study of
SmartChoices.* Cities, Suburbs, Schools Project at Trinity College. http://digitalrepository
.trincoll.edu/cssp_papers/8.

Kaminski, Sarah. 2002. "Magnet Schools: An Effective Solution to Sheff v O'Neill?" *Trinity
Papers.* 21:63–71.

Katz, Jacqueline. 2004. "Historical Memory and the Transformation of City and Suburban
Schools." Educational Studies senior research project, Trinity College, Hartford CT. http://
digitalrepository.trincoll.edu/cssp_papers/27.

Lawrence, Eric. 2002. "Teacher Suburbanization and the Diverging Discourse on Hartford
Public School Quality, 1950–1970." American Studies Senior Project, Trinity College,
Hartford. http://digitalrepository.trincoll.edu/cssp_papers/35.

MacDonald, David. 2005. "The Funding of Interdistrict Magnet Schools in Connecticut: A
Failed Approach to Addressing the Sheff vs. O'Neill Connecticut Supreme Court Ruling?"
Public Policy Studies graduate course paper, Trinity College, Hartford CT. http://digitalre-
pository.trincoll.edu/cssp_papers/16.

Merriam, Alexander R. 1903. *The Social Significance of the Smaller City.* Hartford, Conn.:
Hartford Seminary Press, reprinted in *The Hartford Courant*, July 21, 1903, p. 13.

Moore, Heather. 2005. "Private School Choice and Educational Outcomes in Metropolitan
Hartford." Cities, Suburbs, and Schools Project presentation, Trinity College, Hartford,
CT. http://digitalrepository.trincoll.edu/cssp_papers/36.

Nieves, Nivia, and Jack Dougherty. 2006. "Latino Politicians, Activists, and Parents: The
Challenge of Implementing City-Suburban Magnet Schools." Conference paper presented
at American Education Research Association, Cities, Suburbs, and Schools Project at Trinity College. http://digitalrepository.trincoll.edu/cssp_papers/30.

Orfield, Myron, and Thomas Luce. 2003. *Connecticut Metropatterns: A Regional Agenda for
Community and Prosperity in Connecticut.* Minneapolis, MN: Ameregis.

Pennington, Lis, Emily Steele, and Jack Dougherty. 2007. "A Political History of School Finance
Reform in Metropolitan Hartford, Connecticut, 1945–2005." Conference paper presented at
American Education Research Association, Cities, Suburbs, and Schools Project at Trinity Col-
lege, Hartford, CT. http://digitalrepository.trincoll.edu./cssp_papers/29.

Perkins, Kelli. 2004. "Public Schools and Private Real Estate Markets, 1940–2000." Educational Studies senior research project, Trinity College, Hartford, CT. http://digitalreposi-
tory.trincoll.edu/cssp_papers/28.

Price, Brittany. 2009. "The Usage of Maps in Facilitating Conversations with Stakeholders about Educational Desegregation in Hartford." Educational Studies senior research project, Trinity College, Hartford, CT. http://digitalrepository.trincoll.edu/cssp_papers/26.

Ramsay, Christina, Cintli Sanchez, Jesse Wanzer, and the Educ 308 Seminar with Professor Jack Dougherty. 2006. *Shopping for Homes and Schools: A Qualitative Study of West Hartford, Connecticut.* Hartford: Cities, Suburbs, and Schools Project at Trinity College. http://digital repository.trincoll.edu/cssp_papers/25.

Reynolds, Thomas C. 1994. "Magnet Schools and the Connecticut Experience." Public Policy master's thesis, Trinity College.

Ross, James. 1973. "Realty Bypassing Told by Resident." *The Hartford Courant.* June 21, p. 52.

Reuman, David. 2003. "Effects of an Inter-District Manget Program on Inter-Racial Attitudes at School." Conference paper presented at American Education Research Association. http://digitalrepository.trincoll.edu/cssp_papers/32.

Schofield, Molly. 2002. "Increasing Interracial Relationships." Educational Studies senior research project, Trinity College, Hartford, CT. http://digitalrepository.trincoll.edu/cssp_papers/24.

Shaw, Spencer. 2003. Oral history interview with Jacqueline Katz. City-Suburb Oral History Collection, Hartford Studies Project, Trinity College Library, Hartford, CT.

Sheff v. O'Neill. 1996. 238 *Connecticut* 1, 678 A. 2nd 1267.

Sullivan, Kevin B., and James A. Trostle. 2004. "Trinity College and the Learning Corridor: A Small, Urban Liberal Arts College Launches a Public Magnet School Campus." *Metropolitan Universities.* 15 (3):15–34.

U.S. Census Bureau. 2010. "Average Family Income in the Past 12 Months in 2009 Inflation-Adjusted Dollars." *American Community Survey 2009 (1–Year Estimates).* Retrieved from Social Explorer, Table SE:T59<http://www.SocialExplorer.com>, January 2011.

University of Connecticut Libraries Map and Geographic Information Center—MAGIC. 2010. "Federal HOLC 'Redlining' Interactive Map, Hartford area, 1937."<http://magic .lib.uconn.edu/otl/holc_mashup.html>.

Wanzer, Jesse, Heather Moore, and Jack Dougherty. 2008. "Race and Magnet School Choice: A Mixed-Methods Neighborhood Study in Urban Connecticut." Conference paper presented at American Education Research Association, Cities, Suburbs, and Schools Project at Trinity College. http://digitalrepository.trincoll.edu/cssp_papers/22.

Wetzler, Rebecca. 2006. "The Effects of Health, Mobility, and Socio-Economic Status Factors on Race Gap in Achievement." Psychology senior thesis, Trinity College, Hartford CT. http://digitalrepository.trincoll.edu/cssp_papers/20.

Williams, Jennifer. 2006. "The Unthinkable Remedy: The Proposed Metropolitan Hartford School District." Cities, Suburbs, and Schools Project presentation, Trinity College. http:// digitalrepository.trincoll.edu/cssp_papers/19.

Wilson, Tracey. 2010. "Taking Stock of High Ledge Homes and Restricted Covenants." *West Hartford Life.* 13 (2):36–37.

Winterbottom, Katherine Ellen. 1998. "Beneath the Veneer [racial discrimination in federally subsidized wartime suburban housing]." *The Spectator [West Hartford Historical Society newsletter].* Autumn: 1, 10–14.

Wright, Adelle. 2005. Oral history interview with Meredith Murphy and Aleesha Young. April 11. City-Suburb Oral History collection, Hartford Studies Project, Trinity College. http:// digitalrepository.trincoll.edu/cssp_papers/5.

Young, Aleesha. 2005. "Real Estate, Racial Change, and Bloomfield Schools in the 1960s and "'70s." Educational Studies senior research project, Trinity College, Hartford CT. http:// digitalrepository.trincoll.edu/cssp_papers/18.

7

The Puerto Rican Effect on Hispanic Residential Segregation

A Study of the Hartford and Springfield Metro Areas in National Perspective

Michael Paul Sacks

INTRODUCTION

Households of racial and ethnic minority groups are far from randomly distributed across a metropolitan area. Concentrated in some communities and absent from others, the geography of their residences can be a telling indicator of inequality. This is because place of residence in the United States is closely tied to a wide range of

> "economic and social resources such as affordable housing, quality schools, public safety, transportation, and recreational and social amenities.... Where people live also influences access to jobs that pay family wages, the likelihood that racial and ethnic groups will commingle in schools, places of worship, and commercial establishments—in short, the prospects for minority group integration." (Fischer and Tienda, 2006: 101)

Residential segregation from non-Hispanic whites (for brevity's sake, hereafter, referred to as whites) is, therefore, a measure of both a group's socioeconomic achievement as well as obstacles for future upward mobility (Charles, 2003: 197–199).

Recent scholarship on Hispanics shows the heterogeneity of this broad category and the importance of looking separately at subgroups with different national origin (Landale, Oropesa and Bradatan, 2006: 140). This chapter contributes to this literature with a focus on how concentrated Puerto Rican presence among Hispanics shapes the residential segregation of Hispanics for non-Hispanic whites. The research stems from an attempt to understand how the very high level of such residential segregation in the Springfield and Hartford metro areas might be connected to the unusual predominance of Puerto Ricans among the metro-area Hispanics.

EXPLAINING RESIDENTIAL SEGREGATION

Spatial assimilation theory predicts declining differences overtime between the residential locations of immigrants and native majority group members. Each successive generation is "more acculturated to the U.S. society" and uses growing economic resources to live in more ethnically diverse communities as compared with the first generation (South, Crowder and Chavez, 2005: 499; Iceland and Nelson, 2008: 742–743). This theory predicts that individuals with higher income and education and those with English-language proficiency will be more likely to seek entry into white neighborhoods and have greater success making such moves (ibid.).

In contrast is the segmented assimilation perspective, which emphasizes that "the host society offers uneven possibilities to different immigrant groups based on social factors such as race and SES" (Iceland and Nelson, 2008: 745). Prejudice and discrimination sustain group differences. Current conditions differ in important ways from past immigration flows, for new immigrant communities "flourish and replenish themselves" as result of continual influx of population and are "more racially distinctive than older immigrant groups" (South, Crowder and Chavez, 2005: 499). Moreover, globalization and deindustrialization result in very different economic opportunities for immigrant success than was the case in the past, and this too constrains social mobility (ibid. Veléz, Martin and Mendez, 2009: 122).

Consistent with the segmented assimilation perspective, perceived racial differences among Hispanics are likely to shape residential segregation. According to the 2000 census, Cubans overwhelmingly self-identified as white (84.4 percent), while nearly half of Puerto Ricans and Mexicans chose "other race" for themselves (Iceland and Nelson 2008, 745). Chowder, South and Cravez (2005, 514) found that darker skin color (based on interviewer coding) reduces the likelihood of moving into neighborhoods that are predominantly white. But they discover "skin color among Puerto Ricans is significantly stronger than the corresponding effect among Mexicans or Cubans." While Mexicans show a pattern consistent with the spatial assimilation theory, the authors conclude that "Puerto Ricans . . . are stymied by their dark skin color and may well be experiencing a 'second-generation decline' (and beyond) in their mobility patterns [Gans, 1992], perhaps reflecting their greater absorption into the predominantly African American underclass" (Chowder, South and Cravez, 2005: 516). In earlier research Massey and Bitterman (1985: 326) attributed the greater segregation of Puerto Ricans to the fact that "they are poorer and they are blacker."

Because Puerto Ricans have greatly predominated among the Hispanics who have settled in the Hartford, Connecticut, and Springfield, Massachusetts metro areas, these areas are particularly valuable for studying the distinctive impact of Puerto Ricans. This article begins with an overview of Puerto Rican population growth and dispersion in the United States and how the Hartford and Springfield metro areas fit into this broader pattern. Both metro areas had very high levels of residential segregation of Hispanics from whites. If the segregation could be attributed to the severe poverty of Hispanics in the metro areas, this would be consistent with the classic assimilation theory. Alternatively, the segmented assimilation perspective would predict that that residential segregation was more directly attributable to Puerto Rican predominance among the Hispanics. Such a "Puerto Rican effect" would remain evident after controlling for the influence of group poverty. Data for a broad spectrum of metro areas with varying Puerto Rican representation among the area Hispanics are used to test for this effect.

HARTFORD AND SPRINGFIELD IN NATIONAL PERSPECTIVE

Separated only by a state boundary, the upper edge of the Hartford metro area adjoins that of Springfield. The eponymous central cities of these metro areas are located about 25 miles apart. In 2000 the Springfield metro area had a population of 592,000; the Hartford metro area had about twice the population, ranking 51 in size among all U.S. metro areas. These metro areas have received relatively scant scholarly attention compared with much larger metro areas. They are, however, areas marked by exceptional Puerto Rican influence due to the size of the Puerto Rican population and the very high proportion of Puerto Ricans among area Hispanics. The distinctiveness of Hartford and Springfield can be appreciated by looking at these metro areas in the broader national context.

Puerto Ricans are only a small proportion of the total population of the United States. According to the 2000 census, 10 percent of Hispanics in mainland metropolitan areas (all references, hereafter, are to the mainland population) were Puerto Rican, and Puerto Ricans comprised just 1.5 percent of all metro-area residents. Metro areas like Hartford and Springfield have become more significant areas of Puerto Rican settlement with the overall growth and geographic shift in the Puerto Rican population of the mainland United States during the past 60 years. In 1950 there were about a quarter million Puerto Ricans in the mainland United States. They were overwhelmingly (81 percent) concentrated in New York. By 1980 their number had grown to over 2 million, with the majority outside the New York metro area. By 2000 New York still had by far the largest Puerto Rican population (840,000), but this shrank to a small portion of the overall 3.4 million Puerto Ricans on the mainland (Cruz, 1998: 4; Baker, 2002: 45; Macisco, Jr., 1968; Guzmán, 2001; Rodríguez, n.d.: 9). Since 1980 Puerto Ricans have shifted away from older areas of settlement to small cities; Massachusetts and Connecticut have been important destinations (Whalen, 2005: 39; Acosta-Belén and Santiago, 2006: 86–89).

In 2000 in addition to New York, there were three other metro areas that had at least 100,000 Puerto Ricans: Philadelphia (160,076), Chicago (152,045) and Orlando (139,898). Puerto Ricans in large metro areas, however, tend to be a relatively small proportion of the metro Hispanics. Just one of every three Hispanics in the New York metro area was Puerto Rican in 2000. In 47 other metro areas the Puerto

Rican share among Hispanics was larger than in New York. Topping this list was Springfield, Massachusetts, with 83 percent Puerto Rican among Hispanics. The 65 thousand Puerto Ricans in the Springfield metro area comprised a greater share (10.4 percent) of the *total* population than did Puerto Ricans in New York (9 percent). Indeed, the share of Puerto Ricans in the total population of Springfield was greater than in all but one other U.S. metro area.[1]

In 2000, the metro areas just below Springfield in the percentage Puerto Rican among Hispanics were Jamestown, New York (77.0 percent), Waterbury, Connecticut (75.0 percent), and Hartford, Connecticut (73.1 percent). In both Jamestown and Waterbury, however, the number of Puerto Ricans was relatively small (4,542 and 19,687, respectively) compared with 83,000 in Hartford. The Hartford and Springfield metro areas clearly stand out in the weight of their Puerto Rican populations, making it likely that these locations would reveal any distinctive impact of Puerto Ricans.

PUERTO RICANS IN HARTFORD AND SPRINGFIELD METRO-AREA CITIES

Cities within the Hartford and Springfield metro areas had especially high concentrations of Puerto Ricans.[2] As in other metro areas, selective population movement to the suburbs altered the ethnic composition of cities, and suburbanization has also been shaped by the changing ethnic mix of cities. The political ramifications of Puerto Rican demographic strength were most clear within the city of Hartford. But as this section shows, this city was rather unique.

In 2000 over 80 percent of Hispanics in the city of Hartford were Puerto Rican; Puerto Ricans comprised nearly one-third of the city population. In 2001 Hartford elected Eddie Perez as its first Hispanic mayor and the first Hispanic mayor of a state capital. Perez was born in Corozal, Puerto Rico, and came to Hartford at age 12 in 1969 (City of Hartford Government, n.d.).

This mayoral change culminated a long period of Puerto Rican political mobilization, but it also had a significant demographic underpinning (Cruz, 1998: 174–5). The city of Hartford experienced explosive Hispanic population growth combined with an especially sharp exodus of non-Hispanic whites. In Hartford the shift toward minority predominance came early. By 1970 the Hartford school system was 45 percent black. The city elected the first black mayor in New England, Thirman L. Milner, in 1981 (Grant and Grant, 1986: 78). In 1980 61,000 whites comprised 44 percent of the Hartford population. There were 45,000 blacks, greatly outnumbering the 28,000 Hispanics. White flight was steady and quite extreme: During the 1990s the white share of the city's population declined more than in any other central city in the 102 largest metropolitan areas of the country (Frey, 2003: 167). The result was that by 2000 there was a complete reversal of the 1980 group hierarchy, leaving the city with a small white minority (21.6 thousand) and more Hispanics

(49 thousand) than African Americans (46 thousand). Conditions were particularly propitious for Puerto Ricans to take political leadership of the city.

In his analysis of Puerto Rican involvement in Hartford city politics, Cruz (1998: 5) notes that "[d]emographic concentration facilitated ethnic political mobilization, promoting the development of leaders and organizational efforts and acting as a counterweight to the forces of poverty and marginality." Also important was the fact that Hartford was a medium-sized city, which afforded "easy access to city hall, proximity to elected officials, an accessible media, and small electoral districts that allow direct contact with large numbers of voters even when financial resources are scarce." Puerto Rican influence could be far greater than in cities like Chicago and New York, where Puerto Ricans were found in much greater numbers (Cruz, 1998: 159). Even in Hartford, however, Cruz (2006: 243) notes that just 15 percent of municipal officials were Hispanic, very much lower than their 41 percent share of the population.

Demographic conditions that appear to be of key significance to the political empowerment of Hispanics in Hartford have yet to occur elsewhere in the Springfield and Hartford metro areas. While Hispanics had high representation in the population of other cities, nowhere else did they reach a plurality of the population nor were whites reduced much below a majority of the total population.

With a total population of 157,000 in 1990, the city of Springfield was very close in size to Hartford, but Springfield at this time was still nearly two-thirds white. In the decade that followed Springfield population loss was far smaller than that of Hartford, and by 2000 whites were still nearly the majority of the population. Though they outnumbered African Americans, Hispanics were just over a quarter of the population, much lower than in Hartford.

A similar pattern was evident in two other cities in these metro areas with a particularly large number of Hispanics: Holyoke, Massachusetts, and New Britain, Connecticut. The 2000 census showed that 36 percent of Holyoke's total population (40,000) was Puerto Rican—the highest percentage Puerto Rican of any city in mainland United States (Hartford, with 33 percent Puerto Rican, ranked second) (ePodunk, n.d.). But African Americans were a very small part of Holyoke's population (3 percent), leaving whites in a clear majority in 2000.

New Britain has had a dramatic surge in Puerto Ricans, with their number rising from 10.3 thousand in 1990 to 15.7 thousand in 2000. In the 1990s New Britain was attracting far more Puerto Ricans than the city of Hartford. By 2000, however, whites in New Britain still comprised 59 percent of the population, African Americas were 11 percent and Hispanics were just over 27 percent (up from 16 percent in 1990).

Thus, in these four cities of the Hartford and Springfield metro area with the largest Hispanic populations, Hispanics outnumbered African Americans but, with the exception of the city of Hartford, they remained a small part of the population relative to whites. Only in Hartford did Puerto Ricans gain clear political prominence. There is no question, however, about the very significant demographic weight of Puerto Ricans in these cities and the metro areas as a whole. The areas also shared a similar economic fate that has had profound consequences for the Hispanic population.

HISPANIC VERSUS WHITE
DISPERSION ACROSS THE METRO AREA

The eponymous central cities of the two metro areas have faced severe economic decline. This was particularly evident in Hartford. White exit from Hartford may have created greater political opportunities for Puerto Ricans, but this empowerment, at least up through the 1990s, was of limited value in coping with economic decline (see Cruz, 1998: 208–214). The poverty level of the city of Hartford in 2000 exceeded those of every other major city in the United States with the sole exception of Brownsville, Texas. A variety of studies comparing the central cities of U.S. metro areas show Hartford consistently at or just above the very bottom on indices of economic well being in 1990 and in 2000 (Vey, 2007: 71; Wright and Montiel, 2007; Lewis Mumford Center, n.d.).

Economic decline was closely linked to the extreme erosion of Hartford's population. In 1950 the city population peaked at 177,000; by 2000 there were only 122,000 residents. During the 1990s Hartford's population fell by 13 percent—a decline that exceeded every other comparably sized city in the United States (Glaeser and Shapiro, 2003: 18–19). In the same decade the city of Springfield also lost population, although it was down only 3.1 percent.

Hartford's suburbs, by contrast, were growing. As was the case throughout the nation, whites heading to suburbia were increasingly joined by Hispanics and African Americans (Guzmán, 2001; Wiese, 2004; Suro and Singer, 2002). In 1990 most Hispanics (55 percent) in the Hartford metro area were living in the city of Hartford. Hispanics dispersed widely across the metro area, and ten years later only a minority (43 percent) remained in Hartford. In both the Springfield and Hartford metro areas Hispanics increased their share of the population in nearly every town and city.[3]

Whites were also geographically mobile, but in a way that often reestablished rather than mitigated residential separation from Hispanics. Indeed, in the Springfield and Hartford metro areas the two groups were moving in diametrically opposite directions. Where there was strong Hispanic growth, whites were most likely to be leaving. The greatest white population growth was in areas with the least Hispanic growth.[4] Hispanic growth centered on large towns or cities. Whites, in contrast, tended to sprawl outward from the population centers to the smaller towns.

The differences between whites and Hispanics were especially clear from looking at just those cities or towns in the metro areas where there was a decline of one thousand or more whites in the period from 1990 to 2000 (see Table 7.1). Over many prior decades Hispanics favored residency in these towns and cities, so that by 1990 these locations accounted for 95 percent of the metro-area Hispanics. In contrast, by 1990 nearly half of the whites were already residing elsewhere in the metro area in both Springfield and Hartford.

The top half of Table 7.1 shows the Hartford metro-area and the bottom half shows the Springfield metro area. Whites were clearly exiting from towns and cities that tended to be comparatively large in these metro areas (the median size town or city in these metro areas had a population of about 11 to 12 thousand in 1990).

Table 7.1. Towns or Cities Losing 1,000 or More Whites in the Hartford and Springfield Metro Areas, 1990–2000

	Total Pop. 1990	Population Change, 1990–2000		
		White	Hispanic	Black
Hartford Metro Area				
Hartford	139,739	–20,937	5,123	–4,140
New Britain	75,491	–14,322	6,854	2,320
East Hartford	50,452	–12,527	4,546	5,622
Windsor	27,817	–3,707	452	3,230
Manchester	51,618	–3,680	2,350	2,896
Bristol	60,640	3,615	1,514	627
Vernon	29,841	–3,227	405	635
Bloomfield	19,483	–2,987	128	2,884
Enfield	45,532	–2,875	652	1,440
Windham	22,039	–2,851	2,815	545
West Hartford	60,110	2,492	2,099	1,903
Middletown	42,762	–2,352	874	1,043
Mansfield	21,103	–1,575	320	414
Winchester	11,524	–1,306	195	89
Newington	29,208	–1,259	467	252
Springfield Metro Area				
Springfield	156,983	–25,578	14,815	3,322
Holyoke	43,74	–7,011	2,912	42
Chicopee	56,62	–5,715	2,740	342
Amherst	35,28	–2,359	490	469
West Springfield	27,57	–1,349	791	285
Northampton	29,289	–1,260	317	201

Source: U.S. Census Bureau, Census 1990 STF3 and Census 2000 SF4.

What is particularly notable here (compare columns 3 and 4) is how the white population losses were so consistently associated with growth in the number of Hispanics (and also African Americans, with the exception of Hartford). Whites were moving toward areas of greater ethnic and economic homogeneity. Hispanic growth tended to be greatest in areas where there were already a large number of Hispanics living.

One factor shaping choice of residence is the ability to afford living in the community. Housing is just one of the costs that a poor family must consider. Subsidies provided under the federal Section 8 Rental Voucher Program have increased suburban residency of the poor, but Goetz (2003: 8) notes that "such a voucher does not put a bus line in front of the building, relocate the community college or affordable day care nearby, and bring along the family's network of friends and relatives for emotional and material support." Differences in locational choices are shaped by substantial group differences in socioeconomic resources.

Although residents of the Hartford metro area were wealthier than those in Springfield, this wealth did not seem to have much of an impact on the differences among groups (see Table 7.2). Hispanics were clearly far worse off than whites, with African Americans in an intermediate position. Compared to whites, Hispanics earned only 47 percent of the income of whites in the Hartford metro area and 43 percent in the Springfield area. There was even greater contrast in the figures for those below twice the federal poverty level[5] and for the proportion of children raised in female-headed households. Only about a quarter of Hispanics owned their homes as compared with three-quarters of whites—a factor that contributed to Hispanics being far more likely than whites to change residence within the prior five years. Added to these socioeconomic differences was the fact that the groups differed markedly in their age structure. With a median age of about 40, whites were far less likely to have young children at home than were Hispanics, whose median age was in the low twenties.

It is significant to note that Puerto Ricans differed somewhat more from whites than did Hispanics as a whole (who, of course, were predominantly Puerto Rican). In other words, Puerto Ricans taken separately were somewhat poorer, more likely to have female-headed households, less likely to own homes and had a lower median age. As is shown by data for the nation, Puerto Ricans were in a particularly

Table 7.2. Measures of Racial/Ethnic Differences between the Hartford and Springfield Metro Areas, 2000

	Median Household Income	% Below Twice Poverty Level*	% of Children In Female-Headed Households**	% Owning a Home	% In Same House As In 1995***	Median Age
Hartford Metro Area						
Total population	$52,188	19.7	22.0	70.2	58.3	37.4
Whites	$56,963	12.9	11.9	79.1	63.0	40.2
Hispanics	$27,050	54.5	51.7	26.2	35.2	24.4
Puerto Ricans	$24,454	59.1	57.0	22.2	35.3	23.7
African Americans	$35,103	38.4	52.0	43.7	47.3	30.1
Springfield Metro Area						
Total population	$40,740	29.1	28.5	65.5	57.0	35.8
White	$44,727	21.0	16.8	74.5	62.0	39.2
Hispanic	$19,238	67.8	57.5	23.3	35.1	22.1
Puerto Ricans	$18,022	70.3	60.0	21.1	34.8	21.9
African Americans	$29,075	46.3	55.0	43.6	47.8	27.9

*Among those for whom income known, the % in households with less than twice the official poverty level.
**Percentage of children under 18 living with a female householder, no husband present.
***Percentage of the population age 5 and older living in the same house as in 1995.
Source: U.S. Census 2000, SF4.

disadvantaged economic position among major groups of Hispanic origin other than Dominicans (Ramirez, 2004; Reimers, 2006). Hernández (2002: 162–4) suggests that Dominicans face more severe racial discrimination than Puerto Ricans, who at least have U.S. citizenship in their favor.

The overall economic situation of Hispanics in the Hartford and Springfield metro area was clearly related to the predominance of Puerto Ricans among the area Hispanics. Was the residential separation of Hispanics and whites due simply to group economic differences or was it connected in some other way to the fact that most of the Hispanics were Puerto Ricans? Did the distinctive Puerto Rican composition of Hispanics lead Hartford and Springfield to have Hispanic residential segregation that was very different from other metro areas? To address these questions necessitated comparing Hartford and Springfield with other areas, and this required using a measure of residential segregation that more readily permitted comparisons across metro areas.

RESIDENTIAL SEGREGATION BASED ON CENSUS TRACTS

The ethnic composition of cities or towns is important because of the way in which schools and other community resources are heavily based on these boundaries. It is common, however, to measure the degree of residential segregation by census tract, which averaged 4,200 residents in year 2000. The index of dissimilarity is among the most widely used measures of residential segregation, and often the sole measure used (see, for example, Iceland and Nelson [2008: 748] and Velez, Martin and Mendez [2009]). An important virtue of the index is that it is uninfluenced by the relative size of the two groups being compared—a problem with measures of exposure (Iceland 2002: 120). For these reasons the index of dissimilarity is used in the sections below. In comparing two groups, the index varies from 0 to 100 and can be interpreted as the percentage of one group that would have to move to a different census tract in order for that group to be equally represented in all census tracts of the metro area.[6] If, for example, Hispanics comprised 30 percent of the total metro-area population, the measure shows the percentage of Hispanics that would have to change residence in order for every tract to be 30 percent Hispanic.

Using census tract data for all metropolitan areas, Logan, Stults, and Farley (2004: 6) found that residential segregation of whites from blacks was much higher than the segregation of Hispanics from whites. This difference lessened after 1980, but even in 2000 the white/black index of dissimilarity (65.2) was still considerably above the Hispanic/white index (51.6).[7] In the Hartford metro area in 2000, however, Hispanic/white segregation was at the same level as segregation of whites from blacks, and in the Springfield metro area the black/white segregation was substantially lower than Hispanic/white segregation.

Could Hartford and Springfield metro areas have differed from the overall national trend because of Puerto Rican predominance among the Hispanics? Consistent with classic assimilation theory, the connection seemed plausible if Puerto Rican predominance was associated with an especially large gap in the income of Hispanics relative to whites, and, as noted above, income in turn shaped residential options or choices. Past studies have shown that minority group members with higher income, educational attainment, and English-language skills are less likely to be residentially segregated from whites (Iceland and Nelson, 2008: 745). Residential segregation on the basis of economic and educational status has risen sharply since 1970 (Massey, Rothwell and Domina, 2009: 81–85). Prior research also shows that segregation of Hispanics from whites was highest in Northeast, a region where Puerto Ricans are especially impoverished (Baker, 2002; Jargowsky and Yang, 2006; Santiago and Galster, 1995; Tienda, 1989).

The segmented assimilation perspective points to a more direct role of racial discrimination. Massey and Denton (1993: 151) report that Puerto Ricans were more segregated from whites than are other Hispanic groups and attribute this to "the fact that many [Puerto Ricans] are of African origin. Although white Puerto Ricans achieve rates of spatial assimilation that are comparable with those found among other ethnic groups, those of African or racially mixed origins experience markedly lower ability to convert socioeconomic attainments into contact with whites." South, Crowder and Chavez (2005: 514) find that the dark skin color (as judged by interviewers) among Puerto Ricans was a significant impediment to moving into white neighborhoods. Dark-skinned Mexicans or Cubans are less stigmatized, because they, unlike Puerto Ricans, may be more likely to be characterized as "dark-skinned Latinos, not African Americans, and thus are less likely to experience housing discrimination." Using metro-area data from the 2000 census, Iceland and Nelson (2008: 752) report much lower segregation of whites from *white* Hispanics than from black Hispanics, with segregation from other race Hispanics falling between the two. In contrast to what they faced in their countries of origin, many Hispanic immigrants have been surprised by the extent to which "their national or ethnic identities marked a racial difference in the United States. . . . [T]he category Hispanic has sometimes seemed to offer an escape, an ethnicity rather than a race, and a clear alternative to being black" (Hoffnung-Garskof, 2008: 114; see also Aranda 2007: 120–123).

The racial categorization of Puerto Ricans is also evident among other Hispanics. Smith (2006: 34) finds that first-generation Mexicans in New York "lament and fear the social distress that Puerto Ricans as a group are thought to experience. In imagining a different future for their own children, Mexicans use the readily available American tool, the immigrant analogy, to posit a racialized difference between themselves and Puerto Ricans." Mexican youth distance themselves from what they view as the denigrated status of Puerto Ricans and African Americans in New York through practices ("transnational life") which emphasize their affinity with the community in Mexico from which their families originated (ibid., 163–4; see also Wilson and Traub, 2006: 210, note 13).

To test whether there was a distinct "Puerto Rican effect" on the residential segregation of whites from Hispanics, it is important to consider how much of this segregation can be explained simply by the lower income for Hispanics. Lower income among Hispanics is closely associated with a higher representation of Puerto Ricans among Hispanics. Multiple regression analysis makes it possible to examine the influence of the percentage Puerto Rican apart from or controlling for the impact of the income gap between Hispanics and whites (Blalock, 1960: 328).

Metro areas chosen for consideration included those which, at a minimum, had sufficient Puerto Rican representation for them to be a clearly important component of the Hispanic population, likely to influence the way Hispanics were perceived by whites. This is a difficult figure to judge, but a reasonable threshold seemed to be no fewer than two Puerto Ricans out of every five Hispanics. Forty-one metro areas qualified in the year 2000. Three of these, however, had fewer than 2,000 Puerto Ricans (and a maximum of 4,069 Hispanics) and were excluded because these low numbers were likely to make the measure of dissimilarity unreliable. The remaining 38 metro areas are shown in Table 7.3.

The metro areas are listed in ascending order of their degree of residential segregation of whites from Hispanics (column 1). Hartford and Springfield were just below the top, ranking 3 and 4. These two metro areas were among those with both the highest percentage Puerto Rican among Hispanics (column 2) and the lowest income of Hispanics relative to whites (column 3).

Segregation of whites from Hispanics was closely related to *both* the relative income of Puerto Ricans and Puerto Rican predominance among Hispanics. The higher the percentage Puerto Rican among Hispanics in the metro area, the higher was the level of segregation of Hispanics from whites (r = .71). The lower the income of Hispanics compared to whites, the higher was the segregation of whites from Hispanics (r = -.72). Not surprisingly, the share of Puerto Ricans among Hispanics in a metro area had a close inverse relationship to the income of Hispanics compared to whites (r = -.58). Multiple regression analysis showed that both variables had a strong independent influence on the segregation of whites from Hispanics. (Using the Hispanic/white index of dissimilarity as the dependent variable, the beta coefficients in the regression equation were .469 for the Hispanic/white income ratio and .460 for the percent Puerto Rican among Hispanics, both statistically significant at the .01 level.[8]) In other words, even when the influence of lower income of Hispanics relative to whites was controlled, the percentage Puerto Ricans among Hispanics still showed a statistically significant association with residential segregation of whites from Hispanics.

Finally, Table 7.3 points to the possible importance of regional differences. All four of the Florida metro areas had relatively low levels of white/Hispanic residential segregation. Florida has had a recent surge of Puerto Ricans, who were more middle class and professional than is typical of Puerto Rican migrants (Whalen, 2005: 40). By contrast, 9 of 16 metro areas with the highest segregation of Hispanics from whites were located in Connecticut or Massachusetts. The influence of region is something that requires further study.

Table 7.3. Metro Areas With 40 Percent Puerto Rican Among Hispanics, 2000

Metropolitan Area	Index of Dissimilarity			% Puerto Rican among Hispanics	Hispanic/ White Income Ratio*	Number of Hispanics	Number of Puerto Ricans
	White/ Hispanic	White/ Black	Difference				
1 Reading, PA	72	61	-11	61%	0.51	36,357	22,038
2 Bridgeport, CT	67	53	-13	67%	0.59	56,914	38,307
3 **Hartford, CT**	**64**	**64**	**0**	**73%**	**0.47**	**113,540**	**82,592**
4 **Springfield, MA**	**63**	**49**	**-14**	**83%**	**0.43**	**74,277**	**61,310**
5 Allentown-Bethlehem-Easton, PA	62	74	11	66%	0.60	50,607	33,528
6 Lancaster, PA	62	64	2	72%	0.59	26,742	19,341
7 Waterbury, CT	61	77	16	75%	0.52	26,245	19,687
8 Lowell, MA-NH	61	77	17	61%	0.46	17,242	10,508
9 Philadelphia, PA-NJ	60	57	-3	62%	0.52	258,606	160,076
10 Worcester, MA-CT	60	38	-21	64%	0.48	36,248	23,349
11 New Haven-Meriden, CT	60	55	-5	65%	0.55	53,331	34,509
12 York, PA	58	51	-7	61%	0.66	11,296	6,874
13 Cleveland-Lorain-Elyria, OH	58	64	6	62%	0.66	74,862	46,117
14 Brockton, MA	58	34	-24	56%	0.57	9,524	5,311
15 Buffalo-Niagara Falls, NY	56	63	7	68%	0.52	33,967	22,056
16 New Bedford, MA	56	71	15	68%	0.39	10,395	7,021
17 Harrisburg-Lebanon-Carlisle, PA	55	65	10	62%	0.55	19,557	12,199

18	Trenton, NJ	54	53	-1	41%	0.64	33,898	13,865
19	Rochester, NY	54	58	4	67%	0.53	47,559	32,078
20	Utica-Rome, NY	54	47	-7	63%	0.55	8,125	5,152
21	Atlantic-Cape May, NJ	53	49	-4	49%	0.73	34,107	16,640
22	Jamestown, NY	53	63	11	77%	0.58	5,901	4,542
23	Erie, PA	49	47	-2	58%	0.58	6,126	3,538
24	Vineland-Millville-Bridgeton, NJ	49	69	20	67%	0.69	27,823	18,520
25	Youngstown-Warren, OH	49	54	6	55%	0.73	10,743	5,938
26	New London-Norwich, CT-RI	48	51	3	59%	0.71	13,770	8,155
27	Syracuse, NY	46	51	5	52%	0.56	15,112	7,912
28	Wilmington-Newark, DE-MD	45	57	12	42%	0.66	27,599	11,566
29	Daytona Beach, FL	43	59	15	46%	0.87	31,648	14,577
30	Fitchburg-Leominster, MA	43	66	23	66%	0.61	11,838	7,820
31	Albany-Schenectady-Troy, NY	41	64	23	56%	0.60	23,798	13,306
32	Orlando, FL	41	69	29	52%	0.74	271,627	139,898
33	Newburgh, NY-PA	40	64	24	49%	0.86	42,053	20,507
34	Monmouth-Ocean, NJ	38	44	6	40%	0.81	63,813	25,797
35	Binghamton, NY	37	61	24	47%	0.50	4,495	2,109
36	Dutchess County, NY	33	54	20	46%	0.82	18,060	8,239
37	Ocala, FL	32	67	35	45%	0.87	15,616	6,597
38	Melbourne-Titusville-Palm Bay, FL	25	73	48	41%	0.89	21,970	9,111

*Median household income in 1999.
Source: Lewis Mumford Center; U.S. Census 2000, SF 4.

IMMIGRANT VILIFICATION AND
THE PUERTO RICAN EFFECT

Hispanics in the Hartford and Springfield metro areas were overwhelmingly Puerto Rican. These metro areas also had an especially high residential segregation of whites from Hispanics and very low income of Hispanics relative to whites. Regression analysis of data for 38 metro areas showed that the effect of Puerto Rican presence among Hispanics on Hispanic/white segregation cannot be explained away by the lower income that is also associated with Puerto Rican presence. In other words, a distinct Puerto Rican effect is demonstrated. The argument proposed here is that as Puerto Rican presence among Hispanics rises from moderate (40 percent) to high levels (60 to 80 percent) there is increased racialization of Hispanics. Consequently Hispanics in the metro area face prejudice and discrimination that promotes their residential separation from whites. This supports the segmented assimilation perspective.

The finding that residential segregation was in part explained by the relative income of whites and Hispanics provides some support for the spatial assimilation theory. Massey, Rothwell and Domina (2009: 87), however, have noted that present trends suggest that "racial and socioeconomic segregation will become more important in combination than apart." Local zoning regulations, for example, can effectively restrict the density of residential construction, in turn keeping housing prices high and the supply of affordable housing low. Such "restrictive zoning . . . is associated with higher levels of both racial and class segregation" (Massey, Rothwell and Domina, 2009: 88).

During the 1990s the substantial growth of the overall Hispanic population and the growing dispersion of Puerto Ricans across metro areas have surely contributed to a reduction in the average Puerto Rican share of metro-area Hispanic population. This trend is evident in the 38 metro areas with relatively high Puerto Rican presence among Hispanics. Between 1990 and 2000 the Hispanics who were not Puerto Rican increased by 91 percent, while the number of Puerto Ricans grew by only 58 percent. Data for the United States as a whole show that on average the metro-area residential segregation of Puerto Ricans from whites declined slightly between 1990 and 2000 (Logan, 2002: 9; Vélez, Martin and Mendez, 2009: 129). This decline might be explained by mitigated racialization of Puerto Ricans as they locate within a widening population of Hispanics (Santiago and Galster, 1995: 384). The decline in segregation has brought the average Puerto Rican residential segregation from whites closer to what has been a lower residential segregation of whites from all Hispanics (largely unchanged between 1990 and 2000).

Such progress for Puerto Ricans may now be countered if they are caught in the changed perception of immigrants. Massey (2008) makes a compelling case that immigration policy over the past two decades has had a detrimental impact on Hispanics. The situation has worsened considerably as a result of the response to the September 11, 2001 attack: "The arrival of growing numbers of dark-skinned immigrants over the past several decades has triggered a new round of racial formation in the United States. Latinos, in particular, have increasingly been framed as a racialized 'other' whose presence threatens the culture, values, living standards—indeed, the very existence—of the United States. In keeping with this framing of social reality, discrimination against Latinos has risen to equal or exceed that directed against African Americans (Charles, 2003), with discriminatory treatment being triggered by foreign accent, appearance, and skin color rather than class" (Massey, 2008: 102). Recent more vigorous enforcement efforts against immigrants have profoundly affected Hispanics. The 2007 National Survey of Latinos showed that 33 percent expressed the view that the situation of Latinos had worsened over the past year; this rose to 50 percent in the 2008 survey (Lopez and Minushkin, 2008).

How will Puerto Ricans fare with these changes? A continuing decline in their representation among Hispanics may lessen the extent to which Puerto Rican racialization exceeds that of many other Hispanics. A decline in the distinction between Puerto Ricans and other Hispanics, however, may no longer be advantageous in overcoming discrimination. Indeed, Puerto Ricans may perceive greater incentive to distance themselves from immigrants, despite the likelihood that such a stance is counterproductive. In her examination of Puerto Rican/Mexican relations, Pérez (2004: 175) underscores the perils long associated with such distancing. Puerto Ricans' claim that their citizenship entitles them to preferential treatment "erects barriers of exclusion that prevent Puerto Ricans from seeing their shared location with *mejicanos* and Mexican Americans in Chicago's racialized political economy." Puerto Ricans could find themselves doubly disadvantaged by both lingering racialization and a far more negative immigrant categorization that is also difficult to escape.

NOTES

This is a reprint of a previous article: Sacks, Michael. 2011. "The Puerto Rican Effect on Hispanic Residential Segregation." *Latino Studies* 9(1):87–105.

The author wishes to thank Theresa Morris for assistance with the statistical methodology and two anonymous referees for their constructive comments on a prior version. The paper was originally presented at the Meeting of the Puerto Rican Studies Association, October 1–4, 2008, San Juan, Puerto Rico.

1. Unless otherwise noted, all figures in this section and below are drawn from the U.S. Census 2000, STF1.

2. Further relevant background on the Hartford and Springfield can be found in Black (2009), Grant and Grant (1986), Bauer (1975), Weaver (1982) and Glasser (1997).

3. Such population dispersion was also occurring on national scale: "Between 1970 and 2000 Puerto Ricans gravitated to the South, moved within the Northeast, maintained their presence in the Midwest, and were found in every state of the union. Migration which used to be primarily aimed at New York City now flows directly to other parts of the country" (Acosta-Belén and Santiago, 2006, 86–87).

4. This was calculated from data on the change in the number of whites and the number of Hispanics between 1990 and 2000 in the 58 towns and cities of the Hartford Metro area and the 28 towns and cities in the Springfield metro area. The correlation between white population change and Hispanic population change was -.89 for Hartford and -.98 for Springfield.

5. Given the high cost of living in the urban areas of the Northeast, below *twice* the poverty level seems a more appropriate standard of economic hardship.

6. The measure is equal to half the sum of the absolute differences between the distributions of the two groups being compared across all census tracts of the metro area.

7. The figures represent "the national averages for levels of minority-white segregation . . . , weighted by the number of minority-group members in the metropolitan area, for metropolitan areas with more than 2,500 minority-group members" (Logan, Stults, and Farley, 2004, 6–7).

8. The r square was .67. Multicollinearity was not a problem here, as shown by the tolerance statistic of .518.

REFERENCES

Acosta-Belén, Edna, and Carlos E. Santiago. 2006. *Puerto Ricans in the United States: A Contemporary Portrait*. Boulder, CO: Lynne Rienner Publishers.

Aranda, Elizabeth M. 2007. *Emotional Bridges to Puerto Rico: Migration, Return Migration and the Struggles of Incorporation*. Lanham, MD: Rowman & Littlefield.

Baker, Susan S. 2002. *Mainland Puerto Rican Poverty.* Philadelphia, PA: Temple University Press.

Bauer, Frank. 1975. *At the Crossroads: Springfield, Massachusetts, 1636–1975.* Springfield, MA: U.S.A. Bicentennial Committee of Springfield, Inc.

Black, Timothy. 2009. *When a Heart Turns Rock Solid: The Lives of Three Puerto Rican Brothers On and Off the Streets.* New York: Pantheon Books.

Blalock, Hubert M. *Social Statistics.* New York: McGraw-Hill Book Company, 1960.

Charles, Camille Zubrinsky. 2003. "The Dynamics of Racial Residential Segregation." *Annual Review of Sociology* 29: 167–207.

City of Hartford Government, n.d. "About Hartford's Mayor." (http://www.hartford.gov/government/mayor/biography.asp), accessed on June 9, 2009.

Cruz, José E. 1998. *Identity & Power: Puerto Rican Politics & the Challenge of Ethnicity*. Philadelphia, PA: Temple University Press.

Cruz, José E. 2006. "Latino Politics in Connecticut: Between Political Representation and Policy Responsiveness." In *Latinos in New England*, ed. Andrés Torres, 237–252. Philadelphia, PA: Temple University Press.

ePodunk. n.d. "Puerto Rican Ancestry by City." (http://www.epodunk.com/ancestry/Puerto-Rican.html), accessed on June 9, 2009.

Fischer, Mary J., and Marta Tienda. 2006. "Redrawing Spatial Color Lines: Hispanic Metropolitan Dispersal, Segregation, and Economic Opportunity." In *Hispanics and the Future of America*, eds. Marta Tienda and Faith Mitchell, 100–137. Washington, D.C.: The National Academies Press.

Frey, William H. 2003 Melting Pot Suburbs: A Study of Suburban Diversity. In *Redefining Urban & Suburban America: Evidence from Census 2000, Volume 1,* eds. Bruce Katz and Robert E. Lang, 155–179. Washington, D.C.: Brookings Institution Press.

Gans, Herbert. 1992. "Second Generation Decline: Scenarios for the Economic and Ethnic Futures of Post-1965 American Immigrants." *Ethnic and Racial Studies* 2: 1–20.

Glaeser, Edward L., and Jesse M. Shapiro. 2003. City Growth: Which Place Grew and Why. In *Redefining Urban & Suburban America: Evidence from Census 2000, Volume 1*, eds. Bruce Katz and Robert E. Lang, 13–32. Washington, D.C.: Brookings Institution Press.

Glasser, Ruth. 1997. *Aquí Me Quedo: Puerto Ricans in Connecticut.* Middletown, CT: Connecticut Humanities Council.

Goetz, Edward G. 2003. *Clearing the Way: Deconcentrating the Poor in Urban America.* Washington, D.C.: The Urban Institute Press.

Grant, Ellsworth S., and Marion Hepburn Grant. 1986. *The City of Hartford, 1784–1984: An Illustrated History.* Hartford, CT: Connecticut Historical Society.

Guzmán, Betsy. 2001. "The Hispanic Population: Census 2000 Brief." Washington, D.C.: U.S. Census Bureau.

Hernández, Ramona. 2002. *The Mobility of Workers Under Advanced Capitalism: Dominican Migration to the United States.* New York: Columbia University Press.

Hoffnung-Garskof, Jesse. 2008. *A Tale of Two Cities: Santo Domingo and New York After 1950.* Princeton, NJ: Princeton University Press.

Iceland, John. 2002. *Racial and Ethnic Segregation in the United States: 1980–2000.* Washington, D.C.: U.S. Census Bureau.

Iceland, John, and Kyle Anne Nelson. 2008. "Hispanic Segregation in Metropolitan America: Exploring the Multiple Forms of Spatial Assimilation." *American Sociological Review* 73: 741–765.

Jargowsky, Paul A., and Rebecca Yang. 2006. "The 'Underclass' Revisited: A Social Problem in Decline." *Journal of Urban Affairs* 28: 55–70.

Landale, Nancy S., R. Salvador Oroposa, and Christina Bradatan. 2006. "Hispanic Families in the United States: Family Structure and Process in an Era of Family Change." In *Hispanics and the Future of America*, eds. Marta Tienda and Faith Mitchell, 138–178. Washington, D.C.: The National Academies Press.

Lewis Mumford Center. n.d. "Metropolitan Racial and Ethnic Change—Census 2000, rate of the Cities: Hartford, CT MSA." (http://mumford.albany.edu/census/CityProfiles/Profiles/3280msaProfile.htm) accessed on October 10, 2008.

Logan, John R. "Ethnic Diversity Grows, Neighborhood Integration Lags." In *Redefining Urban and Suburban America: Evidence from Census 2000*, Volume 1, eds. Bruce Katz and Robert E. Lang, 235–255. Washington, D.C.: Brookings Institution Press.

Logan, J. R. 2002. "Hispanic Populations and Their Residential Patterns in the Metropolis." Lewis Mumford Center, mumford1.dyndns.org/cen2000/HispanicPop/.../Mumford Report.pdf, accessed on 12 February 2011.

Logan, John R., Brian J. Stults, and Reynolds Farley. 2004. "Segregation of Minorities in the Metropolis: Two Decades of Change." *Demography* 41: 1–22.

Lopez, Mark Hugo, and Susan Minushkin. 2008. "Report: 2008 National Survey of Latinos: Hispanics See Their Situation in U.S. Deteriorating; Oppose Key Immigration Enforcement Measures." Washington, D.C.: The Pew Hispanic Center.

Macisco, Jr., John J. 1968. "Assimilation of the Puerto Ricans on the Mainland: A Socio-emographic Approach." *International Migration Review* 2: 21–39.

Massey, Douglas S., 2008. "Immigration and Equal Opportunity." In *Against the Wall: Poor, Young, Black, and Male*, ed. Elijah Anderson, 102–119. Philadelphia, PA: University of Pennsylvania Press.

Massey, Douglas S., and Brooks Bitterman. 1985. "Explaining the Paradox of Puerto Rican Segregation." *Social Forces* 64: 306–331.

Massey, Douglas S. and Nancy A. Denton. 1993. *American Apartheid: Segregation and the Making of the Underclass.* Boston: Harvard University Press.

Massey, D. S., J. Rothwell, and D. Thurston. 2009. The Changing Bases of Segregation in the United States. *The Annals of the American Academy of Political and Social Science* 626: 74–90.

Pérez, Gina M. 2004. *The Near Northwest Side Story: Migration, Displacement, & Puerto Rican Families.* Berkeley: University of California Press.

Ramirez, Roberto R. 2004. "We the People: Hispanics in the United States." Census 2000 Special Reports. Washington, D.C.: U.S. Bureau of the Census.

Reimers, Cordelia. 2006. "Economic Well-Being." In *Hispanics and the Future of America*, eds. Marta Tienda and Faith Mitchell, 291–361. Washington, D.C.: The National Academies Press.

Rodríquez, Clara E. n.d. "Puerto Ricans: Immigrants and Migrants: A Historical Perspective." Americans All: A National Education Program. (http://www.americansall.com/PDFs/02-americans-all/9.9.pdf), accessed June 14, 2010.

Santiago, Anna M., and George Galster. 1995. "Puerto Rican Segregation in the United States: Cause or Consequence of Economic Status?" *Social Problems* 42: 361–389.

South, Scott J., Kyle Crowder, and Erick Chavez. 2005. "Migration and Spatial Assimilation among U.S. Latinos: Classical versus Segmented Trajectories." *Demography* 42: 497–521.

Suro, Roberto, and Audrey Singer. 2002. Latino Growth in Metropolitan America: Changing Patterns, New Locations. Survey Series, Census 2000. Washington, D.C.: The Brookings Institution.

Smith, Robert C. 2006. *Mexican New York: Transnational Lives of New Immigrants.* Berkeley, CA: University of California Press.

Tienda, Marta. 1989. "Puerto Ricans and the Underclass Debate." *Annals of the American Academy of Political and Social Science* 501: 105–119.

Vey, Jennifer S. Metropolitan Policy Program. 2007. *Restoring Prosperity: The State Role in Revitalizing America=s Older Industrial Cities.* Washington, D.C.: The Brookings Institution

Weaver, Glenn. 1982. *Hartford: An Illustrated History of Connecticut's Capital.* Woodlands, CA: Windsor Publications, Inc.

Whalen, Carmen Teresa. 2005. "Colonialism, Citizenship, and Puerto Rican Diaspora." In *The Puerto Rican Diaspora: Historical Perspectives.* eds. Carmen Theresa Whalen and Víctor Vázquez-Hernández, 1–42. Philadelphia: Temple University Press.

Wiese, Andrew. 2004. *Places of their Own: African American Suburbanization in the Twentieth Century.* Chicago, IL: The University of Chicago Press.

William, Vélez, Michael E. Martin, and Edgar Mendez. 2009. "Segregation Patterns in Metro Areas: Latinos and African Americans in 2000." *CENTRO Journal* 21: 119–137

Wilson, William Julius, and Richard P. Taub. 2006. *There Goes the Neighborhood: Racial, Ethnic, and Class Tensions in Four Chicago Neighborhoods and Their Meaning for America.* New York: Alfred A. Knopf.

Wright, David J., and Lisa M. Montiel. 2007. *Divided They Fall: Hardship in America's Cities and Suburbs.* Albany, New York: Rockefeller Institute of Government.

8

A Metro Immigrant Gateway

Refugees in the Hartford Borderlands

Janet Bauer

INTRODUCTION

A Bosnian refugee student looked up at my research assistant and asked, "Where are the white people in Hartford?" Drawing on her visions of American space as white, our Bosnian teenager was articulating her firsthand encounters within predominantly minority Hartford neighborhoods. Recent literature on the role of immigrants and refugees in reconfiguring and reinvigorating urban spaces suggests the importance of looking at the nature of the "reception society" and the types of interaction that take place within it. For example, in mid-19th-century Hartford, Irish immigrants were struggling to transform those urban spaces previously defined by earlier, mostly white "natives" through claiming parade routes (Walsh, this volume), as has each generation in their own unique ways. Today, the most recent arrivals to Hartford are placed in an environment increasingly defined not by a middle-class, white majority, but by a racially diverse and largely multicultural (Latino-black) minority.

To adopt a "more interactive model of incorporation," (Zolberg, 1997: 151) which draws attention to the increasing importance of "interaction among immigrant and native minority groups" (Kasinitz et al., 2002: 1020–1), we focus here on the "borderlands" of ethnic interaction, particularly Muslim refugee–Latino interactions, in the metro-Hartford neighborhoods where refugee families are often resettled. We explore how new refugee experiences—and especially refugee notions of ethnic and race relations (or how race works) in America—are affected by being initially placed in Hartford or the immediate, surrounding area.

Our exploration of these issues is based on our ongoing ethnographic research on the various ways in which recent refugee streams have confronted space/place dislocation in this multicultural urban context. These refugees variously deploy far-flung social networks, memory of homeland, and traditional cultural capital in creating unique forms of cultural citizenship and economic adaptation here, while maintaining and making use of their transnational connections and experiences, forged both back home and in places of their pre-arrival sojourn—such as temporary relocation sites in Germany, Spain, Thailand, Kenya, and Israel (cf. D'Alisera, 2004). We do not disagree that different groups and different generations experience Hartford differently (or experience some degree of segmented relocation, particularly in light of their respective communities' very different histories in the area), but we will examine the extent to which the current multicultural and multiracial urban context affects the ways in which various refugee groups are entering American culture and the ways in which intra-communal relations affect or buffer the impact of "mestizo" Hartford for these refugee groups.

We argue that our focus on these non-hierarchal, or "horizontal," relations within refugee groups and between these refugee groups and other immigrant and minority residents of Hartford not only provides insight into refugee adaptation and the changing dynamics of urban racial formations in this majority-minority urban setting, but also illuminates the relationship between the city and its metropolitan area (see Barber, this volume).

STUDYING THE URBAN BORDERLANDS—A METHODOLOGY

Others who research the "new immigrant gateway" cities have established the importance of using ground-up ethnographic approaches, both for understanding these urban landscapes and for investigating the immigrant social networks through which they negotiate their adaptation (cf. Benton-Short and Price, 2008). The discussion in this chapter is based on a collaborative faculty/student ethnographic project (The Hartford Area Refugee Research Project) undertaken from 2001 through 2012, to focus on the integration of refugee groups most recently resettled in Hartford.[1] We conducted community-based, participant observation and controlled life history interviews with multiple members (male and female) of three to five representative families selected from each of the refugee groups— initially, Russian, Ukrainian, Cuban, Khmer, Bosnian, and Kosovar Albanian refugees. We also interviewed service providers in agencies and NGOs assisting refugees in the resettlement process. Interviewees ranged in age from 14 to 75. We initially focused on gender and generational differences in refugee adaptation and included cultural audits or mapping of refugee cultural spaces in the metro area. This research was subsequently extended to focus more specifically on Islam and then on race relations among a wider range of residents and newcomers; and to include newly arrived refugee groups—Kurds, Afghans, Iraqis, Iranians, Sierra Leoneans, Meskhetian Turks, Somalis, and Somali Bantu, and more recently, Nepalis, Bhutanese Lhotshampas, and Burmese Karen. These refugee groups were selected because they are the groups being processed by local agencies. Not surprisingly, they represent the streams of refugees produced by U.S. refugee policy. Our "construction" of refugee social capital in the form of network relations was generated through our interview questions. To date the project includes interviews and multiple visits with over 50 families and 125 individuals.

REFUGE IN THE HINTERLANDS OF CONNECTICUT: IMMIGRANTS AND REFUGEES RESETTLE IN THE CITY

Estimated to be about 4 percent of state residents, and increasingly from Muslim countries,[2] refugees are not the largest group of newcomers. They are, however, more likely than other recent immigrants to be settled into areas nearer Hartford's city center.[3] Over the last 20 years, the refugee streams resettled in the metro area have been processed through Hartford via resettlement agencies such as Catholic Family Services, Lutheran Family Services, and Jewish Family Services—sectarian agencies that have nevertheless been nonpartisan in processing refugees from a wide variety of cultural and religious backgrounds. Our ethnographic samples were drawn from the specific groups resettled here by these area agencies.[4]

Our selected refugee groups speak different languages, come from different cultural and religious backgrounds, experience different degrees of Post Traumatic Stress Disorder (PTSD), enjoy different degrees of community life in exile, and experience different relationships with their homelands. Yet in some respects their adaptation proceeds along a similar path—fleeing from what were once communist countries or from societies where they were persecuted as minorities, surviving upheaval and dislocation, confronting a sometimes ambivalent or even hostile reception society, and adapting to an American cultural experience in the greater Hartford area. Thus, contrasting and comparing their experiences can provide valuable insights into the immigrant experience in second tier destination cities.

While much of the earlier scholarship on immigrants and cities (cf. *Chronicle*, 2004; Davis, 2000; Monahan, 2002) focused on mega cities like Los Angeles or New York, smaller cities like Hartford (population of 124,558 in 2002) and its metro area (population of 1,183,110 people in 2000)[5] remain overlooked. These places are important destinations—both as sites of designated refugee or immigrant resettlement (see Moser, this volume, for Portland, ME) and of chain migration for friends and relatives. Although we will not focus here on "succession," we point out that immigrants have historically re-defined the city and challenged its image as an upper-class white New England enclave, beloved of Mark Twain. It was only during the latter part of the 19th century, when early European colonizers gave way to Irish, German, Polish, and Italian laborers brought to work in local industries like the Colt factories, and then in the 1950s and 1960s, to Puerto Ricans and African Americans from the South, and finally after the mid-1960s to Latin American, South Asian, and Chinese immigrants, who comprise the largest foreign-born populations currently in the state. Since the enactment of the 1980 Refugee Act, Connecticut has become home to an influx of refugees. The changing nature of the immigration imprint (culturally and politically) makes Hartford a useful example of the changing context of race and ethnic interactions in many American cities.

THE FLAVORS OF HARTFORD: IN BLACK AND WHITE

Just under 40 percent of the state's immigrant stock (immigrants plus children born here) reside in the Hartford metro area. These days, when refugees arrive in Hartford, they enter into a "borderland" of culture and language signified by colorful annual public displays (or public cultural assertions), like the St. Patrick's Day Parade, the Italian (Columbus Day) Parade and the three-day Italian Fiesta, the Puerto Rican Day and Three Kings Parades, two West Indian Carnivals, the African American Day celebration, the Chinese and Asian New Year celebrations, South Asian dance festivals, and the Muslim Eid-al-Fitr. These commemorations reflect the diverse population of Hartford (21.5 percent foreign-born) and its metro area (14.2 percent foreign-born with 24.5 percent immigrant stock).

Linguistic diversity also serves as an indicator of this cultural diversity, with140 languages being spoken in Connecticut schools and over 70 of them represented in Hartford-area schools. In addition, about 46.5 percent of Hartford's population speaks a language other than English at home [Spanish is the most prevalent second language, although the majority of Spanish speakers are also competent English speakers and are not labeled as English Language Learners (ELL) or as having Limited English Proficiency (LEP)].[6]

In the 2000 census, more than 43.9 percent of the city's foreign-born population had arrived since 1990 (a higher rate than for the state overall (at 39 percent). More than 44.4 percent of the foreign-born residents had become naturalized U.S. citizens (a slightly lower rate than for the state overall). As the census shows, the metro area, by contrast, has both higher rates of naturalization and a lower ratio of immigrants entering in the last ten years than the city or state averages. There are other noticeable differences between the Hartford metro area and its "anchor," the city of Hartford, where many refugees who are dependent on their resettlement agencies begin their new lives in America.

Perhaps most noticeable are the differences in statistics on racial composition, which show that over the last 20 years, Hartford has become a majority-minority city. While the metro area and even the contiguous suburbs are predominantly white, black and Latino "minorities" dominate the city (see Simmons, this volume). This is especially evident in the school-age population (such as in the school our Bosnian teenager interacts with), as well as in city politics. The racial composition of Hartford itself is 41.4 percent Hispanic, 35.8 percent African American, non-Hispanic, and 17.3 percent white compared to the Metro figures of 13.5 percent Latino, 11.7 percent African American non-Hispanic, and 69.4 percent white (similar to the state racial composition). Metro Hartford has been ranked the third largest U.S. metro area (and the city has been ranked first) in terms of the percentage of residents claiming Puerto Rican heritage (see Sacks, this volume).

The prominence of a visible, nonwhite (or minority) majority in the city reflects a transformation in the urban landscape since the 1950s and 1960s. This is partly the result of cumulative African American and Puerto Rican immigration, which made Hartford the city with the largest "percentage of Hispanic residents north of Florida and East of the Mississippi" (von Zielbauer, 2003). Indeed, the state of Connecticut is home to the highest percentage of citizens born in Puerto Rico (2.1 percent), and Hartford itself has the highest percentage of Puerto Rican–born residents of any Connecticut city (at 15 percent, compared with 1/3 of city residents claiming Puerto Rican identity) (Meija and Canny, 2007). The election of black and Latino mayors in the last 20 years further signifies the growing influence of these otherwise disempowered minorities in the political life of the city, if not in other crucial aspects of everyday life (e.g., economics). Increasingly, Protestant New England steeples have given way to storefront evangelical and Pentecostal churches (with Creole and Spanish services) and mosques, while French, Polish, and Italian social clubs and restaurants have been replaced or joined by Latino and Thai establishments.

THE URBAN BORDERLANDS OF HARTFORD

Most theories of refugee resettlement (whether emphasizing assimilation, accommodation, or assertion)[7] continue to affirm the importance of investigating the context of immigrant and refugee interaction (cf. Zolberg, 1997) and of understanding the "pre-existing ethnic and race relations" (Reitz, 2002: 1005). Although this relational context is generally assumed to be defined by a dominant white middle-class, "American" culture, in Hartford this is nuanced by the prevalence of black (African descended) and Latino cultural or multicultural and political influences, with which refugees must negotiate as they take up residence in the city and begin to configure their own *cultural citizenship,* a term which emphasizes the ability of groups to publicly assert their own forms of culture (Flores and Benmayor, 1997). Upon arrival, refugees are typically placed initially by their agencies in rental apartments in Hartford itself. Cubans, Iranians, Kurds, Afghans, Bosnians, Kosovar Albanians, Iraqis, Afghans, Somalis and Somali Bantu, Meskhetian Turks, Nepalese, Bhutanese, and Karen have been resettled just west of the city center or south of downtown, near the once Italian, and increasingly Latino, neighborhoods. Meanwhile, Russians and Khmer have been placed along Park Street and Farmington Avenue on the Hartford/West Hartford town lines by their respective resettlement agencies.

Where "borders" were once considered "impermeable" or more remote (as in the emblematic case of the Mexican-American border), increasingly cities like Hartford become physical and symbolic points for *entering* American culture. Based on their study, Kasinitz et al. (2002) suggest that immigrant interaction with other immigrants and with "native minorities" (horizontal network contacts) may be more important than their interaction with "native whites" (often representing hierarchical network ties). They argue that theories about segmented immigrant incorporation (and expectations of conflict) are too unrefined, and instead point to the hybrid cultural forms that have emerged from interaction among immigrant and minority youth in New York City. In this sense, the notion of an ethnic "borderland" may convey the impression of energetic intermixing and transformation giving rise to creative forms of incorporation among immigrants and others in Hartford.

And yet, these "borderlands" remain a source of enigma, ambiguity, and uncertainty, marked among other things by what Lugo has called continuous "border inspections" that highlight racialized and cultural differences (2000). On the one hand, refugees and their children often adjust their language and clothing to "ethnic" urban styles and watch *telenovelas*. On the other hand, the impact of this on refugee and minority relations (e.g., Latino/black; Muslim/non-Muslim) is not yet clear. After 9/11 many Muslim refugees in Hartford experienced harassment from coworkers or classmates—often motivating them to further accentuate their distinctiveness through hijab and other forms of "Islamic dress." Interaction in the borderlands is not "unraced" (Bauer and Prashad, 2000) and may result in the "resetting" and reinforcement of "borders" among immigrant and minority communities, especially along racialized cultural lines.

Indeed, the prominence of black and Latino groups in Hartford has an impact on access to neighborhood organizations and the political scene, as well as a range of social services. For example, access to bilingual education, the need for translated materials from service agencies, and community health network concerns are understandably defined by these populations' needs.[8] Thus the issues of diabetes among Hispanics (Condon, 2004) may receive more public attention than PTSD among the Bosnian, who are survivors of rape and torture, or among the Khmer, who were victims of torture by starvation (80–90 percent of Hartford-area Khmer refugees in Greater Hartford are said to suffer from symptoms of PTSD, according to Mary Scully and Theanvy Kouch, Khmer Health Advocates, West Hartford). These populations often bring with them a great deal of "survivor's guilt," which can inhibit day-to-day activities in various ways. For instance, among the Khmer refugee population in Hartford, there has been a proliferation of gambling addiction (Rucker, 2003).

IN SEARCH OF *MESTIZO* HARTFORD:
THE RACIALIZATION OF REFUGEES AND IMMIGRANTS

The implications of the racialized border are complicated in Hartford, where minorities set the cultural tone of the everyday, while white majority culture prevails in structures of state power and economics. The role of the state itself, however, does not lie in "emancipating people from distinctions" (Bauer and Prashad, 2000) and the various resettlement agencies and other NGOs that are directed to "assist" refugee incorporation do not necessarily facilitate day-to-day adaptation or access to resources. Nor do they facilitate the formation of alliances among refugees, immigrants, and so-called "native minorities." The mission of the resettlement agencies is to make the refugees (who presumably arrive with fewer material resources and significantly more trauma than immigrants) self-sufficient within about four months, although different agencies offer different opportunities for continuing services. In fact these organizations have facilitated the development of ethnic-based community organizations to support different ethnic or national groups to define and manage their own needs (including the creation of mutual assistance associations or MAAs, partially funded at various times by state and federal sources). The one local attempt at a coalition of MAAs has been hampered by a lack of funds to assist in the translation and provision of materials in the many area refugee languages.[9]

In the absence of effective institutional brokers, refugees must establish access to individual cultural brokers, often within their own communities, who assist refugees in navigating American culture and bureaucracy. Political and economic opportunities in Hartford can be facilitated by connections to already developed community institutions. For example, Cubans and Kosovars, sharing a common language with other Hispanic and Albanian communities (respectively), have an entrée into some established political and economic organizations.[10] Kosovar Muslims, for instance, have access to (often largely Christian) Albanian organizations, particularly in Waterbury, a neighboring town with a large Albanian population. As a result, refugees groups differ in how they encounter the complex, racially and ethnically mixed, *"mestizo"* Hartford in the two areas in which persistent interaction between refugees and other residents occurs—namely through their work lives and educational experiences.

At least initially, many refugees enter into the American public sphere through their daily interaction with minority (and largely Spanish-speaking) coworkers and colleagues in their neighborhoods, places of work, and schools or classrooms. In fact we first became aware of the importance of the (local/global) Latino connection to refugee adaptation in Hartford when we recognized some common experiences shared by nearly all of our refugee groups: watching Spanish-language television dramas (*telenovelas*) and learning more Spanish than English from coworkers. Refugee children, like Hartford's Bosnian teens, absorb American culture through the hip-hop styles and language of their largely Latino classmates at schools like Bulkeley High. However, while *telenovelas* or even hip hop might provide a touchstone of common experience (especially for the adolescents and teens), ethnic and national cultural forms (the various ethnic or national newspapers, dance, and music) specific to particular groups are especially important for sustaining refugee communities and supporting their unique identities.

Labor, Livelihood, and Social Capital

Our refugee interviewees varied greatly in their educational and professional backgrounds. Many Russians and Ukrainians are highly educated professionals, while many Khmer, Somali, and Karen are unskilled. Considerable variation also exists within refugee communities—e.g., as constituted by particular migrant cohort or migration wave, as well as by generation or age. Yet, as is so often the case with refugees (and immigrants), even the most professionally trained individuals commonly experience downward occupational mobility in the United States. For example, Russian engineers, teachers, and doctors must often retrain through the local community colleges, as one Ukrainian we interviewed did, to become a veterinary assistant.

In contrast to the increase in foreign-born population in Hartford, which contributes to growing diversity in schools, a decline in job opportunities within easy reach of refugee housing draws refugees out of the city in search of employment. Changing economic opportunities conspire to make finding employment around the city challenging—with many of the minimum-wage factory and production jobs having "migrated" to the suburbs surrounding the city (see Chen and Shemo, this volume) or disappeared entirely (see Bacon, this volume). Most often, our refugee interviewees' coworkers were other immigrants who did not speak English well or who (in aggregate) spoke Spanish, leading non–Spanish speakers to complain that they had no opportunities to learn English on the job.

Refugee families often must depend upon unreliable public transportation to reach the more distant, available jobs. Acquiring a car, insurance, and even a driver's license is further impeded by new restrictions on noncitizen access to driver's licenses (so that many Somalis and Meskhetians fly to Arizona and other states thought to offer easier access to acquiring them). The Connecticut Immigrant and Refugee Coalition has been organizing on behalf of noncitizens regarding such matters. However, they have found the collection of official affidavits of complaint difficult among the refugee population. Local labor unions and groups like Justice for Janitors have tried to make inroads into immigrant labor organizing. However, among our refugee groups (especially the Russians and Khmer), there has been a reluctance to engage official or state institutions, given their experiences with state repression.[11]

Regardless of their country of origin, refugees' pre-migration experiences can also have very different effects on their approach to work in the United States. Many older Russians, who had matured under communist regimes, typically expected to retire at age 55 and receive state support. They were not prepared to work, let alone experience a decrease in their professional status. While they appreciated the quality of healthcare and other social services they did utilize, they found the lack of access to resources that then made them dependent upon their children to be frustrating. Other refugees from agricultural communities, especially those who had spent long periods of time in refugee camps (e.g., the Somali Bantu or the Burmese Karen), lacked the kind of work experience relevant to securing meaningful employment in the urban economy.

The contrasting incorporation experiences of different immigrant groups are sometimes explained in terms of comparative histories of discrimination and colonialism, which might reduce opportunities for job advancement (Boswell and Curtis, 1984). It may also be the case that more recent immigrants and refugees remain optimistic about their opportunities in this country and are hence more likely to actively pursue various economic and social possibilities before becoming dissuaded by lack of success over time.

Cubans, Bosnians, and Albanians in particular expressed entrepreneurial aspirations. It may be that a combination of economic frustration under communism and access to an already established community of Hispanic businesspeople (the Spanish American Merchants Association or SAMA) through which to build networks of support have assisted many of the Cubans in starting their own businesses. Cuban refugees seem to enjoy an especially high degree of economic success. Cubans own more businesses (proportionately) in Hartford and have locally higher rates of homeownership and nationally higher rates of education than other Latinos in the community.[12]

Many refugees, like the Cubans, Kosovars, Albanians, and Somalis, often begin working in restaurants, hotels, warehouses, and as janitors before trying to set up individual business—often illegally—as hairdressers or tax preparers, restaurateurs, ethnic-based shop owners, or video store owners. Going into business for themselves with ethnic-themed enterprises has also contributed to the building of their respective cultural communities. Indeed, most Hartford refugee groups developed rich social capital and their own economic ladders. The one exception among our refugee groups are the Khmer, whose past trauma often interferes both with successful employment and with community building.

Today, Franklin Avenue, New Britain Avenue, and Park Street are lined with establishments that have become "hangouts" or "safe houses" for refugees of similar backgrounds. Take for example, Jose, a Cuban balsero (or rafter), who worked several janitorial jobs (including at Trinity College) until he was able, with the help of the SAMA, with its key Cuban membership, to buy a "Cuban" bakery on Park Street, in the cultural heart of Latino Hartford. He began by investing in rental property. Then, despite having to deal with Anglo suppliers with whom he could not readily communicate, he has been able (with assistance from his wife) to give up his janitorial duties to work in his bakery.

Tony, a Bosnian entrepreneur who came to Hartford via New York City, attempted to build an American clientele for his Italian restaurant in the suburb of West Hartford. Without access to other financial backing, he relied on his siblings to pool their resources toward purchasing this business, which, nevertheless, failed within a month of our lunchtime visit. Ali, a Kosovar refugee, worked for some time as a waiter but recently found a job through other Albanians, moving supplies in a warehouse. At the same time, he began classes in Trinity College's community gateway program. He explained to us that while his immediate goal had been to "make lots of money" (partly to fulfill obligations to his family back home), he had altered his strategy, telling his family that he had to focus his future trajectory on being here in Hartford. He sees continuing his education as the one route to achieving his eventual goal of becoming an international businessman who can use his new skills to help his hometown in Kosovo reorganize and build a relationship with America.

Education, Generation, and Identification

Education, even for adults, is often, but not always, seen as crucial to individual and family success. Middle-aged José had no time for education at this point, although other, more highly educated Cuban families place more emphasis on educational achievement. Learning English was considered imperative, although attaining American social fluency was considered to be especially difficult for older newcomers who have lived most of their lives elsewhere. Even the retired (mostly professional) Russian refugees we interviewed have applied themselves to learning English in weekly ESL (English as Second Language) classes offered through local Jewish agencies and other organizations providing services to Russian immigrants. Since the lives of Russian grandparents in West Hartford were largely spent confined to their apartments, making trips to the local Russian grocery stores, and/or visiting with their grandchildren, their ESL classes provided them with one opportunity for interacting with both American "natives" and other Russian refugees. When I was arranging to send student tutors to the Juniper House adult day care center ESL classes, the elder refugees first grilled me on what kind of students I would send (i.e., were they real Americans, meaning were they white Americans without accents?). Indeed, although all my students were native speakers, they included Latinos, blacks, and Asian Americans. While the students were well received and much loved, it seemed that the pre-existing racial hierarchies of American society were already making their impact on these refugees' notions of how to interact with Hartford.

Likewise, the American Place at the Hartford Public Library and Capital Community College in Hartford offer many ESL and other classes for adult refugees. These "schools" are visibly "international" and yet the adult students have little time to spend casual moments with their classmates, as they rush off to their various jobs and family responsibilities. One of the more highly educated Kosovar families seemed to use Capital Community College as a family space, making good use of the library and computer center in their spare time. They applied all their energies to educating the family rather than developing community networks, as others are likely to do.

By contrast, refugee children (born both here and abroad), spend a good deal of their day in the public schools interacting with other students. Young immigrant and refugee engagement with school varies by gender, family background, and their age at immigration. Younger Bosnian teenage girls, sharing their aspirations for furthering their education, seemed particularly interested in the prospect of college, while Bosnian boys demonstrated more interest in obtaining cars, jobs, and money (perhaps reflecting cultural expectations for their familial roles) and have more freedom to roam about the city. Within a year of our initial interviews many Bosnian girls were married and pregnant. Meskhetian Turkish, Iraqi, and Somali Bantu girls also verbalized their intentions to continue their education but were often pressured by their families to leave school before receiving their diplomas in order to marry. Russian parents, who often are highly educated, sometimes considered their children less diligent and less interested in incorporating successfully into American society,

Figure 8.1. A Mixed Ethnic ESL Class Run by Catholic Charities Migration and Refugee Services with a Local Hartford Resident of Color Leading the Class. (Janet Bauer)

preferring instead to hang out with their own friends. As is often the case for Iranian refugee children in the UK (notably reflected in the 2003 film *Second Generation*), the age of the children's immigration to the United States seems to be a factor in this "resistance." Refugee children sometimes feel they had no choice in their parents' decision to flee and therefore hold no real stake in taking up opportunities in this society. They may remain confused about their place and identity, especially when they are still closely tied to friends back home and can easily communicate with them by Skype or other social media, as the Meskhetian girls did.

Reflecting the city/metro contrast in other areas of racial composition, the overall student population in the Hartford School District is 52.2 percent Hispanic, 38.1 percent black, 7.0 percent white, 1.9 percent Asian, and .2 percent American Indian. However, the composition of schools in central Hartford and the south end are heavily Latino, with a slightly higher (if still small) white population (a reflection of white immigrants and refugees, such as the Muslim Bosnians and Meskhetian Turks who live in those areas). For example, Weaver High School in the north end of Hartford is now 90 percent black (African American and Caribbean heritage students) with 8.4 percent of those students from non–English speaking homes, while Bulkeley High School just south of city center is 69.5 percent Hispanic and 22 percent black with 62 percent of students coming from homes where English is not the dominant language.

The student population of Naylor Elementary School (in the south end), on the other hand, is 63.2 percent Hispanic, 15 percent black, and 19.6 percent white (reflecting large numbers of Bosnian and Albanian immigrant families in this school district), with 58.6 percent of the students living in non–English dominant households.

One ESL teacher, whose elementary classrooms included a number of Bosnian and Kosovar students, suggested that the boys who acted out in class when we visited had already "learned bad behavior" from the neighborhood kids. We also witnessed a degree of friction between our Bosnian student guides (who were more fluent in English than Bosnian) and the Bosnian kids in the ESL class over just who was a "real Bosnian." Much of the school friction, however, especially in the middle and high schools that we visited, occurs between nonimmigrant Latino and African American students and refugee students (like the Bosnians—one of the largest refugee groups in Hartford—Afghans, and Somalis). In some schools, like Buckley High, it was clear at that time that new arrivals and ESL students often followed curriculum tracks that "segregated" them from the rest of the school population. However, physical conflicts still occurred, for example, between Puerto Rican students and Bosnian or Turkish refugee students at Buckley High and between African Americans and Somali Bantu or Somalis at Hartford High School.

While it is also clear that Latino culture and styles have become widespread in the school environment, as Kasinitz et al. (2002) suggest, the closest friendships seem to remain among other immigrants, if not within one's own particular group (however that is defined). Even parents, like Azra's, will not allow their daughters to attend school dances where they might mix with other students, although they are of course freer to develop friendships with each other during regular school hours. For some of the older Bosnian children who spent up to six years in Germany on their way to America, German culture and friends also retain a hold on their consciousness; and Meskhetian Turkish Muslim students recount how much more personal freedom they enjoyed as teenagers in Russia. Even Somali Bantu miss their friends and family back in the refugee camps in Kenya.

Both the workplace and the school offer possibilities for experiencing *"mestizo"* Hartford and these experiences do leave their mark. While immigrants have more immigrant associates than "native" associates (Kasinitz et al., 2002), both refugees and their children seem to be (by individual or family choice) directing more attention to developing intra-community networks and relationships. To some extent, new refugees retain their pre-immigration ethnic biases (for example, Bosnians feeling more antipathy toward Polish immigrants than Puerto Ricans, Albanians avoiding Russians—even Russian Jews—because of the association between Russia and their Serbian oppressors).

Inertia and Irruption in Racial Formation

Whether from their own previous experiences or their increasing familiarity with American racial hierarchies, "preexisting ethnic attitudes as well as intergroup boundaries and hierarchies" seems to influence "the social framework" through which refugees encounter others (Reitz, 2002:1008). Some recent events have produced new tensions. For example, at the start of our research, a Bosnian teenager was killed along Franklin Avenue, in an act that was seen as revenge for that young driver striking and knocking down a Latina a few weeks earlier with his car. Following that incident, refugee families became fearful of venturing outside at night and exercised more supervision over their children (see Moser, this volume for the killing of a refugee and its significance in Portland, Maine).

At a more general level, just as the two largest immigrant groups in Connecticut since 1990—Polish and Jamaicans—have contributed to specific residential patterns (moving toward New Britain and the North End of Hartford, respectively), the refugees in our study have begun to establish patterns of residential mobility. On the one hand, this may facilitate proximity between co-nationals and the elaboration of social contacts within their own communities, as when Ali moved to a Nile Street apartment where other Albanians and Bosnians were living. Yet, refugees are also quickly adopting native notions of desirable residential areas, as when a young Russian immigrant disdainfully declared to her mother's "cultural broker" that she did not understand why that woman would live in West Hartford (an affluent Hartford suburb) rather than Avon (an even wealthier one). In the workplace, refugees learn to be afraid of walking outside in certain areas of Hartford and of taking the bus to work rather than driving. One recently arrived Iranian refugee told us that her Latino workmates warned her not to take the bus to her night shift. Initially her coworkers gave her a ride, but within several months the Iranian family moved out of Hartford.

One might expect that their own experiences with ethnic, political, and religious discrimination (both at home and in their places of reception) provide Bosnians, Russian Jews, Albanians, Khmer, Cubans, Meskhetian Turks, Karen, Somali Bantu, and the Bhutanese Lhotshampas a common ground with Latinos and blacks in Hartford. However, any such affinity they might feel is complicated by their interactions in the city—such as complaints directed toward Russian refugees walking the streets and idly sitting in their front yards along Farmington Avenue. Much as other immigrant children told Laurie Olsen (1997), migrants in Hartford have made each other "racial." In order to find their places and form their identities, becoming American has meant succumbing to the ethnic categorization and labeling that circulates through American society. For example, it's not at all clear that the non-Latino refugees make distinctions among Hartford's different Hispanic groups, let alone between different groups of "blacks" in Hartford—such as the Haitians, Jamaicans, Trinidadians, African Americans, and Somalis. Interestingly, among all our refugee groups, it was the Khmer who felt the most affinity with blacks, articulating an appreciation for their common situation in American social strata.

As Hartford's refugees face the challenges of accessing American culture through this multiracial gateway (that holds prospects for intergroup collaboration), the city can become a space of "segregation, producing differences and inequality more than social incorporation" (Silvey, 2008:286). Thus, in general (though, with some generational variation), developing and reestablishing social capital through their own communities (both locally and globally) is the most secure path to refugee incorporation and resistance to cultural subordination in the absence of adequate state and NGO support in Hartford.

THE MOSQUE AS HYBRID SPACE

Religious affiliation has often been proposed as a site of both incorporation and exclusion—something that suggests the continuing salience of religion in a post-secular society (Beaumont and Baker, 2011). In particular a "community's religious experience" may offer the basis for forging a distinct identity and crafting ways of belonging in the face of discrimination (Mohammad-Arif, 2000; Warner and Witter, 1998). Affiliating with communities of coreligionists of different ethnic and religious backgrounds also offers the possibility of inclusion in the larger society (Jonker, 2000). All of the refugee groups we interviewed share religious affiliations with "native" groups: whether as Buddhists (Khmer), Jews (Russians), Muslims (e.g., Bosnians, Meskhetian Turks, Kosovars, Somalis, Iraqis), Hindus (Bhutanese Lhotshampas) or Catholics (Cubans), and Protestants (some Burmese Karen). Yet many of these groups originated from recently communist countries in which religious expression had not been accentuated in the public sphere and their ritual traditions sometimes varied greatly from those of their coreligionists in the United States. To cite a local example, while Russians used Jewish community services, it is not clear that the religiosity of the former organized in the same ways as that of the native-born Jewish population.

However, interesting possibilities for creating community around religious similarities do exist in Hartford, particularly for developing refugee–Latino/Black Muslim interaction[13] at a time when Muslims are seen to be "claiming a place in the public square" (Roozen, Hartford Seminary). Although New England hosts over 30 percent of mosques nationwide and 62 percent of Muslims surveyed claimed mosque membership, American mosque associations are generally dominated by African Americans (30 percent), South Asians (35 percent) and Arabs (25 percent), while our Muslim refugee samples (Kosovars, Albanians, Iraqis, Kurds, Iranians, Meskhetian Turks, and Afghans, Somali and Somali Bantu along with a scattering of Latinos, Iranians, West Indians, and Sierra Leoneans) represent about 44 percent of mosque association participants nationally.[14] In the greater Hartford metro area, there are several mosque associations available to practitioners (for example, in Berlin, New Britain, East Hartford, and Hartford itself, as well as in Windsor, where the Islamic Center of Connecticut represents the region's largest and most conservative Muslim association).

Not surprisingly, however, there are histories of disagreement among various ethno-national groups in the multicultural mosque associations over questions of social practice. The Hartford program Ansar for Kids was one attempt by local

Muslims to reach out to Bosnian refugee youth. Organized by an Egyptian Muslim woman concerned about the difficulties Bosnian children were having adjusting to American culture and school life, Ansar for Kids was originally located in a school building in Hartford. For three and a half hours on Sundays, students were supposed to receive cultural counseling, educational tutoring, and some spiritual guidance. Attendees were predominantly girls, often photographed reading the Koran and wearing, at least in this setting, some type of hijab. They often turned to one of our Hartford-born, female student researchers as a "cultural mentor" to answer questions about school or college. Ansar for Kids, in some respects, was a "safe house" (Pratt, 1990), where these girls received affirmation of their Bosnian culture and developed a rich camaraderie (as did their waiting mothers) in this ethnically segregated setting. Eventually, however, the classes were moved to the conservative South Windsor mosque where Ansar has virtually disbanded in response to rising frustrations from internal disagreements.

One might expect religion to become more important for refugees from formerly communist (and more secular) countries, who have been either persecuted for their religious identities or prevented from engaging in public religious displays—and especially for recently arrived Muslim refugees, who have faced additional difficulties and rejection in post-9/11 America. However, the likelihood that individual refugee families will pursue and strengthen religious affiliations depends upon the intersection of certain conditions: the reception the families or individuals face in the local context, and their connections to situations and events back home (cf. Haddad and Smith, 2002). Relative to their coreligionists, the ritual practices of some groups, such as Kosovars, Bosnians, and Somali Bantu, remain more private, intra-communal, and culturally accented. Before they established the Bosnian American Islamic Cultural Center on Franklin Avenue a few years ago, Bosnians sought their own space for men to say evening prayers during Ramadan—not in the nearby mosque on Hungerford Street but in public school buildings. Among the Bosnian women and girls, we noticed several single pregnant women or teenagers who did not appear to be ostracized. Likewise, the Albanians we met around Hartford marked their holidays in a private family atmosphere (the nearest Albanian mosque being located in Waterbury). Many of the Bosnians, Kosovars, and Meskhetian Turks we have interviewed, having fled former communist countries, had not yet been introduced to the more conservative and sectarian forms of religiosity that are now circulating throughout many religious communities. Bosnians, for example, celebrated religious holidays with family feasts which sometimes included consumption of alcohol during their first years in Hartford. Still, religious rituals play a prominent role in community events. For example, Khmer hold community events under the auspices of the Buddhist Temple, and an all-Russian cultural night I attended took place in the Beth Israel Synagogue on Farmington Avenue, where many Russian and Ukrainian Jewish refugees reside.

Perhaps because Bosnians, Kosovars, Meskhetian Turks (and some other refugees) we interviewed) are relatively recent arrivals or because they do not participate actively in the communities of American coreligionists, they have not yet been pressured to make Islam (or their respective religions) the primary vehicle for asserting their identities, as have some South Asian youth facing discrimination in the United States (Mohammad-Arif, 2000: 85). Presently, they deploy various other strategies and outlets for "belonging," including building and maintaining intra-community relationships. Other communities, like the Afghans, have initiated efforts to organize their own mosque association and a mutual assistance association.

Like other refugees in Hartford, they seek to establish relations with others in their own ethnic and linguistic communities around the city and region, while attempting at the same time to maintain connections with family and cultures left behind—through accessing home language news sources and other media, electronic means such as email, chat room discussions and Skype, or by making personal visits or telephone calls. This can involve participating in religious celebrations or attending weddings. The investment of social and economic resources in maintaining these translocal connections may be understandable in light of the fact that Western NGOs, and American culture in particular, emphasize an egalitarian ideology that "neutralizes differences among different refugee groups" (Daniel and Knudson, 1996: 6). Such a worldview may be unsettling to refugees whose identities are still anchored in their home culture and who have experienced varying degrees of trauma or difficulties in reestablishing trust (Daniel and Knudson, 1996). One additional impact of minimizing participation in the more diverse religious communities with which refugees might affiliate—Christian, Muslim, Jewish, Buddhist or Hindu—is reduced pressure to conform their cultural religious practices to the perhaps divergent expectations of coreligionists from other cultures.

SEGMENTED LOCATIONS: NEGOTIATING SPACE AND PLACE THROUGH TRANSNATIONAL NETWORKS

As Faist (2000) and others[15] continue to suggest, transnational and ethnic-based networks (and sometimes organizations) remain effective ways of balancing the forces and pressures of incorporation and exclusion. It is perhaps their cultural unfamiliarity with American life (as much as nostalgic memory or desire to maintain home identity) and the limits of refugee language facility, which necessitate that refugees utilize social capital (i.e., personal relations and networks among family and co-nationals) to traverse their reception society. The segmentation of refugee experiences and their locations (figuratively and literally) occurs through the maintenance of these local and transnational networks, by which refugee cultural (or ethnic based) communities have been created or transformed.

While refugees typically arrive with fewer resources and greater trauma than "voluntary" immigrants, the line dividing their experiences is often very small. Given similar language and cultural backgrounds, immigrants and refugees in any one ethnic or national-origin community can have very similar adaptation experiences in reception societies (in contrast to other ethno-national immigrants groups) even though different streams of refugees within any national group can also confront different circumstances both in places of destination and within the larger national community. Those immigrant groups who arrive in Hartford to be "embraced" by or take advantage of already established and more sizeable cultural communities may enjoy a different set of opportunities in terms of economic and political assistance, as well as different opportunities for deploying cultural capital within the reception society. These resources allow those refugees to circumvent some of the confines and limitations of incorporation in Hartford.

Despite receiving encouragement to be self-reliant and independent, refugee groups we worked with had to depend upon their own trans-local social networks (inside and outside their communities) to provide them with the information they needed to access benefits, jobs, and social support. For example, as discussed above, refugees in the greater Hartford area looking for residential and employment mobility seek better housing or employment through their personal networks, often resituating themselves to be closer to co-nationals. Women are often central in the processes of resettlement—by making contacts with local cultural brokers or making use of family resource centers at Hartford-area schools.

In many instances, refugees have made use of ethnic religious-based NGOs—for example Jewish Family Services. While these organizations also provide services for refugees other than the ethnic group they represent, the majority of their clients are self-selected by language or ethnicity. Khmer in particular, because of the high rates of PTSD among the adult population, have extreme difficulties forming and maintaining community relations, and are thus heavily reliant on organizations like the Khmer Health Associates (one of only a handful of community based torture treatment centers in the United States). As this organization's data show, their patients describe pronounced and intrusive symptoms that interrupt daily routines and family relationships such as effective communication with their children.

In each of the refugee communities with which we worked there was usually an individual "cultural broker" whose services competed with those of the main NGOs working with that refugee group. While Jewish Family Services resettled many of the Russian Jewish refugees who live along Farmington Avenue in West Hartford, Ada, operating from the back room of her specialty store, filled out immigration papers and did translation for Russian-speaking refugees. Such intermediaries (both individuals and loosely organized interest groups) help refugees negotiate the bureaucratic path to resettlement in the United States. Occasionally refugees are also adopted by American "aunties" who provide financial and other support. For example, Ali received a loan of $1,200 from a sympathetic sponsor to make a last-minute, surprise trip to attend his sister's engagement party in Kosovo.

The larger the community, the more numerous the restaurants, food shops, newspapers, social clubs, and concerts supporting it. This became clear in our visits to similar refugee communities in New York City. The vibrancy of little Albania in the Bronx, the Khmer community gathering at the local Buddhist temple and the numerous Asian food stores, and the pulsating large-screen TVs in Ukrainian restaurants in Brighton beach, for example, can be the basis for increasing chain migration away from smaller destination cities like Hartford. Hartford, though, has become just such a destination site, for a few groups like Bosnians, who have swelled the local (post-census) population with "thousands of additional families," according to local resettlement and refugee assistance organizations whose personnel we interviewed.

Thus the size and history of these refugee groups and the larger ethno-national communities (and organizations) with which they might affiliate in the Hartford metro area vary substantially. For instance, Cubans are a small community but can take advantage of a large Hispanic population and many Latino community resources, while the Khmer are a larger refugee group without a well-established community to support them. The Bosnian community has grown through chain migration to become a sizable community. The Albanian community (both Christian and Muslim)—while sizeable in other Connecticut locations—is relatively small in the city of Hartford, but Kosovar (Muslim) Albanians take advantage of these contacts while maintaining their strongest connections back home. Russian Jews, also a sizeable community, are greeted by established community service and faith-based organizations, although they maintain their distinctiveness within the Jewish community, while Somali Bantus, who were a sizable community with their own ECBO (Ethnic Based Community Organization) just a few years ago, have become fragmented through internal disagreement and outmigration to places like Columbus, Ohio; Lewiston, Maine; and Portland, Maine (see Moser, this volume).

Indeed, intra-community disagreements or prejudices can effectively interrupt access to potential network relations. Bosnians from the town of Bijeljina say they have suffered discrimination from fellow Bosnians from smaller villages. Bijeljina Bosnians are often stigmatized as "gypsies" because of the large number of Roma who lived in that town. Here, they attend social functions at the Cafe Europa in Hartford but have tended to establish residence just to the southwest of Hartford, in New Britain.

Social relationships extending back home and to other pre-arrival destinations are variously maintained through remittances, visits, exchanges or acquisitions of property, telephone calls, and electronic communications. Refugee contact with the homeland is framed by the location of family members (e.g., Russian Jewish refugees citing their children in Israel), the treatment and traumas associated with the homeland (which may be cloaked by nostalgic memories), and the time of their arrival in the United States. Kosovars, who recently arrived in the United States and who were admitted under temporary refugee status, continue to travel periodically to Kosovo, invest in property, vote in elections, and find spouses there. Over time, some of them, like Ali (mentioned above), begin to shift their priorities, while still maintaining commitments to support family back home. Pre-arrival sojourns (to Israel, Germany, Thailand or the Philippines, and Spain or Miami) also contribute substantially to refugee networks, expectations, and sources of identity. Many young

Bosnians in Hartford think of Germany as a home, the place of their childhood memories. While their parents may return to Bosnia to assert property claims and visit relatives, their children choose to spend time in Germany. We were surprised to learn that among all of the refugee groups in our study, most families did not come directly to the United States after fleeing their countries. Likewise, once families have been dispersed throughout the United States, connections are established between co-nationals and family members in Hartford and Miami, Boston, New York, St. Louis, or Chicago.

CONCLUSION: LOCATING AND DECENTERING AMERICA: THE LATIN *ACCENT* IN REFUGEE EXPERIENCES

If global cities are the locus "of networks or flows of capital, people, and culture that connect disparate places across the globe" (Smith 2003: 55), then refugees are clearly a part of this process. Their "transnational citizenship" by which they enjoy cultural and social affiliation in multiple locations is an important element of their local incorporation, providing a new form of nonelite (or "underdog" cosmopolitanism) that can enliven their reception communities (cf. Agustin, 2005). Ali, the Kosovar refugee worker and student, admitted that he had learned some Spanish at his old job as a waiter and that his new Kosovar workmates ridiculed the hours he spent perfecting English paragraphs for his humanities classes. But, all of this is put in different focus when he talks nightly through PalTalk or MSN Messenger with family back home. Hartford, which had moved from the periphery to the center of his world, momentarily slips back on the periphery.

Throughout our research we have routinely visited immigrant restaurants and stores and attended a variety of cultural and religious events (such as weddings, concerts, and Friday prayers). Hartford is alive with a multitude of cultural happenings, many of which remain "invisible" to those outside specific refugee communities. Yet while Ali's experience in the city is inflected with Latino/black (or Caribbean) accents, his experiences do not necessarily take on a hybridized form. Given the necessities and urgencies of refugee life, intra-community relationships and transnational networks, which provide a segmented experience of sorts, become invaluable resources for adapting to metropolitan urban life. Even for the current second generation, as Maira (1999) and Mohammad-Arif (2000) describe for South Asian immigrant youth, the immigrant community of one's family may remain the most important source of identity, often signified by agreement to forgo education and marry within their communities, as some Bosnian and Somali girls have done.

In addition, the American racial and multicultural regime can quickly impinge upon refugee consciousness. While they may still encounter pressures to ground their identity in a distinctly Bosnian, Khmer, Russian Jewish, Cuban/Hispanic, Iraqi, or Kosovar Albanian identity, this generation of refugee youth, perhaps more than previous generations, is positioned to engage nonimmigrant minority cultures and music in ways that may challenge the segmentation in the experiences of refugee communities. Like Kasintiz et al. (2002), we have found the second generation (or immigrant and refugee youth) to be different from their parents, but also likely to define their experiences differently than "native or white" Americans, as well.

Still in search of the meaning of *mestizo* Hartford, and intrigued by the popularity of *telenovelas* for so many of our refugee groups, we retrospectively asked ourselves why we had initially been so perplexed about this. We should not have been surprised to learn that many of the refugees from these very different cultural backgrounds had watched these dramas either back home or on their journeys to Hartford (in Miami—if not Cuba, in Germany on the way to the United States, back home in the Ukraine or Bosnia). For some, the *televnovelas* were nostalgic reminders of a particular moment or experience of childhood; for others they evoked cathartic emotions; for Narin's Khmer mother they visually evoked the Cambodian countryside.

In many ways, the *telenovelas* symbolically reflect the slight decentering of American culture and racial formation in this majority minority city. Viewing them did not necessarily facilitate refugees' engagement with Latino culture or Hartford Hispanics. Yet they did provide refugees a common emotional currency, symbolizing the global reach and cultural potency of this aspect of Hispanic culture. More significantly, our methodological focus on immigrant (horizontal) relationships with so-called "native minorities" in Hartford illustrates what Chacko (2008) describes as the shift from the biracial (black and white) to the multiethnic or poly-ethnic in configuring the logics of inclusion and exclusion in American immigrant gateway cities.

NOTES

1. The following students contributed to this research: Narin Prum, Tooch Van, Daniela Santangelo-Akaratovic, Mary Cavallo, Samilys Rodriguez, Jessica Filion, Kateryna Yeremeyeva, Leila Shulman, Andrea Chivakos, Alissa Phillips, Jessica Hart, Muhammed Umair, Melissa Pierce, Abigail Biller, Eniko Hobor, Janaki Challa, Rosalia Abreu, Channon Miller, Nabila Taj, Jonida Shtembari, and Kristina Mereigh. (Because our Vietnamese student researcher dropped out of the project for personal reasons Vietnamese refugees were not included in our samples.)

2. Figures are from Fix and Passel's presentation, "Immigration and Integration Trends. Immigrants in Connecticut" (January 30, 2004, The Urban Institute, Washington, D.C.). Other data sources indicate that between 1996 and 2001, Connecticut received and resettled on average more than 900 refugees a year (FAIR). Between 2000 and 2009, about 5,637 refugees were sent to Connecticut. If this figure is compared with the total number of foreign-born living in Connecticut during this period alone, they would constitute about 1 percent of the population (FAIR: http://www.fairus.org/states/Connecticut). However, this figure includes neither refugees who moved to the state from other resettlement locations, nor Connecticut foreign-born who were admitted as refugees in previous years (and would have been enumerated as foreign born in subsequent data collections). If these additional figures were to be considered, refugees would account for about 4 percent of the foreign-born population.

3. Specific refugee arrivals by destination city have only recently been made available on the U.S. State Department Refugee Processing website. Figures for one six-month period in 2012 suggest that just under 50 percent of state arrivals are resettled in the city of Hart-

ford, which anchors the metro region. A few years into the 21st century, Hartford's refugee streams were increasingly African and Muslim. For example in 2004, 7 percent of the new refugee arrivals were of European origins, 75 percent were from African countries, and 45 percent were Muslim (from both European and African countries). And, while the total number of refugees in Connecticut and metro Hartford may be relatively small, an acknowledgment of their presence is reflected in the fact that Connecticut now provides driver's license exams in many of the languages spoken by our refugee interviewees, including Albanian, Arabic, Bosnian, Farsi, Vietnamese (but not Khmer), Russian, Spanish, Somali, and Turkish. There are also ample websites devoted to singles as well as "yellow page sites" for most of these CT groups that can be readily "googled." Note that the statistical data on population characteristics presented in this paper is based primarily on data that uses the categories of "foreign-born" or "immigrants"—categories which do not distinguish between refugees (who have a distinct legal status and are generally considered to be involuntary immigrants) and other immigrants. Further challenges to accurately enumerating our selected refugee groups in Connecticut include the aggregation of certain groups like "former Yugoslavians" (obscuring the Kosovar Albanians and sometimes the Bosnians), Somali (without distinguishing between the Somali Bantu and the Somali) and refugees from the former USSR. Cambodians or Khmer also do not appear in many of the aggregate tables—like those noting "place of birth" in the Hartford County samples.

4. Since our refugee groups were selected based on those groups who happened to be resettled by local agencies, they happen to be among the biggest streams of refugees resettled across the United States—with Southeast Asian and Russian refugee peaking in the early 1990s and the other groups peaking after 2000 (FAIR).

5. Some of the immigration figures in this paper, which are gleaned from the U.S. census and other government data sources, are summarized on the Federation for American Immigration Website (www.fairus.org/Research). The use of this data here does not reflect any support for the policy aims of FAIR.

6. Fix and Passel (2004) point out that nationally the majority of LEP students are native-born rather than foreign-born. In Connecticut, although Spanish represents the largest non-English language group (followed by Portuguese, Polish, Chinese, and Haitian Creole), only 29.6 percent of Spanish speakers are ELL students. Perhaps not surprisingly, the language groups representing more recent refugee sand immigrant streams have higher percentages of ELL students—like the Kurds (82.9 percent), Serbo-Croatians, Albanian, Turks, Ukrainians, and Russians (Data Bulletin, Connecticut State Department of Education, "Connecticut's English Language Learners" (2001) and "Connecticut's Limited English Proficiency Students" (1998).

7. See the discussion and summary in *Chronicle of Higher Education* (2004), in *Theorizing Diaspora* (Castles, 2002), and the SSRC Conference on International Migration, as well as many earlier works like Woldemikael (1987) and Bonacich (1973). While the positions represented there are often seen as contraposing "transnationalism" or "cosmopolitanism" against categories constructed by geographical or cultural boundaries—in effect encouraging local assimilation (Dewind and Hirschman 1996)—we, like many other researchers, suggest that immigrants and refugees are attempting to balance these many connections, pressures, loyalties and necessities, locally and transnationally.

8. For example, see the Connecticut State Department of Education reports regarding numbers of bilingual education programs (state mandated for language groups with 20 or more students in a particular school), events held by the Connecticut Immigrant and Refugee Coalition, programs organized by Hartford Public Library (workshops about immigrants and domestic violence or citizenship classes in English and Spanish), and the healthcare coalition events organized by the nonprofit organization Caring Families.

9. However, despite Ferris's report of the increase in the number of local NGOs working with refugees over the last 50 years, the fully funded institutions are not providing the support refugees require for successful incorporation (Ferris, 2003).

10. Sharing a common language, Kosovar Muslims have access to (often largely Christian) Albanian organizations, particularly in nearby Waterbury, a neighboring town with a large Albanian population. (See for example the National Albanian American Council Newsletter discussion of a White House meeting on Kosovo (http://www.alb-net.com).

11. See detailed descriptions of this fear on the Khmer Health Advocates' website (http://www.cambodianhealth.org/healthcrisis.asp). Some of our Russian refugees were wary of participating in our study. One believed that the disposable camera we had given him to record his own life would be sent back to Russia!

12. According to the 2000 U.S. Census of Hartford, those identifying as Puerto Ricans make up 32.6 percent and as Cubans, a mere 5 percent of the total population. Within a five-block radius of Trinity College, we found at least six Cuban-owned businesses. The 1997 U.S. economic census is the latest set of economic data, which recorded that in the Hartford Metropolitan Area, Cubans owned 242 businesses, grossing approximately $300,000 per year compared with Puerto Ricans, who make up the majority of the Hispanic population, owned only 436 businesses grossing about $30,000 per year (The 1997 Economic Census). Moreover, about 25 percent of Puerto Ricans in Connecticut own their homes, while 54 percent of Cubans do.

13. A Latino-Muslim cultural connection is just beginning to receive prominent attention in the literature, as conversions to Islam are on the rise worldwide (including in Mexico) and, significantly, among Latinos in the United States. Part of the attraction of Islam has been linked to dissatisfaction with one's situation (or more specifically, racism and discrimination) particularly in America or as experienced through western cultural and economic influence— referred to as the "other September 11 effect" (Aidi, 2003). This suggests that Islam could become increasingly important as an oppositional identity for new Muslim refugees if their attempts to create more prosperous lives for themselves are thwarted or if their identities become a source of discrimination. Aidi describes a kind of racial or ethnic solidarity being articulated and fashioned around common connections traced to medieval Moorish (Islamic) Spain, often through Latin American popular cultural icons like Shakira (a Lebanese-Colombian singer) or through the statements of political leaders drawing attention to "Islamic Spain as an anchor for their identity" (Aidi 2003: 52).

14. In addition, about 63 percent of converts in the twelve months prior to the Hartford Seminary sponsored survey were African Americans; 6 percent were Latino (from "The Mosque in America," a study produced by Hartford Seminary, found on Muslim Life in America website).

15. See Castles (2002), Bauer (2000), and Glick-Schiller et al. (1992). Pratt (1990) in particular characterizes some of these segmented spaces as "safe havens" or safe houses for preserving necessary parts of one's cultural identity.

REFERENCES

Aidi, Hisham. 2003. "Let us Be Moors: Islam, Race, and 'Connected Histories'" in *Middle East Reports* 29.

Agustin, Laura. 2005. "Still Challenging "Place": Sex, Money, and Agency in Women's Migration." In *Women and the Politics of Place*. Wendy Harcourt and Arturo Escobar, eds.; 271–233. Bloomfield, CT: Kumarian Press.

Bauer, Janet. 2000. "Desiring Place: Iranian Refugee Women and the Cultural Politics of Self and Community in the Diaspora." *Comparative Studies of South Asia, Africa, and the Middle East* 20:180–209.

Bauer, Janet, and Vijay Prashad. 2000. "Dilemmas at the Border: an Introduction." In *Cultural Dynamics* 12 (3):175–181.

Beaumont, Justin, and Christopher Baker, eds. 2011. *Postsecular Cities. Space, Theory, and Practice.* London: Continuum Press.

Benton-Short, Lisa, and Marie Price. 2008. "Migrants to the Metropolis: The Rise of Immigrant Gateway Cities, an Introduction." In *Migrants to the Metropolis. The Rise of Immigrant Gateway Cities.* Price and Benton-Short, eds.; 1–22. Syracuse, NY: Syracuse University Press

Bonacich, Edna A. 1973. "Theory of Middleman Minorities." *American Sociological Review* 38:583–594.

Boswell, Thomas, and James Curtis. 1984. *The Cuban-American Experience: Culture, Images And Perspectives.* Rowman and Allenheld Publishers.

Braziel, Jana, and Anita Mannur. 2003. "Nation, Migration, Globalization: Points of Contention in Diaspora Studies." In *Theorizing Diaspora,* Braziel and Mannur, eds.: 1–21. Malden, Ma: Blackwell.

Castles, Stephen. 2002. "Migration and Community Formation under Conditions of Globalization."*International Migration Review* 36 (4):1143–1169.

Chacko, Elizabeth. 2008 "Washington, D.C.: From Biracial City to Multicultural Gateway." In *Migrants to the Metropolis. The Rise of Immigrant Gateway Cities.* Price and Benton-Short, eds.; 203–225. Syracuse, NY: Syracuse University Press.

Chronicle of Higher Education Colloquy Live. 2004. "Immigrants Reshape American Society and Vice Versa," February 11.

Condon, Garrett. 2004. "Diabetes Forum To Target Hispanics Disease Widely Affects Community; Education Seen As Key." *Hartford Courant.* April 8th.

D'Alisera, JoAnn. 2004. *An Imagined Geography. Sierra Leonean Muslims in America.* Philadelphia: University of Pennsylvania Press.

Daniel, E. Valentine, and John Knudson, eds. 1996. "Introduction." In *Mistrusting Refugees,* Daniel and Knudson, eds. 1–12. Berkeley, CA: University of California Press.

Davis, Mike. 2000. *Magical Urbanism. Latinos Reinvent The US City.* New York: Verso.

Dewind, J., and Hirschman, Charles. 1996. "Becoming American/America Becoming." *Items* 50 (2–3):41–47.

Faist, T. 2000. *The Volume and Dynamics of International Migration and Transnational Social Spaces.* Oxford University: Clarendon Press.

Ferris, E. 2003. "The Role of Non-Governmental Organizations in the International Refugee Regime," in *Problems of Protection: The UNHCR, Refugees, and Human Rights,* Steiner et al., eds: 117–140. New York: Routledge.

Fix, Michael, and Jeffrey Passel. 2004. "Immigration and Integration Trends. Immigrants in Connecticut." Paper presented at the Urban Institute, Washington, D.C., Jan. 24.

Flores and Benmayor, eds. 1997. *Latino Cultural Citizenship: Claiming Identity, Space and Rights.* Boston: Beacon Press.

Glick Schiller, Basch, and Blanc-Szanton. 1992. "Transnationalism: a new analytical framework for understanding Migration." In *Towards a Transnational Perspective on Migration,* Glick Schiller, Basch, and Blanc-Szanton, eds: 1–24. New York Academy of Sciences.

Haddad, Lawrence, and Lisa Smith. 2002. *Muslim Minorities in the West. Visible and Invisible.* Altamira Press.

Jonker, G. 2000. "What is Other about Other Religions? The Islamic Communities in Berlin between Integration and Segregation." *Cultural Dynamics* 12 (3): 311–329.

Kasinitz, Phillip, John Mollenkopf, and Mary Waters. 2002. "Becoming American/Becoming New Yorkers: Immigrant Incorporation in a Majority/Minority City. *International Migration Review* 36 (4):1020–1037.

Lugo, A. 2000. "Theorizing Border Inspections." *Cultural Dynamics* 12 (3):353–373.

Maira, Sunaina. 1999. "Identity Dub: The Paradoxes of an Indian American Youth Subculture." *Cultural Anthropology* 14 (1):29–60.

Meija, Rafael, and Priscilla Canny. 2007. "Immigration in Connecticut a Growing Opportunity." Hartford, CT: Connecticut Voices for Children.

Mohammad-Arif, Aminah. 2000. "A Masala Identity: Young South Asian Muslims in the US." *Comparative Studies of South Asia and the Middle East* 20: 67–87.

Monahan, Torin. 2002. "Los Angeles Studies." *City and Society* 20 (2): 155–184.

Nnaemeka, Obioma. 2004. "Nego-Feminism: Theorizing, Practicing, and Pruning Africa's Ways." *Signs* 29 (2):357–385.

Olsen, Laurie. 1997. "Made in America. Immigrant Students in Our Public Schools." New York: The New Press.

Pipher, Mary. 2002. *In the Middle of Everywhere: The World's Refugees Come to Our Town.* Harcourt.

Pratt, Marie Louise. 1990. "Arts of the Contact Zone." *Second Modern Language Association Literacy Convention.* Pittsburgh, Pennsylvania.

Reitz, Jeffrey. 2002. "Host societies and the Reception of Immigrants: Research Themes, Emerging Theories, and Methodological Issues." *International Migration Review* 36 (4):1005–1020.

Roozen, David. Hartford Seminar, Quoted in "Muslim Life in America." Office of International Information Programs. U.S. Department of State. http://infousa.state.gov/education/overview/muslimlife/living.htm (last accessed 2/3/2013).

Rucker, Patrick. 2003. "Gambling Just as Fast as We Can: A UConn study says that casinos are an obsession among the state's Asian refugee community." *Hartford Advocate,* Oct. 2.

Silvey, Rachel. 2008. "In the Margins of Riyadh: Indonesian Domestic Workers in Saudi Arabia." *In Migrants to the Metropolis. The Rise of Immigrant Gateway Cities.* Price and Benton-Short, eds.; 283–300. Syracuse, NY: Syracuse University Press.

Smith, Michael Peter. 2003. "Looking for Globality in Los Angeles." *Articulating the Global and the Local,* Cvetkovich and Kellner, eds: 55–71.Westview Press.

Valentine, Daniel E., and John Knudsen, eds. 1995. *Mistrusting Refugees.* California: University of California Press, 1995.

Van Haer, Nicholas. 1998. *New Diasporas.* Seattle: University of Washington Press.

von Zielbauer, Paul. 2003. "Hartford Bids A Bilingual Goodbye To A White-Collar Past." *The New York Times.* May 5, p.B1.

Warner, R. Stephen, and Judith G. Wittner, eds. 1998. *Gatherings in Diaspora: Religious Communities and the New Immigration.* Philadelphia: Temple University Press.

Wight, Ellen. 2000. "Bosnians in Chicago: Transnational Activities and Obstacles to Transnationalism." Sussex Migration Working Paper No.2.

Woldemikael, T. 1987. "Assertion Versus Accommodation: A Comparative Approach to Intergroup Relations." *American Behavioral Scientist* 30 (4):411–428.

Zolberg, Aristide. 1997. "Modes of Incorporation: Towards a Comparative Framework." In *Citizenship and Exclusion,* Bader, ed.; 139–154. New York: St. Martin's Press.

9

Re-imagining Portland, Maine

Urban Renaissance and a Refugee Community

Ezra Moser

"Change is the hallmark of American Society, as its cities and urban neighborhoods demonstrate" (Keating et al., 1996, 7).

The evening of April 25, 2009 saw a tragic scene in Portland, Maine. The events took place on Weymouth Street, a small and unassuming thoroughfare straddling the West End and Parkside neighborhoods—one a gentrified community, the other, once the second largest white non-Hispanic ghetto in America (Whitman et al., 1994). Blocks of wood-frame triple-decker tenements lined the street, a ubiquitous typology in lower-income New England neighborhoods, while a Latino bodega abutted its upper corner, an edifice of Portland's changing ethnic face. A 7:37 p.m. phone call to the Portland Police Department reported a seemingly intoxicated African American male brandishing a firearm in the open street. The man described was David Okot of Portland, a 26-year-old Sudanese refugee who had come to America in his teens. Police officers arrived on the scene and confronted Okot. They targeted him with their service weapons and ordered him to show his hands. The police report indicated that Okot turned away from the officers, placed his hand under his shirt, drew a .22 caliber handgun from his waistband and pointed it at them. The officers fired a total of 16 rounds, most of which struck Okot, who died on the scene. Eyewitness accounts, however, claimed that Okot did not draw for or attempt to grab his gun in any manner (for further details concerning this incident, refer to MacQuerrie, 2009). Despite the contested sequence of events, the result was unequivocally tragic—David Okot lay slain, and an already deteriorating relationship between the Portland Police Department and the city's growing refugee community was further exacerbated. The discharging of firearms in the open street is a scene far

Figure 9.1.   Weymouth Street, Parkside—The Setting of the Okot Shooting. (Ezra Moser)

more familiar to war-torn corners of Okot's native Sudan than to Portland, Maine, a progressive "citadel of blue America," with one of the nation's highest rates of residents with college degrees (Conforti, 2007: 323).[1]

This shooting betrays the idyllic Portland, the face the city extends toward the world—one of cultural and historic heritage, maritime New England charm, and an artsy destination replete with independently owned businesses and a variety of urban amenities. The David Okot shooting occurred at the border of Parkside and the West End, two communities that highlight competing visions of the "new" Portland. A portrait of contemporary Portland exposes the dissonance between its re-imagined self—the postindustrial success story of urban renaissance, and its lived self—the one experienced by its everyday citizens. Michel Foucault argues that examinations of power and justice, and in this case, urban planning, should not be "concerned with forms of power at their central locations, but rather with their forms of subjugation at the extremities, the peripheral loci . . ." (Hinkle, 1987: 50). Therefore, to learn anything about the normal is to examine its outlier. Examining the integration and experiences of the refugee community provides an index for the way in which Portland is re-imagining itself. The emergence of a substantial refugee community reflects a new, more diverse Portland, and it is imperative to study whether the city is embracing, navigating, or truly providing for this future.

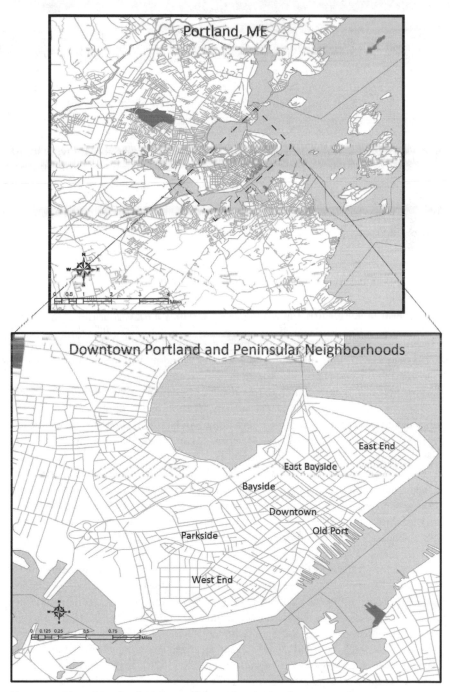

Map 9.1. Map of Portland, Maine, and the Urban Peninsular, 1990 and 2009. (Ezra Moser)

It is both apt and ironic that in 2009 *Forbes Magazine* named Portland the most "livable" city in America (O'Mally-Greenberg, 2009). On one hand this accolade solidifies Portland's status as a city of "renaissance," the culmination of a several-decade trend of economic growth and regeneration that transformed this economically stagnant former port into one of Frommer's top twelve destinations in the world (Frommer's Staff, 2006).

As Conforti (2007) notes, "commercial prosperity and geography endowed Portland with assets that acquired new value in the postindustrial economy: a scenic coastal location, maritime heritage, and distinctive built environment" (322). Portland capitalized on these endowments through regenerative strategies that emphasized a conscious re-imagining and re-engineering of the city as a center of urban diversity, heterogeneity, and vitality.

Richard Florida (2002) posits that in the postindustrial era, "diversity and creativity work together to power innovation and economic growth" (262). This supposed "synergy between production and consumption" has, according to Susan Fainstein (2005), promoted the concept of "diversity" as the guiding mantra for policy makers looking to facilitate urban revitalization (12). Likewise, Sharon Zukin (1995) contends that "culture is more and more the business of cities" (2). Holding these philosophies to be true, Portland developed and followed a seemingly infallible business strategy that transformed the city into the poster child for urban renaissance.

By 1970 Portland was something of a relic. Its economy had declined precipitously following World War II and widespread deindustrialization. The Downtown and Old Port—jewels of the city's contemporary renaissance crown—were all but abandoned, unable to compete with commercial activity in suburban shopping malls. On the other hand, the absence of pro-growth coalitions and a highly racialized landscape left Portland comparatively spared from extensive urban renewal, and community activism during the 1960s and 1970s halted any further destruction to the city's historical cityscape.[2] Early waves of gentrification fueled by this well-intact built environment helped ignite speculative real estate boom in the 1980s, producing one of the nation's "hottest" housing markets. The amount of class-A office space in Portland's downtown doubled during this decade, with 1,000,000 square feet constructed between 1985 and 1988 alone, securing space for the emerging dominance of FIRE industries (Finance, Insurance, and Real Estate) (Knopp and Kujawa, 1993).

The boom turned bust in 1988, however, halting FIRE and construction industries in their tracks, and within three years vacancy rates for downtown office space climbed to a record high of 23 percent (Diesenhouse, 1996). To jumpstart its economy, the city focused its redevelopment efforts on cultivating "culture," investing in its arts and entertainment institutions to stabilize the faltering FIRE industries. The city established a designated "Arts District" and pledged to support local arts groups with public money, through grants and property tax rebates, (Lees, 2003, 620). Local philanthropist and Intel microchip heiress Elizabeth Noyce poured millions of dollars into the Portland Museum of Art, the Maine Historical Society, and similar cultural institutions (Rimer, 1999). Noyce's investments were vital in establishing the nationally acclaimed Portland

Public Market, an indoor farmers' market and retail space, which earned Portland the Downtown Achievement Merit Award from the International Downtown Association (Lees, 2003, 618). Beyond investing in arts, entertainment, and cultural venues, Portland carried its philosophy of creating culture and cosmopolitanism over into its city planning documents, where concepts of diversity, livability, and urban vitality took center stage as the explicit key to its next phase of regeneration. Portland's primary planning document during the 1990s, titled *Downtown Vision: A Celebration of Urban Living and a Plan for the Future of Portland*, is one of the earliest and strongest examples of a conscious engineering of cosmopolitanism and urban heterogeneity on city hall's part. The plan espouses a "Downtown for People—where people of all ages and all socio-economic groups find an exciting, friendly and compassionate atmosphere," and a "Downtown for Opportunity—where a bustling office and retail economy combines with a thriving and diverse cultural, entertainment, and visitor economy to provide a prosperity shared by the whole community," (City of Portland, 1991, 4). As Loretta Lees (2003) notes, the concept of "diversity" is invoked several different times throughout the plan, touting "diverse job opportunities, . . . diverse arts, cultural and educational offerings . . . diverse citizenry" and a "culturally and ethnically diverse community that values its shared history, is proud of its cultural diversity and is working together for a cohesive community" (621). Portland has realized a substantial portion of this "vision" for itself, evidenced by the Old Port's vibrant cobblestone streets and boutiques and Downtown's numerous lofts and thriving art galleries. Any edifice of a "culturally and ethnically diverse community," however, remains elusive to the casual eye.

Portland's contemporary urban fabric has been supplemented and reconfigured by an estimated 10,000 refugees hailing from a variety of nations in Africa, Southeast Asia, the Middle East, and Eastern Europe, the majority of whom arrived from 1990 onward (Cadge et al., 2009, 10; Mamgain, 2003, 113). Given its rapid increase in numbers, to a visitor, this demographic would appear conspicuously absent from much of the landscape of the idyllic Portland. However, to anyone living in virtually any peninsular neighborhood or attending a Portland public school where some 53 languages are widely spoken and enrollment in English as a Learned Language (ELL) programs exceeds 25 percent, the presence of the refugee community is impossible not to notice. Portland is considered a prime destination for refugees, as its small size and relative safety make it an ideal place to raise children, while its extensive social-services infrastructure help their transition to life in America. In 2000 Portland had the seventh highest ratio in the nation of refugees as a percent of its recently arrived foreign-born population (Singer, 2006, 21). The Portland to which these refugees have arrived has been quick to embrace this newfound diversity,[3] but is also a city facing crucial challenges.

Gentrification-induced increases in real estate value and an inadequate supply of new affordable housing construction led to an acute property crisis in the mid 2000s, with vacancy rates dipping below 1 percent. Peninsular neighborhoods have seen the most pronounced impacts of these processes, home to the highest concentrations of rental housing and poverty in the city, but, simultaneously, a tripling in median

Table 9.1. Population of Portland, Maine, and the Urban Peninsular, 1990 and 2009

	1990 Census	2000 Census	2005–2009 ACS Estimates
City of Portland			
Population	64,358	64,249	63,395
% White, Non-Hispanic	96.0%	90.6%	85.0%
% Foreign-Born	5.1%	7.6%	10.5%
% Living in Poverty	14.1%	14.1%	17.6%
Median Gross Rent at			
Percentage of Income	28.4%	26.1%	30.8%
Median Home Value	$109,874	$125,200	$250,035
Urban Peninsula (Census Tracts 1, 2, 3, 5, 6, 10, 11, 12, 13)			
Population	23,405	23,168	22,390
% White, Non-Hispanic	94.2%	86.9%	79.4%
% Foreign-Born	6.4%	10.2%	14.6%
% Living in Poverty	25.6%	23.8%	32.1%
Median Gross Rent at			
Percentage of Income	29.2%	26.1%	32.3%
Median Home Value	$102,708	$127,234	$312,595

Source: U.S. Census.

home value since 1990. Refugees, who invariably arrive in Portland with little financial means and glaring needs, are largely relegated to these peninsular neighborhoods where rental housing is more abundant. Affording these rental units has become increasingly difficult, often necessitating earnings of over $17.00 an hour, a wage far out of reach for these populations. Subsequently, one of the most common situations for newly arrived refugees is to be housed in one of Portland Housing Authority's public and subsidized units, the majority of which are also found in socioeconomically polarizing peninsular neighborhoods. As the city experiences an influx of young urban professionals and creative types that stoke the demand for what they see as relatively inexpensive, urban, market-rate housing, it is simultaneously home to a growing refugee demographic in need of affordable units, with both groups jockeying for space in the exact same neighborhoods.

Critiquing Florida, Fainstein (2005) argues that the abstract notion of diversity has become an unquestioned "mantra for public officials aiming to foster urban resurgence," but one that, as even Florida himself admits, favors a "diversity of elites" (12). Furthermore, scholarly literature (Lees, 2008; Fainstein, 2005; Wyly and Hammel, 2002) emphasizes that gentrification—a concept virtually inseparable from urban renaissance—has increasingly become a tool for de-concentrating and dispersing poverty in order to push forward revanchist and neoliberal agendas favoring the middle and upper classes. However, one former mayor avows that an ethos of civic mindedness has continually been central to contemporary city hall politics, as evidenced by the city's extensive welfare and social-service infrastructure (interview with informant 1, 2010).[4]

Despite *Forbes'* accolade, Portland, as of 2000 had a median household income less than that of its own state, itself relatively poor. Do the benefits of the nation's most "livable city" extend to its refugee populations crowded in the city's housing projects, huddled in the literal shadows of downtown's emblematic postindustrial success? Through the use of scholarly literature, city planning documents, and local interviews, I seek to examine the relationship between Portland and its refugee community in order to determine whether this engineered cosmopolitanism and "celebration of diversity" is an empty gesture. Recalling Foucault, to learn anything about the normal is to examine its outlier, and the experience of the refugee community reveals any dissonance between the city's re-imagined self and its lived experience. Furthermore, considering Portland to be a comparatively blank canvas potentially makes these implications universal. The case of Portland will reveal whether the city of urban renaissance is any closer to the ideal of a socially just city, or merely a distinct morphology of the neoliberal city, disguised by romanticized notions of urban vitality and heterogeneity.

A NEW PORTLAND: THE PROBLEMS FACED

Portland has no illusions about its contemporary reality. The influx of some 10,000 refugees is impossible to ignore in a predominantly white, native-born city. A closer examination of the city's spatial and economic landscape appears to indicate that refugees would be inherently excluded from the benefits of the nation's most livable city. The city's renaissance landscape has made fitting in for this demographic a challenge in the critical realms of housing and employment.

Portland's peninsular neighborhoods are magnets for gentrifying classes and low-income populations. Both groups are drawn, albeit for different reasons, by the benefits of an urban housing stock. ACS census estimates for 2005–2009 indicate that in less than a decade, median home values in these areas rose almost to $200,000 while median gross rent as a percentage of income and poverty rate increased 24 percent and 35 percent, respectively. These neighborhoods may be hotbeds of gentrification, but they are also home to the highest concentrations of refugees, who arrive in Portland in need of affordable housing and access to centrally located social services. Homeownership for newly arrived refugees is virtually out of the question. In 2000 homeownership rates were a fraction of their national averages across all racial categories, but particularly low for minority-headed households, a statistical category that represents the majority of Portland's refugee population (Allen, 2007; City of Portland, 2005). This demographic could only afford 39 percent of the citywide median home sales price, and 72 percent of the average rent for a two-bedroom apartment. With few available options, refugees subsequently occupy approximately 60–70 percent of Portland's public and subsidized housing units, and comprise the majority of the 1,000-plus families on the waiting list (interview with informant 2, 2010).

Access to viable employment opportunities is fundamental to mitigating this unequal access to the city's spatial landscape. It would appear, however, that Portland's renaissance economy is as exclusionary as its housing market. Despite the emphasis on cultural capital and creative industries, the postindustrial urban economy is primarily marked by the dominance and bifurcation of the service sector. This phenomenon is equally evident in contemporary Portland. The five largest industries by employment were in the service sector (as were nine of the top ten), which themselves accounted for 43.4 percent of total employment. As Table 9.2 indicates, the majority of these industries are predominantly high skill, with FIRE industries accounting for more than 10 percent.[5]

The wages of corresponding low-end services offer little consolation, and are often less than half of their high-end counterparts in the same industries.[6] To an extent this is unsurprising, as academic literature posits that the restructuring associated with the transition to a service-sector economy not only exacerbates inequality, but does little to boost the earnings of the lower-income demographics (Logan and Molocht, 2007; Sassen, 1996).

Portland's economy may have flourished in contrast to the rest of Maine, but the city still affords considerably fewer economic opportunities for low-skill workers than many other American cities. Allen (2007) notes that many of the low-skill jobs in Portland, especially much of the accommodation and retail industries, are connected to tourism and therefore seasonal, providing inconsistent employment opportunities that yield very low average earnings (18). The implications of this are particularly problematic for refugee populations. While many refugees were professionals or attained high levels of education in their nations of origin, such qualifica-

Table 9.2. Top Ten Industries by Employment in Portland, Maine, 2008

Industry	% of Employment for Portland, ME
Healthcare	10.7% (3,757)
Accommodation and Food Services	8.8% (3,103)
Educational Services	8.4% (2,942)
Finance and Insurance	8.0% (2,813)
Professional, Scientific, and Technical Services	7.5% (2,653)
Construction	4.1% (1,453)
Administrative Support and Waste Management Services	3.5% (1,231)
Public Administration	3.0% (1,057)
Food & Beverage Stores	3.0% (1,042)
Social Assistance	2.7% (949)

Source: City data, 2008.

tions rarely translate in America. Many refugees also arrive with little proficiency in English, hindering them from entering the job market directly or re-attaining their professional credentials. Research by Allen (2007) revealed that refugees who managed to find consistent employment earned a monthly wage of $1,790 (an annual salary of $21,480), a dismal 44 percent less than the average Portlander. Furthermore, this income would hardly be sufficient to afford Portland's average monthly rent of $850–$1,000. It is telling that in 2000 approximately one-third of Portland's impoverished population were not U.S. citizens, yet foreign-born populations at the time constituted less than 10 percent of the population. This can be construed as generally indicative of refugee populations in the context of Portland, a city whose social geography is otherwise largely homogenous and native-born.

As if refugees have not already overcome incredible adversity by making it to America in the first place, they subsequently find themselves in need of supplementary incomes and short of affordable housing and sufficient employment opportunities and are often relegated to neighborhoods with the highest concentrations of poverty. Furthermore, refugees' educational and professional qualifications rarely translate in the American system, dramatically diminishing their human capital and employment potential. Mamgain (2003) asserts that "occupational integration is key to overcoming poverty," (115). It is difficult to discern exactly how feasible "occupational integration" is for the refugee community in Portland. Does occupational integration constitute simply finding employment or does it imply opportunity for advancement? The economic dominance of the high-end service sectors makes the latter interpretations highly unlikely given that refugees' human capital often does not translate.

Portland's urban renaissance appears to have produced a more polarized than equitable socio-spatial and economic landscape, the effects of which acutely and disproportionately afflict a population as vulnerable as the refugee community. Examining the ground-level realities of this relationship will illuminate precisely how dissonant Portland's re-imagined self is from its lived experience.

A COLLECTIVE EXPERIENCE OF POLICY?

A ground-level examination and interviewees' perspectives reveal that there is not a collective experience of refugee-oriented policy and services in Portland. Interviewees whose line of work was furthest removed from the refugee community itself were less critical of how well the city has provided for it. City-affiliated organizations were associated with stabilizing services, and consequently tended to be most satisfied, believing themselves to be doing their best within budgetary constraints. Community-oriented nonprofit and faith-based initiatives expressed far less satisfaction than city-affiliated agencies, as these organizations tackled complex issues of socio-cultural transitions and socioeconomic integration, which cannot be facilitated by any single provision, such as housing or General Assistance. The refugees and immigrants interviewed believed city services to be misguided or only temporarily necessary, either way, out of touch with the community's long-term needs.

Interviewees associated with city hall were primarily concerned with budget and allocation of resources, indicative of Portland's complicated political reality. Even before refugees arrived en masse, an extensive network of social services were in place, programs that drew "homeless adults, substance abusers, troubled teenagers and disabled people," from communities all across the state and region where "such social welfare programs do not exist" (Conforti, 320). In the 2007 city government payroll, welfare service was the second largest division in terms of full-time employees and was third highest in funding (City Data, 2008). While poorer rural municipalities in northern and western Maine rely heavily on state funds, "property rich" Portland garners little sympathy from the capital and receives modest state funding, forcing the city to install high property taxes in order to finance its overextended social services (Conforti, 320). Initiatives that affect a broad range of constituents, such as housing, welfare, or creating jobs, naturally take a central role, the benefits of which ostensibly extend to the refugee community as much as any other demographic. Refugee-specific initiatives, meanwhile, are forced to rely on federal grant funding to keep their services running.

Nonprofit and faith-based organizations voiced the greatest frustrations, having to provide for long-term needs of their clients, and having limited or inconsistent access to funding. Interviewees cited the three greatest areas of need to be resources for cultural education and language initiatives, employment skills training, and youth programs. These organizations occupy a difficult middle ground, forced to both supplement and navigate city hall's stabilizing, welfare-oriented services, which themselves are constantly threatened by rollbacks. In having to provide for the subsequent issues of acculturation facing refugees, they are keenly aware of this community's specific challenges, but are similarly constrained by budgetary headaches.

In contrast, refugee and immigrant perspectives are far less concerned with fiscal aspects of services available to them, and instead have a clear opinion of which initiatives are necessary or successful and how they can all be improved. Immigrants involved with the refugee community expressed the strongest disapproval of social-service initiatives, believing them to be misguided and overly paternalistic. Refugees themselves, however, invariably utilized these services at one point, and deemed them to be necessary. One informant, director of the city's Office of Multilingual and Multicultural Affairs and herself a Filipino immigrant, believes the city's welfare services–oriented approach relegates refugees to recipients of aid instead of key actors in their own success. Refugee families are "very proud," she says, and do not want to be constantly associated with General Assistance. She claims that "the reality is, if you talk to many of the leaders [in the refugee community], they'll say 'no we don't use [services] . . . somebody else is getting the money but it's definitely not me.' . . ." (interview with informant 3, 2010). One refugee informant cited that city services helped stabilize his own family, but that many refugee families do not understand their temporary and transitional nature, an issue of cultural differences that would be easily mitigated by community engagement, an underemphasized aspect of the city's social services.

Both groups concurred that formulating refugee-specific services without involvement from the constituents themselves is problematic. The director of the Office of Multilingual and Multicultural Affairs asserts that the city's approach is a "white" mentality, assuming that their notions of how to provide for the refugee community will effectively integrate them into Portland's social landscape (interview with informant 9, 2010). Instead, both groups cite mutual education and exposure between refugee and native-born families as simple, imperative solutions. A fundamental realm for implementing such measures would naturally be the city's public schools, which interviewees professed are highly segregated. They cited that ELL programs often serve to further isolate multicultural students, many of whom are kept there until graduation, leaving them with a seriously inadequate education. The ELL initiatives are representative of the refugee experience in Portland: a discord between a vital, well-intentioned service and its implementation.

A study conducted by the Brookings Institution found that "the successful incorporation of refugees into the economic, financial and social mainstream requires local leaders to create an environment both informative to the receiving community and also culturally sensitive to the refugees," (Singer, 26). While the refugees' opinions are vital in formulating political avenues and initiatives that best serve themselves, their differing perspectives exhibit that policy is not necessarily a shared experience in Portland. Furthermore, the opinions from City Hall and the variety of community and faith-based organizations reveal an unclear system of hierarchy and relations in which the latter groups ultimately provide many refugee-specific services. Intriguingly, this indicates underlying and emerging elements of neoliberal urban governance.[7]

Any indication of neoliberal leanings would literally turn Portland's re-imagined self on its head, as the city has long prided itself as a bastion of welfare services. Portland's real estate market was one of the driving forces of its urban renaissance, but its success ultimately cut it off from state flows, forcing the city to become self-sufficient in financing its extensive services. By facilitating the transition to a service-sector and consumption-based economy characteristic of global neoliberal capitalism, Portland acquired neoliberalism's most problematic legacy—a public sector with limited capacity to provide for a comprehensive range of social-service needs and a fragmented hierarchy of urban governance.

An oddly appropriate maritime analogy illustrates this phenomenon in the context of the city's refugee community. Having been cast adrift by state funding, Portland's proverbial ship is sinking under the tremendous weight of its own preexisting institutional frame of services, its hull riddled with the holes left by neoliberalism's structural deficiencies. As Portland sinks deeper, the dissonance between its re-imagined self and its lived experience becomes increasingly apparent, and the refugee community, riding third class in the cargo hold, will be first to drown.

City Hall and its extended coalition of nonprofits and community organizations—the acting captain and his crew—are frantically bailing the water out, but the problem is instead with ship's frame. It is at this juncture that Portland is being examined. To understand the lived experience of the refugee community, the city's outliers, it is essential to examine the grave conditions in the cargo hold. Observing how effective the city's solutions are will further illuminate the lived experience of the refugee community, and whether the captain needs to formulate a better plan, and fast.

STRUGGLING WITH SOLUTIONS: HOUSING AND SERVICES

The city's solutions take the form of housing and social services. Their implementation, however, reveals that the market-oriented strategy of regeneration through gentrification and urban renaissance has created a framework in which government and social services are increasingly unable to mitigate market failures and provide for the refugee community.

According to a PHA estimate, refugees occupy between 60 percent and 70 percent of the nearly 3,000 public and subsidized housing units spread across the city (interview with informant 2, 2010). Refugee service organizations such as Catholic Charities and the Department of Refugee Services actively funnel refugee families into these units when possible, as they provide the most affordable, immediate options. The five largest complexes, however, contain more than 165 units each. They disrupt the urban fabric, are spatially isolated, and have only served to concentrate poverty. Many of these complexes, such as East Bayside's Kennedy Park, expose refugee residents to crime, gang activity, and other negative influences.

Contemporary patterns of subsidized housing construction follow an integrated, mixed-rate model, many of which contain 15 units or less.[8] The emphasis on mixed-rate development theoretically allows the housing market to flourish (by providing market-rate units in centrally located neighborhoods) while keeping its volatile consequences, such as displacement, in check. Scholarly literature, however, indicates that lower-density mixed-income communities often subvert such lofty ideals (Lees, 2008; Wyly and Hammel, 2002). Lees (2008) suggests that the gentrification it necessarily facilitates "is part of an aggressive, revanchist ideology designed to retake the inner-city for the middle classes," and "leads to displacement and socio-spatial segregation rather than alleviating social segregation" (2457). Furthermore, deconcentrating impoverished demographics through socially mixed housing initiatives undermines the vital networks of social capital that such communities may have established (Lees, 2008: 2461).

Perhaps by emphasizing future growth in its housing initiatives, the city is not taking into account the severity of current circumstances for low-income populations. In fiscal year 2009, the city's family-specific homeless shelter experienced a 53 percent increase in secondary migrant refugees requiring its facilities, totaling

300 individuals (City of Portland, 2010: 77). The Department of Refugee Services indicated the arrival of 549 secondary migrants to Portland over the same period. For every two incoming secondary migrants to Portland in 2009, there was essentially one that was homeless for a period of time. Unless temporary shelters are considered adequate housing for Portland's newest arrivals, the provision and construction of affordable housing needs to become an even higher priority. While refugees and city politicians alike agree that spatial integration of subsidized housing is imperative, it appears that these smaller and mixed-rate developments do not satisfy their current demand.

Secondary and nonprofit organizations work to provide a variety of social services, but their relation to the city itself can be complicated. For example, the Office of Multilingual and Multicultural Programs and the Department of Refugee Services were vital initiatives developed with city hall but receive little or no direct funding, relying instead on a variety of federal grants that require a continual re-application process.

The Office of Multilingual and Multicultural programs provides the crucial service of running and managing the Portland Public Schools' English as a Learned Language programs, which some 26 percent of the enrolled student body depend upon. In 2009 alone these programs experienced a net increase of 430 new students, indicating that their reliance on auxiliary federal funding is unlikely to diminish (interview with informant 3, 2010).

The City of Portland Department of Refugee Services is arguably the most refugee-specific organization in city hall. Strictly geared toward secondary migrant refugees, the organization's primary responsibilities include securing housing and providing follow-up services, employment training and placement, and helping clients navigate the city's general assistance bureaucracy.

With public and subsidized units at capacity, securing housing requires the office to hunt in the private market, a task further complicated by the prevalence of large families in the refugee community. The department's director explains that housing a refugee family of ten often necessitates taking two neighboring units out of the market because of the family's size. This exacerbates the already tight market for affordable housing, and many refugee families would have trouble affording one of these units at $1,000 per month, much less two. The Department of Refugee Services is not allowed to subsidize these extra units to appease stubborn landlords, who would have little incentive to rent two units for below-market rates (interview with informant 4, 2010). Clearly a "hot" real estate market confers the majority of its benefits to demographics privileged enough to exercise choice in where they live. Sometimes there is literally nowhere to fit her clients. Even when she is successful, many are ultimately evicted for non-payment. This likely reflects the disturbing rise of secondary migrant refugees, her very own clients, in Portland's family shelter.

Despite consistent grant funding—and servicing 1,459 unduplicated clients in 2009—the Department of Refugee Services can only afford to employ three of its six employees full time. According to its director, the economic downturn of 2008 has severely affected the city and state's budget, as revenues from excise taxes have sharply declined. She predicts that 40 city employees will lose their jobs in 2010. Two years earlier, the city was forced to lay off 96 employees, with 76 of those positions never being replaced (interview with informant 4, 2010).

Her experiences highlight that providing these services requires her to constantly navigate a spatial and socioeconomic landscape littered with legacies of prior policy decisions, precariously tight housing markets, and fiscal debt. She is forced to find room for her clients in a preexisting urban framework that affords little space to accommodate them, despite any cosmopolitan and egalitarian convictions on the city's part. Every refugee client that the city, social services, or the housing market ultimately fails contributes to the dissonance between Portland's re-imagined self of postindustrial success, and a harsh reality of daily struggle, poverty, and unfulfilled American dreams for the New Mainers.

The shortcomings of these efforts illuminate that working against the neoliberal economy's flow is a difficult task for an overextended city government. By investing in a consumer-driven, service-sector economy during its urban renaissance, Portland fashioned itself a framework that would invariably be prone to leaks. The refugee community finds itself vulnerably exposed to both the failures of the market and the increasingly imminent failures of a city government struggling to provision fundamental services such as education. However, if the theoretical neoliberal city supposedly mitigates such failures with a strong coalition of nonprofit organizations, then perhaps Portland has an ideal patch at its disposal.

The State of Maine Department of Health and Human Services (2007) website lists over 40 organizations that serve multicultural families in the Portland area including religious and ethnically specific organizations, consulting firms for multicultural enterprises, mental health services, and legal advocacy groups. These organizations are the refugee community's unsung heroes, primarily handling the difficult task of facilitating socio-cultural transitions for their clients. These responsibilities would likely fall outside the city's stabilizing framework of services, but are nonetheless invaluable. Their community-based nature is more palatable to refugee demographics, because, as an employee of one such organization relays, "It's very difficult to translate into American language how valuable community is to [them]" (interview with informant 5, 2010).

Interviewees highlighted that more assimilated younger generations increasingly eschew cultural traditions and customs such as wearing hijabs or burqas, observing religious holidays or conforming to strict standards of relations with the opposite sex, the effects of which severely strain many refugee families. Gagnon and Lonsdale (2006) imply that "parents and children [are] speaking two different languages, culturally that is" (22). Parents believe that the local school system undermines their efforts to maintain cultural traditions, exercise discipline, and mend this intergenerational gap by supporting the rights of the children over the rights of the parents (Gagnon and Lonsdale, 2006: 24).

City hall would view such socio-cultural conflicts as less of an exigent need and a lower priority than housing, general assistance, or employment training. However, neglecting these issues is highly problematic. One interviewee maintained that the absence of a functioning family unit frequently propels young refugees toward the streets, leading to elevated levels of gang activity, a rapidly growing problem in the community (interview with informant 6, 2010). Gagnon and Lonsdale (2006) discovered that the erosion of these communities' strong cultural capital has led, in part, to a high prevalence of substance abuse in the youth populations of Portland's refugee community, an issue of which parents were unaware, uneducated about, or powerless to stop. One informant, himself a Sudanese refugee, relates an anecdote:

> My mother is active in the Sudanese community and used to always invite other African mothers over for dinner. . . . She would ask them, "How is your son doing?" and they would break down crying. . . . They would say "my son is dealing drugs," or "he's in trouble with the law." . . . This would happen with nine out of every ten families that would come visit (interview with informant 7, 2010).

He has seen several childhood friends end up in prison, and firmly believes that his close-knit family helped him stay on a path toward success. Issues of violent crime and gang activity have become increasingly prevalent in the refugee community, which led to a period of elevated tensions with the police department. This came to a head in 2009, following two tragic and high-profile shootings in which young Sudanese men lost their lives. In one case, the victim, James Angelo, was gunned down outside Mercy Hospital in the West End while on duty as a security guard. Police failed to identify or arrest the shooters, and an outraged Sudanese community wrote a formal letter to city officials saying that "they no longer viewed Portland as a safe city" (Bell and Kim, 2008). This incident was preceded by seven separate unsolved cases involving shootings of Sudanese Portlanders. The David Okot shooting, outlined in the introduction, was highly politicized and controversial as well. Its location at the border between the West End and Parkside highlights that issues with crime literally threatened to spill over into the "idyllic" Portland of urban renaissance. These incidents indicate that Portland's renaissance framework has failed to provide for its refugee community in a very fundamental manner, and certainly calls into question precisely how "livable" the nation's most livable city is for all of its members.

This failure, however, indicates an ideal role for community-based organizations, whose non-affiliation with the city, but knowledge of its systems provide for a vital link for refugee populations. Interviewees believed that the more grassroots the organization, the more attuned it is to its constituents' needs and will likewise be successful in providing for them, one stating that without local and community organizations such as hers, the refugee community would be "in a lot more trouble." The aforementioned Brookings Institution study expounded on the fact that nonprofit and community-based organizations play leading roles in the process of successfully incorporating refugees into American communities (Singer, 2006: 18). One grassroots organization, the West End's LearningWorks, is a $2,000,000-per-year social-service provider that operates language education and job training programs for refugees of all ages and maintains 56 local units of subsidized housing (Hench,

2009). Other similar initiatives such as Bayside's African Culture and Learning Center and East Bayside's Somali Community Center—the latter of which required $500,000 in fund-raising and personal investment to open—were formed by refugees themselves, and seek to specifically address the community's needs (Ross, 2007; Maxwell, 2006). Until Portland allows similar organizations to become leading agents in providing for the city's refugee population—instead of forcing them to be the proverbial cleanup crew—the dissonance between its re-imagined self and lived experience will only grow stronger.

These are not the only avenues for self-empowerment, however, as the experiences of refugee communities facing similar circumstances in other American cities indicate. Somali refugee communities in Minneapolis, Minnesota, and Columbus, Ohio, have found considerable success in establishing ethnic indoor "malls," which spatially imitate their native bazaars and marketplaces (Ali and Arman, 2008). Entrepreneurs lease booth space from which they sell their products, and rent is thus made affordable by the high density of vendors. In Minneapolis, Southeast Asian and Latino refugee communities have carved thriving economic niches through similar practices (Taylor, 2000). In Worcester, Massachusetts, Clark University launched a progressive academic program in which students work with local refugee establishments implementing microfinance loans. This community-university partnership was made possible by a $100,000 grant from Lutheran Social Services, the city's preeminent refugee resettlement program (Dayal, 2010). Even in smaller case studies such as Burlington, Vermont, and Concord, New Hampshire, microfinance loans that facilitate entrepreneurship have been the most successful methods for fostering socioeconomic self-sufficiency for refugee communities, a key to integration (Rathke, 2006; Conaboy, 2007).

In Portland, one of the most successful and empowering programs for refugees stems directly from the private sector. Barber Foods, a large food processing plant on the West End's periphery, employs refugees as 44 percent of its 750-member workforce. The company privately finances an English as a Second Language program for refugee employees along with courses in math and computer science and in 2001 established a college scholarship program named Pathways to Higher Education. This level of commitment to its foreign-born employees is seen as an investment, hoping that the recipients will make their career with the company and become empowered, contributing members to Portland society (Murphy, 2007). Small-scale initiatives that derive from outside the preexisting coalitions of service providers can be the most potent remedies for success and often provide more direct avenues to self-empowerment.

CONCLUSIONS

The 16 gunshots fired at David Okot echoed in the evening air for a matter of seconds, but the dissonance they represented reverberates to this day. This dissonance is between the city of Portland's re-imagined self of urban renaissance, cosmopolitanism, and embedded liberalism, and its lived experience, the latter of which came to an untimely end for Okot. Examining the focal point of this dissonance, the experience of the refugee community, and its relationship to city hall and its renaissance politics, exposes several important conclusions. First, and most evident is that Portland's urban renaissance did not manage to produce a more socially just cityscape, despite having a comparatively "blank canvas," a politically receptive environment, and an extensive welfare and social-service infrastructure. The dissonance indicates that the refugee community's interests are not optimally provided for or being incorporated into the city's socio-political framework. Furthermore, this examination reveals that city hall's political-economic model of urban renaissance exhibits many qualities of a neoliberal city clad in political progressivism and aspirations of cosmopolitanism. Portland is discovering that when an added layer of complexity—a rapidly growing refugee community—is added to its model of urban renaissance, its underlying neoliberal tendencies emerge, and its once successful regenerative framework begins to literally and figuratively tear at the seams.

Investing in a high-end service- and consumption-based economy, while throwing as many social services as possible at the demographics left in the shadow of its success, is neither an effective nor sustainable solution. Unsurprisingly, the ethnic and cultural diversity the city sought to "celebrate" has been largely unable to emerge from these shadows and partake of the festivities. That is not to undermine the efforts of organizations that work doggedly at bridging this gap, but they face the challenge of orchestrating miracles with limited and shrinking resources. Capitalizing on this postindustrial success invariably means tapping into the flow of an increasingly globalized, neoliberal economy, and the city needs to creatively adapt to its pressures and demands.

The most evident implication is that the traditional welfare model needs to be reconfigured in order to adapt to these demands. Mohamed (2001) extensively studied the socioeconomic and political integration of Somali refugee populations in Toronto, Ontario, and his results have significant implications for Portland. Canada provides its citizens with an array of generous social welfare services that would be impossible to find in even the most progressive American cities. Under the precept that stabilization via social services is the key to effective integration, Mohamed's case study demographic should have flourished. His findings, however, indicated the opposite, that Somali refugees did not achieve "significant structural integration, into the social, economic and political structures of Canadian society," and were afflicted by many of the same problems facing Portland's refugee community (Mohamed, 2001).[9] These findings reflect the opinions of Portland's interviewed refugees, whose main desire is simply to have a greater stake in their future. The Office of Multilingual and Multicultural Affairs' director attests that social services that don't emphasize and engender self-empowerment will invariably fail to move beyond the stage of stabilizing its clients. She asserts that "if you don't give [refugees] the tools [to succeed] in the first six months, how do you expect them to stand on their own two feet?" (interview with informant 3, 2010). Stabilizing services essentially aim to "maintain" the refugee community in an increasingly neoliberal, renaissance cityscape with waning available space. Thus, the most imperative avenue for self-empowerment is giving this community the ability to directly participate in the socioeconomic landscape, allowing them to create their own space.

Bolstering initiatives that facilitate self-empowerment through entrepreneurship and the opportunity for socioeconomic integration will allow the refugee community to be the key actors in creating their own success. Portland may have become a distinct—and partially in denial—brand of the neoliberal city, but, intriguingly, exhibits some of the most positive qualities of its theoretical ideal, such as one of the nation's friendliest environments for small businesses (Thomas, 2005). If the abstract notion of "culture" is one of Portland's contemporary sites of production around which consumption is based, then refugee entrepreneurs have much to offer consumers.

If the economic crisis of 2008 effectively halts conspicuous consumption in its tracks, then Portland may be in trouble, as it specializes in producing "culture," which requires a very specific consumer base. However, according to one former mayor, past recessions in Portland merely ratcheted development back as opposed to changing its trajectory altogether (interview with informant 1, 2010). If fabricated versions of urban vitality were sold wholesale to young professionals during the process of urban renaissance, perhaps Portland can capitalize on the opportunity to create an authentic version, this time replete with cultural diversity.

Refugees bring valuable youth and dynamism to an otherwise aging and economically stagnant state. They possess survival skills and have real life experiences that most Americans could not begin to fathom. The city of urban renaissance can undoubtedly harness these assets. In an increasingly globalized world this population provides the global connections necessary to make Portland a truly multifaceted, cosmopolitan, and livable city. Perhaps the presence of the refugee community in Portland has provided Portland in turn with a vital service—a proverbial wake-up call and the opportunity to continually re-imagine and reinvent itself as a city more perfectly in tune with all of its constituents.

The implications of these findings extend beyond Portland. Fainstein (2005) argues that "developing an appropriate physical setting for a heterogeneous urbanity . . . can only go so far in the generation of a just city. Most crucial is a political consciousness that supports progressive moves . . . toward respectfulness of others and greater equality," (16). Portland planned for diversity in a top-down manner and subsequently failed to fully realize its re-imagined vision for itself. Nevertheless, the accolades are far more likely to remain the face of Portland, Maine, in the near future, not the struggles and experience of the refugee community. Likewise, it is unlikely that the paradigm of resuscitation through urban renaissance will diminish as the unquestioned modus operandi of urban planners and politicians, despite its shortcomings.

Examining the case of Portland and the experience of its refugee community demonstrates that planning for diversity requires investing in its interests, listening to its needs, and fostering direct participation. The richest tapestry of urban fabric is woven with its entire population, and the largest threads are not always the most vibrant.

NOTES

1. In introducing the concept of the refugee community, it is of paramount importance to understand that this terminology is by no means intended to construe this demographic as a monolithic bloc. Conversely, the most distinguishing characteristic of this population is its diversity. While certain patterns of settlement and spatial realities have materialized, it is important to recognize that attempting to consolidate such a vast array of cultures and experiences into a single "community" is ultimately inaccurate.

2. For reference and more information concerning Portland's economic historical trajectory, urban renewal in Portland, and the early stages of the city's renaissance, refer to Fishman (1980), Barry (1982), Bell (2009), Conforti (2007), and Bauman (2006).

3. According to research by Cadge et al. (2009), Portland provided an exceptionally welcoming political environment for its immigrant and refugee communities. Cadge et al. (2009) asserts that Portland "wholeheartedly included immigrants in its political and economic agenda," and integrated them "as part of working to recreate itself as a multicultural, welcoming, and tolerant place to live" (2 4).

4. All interviewees retain anonymity per standard sociological practices and have been given informant numbers.

5. Real estate (not depicted in Table 9.2) accounts for 2.6 percent of total employment in Portland, ME (928 persons), and is the eleventh largest employer by industry (City Data, 2008).

6. For example, in healthcare, the largest sector in Portland, the mean salary of practitioners and technicians was more than twice as much as that of "support occupations" ($56,350 compared to $21,580)(Bureau of Labor Statistics, 2001).

7. A characteristic of the contemporary "neoliberal city" is a diminished municipal government flanked by a coalition of nonprofit and community-based organizations to provision social services. For more information, refer to Eick (2007).

8. The PHA database cites 58 individual housing developments that include units subsidized on the peninsula, of which 32 contain 15 units or less (interview with informant 2, 2010).

9. Mohamed's study found that "as recent migrants, Somali refugees have not achieved significant structural integration into the social, economic, and political structures of Canadian society. Dependence on social welfare assistance, a high rate of unemployment, limited educational pursuits, and social and residential segregation are features common among Somali refugees in Toronto . . . factors that hinder their effective integration" (Mohamed, 2001).

REFERENCES

Ali S. B., Arman, A., 2008, "Somalis in Columbus." (*Islamic Horizons*, 1 September, 2008).
Allen, R., 2007, *Sometimes It's Hard Here to Call Someone to Ask for Help: Social Capital in a Refugee Community in Portland, Maine*. PhD. Massachusetts Institute of Technology.

Allen, R., 2006, Employment and Earnings Outcomes for Recently Arrived Refugees in Portland, Maine. *Special Publication for the Maine Department of Labor.*

Barry, W., 1982. *A Vignetted History Of Portland Business.* New York: Newcomen Society.

Bauman, J., 2006, "A Saga of Renewal in a Maine City: Exploring the Fate of Portland's Bayside District." *Journal of Planning History,* Vol. 5.4, 329–354.

Bell, T., 2009, "Rethinking an Urban Vision." (*Portland Press Herald,* 26 April, 2009).

Bell, T., Kim, A., 2008, "Sudanese Decry City's Inaction Against Growing Violence 'Why is This Happening?'" (*Portland Press Herald,* 8 September, 2008).

Bureau of Labor Statistics, 2001, *2000 Metropolitan Area Occupational Employment and Wage Estimates: Portland, ME MSA.* Retrieved 22 April 2010 from http://www.bls.gov/oes/2000/oes_6400.htm#b41–0000.

Cadge, W., Curran, S., Jaworsky B. N., Levitt, P., Hejtmanek, J., 2009, The City as Context: Spaces of Reception in New Immigrant Destinations. In: *American Sociological Association Annual Meeting, Sheraton Boston and the Boston Marriott Copley Place, Boston, MA.* Boston, MA. Available from http://www.allacademic.com/meta/p242725_index.html.

City Data, 2008, *Work and Jobs in Portland, Maine (ME) Detailed Stats: Occupations, Industries, Unemployment, Workers, Commute.* Retrieved 21 April 2010 from http://www.city-data.com/work/work-Portland-Maine.html#travelTimeToWork.

City Data, 2008, *Portland, Maine: Profile.* Retrieved 21 April 2010 from http://www.city-data.com/city/Portland-Maine.html.

City of Portland, 2005, *2005–2010 Consolidated Housing & Community Development Plan.* Available from http://www.portlandmaine.gov/planning/2005–2010consolplan.pdf.

City of Portland, 2005, *Analysis of Impediments to Fair Housing Choice in the City of Portland.* Available from http://www.portlandmaine.gov/planning/fairhousing.pdf.

City of Portland, 2010, *Draft of Five Year Strategic Plan 2010–2015.* Available from http://24.39.51.187/planning/conpla021810cleanacceptedchgs2.pdf.

City of Portland, 1991, *Downtown Vision: A Celebration of Urban Living and a Plan for the Future of Portland.* Available from http://www.ci.portland.me.us/planning/downtownvision.pdf.

City Of Portland Department of Refugee Services, 2009, *Department of Refugee Services Year-End Report FY 2009.* Available from http://www.ci.portland.me.us/hhs/hhsrs.pdf.

Conaboy, C., 2007, "Fashioning Their Lives: Somali Refugees Notch Successes But Still Face Challenges." (*Concord Monitor,* 5 August, 2007).

Conforti, J., 2007, *Creating Portland: History and Place in Northern New England.* Durham, NH: University of New Hampshire Press.

Dayal, P., 2010, "Small Loans, Big Ambitions: Microfinance Class at Clark to Help Refugees in Worcester Start Businesses." (*Worcester Telegram & Gazette,* 7 February, 2010).

Diesenhouse, S., 1996, "Real Estate: A Philanthropist Invests in Downtown Portland, Me., Hoping to Help Stem the Flight to the Suburbs." (*New York Times,* 14 February, 1996).

Eick, V., 2007, "Space Controls: The New Peace-Keeping Functions of Non-Profits." In Helga Leitner, Jamie Peck, Eric Sheppard (Eds.), *Contesting Neoliberalism: Urban Frontiers* (pp. 266–290). New York: Guilford.

Fainstein, S., 2005, "Cities and Diversity: Should We Want it? Can We Plan for It?" *Urban Affairs Review,* Vol. 41.1, 3–19.

Fishman, J., 1980, *Renaissance For Who?: Urban Renaissance in Portland Maine.* B.A. Hampshire College.

Florida, R., 2002, *The Rise of the Creative Class.* New York: Basic Books.

Frommer's Staff, 2007, *Frommer's Top Travel Destinations for 2007.* Available from http://www.frommers.com/articles/4056.html.

Gagnon, S., Lonsdale, A., 2006, *Defining Substance Abuse in the Sudanese and Cambodian Refugee Communities:* Final Report. State of Maine Department of Health and Human Services: Office of Substance Abuse. Available from http://maine.gov/dhhs/osa/prevention/community/spfsig/documents/subpops/camsud.pdf.

Hench, D., 2009, "What's in a Name? Learning Works Leaves No Doubt." (*Portland Press Herald,* 9 April, 2009).

Hinkle, G., 1987, Foucault's Power/Knowledge and American Sociological Theorizing, *Human Studies,* Vol. 10.1, 35–59.

Informant 1, 2010, Telephone Interview, 20 March.

Informant 2, 2010, Telephone Interview, 23 March.

Informant 3, 2010, Telephone Interview, 8 April.

Informant 4, 2010, Telephone Interview, 24 March.

Informant 5, 2010, Telephone Interview, 20 March.

Informant 6, 2010, Telephone Interview, 20 April.

Informant 7, 2010, Telephone Interview, 24 April.

Keating, W. D., Krumholz, N., Star, P., 1996, *Revitalizing Urban Neighborhoods.* Lawrence, KS: University of Kansas Press.

Knopp, L., Kujawa, R., 2003, "Ideology & Urban Landscapes. Conception of the Market in Portland, Maine." *Antipode* Vol. 25.2, 114–139.

Lees, L., 2003, "The Ambivalence of Diversity and the Politics of Urban Renaissance: The Case of Youth in Downtown Portland, Maine." *International Journal of Urban and Regional Research,* Vol. 27.3, 613–34.

Lees, L., 2008, "Gentrification and Social Mixing: Towards an Inclusive Urban Renaissance?" *Urban Studies,* Vol. 45, 2449–2470.

Logan, J., Molotch, H., 2007, *Urban Fortunes: The Political Economy of Place.* Berkeley, CA: University of California Press.

MacQuerrie, B., 2009, "Fear Envelops a Refuge of Immigrants in Maine." (*Boston Globe,* 13, July, 2009).

Mamgain, V., 2003, "Off the Boat, Now Off to Work: Refugees in the Labour Market in Portland, Maine." *Journal of Refugee Studies,* Vol 16.2, 113–146.

Maxwell, T., 2006, "Help in a New Home: With Few Groups to Help African Refugees Adjust, the Community Creates Its Own Agency." (*Portland Press Herald,* 2 June, 2006).

Mohamed, H. A., 2001, *The Socio-cultural Adaptation of Somali Refugees in Toronto: An Exploration of Their Integration Experiences.* EdD. University of Massachussetts Amherst.

Murphy, E., 2007, "Language Skills Hinder Refugees Helping Them Acclimate to a New Culture Could Ease Maine's Chronically Strained Labor Market." (*Portland Press Herald,* 14 January, 2007).

O'Mally-Greenberg, Z., 2009, "America's Most Livable Cities." (*Forbes,* 1 April, 2009).

Rathke, L., 2006, "Refugees Find Business Success: Programs Help People Overcome Obstacles to Getting Ventures Started." (*Albany Times Union,* 26 March, 2006).

Rimer, S., 1999, "Portland Journal: An Idea + a Philanthropist = A Market." *New York Times,* 1 January, 1999).

Ross, A., 2007, "Immigrants Find New Use For Old Store: The Portland Appliance Building is becoming a Somali Community Center." (*Portland Press Herald,* 23 June, 2007).

Sassen, S., 1996, "Service Employment Regimes and the New Inequality." In Enzo Mignone (Ed.), *Urban Poverty and the Underclass: A Reader* (pp. 64–82). Cambridge, MA: Blackwell Publishers Inc.

Singer, A., 2006, From There to Here: Refugee Resettlement in Metropolitan America. *Brookings Institution*. Available from http://www.brookings.edu/metro/pubs/20060925_singer.pdf.

State of Maine Department of Health and Human Services, 2007, *The Multicultural Resource Guide*. Retrieved 24 March 2010 from http://www.maine.gov/dhhs/oma/Multicultural Resource/resguide.pdf.

Taylor, K., 2000, "Somali Mall is Much More Than Stores." (*Minneapolis Star Tribune*, 25 May).

Thomas, G. S., 2005, "Where to Go for America's Hottest Small Biz Market." (*American City Business Journal*, 10 January, 2005).

Whitman, D., Friedman, D., Linn, A., Doremus, C., Hetter, K., 1994, "The White Underclass." (*US News & World Report*, 9 October, 1994).

Wyly, E., Hammel, D., 2002, Neoliberal Housing Policy and the Gentrification of the American Urban System. Unpublished manuscript, Department of Geography, University of British Columbia, Vancouver, BC; Department of Geography and Geology, Illinois State University, Norman, IL.

Zukin, S., 1995, *The Cultures Of Cities*. Malden, MA: Blackwell.

III

RENEWING HARTFORD:
GLOBAL AND
REGIONAL DYNAMICS

10

Shifting Fortunes

Hartford's Global and Regional Economic Dimensions

Xiangming Chen and John Shemo

INTRODUCTION

Are larger cities inherently more global than smaller ones? There is little doubt that New York and even Boston are more global or globally connected than Hartford, the much smaller capital city of Connecticut with about 120,000 people located between these two major centers. But this does not mean that Hartford or other cities of a smaller scale lack global features and connections that matter a great deal to their fortunes in the past, at the present, and into the future (see Chen and Kanna, 2012). Given the demonstrated global features of Hartford's history, such as immigration (Walsh, Bauer, this volume), we build on this global history here to demonstrate the persistent influence of global economic forces on Hartford's shifting fortunes. We do so by revealing the latent and unexpected features of Hartford that impart a strong sense of globalism to the city, perhaps to the point of rendering the city quite global in economic terms. In addition, we use this global lens to examine how Hartford's local and regional economic fortunes have shifted as its ties to the global economy have changed. By doing so, we show that Hartford has been a lot more global(ized) with serious consequences than hitherto recognized and understood. In conclusion, we suggest how the economic globalism of Hartford, coupled with some regionalizing conditions, presents both opportunities and constraints for turning the city's economic misfortune around.

Cities operate today in a more complex—indeed global—world. This shift calls for using a somewhat different lens for understanding a city: we must now see it not just for its internal dynamics, but also in ways it works in a large and expanding global economy. While cities continue to be important local places, the workings of those places today are increasingly affected by powerful forces that lie outside them: economic decisions made by people who do not themselves reside in those cities.

Companies in Hartford may use a supplier in Shanghai via East Hartford (e.g., Pratt & Whitney, see below) and sell its products or services to assemblers or customers in Middletown, Connecticut, or Shanghai, China. These firms and people working for them, as well as the families depending on them, are influenced by the workings of the local and regional economies in the broader global arena. These interconnections span and penetrate multiple geographic boundaries to pull and insert companies and individuals into the global economy directly or indirectly. To help make a little general sense of these global-local economic connections, we provide a short theoretical overview of the relevant scholarship (drawing from Chen, Orum, and Paulsen, 2012) to guide our case study of Hartford.

CITIES IN A GLOBALIZING WORLD

Peter Hall (1966), a British geographer, laid the groundwork for global perspectives on cities. He focused on eight of what he termed *world cities*. These cities are: Hong Kong, London, Mexico City, Moscow, New York City, Paris, Randstad Holland (the sprawling urban complex that includes Amsterdam, Rotterdam, and The Hague), and Tokyo. He portrayed these cities as national centers of government, trade, and professional talents of all kinds. However, Hall's idea did not catch on until the early 1980s. At that time, the geographer John Friedmann proposed a more refined and productive research agenda for understanding world cities. Friedmann argued that world cities represent a small number of urban regions, and that they lie at the top of an urban hierarchy, or hierarchy of places. This urban hierarchy exercises world-wide power over production and the expansion of markets. With their control over production and employment in the economy, world cities also become the major sites for the concentration and accumulation of international finance. Friedmann identified several world cities, including New York, London, Tokyo, Paris, Randstad Holland, Hong Kong, Mexico City—all originally identified by Peter Hall—but also a number of other major international cities in his study.

A few years later, sociologist Saskia Sassen brought a definitive touch to the study of the global city, with the publication of the book *The Global City: New York, London, Tokyo* in 1991. According to Sassen (1991), global cities function as: (1) highly concentrated command points in the organization of the global economy; (2) key locations for finance and specialized services, which have replaced manufacturing as the leading industries; (3) innovative sites of production in these leading industries; and (4) markets for the products and innovations of these industries. From her perspective, the hallmark of a global city is the growth and extent of its producer services, which include accounting, banking, financial services, legal services, insurance, real estate, computers, and information processing. Producer services, she argues, are highly concentrated in the central locations of cities of considerable size because they require diversified resources, centralization of information, and easy access to the concentration of the headquarters of large manufacturing firms. Having identified these clear criteria and characteristics of a global city, Sassen (2006) also went on to examine such major international cities as Miami, Toronto, and Sydney, which, she claims, exercise global city functions but are not full-fledged global cities. This conception, taken literally, may disqualify dominant manufacturing centers in China like Shanghai and Shenzhen, and prominent political or administrative centers like Beijing and Delhi, as global cities. A broader and more open definition of the global city is more realistic. Going beyond the finance-based criteria, as Sassen has also done, would bring these cities back into the realm of global city studies as they host the headquarters of both multinational corporations (MNCs) and international organizations.

One central proposition among the insights and contributions from Sassen's work particularly stands out: the dominant influence of global cities coexists with undesirable local consequences. Examples of this include the growing income inequality between white-collar professionals in high-paying producer services jobs and minority workers in low-end commercial services, and the striking spatial disparity between the renewing and booming downtown and the physical decay of peripheral areas.

By taking a global perspective on the city, Sassen and other scholars have questioned the assumption that a city represents a bounded territory of the sovereign state, and pointed to the need to re-imagine the relationship between local places in a globalizing world. While they acknowledge the powerful impact of globalization, some geographers and sociologists insist on the persistence of local diversity and identities. The British geographers Ash Amin and Nigel Thrift (1994), for example, suggest that global dynamics, such as the flow of capital or money across borders, inevitably encounter places that are themselves distinctive, with unique histories and complex patterns of economic institutions and cultural traditions. Thus, according to some alternative views, the process of globalization does not imply homogeneity among places, but instead a continuation of the significance of territorial diversity and difference.

Besides New York and London or a small number of other global cities that occupy the top tier of the global urban hierarchy, there are many cities arrayed on the middle and lower rungs (see Chen and Kanna, 2012). An implicit assumption of the global city perspective is that many of these cities would compete to move up and possibly join the exclusive club at or toward the top. From a counter or alternative perspective, Brent Ryan (2012, emphasis original) conceptualizes some old and deindustrialized American city-regions like Detroit as going through a *de-globalizing* process. Despite its glorious past as a top exporting city of the United States, Detroit has become stuck in a *de-globalizing* or re-localizing groove. To this end, Detroit has since the 1990s built four casinos as an alternative economic engine, but without much success. This is similar to what Nick Bacon has termed *podunkification* (see chapter 3). While Hartford is unlike Detroit in terms of having one severely eroded dominant industry, they both represent old American cities that have deviated from or run opposite the track and direction of a global city, becoming in a way victims of the competitive global economy. Yet Detroit has taken some realistic and drastic measures since the 2008 crisis. Mayor David Bing has implemented the so-called Detroit Works that would relocate residents from supposedly vacant neighborhoods to "seven or nine urban villages" through incentives such as continued city services like fire engines, water, and electricity. The hollowed-out areas are then set aside for "future development." This "clean or blank slate" approach amounts to a large-scale remaking of a major American city or of the many smaller living places in the city. Detroit has also transformed some empty urban spaces into agricultural farms or gardens, even though the city's severe economic misfortune has recently forced the State of Michigan to take over its finances through an appointed manager. But none of these saved Detroit from filing for bankruptcy in July 2013.

To anticipate how a smaller city like Hartford can respond to its own more recent economic challenges, we first take a historical look at the origins of its early economic fortunes.

THE ROOTS OF HARTFORD'S GLOBALLY CONNECTED AND COMPETITIVE INDUSTRIES

At their respective peaks, Hartford's manufacturing and insurance industries defined and anchored the dual economic foundation of Hartford and its surrounding region. Hartford began as a manufacturing center around 1836 when Samuel Colt founded the Colt Manufacturing Company, which initially operated in Patterson, New Jersey, until the early 1840s and didn't move to Hartford via New Haven until 1848. Its first rented space was close to the present-day Convention Center, and in 1854 it moved to the new complex in Coltsville, where it became the world's largest single privately owned factory at the time making firearms sold around the world.[1] Coltsville is being turned into a historic landmark today to mark its glorious manufacturing past.[2] Hartford's manufacturing reputation and capacity didn't reach its zenith until around the mid-20th century, with Pratt & Whitney emerging as a world leading producer of large commercial jet engines. This century or so marked Hartford's golden era of manufacturing, which also featured a sizeable production of hand tools, typewriters, and bicycles. The other leg of Hartford's economic base, insurance, has had a longer life than manufacturing, having started around 1800 and remaining viable through today, whereas manufacturing has sustained a severe and irreversible decline since the 1960s. To understand the different trajectories of manufacturing versus insurance and their critical importance to Hartford's economic fortune over time, we first trace their once globally competitive nature and status to their local and regional roots.

Making Things Early and Well

Like all places in New England and beyond, the Hartford region in the early 1800s was primarily rural and agricultural. From the soil and grain, liquor from the distilleries along the Park River was made and became the earliest product that was sent abroad. According to the *Gazetteer* of Connecticut in 1819, "There is no town in the United States where there is as great a quantity of spirit made from grain as in East Windsor" (cited in Day, 1935: 3). Not far from East Windsor, Hartford was a small town by today's standards as it barely had 7,000 people. Around this time, the agrarian economy characterized by limited soil capacity and hard manual labor drove more people in the large and small towns in Connecticut to pursue manufacturing and trading what was made. As early as the mid-1700s, farmers and traders in the Hartford region began to sell pickled beef to the Caribbean to feed slaves. This early entry into global commerce spurred local manufacturing growth and stretched its global dimensions. Tinware was made in Berlin and sold as far west as Detroit, as far north as Canada, and as far south as New Orleans. The local clustering of production emerged and spread to: hats in Danbury, clocks in Bristol, combs in Meriden, and hardware in New Britain. Spurred by the growth of turnpike roads and machinery operations, New Haven became the center of carriage production, including reportedly the largest factory in the world. Its carriages were marketed well beyond the United States to the Caribbean, South America, and even the islands of the Pacific (Day, 1935). Early investors in Hartford financed growth of textile mills in towns and places where water power was more easily harnessed, including Manchester (silk), Thompsonville (carpet), and Rockville and Willimantic (cotton thread). For Hartford itself, pioneering manufacturing took place in distilleries and tanneries along the Park River. Pliny Jewel opened the first really significant factory in 1826 to make the leather belts that transmitted power from water wheels and gear assemblies to individual machines in the first-generation factories in the region. Pitkin Brothers Iron Works was also representative of the early manufacturing growth in the 1830s when steam power was harnessed successfully.[3] Looking back, we see this period as the first blossoming of industrial production in Hartford and its surrounding region (also see Walsh, this volume).

Two other developments characterized and solidified this period of manufacturing boom. One was the invention of more refined machinery that replaced manual labor and raised productivity. The milling machine, for example, could work and finish small parts to fairly exact specifications. First used for Whitney muskets and North pistols, this new machine was then employed as a precision instrument to make Sharps rifles and Colt revolvers (Day, 1935). The gun industry in fact ran from New Haven through Hartford to Springfield, covering the Connecticut River Valley, with Eli Whitney factory in New Haven, Colt in Hartford, and the Springfield Armory driving technical innovation (see Walsh, this volume). On a different front, the textile industry expanded rapidly and became the most dominant industry in both output and employment in Connecticut by around 1850, followed by the boot and shoe making industry. Tool and die makers also grew with steam-powered printing, which led to Hartford becoming a major publishing center. This further and wider industrial growth benefited from the construction of the railroad that connected New Haven to Hartford in 1840 and extended to Springfield, Massachusetts, in 1844. By around the mid-19th century, the combination of favorable conditions had solidified the strong root of manufacturing in and around Hartford and ushered in a long century of industrial growth and economic prosperity.

Insuring the Right Things at the Right Place

One would think that the growing wealth associated with rapid industrialization would generate the need for insurance against the risk of financial loss. In Hartford and Connecticut, however, insurance pre-dated some industrial growth due to the city's location on the early trade route. Following the export of pickled beef to the Caribbean in the mid-1700s, sea-borne trade was extended all the way by sloop navigation along the Connecticut River to the port of Hartford whose residents were actively involved in the trading business. Since regional and global ocean trade entailed the risks of financial loss from sea storm, pirates, and other threats, Hartford became the first place where a plan was developed with a contract among people other than the owner of the vessel to share these risks. If this was some kind of origin of modern insurance, it became formalized through the incorporation of the Hartford Fire Insurance Company in 1810, before much of the early wave of manufacturing activity. In 1834, the young Hartford Fire Insurance met its initial big test. After the great New York fire broke out that year, the Hartford Fire Insurance's President Eliphalet Terry managed to pay all the claims against his company even by throwing in his own money, as there was not enough company cash to do so (Welch, 1935). This early development of insurance was also linked to banking in Hartford, which became the second most important banking center in New England, behind only Boston.

Over time insurance became more and more central to Hartford, whose fire insurance companies fulfilled their obligations after the devastating Chicago fire in 1871. Of the eight fire insurance companies in Connecticut after 1871, four were located in Hartford and accounted for more than two-thirds of the total assets. By 1907, the number of fire insurance companies in Connecticut grew to 14, 12 of which were based in Hartford (Welch, 1935). Life insurance did not become a corporate business in Hartford until the 1850s. The Travelers, established in Hartford in 1864, began to sell life insurance in 1865. Unlike their global reach today (see later), the insurance companies at that time did not allow their insured customers to travel even to other parts of the United States and Canada so the policies would not forfeit. The Supreme Court reinforced this state-level regulation of insurance by upholding that insurance was not a transaction of commerce against the appeal of the *Paul v. Virginia* case in 1869. By around 1930, the total amount covered by the policies issued by the life insurance companies in Connecticut, mostly based in Hartford, reached $10 billion, up from $1.2 billion in 1914 (Welch, 1935: 35). While this early history of the insurance industry paralleled much of the development of manufacturing, it reflects upon an even denser concentration of insurance companies in Hartford that has sustained the city as a much more dominant insurance center relative to its small population base and declined manufacturing sector.

A LONG TRANSITION IN THE GLOBAL ECONOMY

The Rise and Fall of Manufacturing

Once we have traced how manufacturing and insurance started in Hartford by the mid-1800s, it is easier to see it on a century-long trajectory of growth and prosperity. In regard to the manufacturing industry, pioneering manufacturers like Samuel Colt experimented with interchangeable parts. This laid the foundation for today's assembly line manufacturing. New techniques employed in his firearms factory made mass production possible as well as Hartford a frontier of precision manufacturing. In terms of the insurance industry, the simple trade along the Connecticut River in spices, coffee, and rum was distributed from warehouses in Hartford's thriving merchant district. To deal with the risks of fires, pirates, storms, and accidents that might threaten ships sailing from Hartford to England, the West Indies, and the Far East, local merchants developed the concept and method of modern insurance. As a corollary, banking made it easier and more efficient for Hartford investors in manufacturing and insurance to study and then copy British precedents. There was strong evidence that Hartford was then a globally important economic center despite its small size relative to such international commercial centers as London and New York.

The early globally linked manufacturing and insurance industries would propel and sustain the small city of Hartford on an upward economic climb for decades to come. This long boom was marked by the birth and dominance of a few key companies that have called the Hartford region home. Pratt & Whitney may be the most illustrative example of the region's manufacturing prosperity in the first half of the 20th century and of its challenges since then (see a later section). The company's storied history began during World War I, when Captain Frederick Rentschler oversaw production of aircraft engines for the U.S. Army. That experience caused him to explore the lucrative opportunities of global commerce through designing aircraft engines. In 1925, Rentschler co-founded Pratt & Whitney in Hartford,[4] drawing upon the machine-tool skills of the young Pratt and Whitney who had worked for Colt as machinists before forming their own partnership to make tools. Like what Colt did, Pratt & Whitney led the world in making precision machines with interchangeable parts (see Figure 10.1) and turned out nearly ten thousand different kinds of machines for making all kinds of things.[5] In a way, Hartford was the high-tech manufacturing capital of the world in its heyday, or what might be called the "Silicon Valley of the Time."

In 1929, needing more space, Rentschler moved its facilities across the Connecticut River to its present location in East Hartford. This established a long tradition of aircraft engine manufacturing after building the company's first engine, the 425-horsepower R-1340 Wasp. With this audacious start, Pratt & Whitney went on to define the industry standard of aviation technologies and thus put the Hartford region on the global map of advanced manufacturing. Contributing greatly to the manufacturing prowess of Hartford in those years was the typewriter industry. While

Figure 10.1. Aerial View of Pratt & Whitney, 1930. (Connecticut Historical Society)

Figure 10.2. Display window at Underwood Typewriter in 1910. (Connecticut Historical Society)

headquartered in New York City, Underwood, a typewriter producing company, had produced five million typewriters in Hartford by 1939 (see Figure 10.2). It was in Hartford where its factory was turning out typewriters at the rate of one each minute at its peak, and many of these machines were exported. Major manufacturers like Pratt & Whitney and Underwood made a small city like Hartford much bigger in economic size and influence nationally and internationally.

Much more than insurance, manufacturing strength drove Hartford's growth and prosperity halfway through the 20th century. Relative to insurance, manufacturing decline since that point has contributed more to Hartford's long economic deterioration. Together with insurance, the rise and fall of Hartford's manufacturing capacity reflects the city's uneven shift along two different tracks of its globally linked economy over the past several decades. From a long historical and global perspective, Hartford developed as a rare small city that rode on manufacturing and insurance as a pair of powerful wheels. In this respect, Hartford differs considerably from Springfield, Massachusetts. Located 30 miles north in the Connecticut River Valley, and sharing a history with Hartford, Springfield has experienced a protracted decline in its once dominant manufacturing economy, without a strong alternative sector to cushion the fall (Forrant, 2012). Hartford's similarities to Springfield in size and manufacturing dominance, as well as their geographic proximity, are more than offset by Hartford's distinctive status as a strong citadel of insurance. This distinction has lengthened and complicated Hartford's long transition vis-à-vis and in dynamic interaction with global, regional, and local economic and political forces that continue to challenge the city.

As a small city blessed by the long coexistence and co-prosperity of strong manufacturing and insurance, Hartford should not have fallen too precipitously when it began to lose manufacturing capacity in the 1950s. What has actually happened is quite another story. Rising production costs in the old American manufacturing belt, coupled with growing international competition, eroded the industries in Hartford and pushed them to leave the city at an accelerated pace, but for somewhat different reasons. Typewriters were replaced by the early computers, while textiles and machines could be made more cheaply elsewhere. With the quick loss of manufacturing employment, Hartford's population declined for the first time in history, from its peak of 177,393 in 1950 to 162,178 in 1960, and this demographic loss has persisted ever since, ending with about 120,000 people still living in Hartford today. As direct evidence of the growing misfortune of manufacturing, major brand-name companies like Colt, Royal, and Underwood (both typewriter makers) closed down their local factories in the 1960s and 1970s, and so did other lesser known manufacturers (Walsh, this volume). To highlight the growing location-specific influence of global competition and connections, the traditionally competitive and profitable machine tool factories in and around Hartford (and Springfield) in the Connecticut River Valley based on long-standing craftsmanship lost out to the up-and-coming Japanese firms, although some of them also adopted the Japanese "lean production" techniques. These powerful distant forces drove some manufacturing jobs from Hartford to its adjacent suburbs like East Hartford or to the American South where production costs were lower, but a growing portion of the old manufacturing sector was lost forever, leaving behind brownfields on the urban landscape and creating more pressure on the other parts of the local economy to pick up the slack.

It turned out that not only did the other sectors like insurance failed to compensate for the first stage of decline in older or more traditional manufacturing during the

1960s and 1970s, but that the already eroded manufacturing sector actually went into a second phase of deterioration characterized by the loss of jobs in more advanced and high-end industries. Before this happened, major divisions including Sikorsky helicopter and Pratt & Whitney of Hartford-based United Technologies Corporation (UTC) benefited handsomely from increased defense spending during the 1980s. The collapse of the former Soviet Union, coupled with the economic recession in the early 1990s, had a major negative impact on what was left of the manufacturing sector in the Hartford region, forcing major employers like Pratt & Whitney to lay off production workers. Figure 10.3 captures this trend of declining manufacturing employment in the part of Greater Hartford including East Hartford where Pratt & Whitney was located. In fact, the number of Pratt & Whitney production workers in and around East Hartford dropped from the peak of around 40,000 in the 1960s to about 6,000 in 2000 and only some 3,000 today (Lee, 2011). This significant reduction of jobs at one major company contributed a lot to the manufacturing sector of the Hartford region shrinking to its historical low (see Figure 10.3).

Relative to manufacturing, Hartford's substantial insurance sector, as part of the broader professional service economy characterizing postindustrial cities, has weathered the rising business cost and tough global competition better since the economic turn for the worse in the 1960s. When the manufacturing sector was increasingly exposed and vulnerable to lower-cost international competitors, especially those in East Asia, the insurance industry was relatively insulated due to its much heavier domestic orientation and market emphasis. If there was any competition from international insurers during the 1960s and 1970s, it paled in comparison to the very advanced and efficient position of American insurance companies that reflected the broader sophistication of the high-end professional services of the U.S. economy. The lack of, or at least weakened state of, global competition allowed the traditional strength of Hartford's insurance sector to sustain itself into the era of greater global competition in the 1990s and 2000s. This relative strength, however, was not enough to counter the cyclical impact of recession and external shocks. The recession of the early 1990s took a heavy toll on the advanced service sector including insurance companies in the Hartford region, leading to a heavy loss of jobs (see Figure 10.3) just as in the manufacturing sector. The recovery from the mid-1990s was short-lived as the dot-com crash in 2000 and 9/11 in 2001 triggered another period of steady decline.

The global economic crisis of 2008 caused still another round of job loss in both professional services and manufacturing. While global economic impact no longer spares Hartford's insurance industry, it remains in better employment shape relative to other sectors, again due to the dual advantage of concentration and resilience. In May 2010, for example, the percentage of people working as insurance underwriters in the Hartford-West Hartford-East Hartford region[6] were so disproportionately large as to register a location quotient of 5.7 relative to the national average.[7] The same source also reported that Hartford-West Hartford-East Hartford had 35,490 jobs in business and financial operations in 2010, accounting for 6.5 percent of local area employment, significantly higher than the 4.8 percent share nationally.

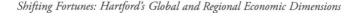

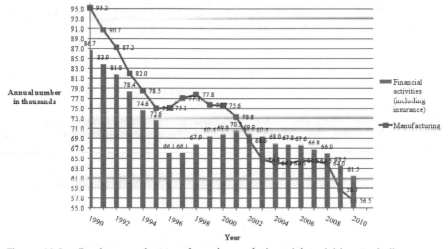

Figure 10.3. Employment in Manufacturing and Financial Activities (Including Insurance) in the Hartford-East Hartford-West Hartford Region, 1990–2010. (Xiangming Chen)
Source: Graphed from Bureau of Labor Statistics online data series.

SMALL URBAN SCALE AND GLOBAL ECONOMIC STRENGTH

By taking a global perspective on Hartford's economic history, we see a temporal story of two key industries—manufacturing and insurance—that prospered together through the 1950s and have fared differently since then. While manufacturing has experienced a continued decline through different stages, the insurance industry has held steady based on both its historical strength and the overall postindustrial growth of advanced services in the United States. Yet this tale of two industries has unfolded in more complex ways and across local, regional, and global scales, featuring the sustained interaction between the city's small urban scale and global economic strength. We illustrate this salient attribute of Hartford from a few analytical and statistical perspectives.

First of all, what makes any city globally influential is less its own scale and more the economic size, standing, and connectivity of its key companies. The Hartford region hosts the headquarters of several Fortune 500 Companies in 2010: United Technologies (37), Aetna (65), Hartford Financial Services (97), Waste Management (196), Northeast Utilities (385), and Stanley Black & Decker (435). Since corporate headquarters are critical to their host cities in terms of symbolic significance and real financial and employment benefits, the mixture of six highly ranked manufacturing, insurance, and service companies calling the Hartford region home elevates it to a much more important global position relative to its size. Using comparative information, Table 10.1 shows that Hartford in 2005 ranked eleventh globally and third nationally among the most important and powerful insurance centers in the world.

If not for the dense concentration of major insurers and their combined assets locally, Hartford would never be at a level comparable to several of the global cities in Table 10.1 such as New York, London, Paris, and Zurich.

While the above information helps place Hartford quite high in the global economic hierarchy, we use other evidence to demonstrate its relational strength based on two-way investment and trade ties with foreign companies and countries. The Greater Hartford region is home to 32 international companies from 14 mostly Western industrialized countries.[8] Four of these are the North American headquarters of the respective foreign companies, while a number of others are important sales, service, and technology centers. While some foreign companies in the region have been relatively recent acquisitions, such as Sovereign Bank and TD Bank, the vast majority on this list have long-standing roots here. The Hartford region's total exports in 2008 exceeded $10.4 billion, $4 billion of which went to the European

Table 10.1. Cities Ranked by Assets of the World's 50 Largest Insurers, 2005.

Rank	City	Assets	Percentage of Top 50
Total for Top 50		8,324,240	100.00
Total for US		2,760,140	33.16
Top 15 Cities in the World (ranked by assets)			
1	Munich	1,374,460	16.51
2	New York	1,251,180	15.03
3	London	938,180	11.27
4	Paris	759,880	9.13
5	Zurich	553,280	6.64
6	Toronto	388,110	4.66
7	Newark, NJ	381,940	4.59
8	Tokyo	352,370	4.23
9	Trieste	317,660	3.81
10	The Hague	311,160	3.74
11	**Hartford, CT**	**259,740**	**3.12**
12	Omaha, NE	181,860	2.18
13	Northbrook, IL	149,730	1.80
14	Columbus, OH	116,880	1.40
15	Philadelphia	110,380	1.33
Top 10 Cities in the United States			
1	New York	1,251,180	15.03
2	Newark, NJ	381,940	4.59
3	**Hartford, CT**	**259,740**	**3.12**
4	Omaha, NE	181,860	2.18
5	Northbrook, IL	149,730	1.80
6	Columbus, OH	116,880	1.40
7	Philadelphia	110,380	1.33
8	St. Paul, MN	109,680	1.32
9	Columbus, GA	52,910	0.64
10	Warren, NJ	43,130	0.52

Source: Adapted from Sassen (2012: A.4.6a)

Union, with Germany being the largest single-country trade partner with the Hartford region. The Hartford region has been a major exporter of transportation equipment, the bulk of which are aircraft and related products. In 2008, the value of such exports exceeded $4.4 billion and accounted for over half of Hartford's total exports.

This placed the region number six on the list of the top metros in the nation for exporting transportation equipment, behind only Detroit, Los Angeles, New York, Cincinnati, and Miami (U.S. Department of Commerce). This reflects the competitive strength of Pratt & Whitney and Hamilton Sundstrand, which is also part of United Technologies and headquartered in Windsor Locks. Pratt & Whitney supplies the engines for the Airbus A380 as part of a joint venture with GE Aviation. Hamilton Sundstrand is responsible for supplying 13 major systems/components for the new Airbus A380, which is expected to generate more than $3 billion in revenue. The company also built the power distribution center for Airbus Military's A400M transport aircraft, which made its maiden flight in November 2009. Headquartered within the old Hartford County boundary in Plainville, GE Industrial Solutions manufactures and services a variety of products in electrical equipment in 27 countries. Measured by inward/outward investment and exports, the Hartford region has been heavily plugged into the global economy with a primary orientation to the European Union, as a player more significant than expected for a city of its size.

Given the Hartford region's strong connections to the global economy, it is expected to perform correspondingly well according to certain important economic criteria. This relationship has become visible in city-regions that are favorably positioned and integrated in the global economy as drivers of growth and leaders of innovation (Chen, 2007). While more of these cases are dynamic regions in emerging economies like China, a number of the older regions in industrialized countries continue to be productive. The Hartford region happens to be one of them. According to the 2010 Transatlantic Economy report published by the Center for Transatlantic Relations at John Hopkins University, the Hartford region ranked as the number one region in the world in terms of labor productivity, the number one region in terms of per capita R&D expenditure by business, and the number eight region in terms of per capita R&D expenditure by government. On the 2008 World Knowledge Competitive Index for 145 regions across 19 knowledge economies compiled by the Centre for International Competitiveness (Huggins et al., 2009), Hartford was the third most competitive knowledge region in the world, behind only the San Jose (where Silicon Valley is located) and Boston metro areas. On an index of labor productivity (output per employee), Hartford scored first, ahead of San Jose. In addition, on an index of per capita research and development expenditure by business, Hartford also ranked first, before Bridgeport-Stamford. On an index of patent registrations per one million inhabitants, Hartford ranked 16th among the top 20 regions in the world, behind Tokyo and Osaka and 13 other U.S. metro areas and ahead of the South Netherlands, Kyoto, Baden-Württemberg (Germany), and Shanghai (Huggins et al., 2009). In 2009, CNNMoney ranked the Hartford metro area the fifth best place among all large metro areas for launching a small business.

The very recent evidence above seems to turn Hartford as a distinctive city into a peculiar and puzzling case of contradictions. How can a small and aging city-region with severely eroded manufacturing and a weakened professional service sector dominated by insurance sustain its high national and global rankings on a wide set of meaningful indices? One easy answer to this question is the collective advantage of spatially concentrated educational resources that produce rich human capital. To prove the point, with 32 colleges and universities, the Hartford-Springfield Corridor ranks just behind the Boston metro region for the heaviest concentration of institutions of higher learning in New England, which has shifted more to education as the main driver of economic development. Instead of stopping with this convenient explanation, we take an in-depth microscopic approach to probing some sources of the Hartford region's economic competitiveness through a spatially grounded case study of Pratt & Whitney, with some comparative reference to local insurance companies that have gone global.

PRATT & WHITNEY: FROM LOCAL
TO GLOBAL AND BACK

More than any other local company, Pratt & Whitney has defined and redefined the global nature and connectivity of the Hartford region's economic transformation. By focusing on Pratt & Whitney both locally and globally, we aim to show how the changing strategy and practice of a major corporate player can both mediate and reshape the complex and multifaceted relationship between the local and global economies. Scholars have conceptualized this relationship as interdependent and interpenetrating in varied ways including a discussion on "*glocalization*," which refers to the localization of global dynamics (see Robertson and Khondker, 1998). While it is easy to measure the global integration of national economies through trade and investment flows, it remains empirically difficult to clarify how global and local economics are linked in different regional contexts (Chen and Sun, 2007). To insert a regional perspective on Pratt & Whitney as it moves back and forth between the local and global scale, we also shed light on the "crucial middle" role of regions in bridging and integrating global and local economies. This exercise will help reinforce a prominent theme of this book that regional dynamics and processes are critical to understanding how the city of Hartford or a locally headquartered company responds to economic and political challenges from different origins (see Bacon and Chen, introduction, this volume; Walsh, this volume; Rojas and Wray, this volume).

A global company with 52 locations worldwide today, Pratt & Whitney had its humble beginnings in the heart of the Hartford region—the city of Hartford itself—in 1925. This was not a single random event. As mentioned earlier, Hartford was a core part of the birthplace of the American machine tool industry in the Connecticut River Valley, ideally suited to accommodating precision manufacturing that was crucial to making aircraft engines. With a few machine tools, a little start-up money, and some family connections, Frederick Rentschler and a few of his former colleagues started Pratt & Whitney Aircraft at the old Pope-Hartford auto plant on Capital Avenue, a space then filled with cigar tobacco (see endnote 2). With the success in assembling the first engine of 425 horsepower named Wasp for the U.S. Navy in 1925, Pratt & Whitney was off on a great start for decades of building new generations of aircraft engines through physical expansion and technological innovation. As part of its initial growth beyond the original space, Pratt & Whitney in 1929 moved across the Connecticut River to an 1,100-acre parcel of land in East Hartford, where it has maintained its corporate headquarters ever since (Sullivan, 2008).[9]

From its relatively small and humble local roots, Pratt & Whitney would quickly become linked to the global economy given its unavoidable role as the primary manufacturer of engines for fighter planes during World War II. As allies of the United States fighting Nazi Germany, both France and Great Britain placed huge orders for engines totaling hundreds of thousands of horsepower a month around 1940, so much so that they financed two additions of 280,000 square feet and 375,000 square feet to Pratt's East Hartford plant, respectively. Thanks to the government's orders during the war, Pratt & Whitney and its licensees built a total of 363,619 engines totaling 603,814,723 horsepower, which accounted for half the horsepower required by the American air forces. By the end of the war, Pratt & Whitney grew to about 40,000 in total employment and five million square feet of factory and office space, mostly in and around the Hartford region (Sullivan, 2008).

The immediate postwar years were tough for Pratt & Whitney due to the major reduction in government work, and the company was forced to significantly shrink its workforce. As the 1950s came along, Pratt & Whitney rebounded and grew again from the combined demands of the engine for the B-52 bomber, the early development of the space program, and other large industrial engines. But it was the onset of the commercial jet age in the 1960s that set Pratt & Whitney onto a steady path of growth. The company first launched JT8D, one of the two most produced commercial jet engines that powered Boeing 727s and 737s and McDonnell Douglas (MD) DC-9s and MD-80s, some of which have flown into the 21st century. The use of JT9D and its improved model on Boeing 747s in the 1970s ushered in a new era in commercial aviation history. The introduction of PW4000 for Boeing 767s and 757s in the 1980s kept Pratt & Whitney as the leader for new and improved engines (see Sullivan, 2008: 62–67 for timelines of Pratt & Whitney's highlights and world aviation events).

Major Restructuring, Global Expansion, and East Hartford Again

The 1990s marked the dawn of another new era for Pratt & Whitney that, more than any previous decade, has restructured the company internally, extended its global reach, and shed a spotlight on East Hartford (though, see Bacon, this volume, for an alternative take). This set of developments reveals a lot about stronger global-local economic connections mediated by corporate restructuring and regional thinking. It began with the introduction of lean manufacturing, quality control, and inventory reduction that led to the closing of Pratt's plants in North Haven and Southington in Connecticut and the consolidation at its East Hartford and Middletown sites, with the painful consequence of shedding around 10,000 jobs. This workforce reduction by a key employer contributed a lot to the declining manufacturing employment shown in Figure 10.3. In addition, Pratt moved the bulk of the equipment and people of its Government Engine Business division from Florida back to Connecticut. These corporate consolidations helped position and prepare Pratt & Whitney to spread its wings globally on an unprecedented scale.

The global seed of Pratt & Whitney was sowed back in late 1928 when a small Canadian branch of Pratt & Whitney was incorporated and opened its doors in a Montreal suburb. Starting out with only 10 employees and putting engine kits from the United States together for the Canadian market, Pratt & Whiney Canada developed engine service as a core business for many small operators flying in the wilds of Canada. Over the course of eight decades, Pratt & Whitney Canada has grown to a global operation that supports 42,000 engines on 23,000 aircrafts among 9,000 operators in 190 countries on six continents (Sullivan, 2008: 78). Since the 1990s, Pratt & Whitney has stretched its global footprint far beyond the traditional industrialized countries of Canada and Western Europe to the rapidly growing aviation markets, especially in Asia. Although having fewer employees than its peak of 40,000 during World War II, Pratt & Whitney now has a global workforce of 36,000 who support more than 11,000 customers in 195 countries. Pratt's large commercial engines power over 50 percent of the world's commercial airliners and its systems can be found on more than 90 percent of the world's aircraft.[10] Today Pratt & Whitney operates at 52 global locations including the United States that comprise seven engine centers, 16 repair centers, 22 EcoPower© engine wash centers, and other line maintenance, specialty, and engineering service centers.

To understand Pratt & Whitney's recent global expansion and its local and regional feedback loops, we zero in on its newer locations, primarily the Engine Maintenance Facility in Shanghai as displayed on Map 10.1. China has become the world's largest and fastest-growing aviation market, where regional airlines compete against one another flying relatively short routes on hundreds of Boeing 737s and Airbus 320s, many of which carry the CFM56 engine. In response to the huge demand for servicing and repairing these aircraft engines, Pratt & Whitney in 2009 made a big move in China by entering another joint venture with Shanghai-based China Eastern Airlines, the largest of the major regional airlines. Drawing a total investment of $99 million, Shanghai Pratt & Whitney Aircraft Engine Maintenance Co. Ltd. was designed to provide professional aircraft engine maintenance, repairing, and overhauling services for the aviation companies in China, satisfying their demand for maintenance and repairing of the CFM56 engine. The center comprises approximately 25,000 square meters

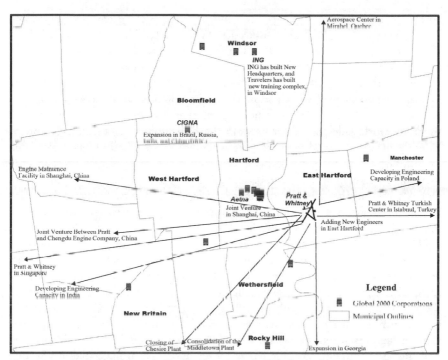

Map 10.1. Pratt & Whitney's Regional Base and Global Reach, with Hartford's Insurance Companies' Regional and Global Moves

(275,000 square feet) and features a 10-meter test cell with capability of testing engines up to 75,000 pounds of thrust. It was planned to repair or overhaul up to 300 engines annually and engage about 800 employees in two to three years. The center uses the lean manufacturing principle and an advanced information technology infrastructure that assists with materials, inventory, cost, and quality, and scheduling, which are comparable to the standards back in East Hartford. On two separate visits to the Shanghai center in 2011 and 2012, the first author of this chapter was struck by its state of the art equipment and technology, as well as its "green" building certification as Leadership in Energy and Environmental Design (LEED) by the U.S. Green Building Council.[11]

Soon after setting up the Shanghai center, Pratt & Whitney opened up a similar center in Turkey in 2010 that also would service the CFM56 engine. In the meantime, Pratt & Whitney has either already been in or is planning to expand further in other parts of Asia and Europe (see Map 10.1). By the second decade of the 21st century and approaching its 100-year anniversary, Pratt & Whitney has become a true global company, with its globalization accelerating over the two most recent decades.

As Pratt & Whitney has been globalizing, it has been undergoing a dual process of reorganizing and innovating at home that both accompanies and fosters the company's global expansion. On one hand, Pratt & Whitney has recently closed its engine center in Cheshire, Connecticut, which assembled and overhauled the PW4000 engine, and moved 300 of the 390 workers to the Middletown plant or East Hartford. The company also put a small number of these workers through machining training so they could function at the Middletown plant. As Pratt & Whitney acknowledged, the Cheshire plant was closed because the work had been moved to Asia (Lee, 2011). The new global engine centers are being supported by Pratt's worldwide part repair network that can service engines quickly and efficiently, saving time and money and thus rendering the Cheshire plant obsolete.

Differing from this global-local rebalancing, Pratt & Whitney has also been focusing on leveraging its home-base engineering talent to elevate its long-term global competitiveness in the commercial aviation industry. Having spent $1.5 billion in R&D investment and many years of risky and trial-error engineering, Pratt & Whitney has recently unveiled the new PurePower engine with the initial GTF (for geared turbo fan) that saves 16 percent in fuel burn and reduces noise by 50 percent. Since getting the Canadian aircraft-maker Bombardier as the first customer for GTF in 2007, Pratt & Whitney has secured orders from Mitsubishi for its Regional Jet and from Airbus customers like Lufthansa. Since each of the hundreds of GTF engines on order will sell for $12 million to add up to a great return on sunk investment, Pratt & Whitney has decided to add many new engineering jobs at its East Hartford headquarters (Saporito, 2011). This innovative engine technology not only has renewed Pratt & Whitney's leading position in global commercial aviation, but also revitalized its hometown corporate base through creating high-paying, knowledge-intensive jobs in the Hartford region. However, these engineering jobs generally do not match the local human capital level in East Hartford and thus contribute relatively little to its employment picture and everyday life.

INSURANCE GOING GLOBAL AND REGIONAL

To continue the theme that the tale of two industries (manufacturing and insurance) is key to tracking and deciphering Hartford's shifting economic fortunes, we offer a brief analysis of how the major insurance companies have navigated global and regional economic spaces while undergoing corporate restructuring in recent times that can shed more comparative light on the past and present of Hartford. Compared with U.S. multinational manufacturing companies in general and Pratt & Whitney in particular, Hartford-based insurance companies started going global later and have not globalized as extensively. Since the 1990s, however, Hartford's insurance sector has become far more globalized than at any other time in its long history, in both outgoing and incoming directions.

German and Dutch insurance companies have become critical to the Hartford economy. Following the Lehman collapse at the height of the financial crisis in October 2008, Germany's Allianz SE made a $2.5 billion investment in The Hartford, acquiring 24 percent of the company, but the investment hasn't done so well. HSB Group, including the Hartford Steam Boiler Inspection and Insurance Company, founded in 1866 and formerly a subsidiary of AIG, was bought by Munich Re of Germany for $739 million in April 2009. With its U.S. headquarters in the Hartford region, Dutch banking giant ING Financial Advisors and ING Retirement Plans owns several life insurance carriers in the United States and acquired Aetna's financial services and international businesses in 2000, but subsequently decided to split its banking and insurance divisions.

Aetna in turn has led the region-based insurance companies in entering global markets, starting with its foray into China in 1993. In 1997, Aetna formed a joint venture with China Pacific Insurance Company, the second largest insurer in China, to provide life insurance products to individual Chinese citizens and foreign nationals in the Shanghai region. While Aetna sold Aetna Pacific Life Insurance Company to ING in 2000 as part of its global restructuring mentioned above, it has retained its international health business, Aetna Global Benefits. In March 2008, Aetna opened its representative office in Shanghai and started to actively explore its strategic development options in China. Cigna, which relocated its corporate headquarters from Philadelphia to Bloomfield in 2011, has been exploring market opportunities in the BRIC (Brazil, Russia, India, China) countries (see Map 10.1). Six years after establishing a foothold in China in 2003, Cigna began to offer its first comprehensive healthcare product there through Cigna & CMC Life Insurance Company Limited, a joint venture between Cigna and its Asian partner, China Merchants Group (Bordonaro, 2009). It also became the first U.S. insurance company to be licensed to operate in India in 2011. Cigna also entered a partnership with Gama Saúde, Brazil, which has 20,000 doctors, hospitals, and healthcare professionals in Brazil, to further expand its coverage of more than 850,000 employees who work outside their home countries in 200 nations. Furthermore, Cigna bought FirstAssist Insurance Services, a British insurer, from Barclays Private Equity for $71 million, to add another product line to its growing global portfolio (Sturdevant, 2011).

The two-way flow of insurance capital between Hartford and the international insurance markets, especially involving rising global cities like Shanghai, highlights the global economic dimensions of the Hartford region revealed by Pratt & Whitney. The evidence not only reinforces Hartford's past and present position as a highly ranked global insurance center (see Table 10.1), but also reveals the unfavorable conditions and limitations of the city's small size for sustaining the density of insurance capacity.

To the extent that Pratt & Whitney has coordinated and balanced its global expansion with its local (East Hartford) and intra-regional consolidations, we can take a comparative look at how insurance companies have dealt with both operation and employment in the headquarters city of Hartford in relation to the larger region and even the state of Connecticut that are also insurance heavy. Connecticut is the state in the country that has had the largest share of its employment in insurance or most dependency on it, with an average of about 3.3 percent during 1995–2005, while the other four of the top five states (New Hampshire, Wisconsin, Iowa, Nebraska) averaged less than 2.3 percent (Connecticut Economic Resource Center, 2006: 19). When Connecticut lost 138,000 manufacturing jobs between 1985 and 1999, insurance, together with finance and real estate, which make up the so-called FIRE sector, gained 10,300 jobs (Forrant, 2002). Within the state, Hartford and the neighboring towns have the heaviest concentration of insurance employment, followed by the Greenwich and Stamford region bordering New York state, while insurance's presence is relatively light everywhere else in the state. While the largest share of the office spaces of the major insurance companies may be located in downtown Hartford, the neighboring towns like Avon, Bloomfield, Glastonbury, Simsbury, and South Windsor had a higher (15) percentage of their residents employed in insurance compared to 5–10 percent for Hartford, according to the 2000 Census (Connecticut Economic Resource Center, 2006). As part of this regional spread of insurance activities, several insurance companies have recently moved their operations to nearby suburban towns.

MetLife has joined Cigna in a large suburban campus in Bloomfield. Travelers has built a new training complex in Windsor, leaving a huge incentive package reportedly offered by the city of Hartford on the table. The life insurance division of The Hartford operates mostly out of Simsbury. In 2007, the large financial and insurance firm ING moved most of its workers (about 2,200) from Hartford to its new 475,000-square-foot headquarters in Windsor, just north of Hartford. At the end of 2010, ING relocated the last 150 or so employees from downtown Hartford to Windsor (Gosselin, 2010). This pattern suggests that as these insurance companies have become more globalized, they have regionalized more across Greater Hartford and are less confined to their original downtown locations. While there is no sufficient evidence to establish a strong and direct association between globalization and regionalization around Hartford for the insurance companies, and for major manufacturers like Pratt & Whitney, for that matter, it behooves us to examine the often controversial conditions under which downtown-based companies have moved to the surrounding region, which may shed additional light on Hartford's local-regional nexus.

Most manufacturing and service companies in the United States either started in or moved into central cities where they maintained corporate headquarters for decades until the 1950s. Then a growing number of them began to move out of downtowns of large or small cities. From the largest headquarters city of New York, General Foods moved to White Plains in 1954, and IBM relocated to Amonk in 1964 (Whyte, 1979). The trend accelerated in the 1970s, when some companies moved to the sun belt of the South and Southwest, while more headed for the suburbs. While there is no detailed data on companies moving out of downtown Hartford during these periods, two indicators over time provide a proxy gauge of the city's declining economic centrality as a headquarters location. In 1963, 21 percent of the people holding jobs in Hartford were employed in manufacturing, but the figure dropped to 7 percent by the early 1980s. In 1960, 48 percent of the jobs in Hartford were held by Hartford's residents, while the figure was only 23 percent by 1980 (Neubeck and Ratcliff, 1988: 303).

This job loss is somewhat counter-intuitive or ironic given the boom of new construction and the prosperity of the major insurance companies in downtown Hartford in the mid-1970s. The historical spatial legacy, coupled with the then economic reality, revealed the unfavorable conditions that would gradually push more companies to move out of downtown Hartford. With its boundaries historically drawn very closely around the central city, Hartford has had little land to develop to accommodate more economic activity. The growth of the insurance business offered few opportunities to the lower educated and lower class local residents who had lost manufacturing jobs (Neubeck and Ratcliff, 1988). With their economic power and political influence, the insurance companies in Hartford, together with smaller real estate developers, secured sufficient tax incentives from the city government to keep some of their presence and operations downtown, despite its overall continued decline. This lasted more or less until the most recent decade during which some of the remaining insurance companies in downtown reduced their staff.

Relative to manufacturing as exemplified by Pratt & Whitney, the insurance sector of Hartford has regionalized later and with fewer global connections. This may have something to do with the fact that employment in insurance, as part of the overall finance activity category, remained more robust from the mid-1990s to the financial crisis of 2008 (see Figure 10.3). Since these trend data pertain to the broad region including the city of Hartford, they have already factored in the large spatial spread of insurance jobs for quite some time. In addition, insurance has a lesser need for face-to-face contact that is critical to large investment institutions located in downtown Manhattan (Whyte, 1979; Sassen, 1991). Much of the work at Travelers and ING involves large numbers of their employees using computers to process claims in suburban office buildings. Major insurance companies have also experienced regional mobility across inter-local municipal boundaries, however in a different way than manufacturing, especially between Hartford and its contiguous or adjacent suburbs.

CONCLUSION

In this chapter, we have attempted to weave three previously unrelated facets of an under-told story about Hartford's economic fortunes. First, we have shown Hartford's early and recent economies to be more globally linked and positioned than assumed. Second, we have spun a tale of how two dominant industries of manufacturing and insurance have shaped the direction and performance of the Hartford regional economy through good and bad times. Third, we have revealed some of the interstitial spaces between the global and regional economic activities of major manufacturing and insurance companies that both connect Hartford to and isolate it from the suburban towns. The three themes have converged to drive one obvious point home: Hartford is too small and limited to fully take advantage of the much larger global and regional economic opportunities. This is akin to how Tom Condon (2008: C4) put it in *The Hartford Courant*, "Hartford may be too small to solve his own problems; it is hard to be an inner city without an outer city" (also see Condon, this volume). With 18 square miles, Hartford as a municipality is only one third of the territorial size of Denver International Airport, which occupies 53 square miles. Looking slightly beyond this well-recognized spatial constraint, we see earlier lessons and new opportunities emerging from our integrated analysis that may point to regional solutions to renew the economic fortune of the Hartford region.

Two lessons about manufacturing can be derived from understanding the history of Pratt & Whitney and its recent global and regional restructuring. First, while the overall decline of manufacturing employment in old American cities like Hartford has been inevitable, it has had a "ripple effect" as each eliminated production job can lead to the loss of four more indirect jobs in retail, business services, and housing construction. It was projected that of the Pratt & Whitney workers who might lose jobs in 2001, 20 percent (2,285 people) would remain unemployed for at least 26 weeks and 4.6 percent (521 people) would be unemployed after one year. In addition, since 75 percent of Connecticut Pratt & Whitney workers were over 45 and the average seniority in the plants was 22.1 years at the time (Forrant, 2002: 128–31), it would be somewhat difficult to retrain some of the seasoned machinists for other tasks, although Pratt made a best effort to do so when it closed the Cheshire plant in 2011. On the other hand, once the R&D for the new GTF engine is completed by engineers in East Hartford and orders are placed (see earlier), it can generate new jobs multiple times over in assembling, parts supply, and engine overhaul (Saporito, 2011). Since aircraft engine manufacturing is human and physical capital intensive, highly skilled, and highly efficient, it can continue to be based in Connecticut, which remains competitive for manufacturing when high labor productivity and non-labor efficiency are factored in (L. Chen, 2011). However, it is important to note that not all the newly hired engineers will live in East Hartford and thus produce multiplier effects locally; similarly not all the new production and service jobs related to the new engine will be regionally based, including at the Middletown plant.

The comparative lesson from the insurance sector is how to leverage its broad region and state-wide dominance to help Hartford, which remains the center of the industry, and create other location benefits. With only 4.4 percent of the total employment in Connecticut, insurance carriers accounted for 6.4 percent of the gross state product (GSP) and 8.5 percent of the total wages and salaries (Connecticut Economic Resource Center, 2006). However, the industry continues to face a gap between its increasing global growth and predominantly high salaried employment versus the lower-income and lower-skilled pool of job-seekers in Hartford. In 1998, Aetna donated $10 million to Shanghai Jiao Tong University to establish its business school and named it Aetna School of Management. Other insurance companies have brought scores of lower-paid software engineers from India to Hartford, where they work on the companies' information systems and stay on special temporary visas. While some of them live in downtown apartments in Hartford, others, primarily those who have brought their families, have settled in nearby suburban towns like East Hartford, which hosts the second most Asian (including Indian) tract in the

2010 Census for Connecticut. The hiring of the Indian software professionals in Hartford-based insurance companies confirms the shortage of software professionals in the local labor market.

To deal with the challenges created by Hartford's legacy of having lost its manufacturing sector and sustaining a viable insurance industry, we can look back to search for clues and look regionally for solutions. Of the mid-sized old manufacturing cities including Hartford that were similar in 1960, some like New Haven, Providence, Fort Wayne, and Grand Rapids have made some sort of comeback through the 2000s, while Hartford and Springfield, as well as Waterbury, have faltered. Among the factors that have contributed to these variations in success, leadership, and regional collaboration over long periods of time, diversification and innovation through university research and entrepreneurship stood out (Condon, 2011). The lack of municipal leadership for regional cooperation aside, physical regional and global connectivities are also lacking. The outdated rail service between New Haven and Springfield is being upgraded, but slowly. Located 20 miles north of Hartford, Bradley International Airport (BDL) flies nonstop to 31 domestic destinations, has 100 daily departures, and serves over five million passengers annually. Bradley International Airport is something of a misnomer given that BDL only has nonstop international service to Canada and Puerto Rico. Northwest Airlines (now part of Delta) started a nonstop passenger service to Amsterdam in 2007, but had to discontinue it in 2008 as fuel skyrocketed to $150 a barrel. The nearest airports to provide nonstop air service to multiple international destinations are Logan in Boston and JFK and LaGuardia in New York. Since Hartford is embedded in a much larger region filled with both favorable and unfavorable conditions and global connections, the time has come to reconfigure them through a real regional approach to economic development and service delivery. Jason Rojas and Lyle Wray pick up the regional story in the next chapter.

NOTES

We would like to thank Nick Bacon '10, Tom Condon, Chris Duffy, Laura Hua, Jason Rojas, Ron Spencer, Gaurav Toor '14, Andrew Walsh, Lyle Wray, and an anonymous reviewer for their helpful comments on earlier drafts of this chapter.

1. Thanks to Andrew Walsh (see his chapter on Hartford's more complete history, this volume) sharing with me his encyclopedic knowledge about Hartford's history, including this information on the origin of Colt Manufacturing.

2. Information extracted from http://www.cttrust.org/index.cgi/7518, April 2012.

3. Ibid.

4. Rentschler's manufacturing connection with Pratt and Whitney in Hartford goes back much further. In 1860 Francis Pratt and Amos Whitney were master machinists who started a machine tool company in Hartford. It was later acquired by Niles Bement Pond, a very large machine tool company. Rentschler's brother Gordon and good friend Edward Deeds were on

the board of Niles Bement Pond. In 1925 he convinced them to let their Pratt & Whitney subsidiary invest in his fledgling company and give him space in their building in Hartford. That is how Rentschler came to Hartford and started Pratt & Whitney Aircraft. Rentschler ended the relationship in 1929, but the separation agreement allowed him to keep the name. Interestingly, Pratt & Whitney Measurement Systems Inc., successor to the tool company, still exists, in Bloomfield.

5. We are grateful to Tom Condon and Andrew Walsh for providing and verifying this episode of Pratt and Whitney's early work experience with the machine-tool industry, and to Walsh again for illuminating Pratt & Whitney's key role in making Hartford globally advanced and known for manufacturing precision machines.

6. The Hartford-West Hartford-East Hartford Connecticut Metropolitan Statistical Area includes Andover town, Ashford town, Avon town, Barkhamsted town, Berlin town, Bloomfield town, Bolton town, Bristol city, Burlington town, Canton town, Colchester town, Columbia town, Coventry town, Cromwell town, East Granby town, East Haddam town, East Hampton town, East Hartford town, Ellington town, Farmington town, Glastonbury town, Granby town, Haddam town, Hartford city, Hartland town, Harwinton town, Hebron town, Lebanon town, Manchester town, Mansfield town, Marlborough town, Middlefield town, Middletown city, New Britain city, New Hartford town, Newington town, Plainville town, Plymouth town, Portland town, Rocky Hill town, Simsbury town, South Windsor town, Southington town, Stafford town, Thomaston town, Tolland town, Union town, Vernon town, West Hartford town, Wethersfield town, Willington town, and Windsor town.

7. The location quotient is the ratio of the area concentration of occupational employment to the national average concentration. A location quotient greater than one indicates the occupation has a higher share of employment than average, and a location quotient less than one indicates the occupation is less prevalent in the area than average. The location quotient of 5.7 was reported by the Bureau of Labor Statistics in its news release on occupational employment and wages in the Hartford-West Hartford-East Hartford region, July 28, 2011.

8. The list includes Carvel Corp (supermarket headquarters) from Bahrain; Allied World Assurance from Bermuda; Embraer (service center) from Brazil; Bombardier Business Aviation and TD Bank from Canada; Lego from Denmark; Alstom (engineering and customer service center), AXA Equitable, TLD, and Zodiac Aerospace Group from France; Ahlstrom from Finland; Eppendorf Mfg (shared service center), Henkel Loctite (North American Headquarters), Lipold (North American production facility), MTU (Aero Engines North America design center), PTR, and Trumpf, Inc from Germany; Permasteelisa Interiors from Italy; Konica (training and business service center), Honda (distribution center), Mazak (Northeast Technology Center), Westinghouse Electric (nuclear power plant design and service) from Japan; ING, Philips, and KPMG from the Netherlands; Sovereign Bank from Spain; ABB and Swiss Reinsurance from Switzerland; Citizen's Bank, Signature Flight Support, Scapa, and Tilcon from Great Britain.

9. A detailed history of the origin and early growth of Pratt & Whitney was provided by Mark Sullivan's book *Dependable Engines: The Story of Pratt & Whitney* published in 2008.

10. Information extracted from http://www.pwsingapore.com.sg, August 2011.

11. Most of this information was obtained by the first author during two visits to the Shanghai engine center in June 2011 and June 2012. Thanks to Pratt & Whitney in East Hartford for arranging and Pratt & Whitney in Shanghai for hosting these visits that also included a group of Trinity College faculty and students in the "River Cities of Asia" program.

REFERENCES

Amin, Ash, and Nigel Thrift. 1994. "Living in the Global." Pp. 1–22 in Ash Amin and Nigel Thrift, eds. *Globalization, Institutions and Regional Development in Europe*. Oxford: Oxford University Press.

Bordonaro, Greg. 2009. "Cigna Grows China Connection." HartfordBusiness.com, November 30.

Chen, Lei. 2011. "Is State Bad for Business?" *The Hartford Courant*. July 17: C1, C5.

Chen, Xiangming, 2007. "A Tale of Two Regions in China: Rapid Economic Development and Slow Industrial Upgrading in the Pearl River and the Yangtze River Deltas." International Journal of Comparative Sociology 48 (2–3): 167–201.

Chen, Xiangming, and Jiaming Sun. 2007. "Untangling a Global-Local Nexus: Sorting Out Residential Sorting in Shanghai." *Environment and Planning A* 39 (10): 2324–2345.

Chen, Xiangming, and Ahmed Kanna, editors. 2012. *Rethinking Global Urbanism: Comparative Insights from Secondary Cities*. New York: Routledge.

Condon, Tom. 2008. "City, Town Challenges Cry Out for Regional Solutions." *The Hartford Courant*. March 16: C4.

Condon, Tom. 2010. "Hartford: Bigger is Better." *The Hartford Courant*. September 26: C5.

Condon, Tom. 2011. "Cities: Hot Or Not?" *The Hartford Courant*. March 20: C5.

Connecticut Economic Resource Center. 2006. *Connecticut's Insurance Industry: Economic Impacts & Contributions*. A report. December.

Day, Clive. 1935. *The Rise of Manufacturing in Connecticut, 1820–1850*. New Haven: Tercentenary Commission, Yale University Press.

Forrant, Robert. 2002. "The International Association of Machinists, Pratt & Whitney, and the Struggle for a Blue-Collar Future in Connecticut." *IRSH* 47: 113–136.

Forrant, Robert. 2012. "Staggering Job Loss, A Shrinking Revenue Base and Grinding Decline: Springfield, Massachusetts in a Globalized Economy." Pp. 75–90 in Xiangming Chen and Ahmed Kanna, eds. *Rethinking Global Urbanism: Comparative Insights from Secondary Cities*. New York: Routledge.

Friedmann, John, 1986. "The World City Hypothesis." *Development and Change* 17: 69–83.

Friedmann, John and Goetz Wolff. 1982. "World City Formation: An Agenda for Research." *International Journal of Urban and Regional Research* 6: 304–344.

Gosselin, Kenneth R. 2010. "ING Pulling Rest of Workers from Downtown Hartford." *The Hartford Courant*. December 3: A14.

Hall, Peter. 1966. *The World Cities*. London: Weidenfeld and Nicolson.

The Hartford Courant. 2010a. "City & Town: Talk, Walk." September 24: B6.

The Hartford Courant. 2010b. "Moving to Windsor: ING Pulling Rest of Workers from Downtown Hartford." December 3: A14.

Huggins, Robert, Hiro Izushi, Will Davies, and Shougui Lou. 2009. *World Knowledge Competitiveness Index 2008*. Centre for International Competitiveness, University of Wales Institute, Cardiff, Wales, United Kingdom.

Lee, Mara. 2011. "Pratt Keeps Workers After Closing Cheshire Plant." *The Hartford Courant*. August 1: A8.

Neubeck, Kenneth J., and Richard E. Ratcliff. 1988. "Urban Democracy and the Power of Corporate Capital: Struggles over Downtown Growth and Neighborhood Stagnation in Hartford, Connecticut." Pp. 299–332 in *Business Elites and Urban Development*, edited by Scott Cummings. Albany: State University of New York Press.

Robertson, Roland, and Habib Haque Khondker. 1998. "Discourses of Globalization: Preliminary Considerations" *International Sociology* 13: 25–40.

Ryan, Brent. 2012. "From Cars to Casinos: Global Pasts and Local Futures in the Detroit-Windsor Transnational Metropolitan Area." Pp. 91–106 in Xiangming Chen and Ahmed Kanna, eds. *Rethinking Global Urbanism: Comparative Insights from Secondary Cities*. New York: Routledge.

Saporito, Bill. 2011. "How to Build a Job Engine." *TIME*. May 30: 41–44.

Sassen, Saskia. 1991. *The Global City: New York, London, Tokyo*. Princeton: Princeton University Press.

Sassen, Saskia. 2012. *Cities in a World Economy*, 4th edition. Thousand Oaks, CA: Pine Forge Press.

Sturdevant, Matthew. 2011. "Cigna Adds to Its Global Portfolio." *The Hartford Courant*. December 3: A8.

Sullivan, Mark P. 2008. *Dependable Engines: The Story of Pratt & Whitney*. Reston, VA: American Institute of Aeronautics and Astronautics, Inc.

Welch, Archibald Ashley. 1935. *A History of Insurance in Connecticut*. New Haven: Tercentenary Commission, Yale University Press.

Whyte, William H. 1979. "End of the Exodus: The Logic of Headquarters City." Pp. 83–90 in *Hartford, the City, and the Region: Past, Present, Future*, edited by Sondra Astor Stave. Hartford: University of Hartford.

11

A Tragic Dialectic

Politics and the Transformation of Hartford

Clyde McKee and Nick Bacon

INTRODUCTION

Since the inception of modern thought, historically produced social life has too often been uncritically understood as organic—as unmediated embodiments or reflections of nature. At both the formalized academic and everyday ideological levels, the monumental events of history are still commonly interpreted as "fate," while everyday tragedies are abstracted in perception as either the inevitable consequence of the cosmic or as the completely relative determination of (a-social) individual choice. Yet, in modern civilization, built and reproduced as it is by structural configurations of particular states, industries, and citizens, life is determined by specific constellations of historical and contemporary social practices. Thus, it is crucial to understand the *political*—the objectification of particular social actions within a given historical context and moment. It is only in this way that we can understand the causality of the event and the meaning of the situation, be our object of study a drone battle in a neo-imperialist war or the everyday drudgery of mechanized housekeeping.

What does this mean at the scale of a city or region? How do political actions, activities, and processes manifest, be they in the form of local political decisions or reified global forces—as consequences or opportunities for particular cities? In this essay, we look at how the city of Hartford has been transformed by political actions in an age of unprecedented uneven development at the global and local scale. Following the Civil War, this core state and industrial capital was commonly celebrated as one of the most prosperous and beautiful cities in America. Yet, by the year 2000, Hartford was ridiculed as the second poorest city in the nation, even as it remained the capital of the nation's wealthiest state as measured by per capita income (see Simmons, this volume; Horan, 2002) and the most productive city in the world

219

as measured by per capita GDP (see Bacon and Chen, introduction, this volume). Understanding Hartford's tragic dialectic, and how that dialectic can be controlled in the future, is the subject of this chapter.

THE CONSTITUTION STATE

Connecticut gained the nickname "Constitution State," because it was here that the United States' first state constitution was drafted. Based upon the political theory of the Mayflower Compact, Connecticut's first laws, *The Fundamental Orders* (1638–1639), empowered a select few white, male, church-certified, landowners to create a polity and govern it. This pioneering social contract designated Hartford and two other colonies as independent polities with sovereign residents, while also formally provisioning for the future possibility of further internal division/differentiation, rather than unification. By structuring the colony's municipalities in a way which only allowed for their further political subdivision (rather than annexation), Connecticut failed to anticipate inevitable geographic and demographic expansion. They also blundered in giving all their created units equal representation, failing to envision that Hartford in 1950 could have approximately 177,000 residents locked within 18 square miles with the same number of representatives (two) as the little town of Union, population: 600. All of this state's 169 towns and cities are now incorporated and cannot realistically expand their boundaries and increase their taxable grand lists. The founders of towns in Texas, Florida, Tennessee, and Maryland did not make the same mistakes as those of New England. They allowed for annexation to accommodate growth (see Rojas and Wray, this volume).

One of the most important decisions made by Hartford leaders occurred in 1870. The state constitution of 1818 required that legislative sessions alternate between Hartford and New Haven. Although the city's debt was $3,000,000, Hartford's leaders, with the approval of residents, offered the state $500,000 to build a permanent capitol in Hartford, and offered the trustees of Trinity College $600,000 to abandon its site adjacent to Bushnell Park for its present campus on Vernon Street (Weaver, 1982: 98–99). The consequences of this decision are disputable. On the one hand, it is almost tautological to say that designating Hartford the *sole* epicenter of state political power strongly supported the city in also becoming the *insurance* capital of the world, and thus that the move had a dramatic positive impact on regional and even global civil society. On the other hand, at the local level, the move was negative in the long term. Irreplaceable urban fabric—Victorian tenements and colonial mansions alike—were obliterated to make way for the erection of an alienated urban space made up of blank government buildings and private offices. Because state office buildings cannot be taxed by the city to improve its grand list, this decision has made it difficult for the city to balance its budget (see Carbone and Brody, 2002). One could also make the case that had Trinity College stayed in its original location, it could have sustained and increased downtown Hartford's vitality, as Yale has arguably done for New Haven.

THE CLASH OF THEORIES AND PRACTICES

There were three sharply contrasting movements during the late 1800s that influenced theories and practices of local governments in certain parts of the United States, including Hartford. These were urban boss organizations, the decisions of "home rule" judges, and the "Model City Charter" advocates.

There is extensive literature related to the domination and demise of big city bosses.[1] They gained major influence by effectively meeting the pressing needs of thousands of Irish, Italian, and other European immigrants. On the other hand, home rule, by which local governments exert political dominance, has typified Connecticut politics since the 18th century. The history and theory of the Model City Charter movement can be found in the publications of the National Civic League (which changed its name in 1986 from the National Municipal League). The synthesis of these three movements is new and challenging for contemporary actors seeking to change the structure of Hartford and its region.

The Political Bosses

Droves of immigrants from Europe were caught up in the "push-pull" forces that began with the Pilgrims at Plymouth and the Puritans in Boston. These forces included potato famines, wars, religious persecutions, social class rigidity, desires to explore and develop new lands, exploitation of people and land, demands for increased international trade, and desires for wealth, salvation, and work. Urban bosses arose to address two major problems: (1) the immediate needs of immigrants for food, housing, income, community, and a way to learn English; and (2) the equally pressing needs of the heads of businesses for cheap laborers to dig sewers, lay trolley tracks, and later to make guns, bicycles, and cars. These urban bosses were brokers and personnel directors, who developed the political parties created by those federalists and anti-federalists who negotiated to create a national constitution. Party bosses also arguably created the theories and practices of responsible party government, because some form of party is necessary to organize individuals and produce public policies based on the principle of majority rule.

In Connecticut, Democratic and Republican bosses played major roles in selecting, nominating, and electing outstanding national and state leaders during the mid-20th century. They also controlled productive patronage systems needed to fill positions in local government. For example, during the late 1900s some young graduates of law schools would seek the advice of some local bosses for employment. Some of these bosses would tell them that if they volunteered for certain difficult-to-fill positions— such as the commission on aging, the library board, the youth commission, or the task force on energy consumption—the boss would arrange for them to earn a living by doing title searches in city hall. He might say, "If you do good volunteer public service, gain valuable experience, and develop name recognition, I might recommend you as a candidate for the state legislature. If you serve in the General Assembly with distinction and become a leader, I might be able to recommend you for appointment as a judge." On a lower level, today's mayors and town managers often ask local party leaders to help them find good candidates to serve as crossing guards to provide safety for children going to and coming home from school. At the highest levels, party bosses select outstanding delegates to participate in constitutional conventions.[2]

The Home Rule Law

To gain insights into basic questions, we need to understand the evolving theory of home rule law and how this theory applies to Hartford (see also, Rojas and Wray, this volume). During the second half of the 19th century there were two competing theories of the authority of local governments: the Cooley Doctrine and the Dillon Rule. The Cooley Doctrine grew out of the decision of Michigan Supreme Court Judge Thomas Cooley's decision *The People ex rel v. Herlbut* (1871). In this decision the court agreed unanimously that the state legislature had no authority to interfere with city operations. Judge Cooley used English common law and the right of local government to inherit English traditions. This Cooley Doctrine was replaced generally by the decision of Iowa's Chief Justice John Dillon. In his decision in *The City of Clinton v. The Cedar Rapids Missouri River R.R.* (1868), Dillon presented a comprehensive argument that local governments are "mere tenants at will of the legislature."

Other judges refined the Dillon Rule using these guidelines: Authority given to local government must be expressly defined, necessary or fairly implied, or essential to the declared purposes of local government. When a local government's authority is questioned, its authority should be denied. Giving added strength to this theory was the decision of the U.S. Supreme Court in *Hunter v. Pittsburgh* (1907), which held that state governments can both confer and withdraw the authority and privileges of their local governments.

The concept of home rule was first introduced to Connecticut in Public Act 317, "An Act Providing Home Rule For Cities and Towns and Other Municipalities" (1915). It was repealed. In 1951 and 1953, Public Act 338 "An Act Concerning Home Rule" created the basis for this state's present home rule law found in Article Ten of the 1965 State Constitution. Before this article was added to the current constitution, the basic theory that "local governments are creatures of their state" was tested in three early court decisions: *Noyes v. Ward* (1848), *City of New London v. Brainard* (1853); and *Webster v. Harwinton* (1864).

It has now been established that home rule means a city or town has authority under guidelines of the state legislature to frame, adopt, and amend its charter. A current question is whether or not Dillon's Rule should be modified—and if so, how?

The Model City Charter

In 1894, the National Municipal League was created to check the influences of city bosses and conflicting decisions of state judges regarding home rule. The main strategy of the leaders of this league was to use the established practices of business corporations and apply them to local governments. In this theory, a nonpartisan board should hire a nonpartisan, professionally trained, and experienced chief executive to manage the local government's various departments (e.g., police, fire, finance, records, personnel, and public works). This board of directors, called a city council, would be a small (7–9 members) group elected at-large rather than by districts. The head of this council would be a ceremonial mayor, who would not be a policy leader. A basic assumption was that "there is no Democratic or Republican way to repair a road." Such a notion departs radically from the structures of our national and state governments. There is no separation of authority and power into three branches. There are no checks and balances—no separate election of the chief executive. And there is relatively little opportunity for citizens to participate directly in making policy, a function which is instead executed by the city council.

This league's first model city charter was published in 1900 and became known as "the council-manager plan." In general, the various iterations of the model have been adopted by smaller and medium sized cities such as Hartford. For instance, in 1912, it was adopted by Sumter, South Carolina, and by Dayton, Ohio, two years later. By 1915 this council-manager plan had been adopted by 82 of the leaders of cities, and by double this number in 1920. This model city charter has been revised and published by the National Civic League in seven editions. Each new edition has contained various options related to roles of the mayor, the way the mayor should be selected, and the specific authority of the council relating to the authority of the mayor and the manager.

In 1947, the classic council-manager plan recommended by the National Municipal League was adopted for Hartford by a majority of the city's voters and approved by the state legislature. There are two theories as to why the traditional weak-mayor commission form was abandoned. The first asserts that following World War II, Hartford, which had played a major role in producing war equipment and supplies, had neglected its own needs and should hire a professional executive who would understand the city's needs and advise the council on what policies should be approved. The second theory supports the reasoning that Connecticut had been a Republican state whose leaders were fearful of the expanding strength of the Democrats. They believed that if they could persuade the city's voters and the state legislature to have the capital city adopt an official nonpartisan form of government, this would permanently cripple the Democrats.

PARTISAN TAKEOVER OF COUNCIL-MANAGER GOVERNMENT

There are general principles used to evaluate governments: form should follow function and formal and informal structures and practices should coincide. Hartford's reformers did not foresee that the new nonpartisan council-manager form would give a Democratic boss a wonderful opportunity to build a powerful political machine. Hartford lawyer John M. Bailey, whose family lived in the city, set up a law office and hired a small group of attorneys, some of whom became outstanding federal and state judges. But, Bailey decided to focus on politics rather than law.

He opposed Hartford's adoption of the nonpartisan council-manager form but once it was adopted he developed a strategy to take it over and strengthen the Democratic Party. His plan was fairly simple. First, he selected a group of Hartford citizens he believed would make good members of the city council. Next, he told them that he could help them get elected by getting them signatures for their candidates' petitions and raising money they needed for filing fees. Once he had his "nonpartisan" team organized, he delivered the votes to get them elected. After all his candidates were elected, he created what was known as "the Bailey Room" at the Parma Restaurant located behind city hall. Before each council meeting Bailey would convene the "nonpartisan" council members at a dinner meeting to have a discussion of what policy issues they had in mind and which ones should be approved for the city manager's implementation. Members of the new council were instructed that they were not to interfere directly in the manager's administration of various departments.

Members of the press were invited to attend these "Bailey meetings," but there was a strict understanding that what reporters learned was off the record. Thus, reporters had to base their news reports on what took place at the public council meeting. The result was that council meetings ran very smoothly because all debate had already taken place. And, members of the city council did not interfere with the administration of the government by the city manager.

The classic council-manager form of government is based on the assumptions that local elections will be nonpartisan, have votes counted at-large rather than by districts, and be held at times separate from partisan elections for state and national candidates. Connecticut's state statutes have long held that local governments with at-large elections must have "minority representation." This means that city councils with nine partisan seats must reserve three seats for members not of the majority party. But with Bailey's takeover of all nine seats on Hartford's council with "nonpartisan" members, it was obvious that there were no seats for minority Republican representatives. State Republican leaders made this lack of representation an issue, but the only solution was for the Bailey Democrats to agree to scrap nonpartisan elections for partisan elections. Next, there was an issue over the way the mayor was elected. The classic form of council-manager government asserts that the manager is the chief executive and that the mayor is just the member of the council who gets the most votes. It was soon recognized, however, that the office of mayor should not be left to chance. Candidates interested in becoming mayor developed a strategy of running by asking the CEO of the *Hartford Times*, the dominant daily paper in Hartford, "What do I have to do to get your paper's support for election to the council?" Answer: "Promise not to raise local taxes." Result: The charter was soon changed to separate the elections for mayor and candidates for the city council. But the office for the new mayor only was paid a small stipend upon which one could not subsist. It devalued the mayoral role and forced incumbents to only work part time. That was just one of many issues that influenced voters to support the abandonment of council-manager government and the adoption of a strong mayor system in which the mayor is a generously compensated full-time chief executive.

THE STRUCTURAL IMPACT OF A
UNITED STATES SUPREME COURT DECISION

The U.S. Supreme Court's decisions in *Baker v. Carr* (1962), *Reynolds v. Sims* (1964), and *Westberry v. Sanders* (1964) transformed Connecticut's political system. This radical change, which greatly improved opportunities for Hartford because it increased this city's number of representatives in the House, took place in the 1965 constitutional convention. This convention was necessary to replace the traditional unit representation model with the "one person-one vote" national requirement.

The Constitutional Convention of 1965[7]

The leaders of the Republican and Democratic parties were in complete control of the 1965 Convention. There were 84 delegates, 42 from each party. The party leaders agreed that there would be a requirement that all proposals for changing the 1818 Constitution must have the approval of two-thirds of the delegates. They also agreed that the proposals be presented to citizens in meetings throughout the state for debate and comment. Although the main issue before the convention was reapportionment of each town and city as directed by the U.S. Supreme Court, there were 240 proposals. These included reducing the number of legislators in the House, having annual sessions of the legislature, and increasing the authority of the governor.

Steps taken to change the state's constitution as it pertained to local government are of particular importance. The concept of home rule was given constitutional status in Article 10. This revised article also enjoined the General Assembly from passing any special acts related to a specific town or city. The General Assembly was given express authority to legislate with reference to regional governments and inter-municipal compacts. A current issue is whether or not this article should be amended to enable the General Assembly to give special authority and power to Hartford and Connecticut's other major cities.

Article 8 on Education received extended deliberation. The old 1818 Constitution lacked reference to free public education. There was general agreement among the convention delegates that the new constitution must recognize governmental responsibility for education. Education was equated with the state's Bill of Rights. The difficulty here was defining the difference between state and local responsibility in this area. This question was to become an enduring issue for Hartford in several court cases.

The 1959 Election

The 1959 campaign for governor marked the high point of success for Connecticut's Democratic Party. Under the leadership of State Chairman John Bailey, the Democrats in their party platform and campaign speeches pledged that if they won the office of governor and majorities in both houses of the legislature, they would make two radical reforms: they would abolish the inefficient county governments, as well as the corrupt local justice of the peace courts. They achieved both objectives and kept both pledges. The responsibilities of the abolished counties were divided between the state and local governments while the judicial responsibilities of the justice of the peace courts were shifted to the state's circuit courts. These changes increased the responsibilities of the city manager and city council of Hartford but did not sufficiently increase their authority or financial resources. As the needs of the state and local governments grew, the void left by the abolished counties became more evident.

To fill this void the state legislature used its constitutional authority to create the Department of Community Affairs, regional councils of governments, and regional planning agencies. These organizations had the responsibility to develop plans for conservation and development throughout the state. There were serious weaknesses in these organizations. The councils of government consisted of appointed local representatives who had few professional skills and received no financial compensation. The regional planning agencies hired trained planners but they had no authority to implement their plans. Particularly important, these organizations had no authority to infringe upon the jurisdiction that local governments possessed from their home rule charters.

The state legislature missed a huge opportunity in October, 1967. After three years of careful research and planning, the Capitol Regional Planning Agency (CRPA), which was composed of representatives from 30 of the towns and cities in Hartford's metropolitan area, published a major report prepared by The Regional Affairs Center at the University of Hartford. In its report, titled "Governmental Organization in the Capitol Region," the CRPA described, analyzed, and evaluated seven types of regional governments: voluntary metropolitan councils, intergovernmental agreements, urban county, limited purpose special districts, multi-purpose special districts, city county consolidation, and metropolitan federation. The report next evaluated how these forms were actually working in 13 regions throughout the United States. In the final section of its report, the CRPA reduced the optional types to five, used seven criteria to evaluate each, and then recommended that the state legislature create regional federated governments.

Why was this recommendation not adopted? The short answer is that fiscally conservative Republican Thomas Meskill won the office of governor in 1970. Faced with significant debt created by the two previous Democratic administrations, Meskill began his term by announcing that he was going to abolish all non-essential state agencies, which included the Department of Community Affairs. The long answer requires us to appreciate a dominant global and national phenomenon which was structuring economic and political conditions at this time. The 1970s ushered in globalization, along with profound economic restructuring and neoliberalism. The national welfare state was severely eroded and replaced with a newfound reliance upon municipal governments for the most basic financialization, planning, and implementation of urban strategies. Due to its reliance upon private-sector companies and competitive practices, some theorists (e.g., Harvey, 1989) have called the resulting phenomenon *entrepreneurial urbanism* (see Bacon, this volume, for a more detailed discussion).

HARTFORD'S THREE FAILED EXPERIMENTS WITH PRIVATIZATION

The failure of Connecticut's public institutions to fill the void left by the abolition of country government motivated Hartford's major private corporations to create their own solutions, but these approaches failed as well.

The Greater Hartford Process

The first failed experiment was the Greater Hartford Process, a regional master plan funded and partially implemented by a selection of Hartford's business elite. As globalized capitalism first spatialized in the United States, urban designers in collaboration with big business and government attempted to strengthen urban regions and build new towns in order to maximize location advantage and urban competitive potential. For instance, before James Rouse began construction of his planned city of Columbia, Maryland, he created a model based on strong neighborhoods organized within a cohesive urban system. Each neighborhood was designed for 2,000 to 5,000 residents—small enough that inhabitants could get to know each other and develop cooperative relationships. Every neighborhood would have an elementary school, swimming pool, convenience store, park, and playground. Two to four neighborhoods holding 10,000 to 15,000 persons would make up a village. Each village would have a middle school and high school, a commercial center with a supermarket, pharmacy, barber shop, cleaners, and professional offices, gas station, and one major facility to serve the entire city. The city would have seven villages surrounding a downtown core. This core would have a major mall, a variety of restaurants, office buildings, a medical clinic, a music pavilion, and a dinner theater. City residents could enjoy any of the major village facilities. These included a major ice skating rink for hockey and general family use, a large outdoor and indoor tennis complex, a health center with squash courts and an indoor track, and two 18-hole championship golf courses. Rouse wanted each resident to be able to identify with and have pride in a neighborhood, village, place of employment, and city.[4] To ensure the reproduction of this "practical utopia," there would also be a large area for industrial and commercial development.

Hartford saw mixed results when it tried to apply Rouse's criteria for a "good city" to its region. As James Rouse was celebrating the fifth anniversary of his planned city of Columbia, Maryland, business leaders in Hartford were planning to bring his theories and practices to Connecticut. Using the advice of the American City Corporation, a subsidiary of the Rouse Corporation, Frazier Wilde formed a 17-member board of directors composed of various leaders in Hartford. Members of this board created two nonprofit service corporations, the Greater Hartford Process, Inc. and the Greater Hartford Community Development Corporation, which became known as DevCo. It was DevCo's responsibility to obtain financing, acquire land, engage in site planning, and develop and follow recommendations suggested by residents of the Hartford region.

To provide a basis for these two corporations to begin their work, the Board of Directors of Greater Hartford Process endorsed eight "basic principles": "Bring the Essential Parties To The Table; Set Forth A Believable Image of a Region That Works; Unite Planning and Development With A Commitment to Carry Out the Plans; Recognize the Inseparability of Social, Economic, and Physical Planning and Development; Use Physical Development as the Opportunity for Positive Social Change; Work at a Large Enough Scale; Create and Capture Values; Establish a Continuing Process" (American City Corporation, 1972).

On December 7, 1966, James W. Rouse, President of the Rouse Company, gave a speech before the U.S. Senate Committee on Government Operations. In this presentation, he described the problem of urban sprawl. He argued that it is inefficient, ugly, oppressive, and inhuman. He said that as a mortgage banker and developer he had seen this problem throughout America. Rouse explained how he began to build his planned community of Columbia, Maryland. He said he began with these questions:

> "Why not build a rational city?" "Why not bring together in orderly relationship the pieces of urban growth to one another?" "Why not arrange them with respect for the nature of man?" "Might not the interaction of these purposes strengthen each?" "Might not such a city be such an appealing place to live and work or run a business that it would be profitable indeed to produce it?"

Rouse told the senators that his team built a model of his city planned for 100,000 residents, that they estimated that they needed at least 14,000 acres at a cost of a $25 million mortgage over a 20–year period. Since Rouse had a relationship with the CEO of the Connecticut General Insurance Company, he asked this company to loan him money to purchase the needed land and to become a co-owner of the planned city. Rouse said his team had four main objectives: (1a) to create a real city; (2a) to respect the land; (3a) to provide the best possible environment for the growth of people; and (4a) to make a profit. Next, to understand why the Greater Hartford Process failed we need to understand what DevCo announced that it would not do:

(1b) condemn land; (2b) act outside the legal framework of local government; and (3b) disrespect local zoning, site planning, utilities, and other conditions under local control. DevCo pledged it would not itself administer any program or deliver any services. It stated "The only power DevCo has is the power of ideas." How powerful are ideas without authority to implement them?

After announcing its principles and what it would not do, DevCo announced that it would accept responsibility for three projects: (1) create a "renewing community" placed within the older areas of the inner city; (2) organize "an expanding community" designed to contain urban sprawl; and (3) plan a totally "new community" located somewhere within the 700 square miles of the capital region. In addition, this corporation announced it would make a region-wide effort to create "new social and economic values," give "local government a stronger economic base," and challenge "institution and community agencies to respond to changing community patterns to change their delivery systems."

Had DevCo committed itself to just its first two projects it might have been successful, because these would have allowed it to work closely with the officials of Hartford. It was the announcement that it planned to build a totally new community that really got public and non-public officials excited. Where would it be located? What would land be worth before it got started? Could this land be purchased now and sold later? Most pressing, was the question of how this company could even pull off its commitments if it acknowledged publically its lack of real authority or power.

These decision makers could have learned lessons from the key players, who persuaded the voters of Hartford in 1947 to switch from the weak mayor-commission form of government to the classic council-manager form. These players included the CEO of *The Hartford Times*. While speculators were trying to find out where DevCo would build its "new community," its agents were spending millions to covertly purchase land in the town of Coventry, located near the expanding University of Connecticut. Governor Thomas Meskill, who was not associated with the Board of Directors of Process or DevCo, announced prematurely that their "new community" would be constructed in Coventry. The mistake of publishing a stolen memo became one of the primary determinants contributing to the destruction of plans for the three new planned communities in Greater Hartford. In January 1975, the *Hartford Courant* published an in-house staff memo that a reporter took without permission from the desk of the president of Greater Hartford Process. This "think piece" (Pazniokas, 1975) expressed concern about the impact on Hartford of its rapidly growing Puerto Rican population and whether this ethnic group should be treated with "benign neglect" (see Simmons, this volume). The publication of this memo inspired an estimated 1,000 Latino demonstrators to converge on the opening of the city's new $35 million civic center and blocked its scheduled events. Spanish-speaking students shut down their schools. The Director of the Puerto Rican Department of Migration flew into Hartford and rebuked the president of Greater Hartford Process, demanding that the author of the controversial memo be fired.

Following Governor Meskill's disclosure that Coventry had been selected to become a new planned community, the selectmen of this town announced a call for a town meeting to give citizens of their community an opportunity to express their opinions related to becoming a "new community." The (first-listed) author and his wife decided that they would also attend this meeting even though they did not live in the town or own any property there. They covertly made a tape of the entire discussion by town residents, and were shocked after reading an article on this town meeting the next day in *The Hartford Courant.* This entire article (Young, 1973) was devoted to the opinion of a single resident's subjective account of why a reified Coventry opposed becoming a "new community." Not reported were any resident comments which favored becoming a new community. From our (the first-listed author and his wife's) own account, some attendees made such statements as "this plan could greatly improve our schools," "improve our health care," "raise the value of our homes," etc.

It seemed clear that the reporter had either falsely reported on the content of the meeting or had not attended it at all. Moreover, we might speculate that the peculiar interest of DevCo's then president in obtaining our recording of the meeting implies that perhaps no one on his staff had attended either. Governor Meskill's disclosure of the intended location of the "new community," the purloined article published by *The Courant,* and the biased reporting of the Coventry town meeting killed the project in its entirety. Business leaders lost interest in investing in Coventry and refused to put money in any more of their company funds. DevCo sought to sell all of the land it had purchased, and its employees began to look for new jobs.

A valuable opportunity for Hartford and its region was lost. The extent of this missed opportunity can perhaps be estimated by comparing three recent reports attempting to quantify qualitative conditions of American cities. The August 2010 issue of *Money Magazine* ranked Columbia, Maryland, with 155,000 residents, the second best city in the United States. Meanwhile, the August 2010 issue of *Connecticut Magazine* ranked Coventry the 17th worst small town in the state, out of the 22 towns in its category. Last, *24/7 Wall St.* gave Hartford the bronze slot in "America's Dead Cities" (August 23, 2010). Although all three ranking systems may lack properly objective methodologies and may misrepresent urban conditions by absolving their categorical reasoning of context (e.g., regional/local socioeconomic conditions), we have to ask ourselves how critical this missed opportunity must have been. Might Hartford's adoption of the Columbia model have changed these rankings?

The Bishops

The second failed model of privatization is "the Bishops." Who were these so-called Bishops? Their implicitly absolutist title may fit well enough the group's form, role, power, and genesis. However, in this section we show how the fundamentally flawed regime failed.

On January 23, 1983, The *Hartford Courant* ran a headline with the pithy title: "The Bishops of the Board Rooms Set City's Course." After announcing that the so-called "Bishops" were directly constructing Hartford's public policy, the *Courant* had its reporters spend six months interviewing dozens of informed residents to define this city's power structure. These reporters used the classic definition of power outlined by the sociologist C. Wright Mills in his book *The Power Elite* (1956). By "power" Mills meant "those who are able to realize their will even if others resist it" (Mills, 1956: 9). The *Courant* reporters similarly followed the guideline to distinguish between those who really exercise power from those who, because of their prominence, were merely believed to have it.

In their first article titled "The Powerful in Hartford," (Martin, 1983) a staff writer wrote that the heads of about 15 major financial corporations in Hartford made an unprecedented commitment of $11 million in low-interest loans to produce 1,000 rehabilitated housing units and to aid existing neighborhood businesses. This writer described "the powerful" as a cohesive group of white, male, corporate executives who lived outside the city but who met secretly for breakfast each month in one of the corporations' downtown executive rooms, in order to plan, discuss, and implement projects investigated by their private staff. Their decisions were thought to profoundly affect Hartford's fabric and character by influencing (1) who lived and worked there; (2) what the city would look like; and (3) which neighborhoods would be saved and which would be demolished or left to deteriorate. Despite the suburban residency of its members, part of the justification for the powerful influence of the "Bishops" was that Hartford corporations and businesses paid about three quarters of the city's municipal property taxes.[5]

Although very powerful, "the Bishops" would not have existed were it not for the city's fragmented government and its lack of adequate resources to focus on projects needing special attention. Once elections were made partisan and members of the city council were given special titles and functions, Deputy Mayor and Majority Leader Nicholas Carbone became the city's link to John Filer, who was chairman of the Aetna Life and Casualty Company and was regarded as "First Among Equals." Carbone and Filer had a harmonious relationship partly because Filer had served a term in the state senate and understood how politicians of that era thought and worked.

Aside from the weakness of Hartford's government, there were other reasons for the formation of "the Bishops." The corporations represented by this group had been investors in the Greater Hartford Process, which had failed in its attempt to apply the Columbia model to Hartford's region. The heads of these corporations saw that by creating an informal decision-making group within Hartford they could avoid the problems associated with Coventry. Next, the head of Hartford's Chamber of Commerce had long advocated corporate social responsibility. During the Bailey era, Bailey had persuaded the head of Travelers Insurance Company to encourage some of his employees to serve Hartford in elected and appointed positions. He did this by making it company policy that those employees who served in the city's government could take off as much time as they needed to do their public work and that their service would advance their professional careers rather than handicap them. Finally, the "Bishops" wanted Hartford to change its tax policy, which taxed business property at a rate they thought unfairly high.

Why did the "Bishops" fail? First, for better or worse, the articles published by the *Courant* profiled the individuals in this group and exposed their specific activities to the public in a somewhat negative light. Second, three members of the radical third party "People For Change" were elected to the city council, and introduced resolutions highly critical of the business policies of the corporations represented by "the Bishops" (see Simmons, this volume). These two situations combined with other economic factors (see Chen and Shemo, this volume) influenced some of these corporations to move their headquarters out of Hartford, merge with other corporations, or go out of business. As their corporations dissolved, so too did the so-called "Bishops."

Educational Alternatives, Inc. (E.A.I.)

In 1994, Hartford attracted national attention when it privatized the management of its entire public school system. With 26,000 students, the Hartford school system was the second largest in New England. However, despite its gargantuan size, its bounds did not extend into any suburban district. Given that Hartford's school system was enclosed entirely within the bounds of the vastly undersized and overimpoverished central municipality (see Bacon and Chen, this volume), many informed citizens unsurprisingly regarded it as Greater Hartford's worst. There were declining test scores, deteriorating facilities, serious social problems, deep budget cuts, constitutional violations, and serious union-management conflicts.

Hartford's charter prescribed a partisan council-manager form of government with a separate nonpartisan nine-member board of education with members elected at-large. Although the city manager prepared the city's budget for approval by the city council, the budget for the school system was prepared by the school superintendent for approval by the school board. The school budget was then presented to the city council for lump-sum approval as part of the city's total budget. In other words, though Hartford's general government was politically separate from the school system, these two systems were intimately connected financially. The result was a fragmented political system that was difficult for the citizens of Hartford to understand and for elected officials to operate.

Because all local government budgets are required by state law to be balanced, Hartford's revenue, which was primarily generated from local property taxes, either had to be raised or the city needed to severely cut services. A significant number of the candidates elected to the board of education were fiscal conservatives, who had campaigned on pledges to reduce the school budget by opposing the demands of the teachers' union representatives. Some board members asserted that teachers were misclassifying their students as "needing special education" so that they could receive higher salaries and be assigned special teaching assistants. To support this assumption, members of the board pointed out that Connecticut's average expenditure per student was approximately $6,000, while Hartford's average cost per student was approximately $9,000 (though, see Dougherty, this volume, for a more nuanced understanding of Greater Hartford's educational financing and structure).

Following the request of the school board, the school superintendent contacted Education Alternatives, Inc. (E.A.I.), a Minneapolis-based, private, for-profit management and consulting firm, to help reform Hartford's school system. In addition to members of the school board, administrators, teachers, union representatives, and various parent organizations met with representatives of this private company. Although they were not directly involved, some members of the city council expressed support for hiring E.A.I. In the end, a five-year management contract was approved by the board of education in a 6–3 vote. The company agreed to invest $20 million immediately to upgrade the school's infrastructure, downsize the school's top-heavy bureaucracy, and reduce the number of students classified as "needing special education." E.A.I. also promised to save as much as $3,000 per pupil—thus cutting spending down to the state average. These savings would be interpreted as profits, and would be divided between the company and the city. As a final safeguard, the contract included a provision allowing the city to review and revise it on an annual basis.

Yet, this experiment in privatization ultimately failed. Why? First, various parent groups asserted that E.A.I. had not listened to their recommendations and that they saw no improvement in their children's educational development. Second, representatives of E.A.I. asserted that the superintendent, the school board, and representatives of the teachers' union failed to cooperate with them. Third, proposals to reduce teacher employment generated a significant employee morale problem. Fourth, the *Courant* (1995) published the "high expense accounts" that representatives of E.A.I. were submitting for their interstate travel, hotels, and food. Finally, there was growing public sentiment that the city's schools should not be used for profit. After E.A.I. agreed to reduce the scope of its management plan, its contract was terminated.

PLANNING TO AVOID FUTURE MISTAKES

The big lesson from Hartford's mistakes and missed opportunities is not necessarily that privatization by its nature generates failure. There are numerous case studies that reveal how government services can be improved by such models. For example, city managers have demonstrated how unionized public trash collection can be made more efficient and effective by having public employees compete with private trash collectors for expanded service areas (Osbourne and Gaebler, 1992).

Instead, we must understand that each case study discussed in this chapter represents an earnest problem-solving strategy to counter forces over which Hartford and its region in truth have little control. Globalization has led to locally significant trends such as deindustrialization, suburbanization, immigration, and socioeconomic immiseration. Moreover, it has led to what some have called *glocalization:* the contradictory tendency under globalization for deteriorating national and regional government and a concomitant reliance on local municipalities and private entities (see Moser, this volume). In Greater Hartford, glocalization, retrofitted as it is to 18th-century municipal balkanization, has led to a lack of funds and interest in Hartford's urban core.

Thus, the urban and regional strategists of Hartford and its surrounding metropolitan sprawl face seemingly impossible challenges, for which there are only so many options. Yet, wise leaders learn how structural forces over which they have no direct control serve to limit their authority, power, and influence. More important, they understand that these forces only determine their choice of options, but never annihilate them completely. Thus, we can learn from the mistakes and missed opportunities of those who ruled before us, and conceptualize/implement realistic plans to improve cities like Hartford. We can avoid some of the aforementioned mistakes and missed opportunities by situating ourselves as ideally as possible to use the resources we do have, and to efficiently respond to those opportunities that do arise, however limited they might be.

NOTES

Clyde McKee was originally the single author of this contribution. However, he tragically died before the chapter could be completed. Nick Bacon thus finished the piece without collaboration from McKee, trying to as truly as possible keep with McKee's argument and views. We must disclose that Bacon and McKee differ profoundly in age, theoretical background, and perspective. The reader should thus be aware that, while the content of the article is assuredly factual, there are a number of instances in which both co-authors might very well object to the language or implications of a given statement.

1. See Lee S. Greene. 1964. "City Bosses and Political Machines." Special Edition, *The Annals of The American Academy of Political and Social Science*, 353.

2. For a detailed review of machine politics, see ibid.

3. For a detailed review, see Bosworth, Karl A. 1966. "1965 Constitutional Convention: Its Politics and Issues." *Connecticut Government,* 19: 1–6

4. It should be noted that the first listed author and his family of six children lived in and studied Columbia during 1971–1972.

5. This statistic should be taken with a grain of salt. For a more critical account of the city's financials in the 1980s, and how the city and its residents were often exploited for sheer corporate and suburban gain, see Neubeck and Ratcliff, 1988.

REFERENCES

24/7 Wall St. 2010. "America's Ten Dead Cities: From Detroit to New Orleans."

American City Corporation. 1972. The Greater Hartford Process. Columbia, MD.

Bosworth, Karl A. 1966. "1965 Constitutional Convention: Its Politics and Issues." Connecticut Government, 19: 1–6.

Brady, Andrew, and Patricia Grandjean. 2010. "Rating the Towns, 2010." Connecticut Magazine, August Issue.

Capitol Region Planning Association. 1970. Pp. 233–252 in "Governmental Organization in the Capitol Region."

Carbone, Nicholas R., and Evelyn Brody. 2002. "PILOTs: Hartford and Connecticut." Pp. 233–252 in n ed. Evelyn Brody, Property Tax Exemption for Charities: Mapping the Battlefield. Washington DC: The Urban Institute Press.

Greene, Lee S. 1964. The Annals of the American Academy of Political and Social Science, 353.

The Hartford Courant. 1983. "The Bishops of the Board Rooms Set City's Course." January 23.

The Hartford Courant. 1995. "Gouging the City for Expenses." May 17: A.14.

Harvey, David. 1989. "From Managerialism to Entrepreneurialism: The Transformation of Governance in Late Capitalism." Geografiska Annaler 71(1): 3–17.

Horan, Jim. 2002. "A Tale of Two Connecticuts." Connecticut Association for Human Services. Accessed at: http://www.cahs.org/publications/Essay.pdf.

Martin, Antoinette. 1983. "The Powerful in Hartford: 'Bishops' of the Board Rooms Set City's Course." Hartford Courant, January 23: 17.

Mills, C. Wright. 1956. The Power Elite. New York: Oxford University Press.

Money Magazine. 2010. "Best Places to Live," August Issue.

Neubeck, Kenneth J., and Richard E. Ratcliff. 1988. "Urban Democracy and the Power of Corporate Capital: Struggles Over Downtown Growth and Neighborhood Stagnation in Hartford, Connecticut." In Business Elites and Urban Development, edited by Scott Cummings. Albany: SUNY Press.

Osbourne, David, and Ted Gaebler. 1992. Reinventing Government: How the Entrepreneurial Spirit is Transforming the Public Sector. Boston: Addison-Wesley.

Pazniokas, Mark. 1975. "Memo Casts Doubt on Commitment to City Residents' Needs." Hartford Courant. May 22.

Rouse, James W. 1966. "New towns from old cities." Statement before the Executive Reorganization Subcommittee, Senate Committee on Government Operations. Baltimore, MD: December 7.

Weaver, Glenn. 1982. Hartford: An Illustrated History of Connecticut's Capital. Lincoln: Windsor Publications.

Young, Thora. 1973. "DevCo Agent, Resident Clash at Meeting." Hartford Courant, Oct 12: 18C.

12

Metropolitan Hartford

Regional Challenges and Responses

Jason Rojas and Lyle Wray

INTRODUCTION

What is the Metropolitan Hartford Region and what should it mean to the average resident, taxpayer, worker, town, or business? It can be argued that the region exists on paper alone for academic, administrative, or theoretical purposes. Connecticut is well known for the sacredness which it attributes to the local, and for its odious stance on "intrusions" by higher branches of government. Thus, the "constitution state" has long been known as a "state of towns . . . a republic of republics . . . where the people have long atomized their political life breaking the state into smaller and smaller units" (Lancaster, 1930: 693). This glorification of local control supports a mind-set that the 169 towns of Connecticut and the subset of 30 towns and cities making up the Capitol Region Council of Governments (CRCOG) can continue to function independently of each other. It does so in spite of the reality that no town is completely self-sufficient. Whether the validity of local control is real or imagined, one outcome in metropolitan Hartford, and in several other New England city-regions, is a continual decline in the economic and social well-being of the core city.

An overreliance on property taxes as the primary revenue source for local service delivery has led to the permanent inability of Hartford and other poorer munici-palities to meet the basic needs of their inhabitants. Here, and increasingly in the region's suburbs and peripheries, this crisis has been exacerbated by negative social and economic changes, such as increasing poverty (Hershberg, 1996). In these cores and sub-cores, there has emerged a crisis of sheer survival which cannot be solved by local means alone. What must be understood, however, is not simply that Hartford cannot solve its own problems without outside suburban altruism. Rather, what is crucial to understand is that the region's misguided localism has contributed to Hartford's concentrated immiseration. Moreover, it is this same localism which has led to the region's mischaracterization of regional crises as local problems in the first place—a mischaracterization which is all the more insidious because it justifies the decisions of the region's municipalities to not solve collective problems that they wrongly see as those of "other towns." This failure to acknowledge the regional nature of urban problems and the subsequent lack of effort to ameliorate them, has allowed once manageable ills to spread and intensify to unprecedented levels both within and beyond the bounds of the inner core.

Urban problems are inherently regional. They take place not in one locality, but in many. Thus, by their very nature, urban crises are metropolitan and cannot be solved at the local scale. How do we address these local policy questions that are in fact regional when Hartford lacks a clear sense of what its region even looks like? How can a regional approach to urban problems succeed in an environment where there are multiple definitions of what Metropolitan Hartford is (see Map 12.1)? Hartford is home to less than 15 percent of its region's population, and the next largest municipality has little more than 7 percent. While the region retains critical functional linkages to its core city, it is nevertheless becoming increasingly isolated politically, socially, and economically. Metro Hartford is a region unsure of its identity because of an underlying belief that the suburbs do not need Hartford, while at

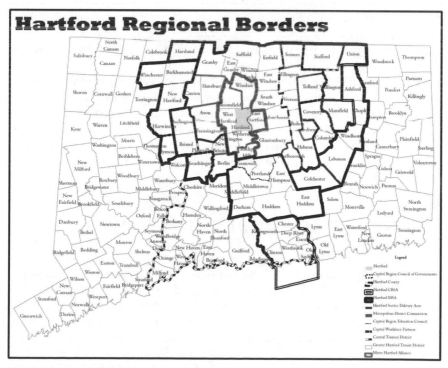

Map 12.1. Hartford Regional Borders

the same time recognizing that there's no such thing as a "suburb of nowhere" (Metro Hartford Regional Assessment, 2006). Nevertheless, how the metropolitan region is defined depends on who is asking and why. As we will see later on in this chapter, there are a number of "regional" entities that are intended to address specific urban policy questions in Greater Hartford, but they fall short in sustaining the region's economic competitiveness.

Domestically and globally, core cities often offer leadership for a metropolitan regional direction in responding to emerging challenges. In an age of exponential competition among regions in a global economy, metropolitan areas anchored by core cities are increasingly becoming the critical units for determining national capital investments (Levine, 2001). Yet, the Hartford metropolitan region is best understood as having a *polycentric* character. This type of region lacks a singular city that can serve as a total economic, political, or social focal point for the broader metropolitan area. It is rather constituted by many proximate but historically and politically distinct cities, all of which may be physically separated by space, but which nevertheless do maintain strong functional linkages (CERC, 2007).

The unique challenge for metropolitan Hartford is the combination of its core city's extreme smallness and the anarchic subdivision of the rest of the region into an absurdly large number of tiny, but politically separate, municipalities. The absence of a large core city or county makes it more difficult to develop a critical mass of human, economic, and political capital to arrive at strategies capable of address-ing inherently regional dilemmas. Inter-jurisdictional cooperation is easier with a larger core government with surplus service capacities that it can potentially sell on the margins. It is also easier in states with larger counties anchoring metropolitan regions. Thus, cities like Chicago, Portland, and Seattle are structured in such a way that they can continue to serve as regional cores. Though Hartford remains a major employment center and is home to significant political, economic, cultural, and recreational assets, it does not share the specifically regional attributes of these aforementioned cities. Such contrasts are crucial to acknowledge, because they reflect the political, social, and structural dynamics around which a metropolitan regional agenda for Hartford must be developed.

THE FRAGMENTED METROPOLIS

The second decade of the 21st century finds Connecticut's capital city and surround-ing region facing a number of challenges in an increasingly competitive national and international economic context. Many of the challenges faced at the metropolitan level, from moving people and goods to creating an ever more skilled workforce, de-mand regional responses that are well beyond the capacity of any single municipality. Yet the region's political mechanisms are, in many cases, fragmentary or incomplete to meet these challenges. In order to remain economically competitive against growing pressures from other regions of the country and world, there needs to be a reset and upgrade of current governance and services delivery systems that allow for expanded metropolitan regional planning, and policy development and implementation on key challenges (Hershberg, 1996). It should be acknowledged from the outset that this paper is not advocating exploration of a general purpose regional government. What this paper explores is how we work within an existing political and organizational framework while utilizing and reallocating existing resources that advance economic and social development for the region. Metropolitan *governance* may be pursued without moving to metropolitan *government* (Parks and Oakerson, 2000).

An ability to respond at the metropolitan regional level is critical to effectively responding to significant policy initiatives in metropolitan Hartford that are regional in nature, particularly in the areas of the dispersion of poverty, urban decay, land use, economic development, housing, and sustaining environmental quality. Regions are in direct competition with other regions that often have economies of scale and centralized decision making, which in turn allows for better adaption to changing demands (Chen and Shemo, this volume; Wallis, 1995).

When analyzed in the context of globalization, there are three interrelated trends that demand the metropolitan Hartford region and the state recognize and develop a coordinated response. Wallis (1995) discusses the globalization of production, consumption, and investment that is increasingly defining the postindustrial economic and social environment in which cities must compete. This system is one in which production can be relocated to areas where there are lower costs and more development opportunities, in an effort to meet the growing consumption demand created by emerging economies. This in turn fuels the mobility of capital to areas where investment can be best realized and exerts increased pressure on natural resource systems. To put it simply, metropolitan regions cannot count on past glories and current assets to shelter them from a grueling global competition for investment and talent.

Metropolitan Hartford is a lot like other urban areas of the United States that are seeing increasingly spatialized inequalities. Divides have been widened by a host of drivers. For instance, the federal policy of the last 50 years has contributed to the abandonment of core cities and the migration of capital, labor, and jobs to select suburban communities. Federal taxes, housing, and transportation policy have all encouraged this movement, resulting in increased economic, social, and racial isolation in many cities and regions (Mazey, 1997). This leaves Hartford in a situation that can be understood as what former mayor of Albuquerque, New Mexico, David Rusk described as a city facing the "Point of No Return." The qualities that make up this descriptor were assigned to 24 U.S. metropolitan areas in Rusk's 1993 book *Cities Without Suburbs*. By 1990 these identified core cities had experienced major population loss, faced significant racial isolation in comparison to surrounding suburbs, and had residents whose average incomes levels were less than 70 percent of suburban income levels. Passing the "point of no return" is determined by whether the central city in a metropolitan area was structurally capable of closing its economic/social equity gap by even a single percentage point over any period of time (Rusk, 2000).

The current state of fragmentary government in the metropolitan Hartford Region undercuts our regional prosperity because of the great divide of community wealth, both political and economic, between resource rich suburbs and resource poor urban locales (and increasingly certain inner-ring suburbs [Metro Patterns, 2003]). Regional fragmentation has been increasing since the 1960s. In response the state initially increased its efforts to expand regional collaboration by studying the feasibility of metropolitan government in Connecticut. Among the primary findings of such studies, was that there was no comprehensive "political base" from which to advance coordinated planning. Thus, while some progress was made in creating regional solutions, most efforts were rejected by local officials because they felt the state was dictating how the local government should operate (Public Research and Management, 1975). This fragmentation balkanized metropolitan Hartford, resulting in a disconnected regional economy with an inadequately trained workforce confined to urban core areas. What resulted was a limited transportation network that exacerbated congestion and could not connect workers with jobs, along with diminished urban service delivery systems in precisely those areas where assistance was needed most (Judd and Swanstrom, 2008).

In the 2000 update to *Cities Without Suburbs*, metropolitan Hartford fell into a category in which the city-suburb economic gap, as well as racial segregation, continued to grow. Population loss from Hartford's historical high point of 177,397 in 1950 was 21 percent by 1990 and 31 percent by 2000. Meanwhile, the percentage of Hartford's black and Hispanic population was 66 percent in 1990 and increased to 81 percent in 2000, while city income as a percentage of suburban income dropped from 53.1 percent in 1990 to 46.3 percent in 2000 (Rusk, 2000). These data exemplify how Hartford, despite decades of state intervention in education, public safety, economic development, and housing, continues to face social and economic conditions disproportionately isolated within its inflexible political boundaries of 18 square miles.

With a governing framework based on an 18th-century system of strong town home rule, how does the metropolitan Hartford region address the increasingly complex and inherently trans-local challenges of the 21st century? Which politically acceptable solutions and mechanisms can be brought forth at a regional scale in a timely manner to meet the challenges facing the region? What are some of the important factors that either facilitate or constrain the metropolitan Hartford region's ability to address important issues at the metropolitan regional scale? What has been the history of metropolitan Hartford's institutions and programs that address regional scale issues to date?

OBSTACLES TO REGIONALIZING HARTFORD: HISTORY, ABOLITION OF COUNTIES, AND CONSTITUTIONALLY PROTECTED TOWN HOME RULE

There are perhaps three key interconnected obstacles to moving a regional agenda in metropolitan Hartford and in Connecticut. The first concerns the ability of places like Hartford to grow beyond their current political boundaries. The area within Hartford's municipal boundaries is extremely small, as annexation has not been and is not currently a viable policy option for cities in Connecticut, New England, and other states where there is no unincorporated land to annex. The region is further limited since it functions in a political reality where town boundaries are virtually unalterable, having been cemented in place for hundreds of years. This very fact eliminates annexation as a policy option for dealing with regional challenges (Rusk, 2000).

The inability to annex and grow the area of a city and region determines a city's elasticity in the context of Rusk's use of the concept. Annexation, in which large communities absorb undeveloped land or smaller neighboring communities, has been a primary driver of metropolitan growth throughout the United States. Cities of comparable size to Hartford in 1950: (1) Nashville, Tennessee (22 square miles) and (2) Raleigh, North Carolina (11 square miles) grew to 69 square miles and 473 square miles respectively by 2000. This allowed these cities to grow both geographically and demographically, and helped mitigate the racial and economic isolation which limits Hartford's social progress (Rusk, 2000).

A regional agenda for metropolitan Hartford is further complicated by Connecticut's decision in 1960 to become the first state in the country to abolish its counties. Moreover, Connecticut did not replace counties with an intermediate general-purpose government that had any authority to provide appropriate scale and consolidation for delivering services. It could be argued that this decision further accelerated local fragmentation as town and cities were left to fill the void for service delivery. By the time of abolition, county governments had little functional authority left apart from operating the county jail systems, along with a few minor miscellaneous administrative responsibilities. Counties had no taxing authority and not even one function over which they held exclusive authority (Levenson, 1966). The motivation to abolish counties was partly driven by a perception that the system was corrupt and utilized an unnecessarily high level of bureaucracy (Tondro, 1999). This historical skepticism is in many ways still indicative of the contemporary sentiment expressed toward any notion of regionalism in Connecticut. It is a practice, and perhaps a psychological phenomenon, deeply rooted in the state's historical narrative of local control that continues today and limits the ability of government to respond to regional policy demands.

If we combine these two obstacles with the third, home rule, we get a clearer understanding of why governance is structured the way that it is in metropolitan Hartford, and why this phenomenon plays a critical—if not absolute—role in any discussion related to advancing a regional agenda. Home rule is the notion that municipalities should continue to maintain authority to operate autonomously with as little state interference as possible (see McKee and Bacon, this volume). In Connecticut, this legalized conception of local jurisdictional independence dates back to colonial times, when Hartford, Wethersfield, and Windsor joined to become the Connecticut Colony, while still retaining rights to self-government in each joining municipality, but in fact became far more important during the massive waves of further municipal balkanization in the 18th and 19th centuries. Thus the local governance debate has gone on in one way or another for more than three centuries. And the debate continues today despite the 1864 Connecticut Supreme Court ruling in *Webster v. Harwington* that the authority of towns "instead of being inherent or reserved, have been delegated and controlled by the supreme legislative power of the state from its earliest organization" (Collier, 1992: 180).

Increasing urbanization continued through the 1800s and the interests of rural areas in limiting state intervention in local affairs began to intensify (Grumm and Murphy, 1974). The home rule movement was initiated by Michigan Supreme Court Justice Thomas C. Cooley in an 1871 court case *People v. Hurlburt*. Cooley argued that there was a reasonable expectation that citizens would want to place some limitations on the authority of state government to supersede day-to-day decision making at the local level. Furthermore, he also argued that when a matter is clearly within the purview of a local government, no state rule or law should override the ability of a local government to address it (Brookings Institution, 2003).

There is also legal theory and case law that challenges home rule. Most seminal was Dillon's Rule, which emerged from an 1868 Iowa Supreme Court case presided over by Judge John F. Dillon. His 1911 *Commentaries on the Law of Municipal Corporations* has served as the basis for our current system in which local municipalities are provided with limited authority to exist and function through the granting of charters by their state. This confirmation of state dominance over local governments was not without consequence. The local governments were unable to adequately address local issues; therefore, state legislatures were often burdened with numerous requests for special legislation by towns to provide them the legal authority to perform functions not expressly granted by a state (CACIR, 1987). Year after year the Connecticut legislature would have to consider countless such requests, to the point that by 1953 legislative session the number totaled 836. This accelerated agitation for home rule in Connecticut, leading to the 1957 Home Rule Act, which granted towns and cities the authority to develop local ordinances as well as the structure of government that they felt was best for their communities (Spiegel, 1992).

The home rule Act prescribed how a town would go about making changes to its charters, but also provided some protections to local governments by prohibiting the legislature from passing special legislation aimed at diminishing their power or dictating how the town should be organized, unless expressly requested by its municipal government (CACIR, 1987). A 1965 amendment to the state constitution included provisions for home rule, but still confirmed that ultimate authority rested with the legislature. The amendment still did include enabling language that allowed municipalities to determine how and whether they should form regional governments or participate in regional compacts for the provision and delivery of service (Horton, 1993).

Thus, while it is clear that the state largely holds the ultimate authority over decision making at the local level, the political reality remains that towns have a constitutional right to have the least amount of interference possible, and in effect, to make all decisions they feel are local and within the purview of local government.

Regardless, there is one commonality for all states regarding home rule, i.e., none of them give actual local autonomy in the manner that is perceived (Frug and Barron, 2008). Despite this allegiance to home rule there are a number of ways in which regional cooperation has taken hold.

METROPOLITAN REGIONAL CHALLENGES

Every metropolitan region rightly sees itself as unique in geographic, demographic, and historical terms. Yet there are many shared challenges across U.S. metropolitan regions that can offer lessons on how to address challenges at a metropolitan regional scale. This section examines some common metropolitan challenges and a portfolio of options that regions have for responding, before finally identifying actual examples of regional responses to date that can serve as a foundation of moving forward. The challenges we examine include the movement of people and goods, public service optimization, environmental preservation, and competitive workforce.

Moving People and Goods

In the Hartford metropolitan region, very few people use public transit on a significant percentage of community trips. For instance, under 2.5 percent of the region's population uses public transit to get to work (Capitol Region Council of Governments, 2001). No rapid transit, light rail, or bus rapid transit presently exists in the region (although the first rapid transit line from Hartford to New Britain is under construction [Busway Fact Sheet, 2011]). In contrast, many metropolitan regions around the country have been adding intercity rail and regional rapid transit to provide mobility options to drivers driving cars alone and to concentrate development in more sustainable land use patterns.

At the "big picture" level, there are steps in process to better connect the Hartford metropolitan area with the $800 billion dollar economy of the New York City metro, situated little more than 100 miles away. By 2016 more frequent intercity rail service at 30 minute intervals, together with the rapid transit line cited above, can provide for significant economic benefits in construction and labor market expansion (Stacom, 2011). Intercity rail and rapid transit can also address the high levels of per capita land consumption with new developments taking private and public investments farther from historic center areas and leaving underinvestment and aging infrastructure behind.

Currently in the Hartford metropolitan region, there is very little local money invested in metropolitan regional transit or commuter rail. By contrast, nationally, a major trend is for more local funding to speed up metropolitan regional transit options with transit and transit-oriented development, expanding from coast to coast (Transit and Regional Economic Development, 2011). A large majority of referenda for transportation and transit improvements have been passing despite challenging economic times (2010 Transportation Ballot Measures, 2010). The result is that for San Diego and Los Angeles Counties some 60–70 percent of transportation funding comes from local sources to supplement federal spending (personal communication at National Association of Regional Councils annual meeting, 2011).

Commercial aviation is another important part of metropolitan regional mobility. Commercial aviation links our regional economy with other regions in the country and the world. The Hartford region is served by Bradley International Airport (BDL), which until recently has been operated as a unit of the state department of transportation. Overall trends for the past decade have been negative at BDL airport in passenger and freight volume, for example, as they are still below 1999 levels (Kane, 2011). Legislation passed in the 2011 session by the General Assembly and signed by the governor creates an airport authority to operate a number of airports, including BDL. The legislation was designed to provide more flexibility to respond to the rapidly changing and turbulent world of commercial aviation, with the advent of more competition and more point-to-point flights rather than a predominantly hub-and-spoke airline system. Time will tell whether a more entrepreneurial approach emerges from the new authority in securing new international and national routes for the airport, providing more amenities within its pedestrian complex, and leveraging economic development around its perimeter.

Public Service Optimization

Metropolitan regions compete for investor funds on the price, performance, and predictability of public service, among other factors. Having public services working at an optimal scale for efficiency and effectiveness is a challenge addressed by many regions. The metropolitan regions in Connecticut have a number of challenges to address in this area. For example, there are more than 104 centers to answer 911 calls that could be served by far fewer (and in fact are in many states). There are more than 164 school superintendents for a general population of 3.3 million people. The list continues on in the same fashion for any of a number of public services delivered at the local level. No precise estimate has been made of the cost of having services at a less than optimal scale but an educated guess is that the cost would be substantial. There is generally no data on the performance of these smaller units against that of larger service units. While the price of government (through taxes and fees) and regulatory predictability continue to be important factors in business location and investment decisions, public service optimization is likely to rise to greater visibility and response.[1]

Competitive Workforce

The metropolitan Hartford region has long been home to a highly skilled and well-educated workforce, hosting numerous financial service, precision manufacturing, healthcare, and aerospace companies that have provided a higher standard of living for generations (See Walsh, Chen and Shemo, this volume). The region is at the heart of New England's compact "Knowledge Corridor," which stretches from Middletown, Connecticut, to just north of Springfield, Massachusetts. The corridor is home to 32 colleges and universities that collectively produce 26,000 graduates per year. Its smaller sub-regions in many ways act as one, as 45,000 people cross the border each day to work (Greenlee, 2004). Workforce is also an inherently regional issue with a great deal of workforce mobility across the region cutting across the Connecticut-Massachusetts border, as is shown in Map 12.2.

At the same time, there is a major regional concern over an access and skills gap that leaves many in Hartford disconnected from job opportunities paying a "family living wage." Worse still, this is coupled with highly publicized "achievement gaps" in academic performance by class and race. There is a very real concern that the next generation of workers will not possess the same high level of education as the retiring generation. This generational incongruity will inevitably cause serious problems for high value added employers. Concern was heightened when data collected by Connecticut's Departments of Education and Higher Education 2010 showed that upward of 72 percent of Connecticut high school graduates attending state community colleges and 65 percent of Connecticut high school graduates attending

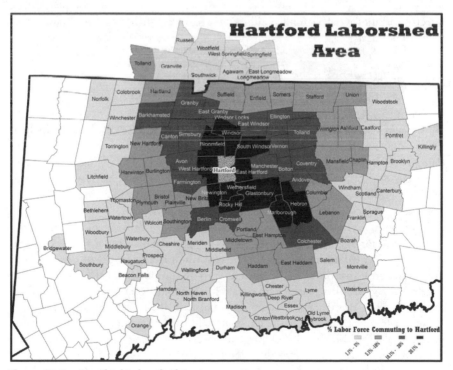

Figure 12.2. Hartford Laborshed Area

one of Connecticut's four state universities needed to enroll in remedial or developmental math or English courses (Megan, 2010). Similarly, the precision machinists workforce averages more than 55 years of age and the state is among the oldest in the United States (Connecticut Indicators: Aging and Work, 2008). Replacing this skilled workforce after the coming wave of "baby boomer" retirements will pose a significant obstacle to business recruitment and retention, which is particularly concerning given the anticipated manufacturing and production growth at Hartford-based United Technology Companies Pratt & Whitney, whose aircraft engine business results in an extensive system of suppliers and maintenance manufacturers that employs thousands of workers (see Chen and Shemo, this volume).

How will a region with a disconnected regional education system, made up of dozens of economically and racially segregated independent school districts, educate a future workforce increasingly composed of graduates from low-performing public schools? What is relatively unique is not the set of challenges faced. Indeed, the list above could easily describe any number of American postindustrial cities hit with industrial job losses and rapid and widespread suburbanization. What is particular to Hartford is the historical and structural context within which its region must work to come up with effective responses to these challenges. Hartford and other urban core areas in Connecticut differ from many other American cities in that they been left to deal with their public policy challenges on their own. They completely lack effective or appropriately funded sub-state structures, such as counties and other regional polities.

METROPOLITAN REGIONAL RESPONSES TO DATE

This chapter now turns to the relevant distinguishing features of the metropolitan Hartford region and to the responses to its challenges that have been mounted to date. The following is not meant to be an exhaustive list, but is rather meant to showcase some of the major categories of response. This should help lay the groundwork for a review of efforts to date in the metropolitan Hartford region and point to possible ways forward for more effective regional responses.

Metropolitan Hartford has a regional layer of service delivery and coordination which is extraordinarily fragmented. This is because the delivery of services is organized and executed at the local level. The end result is a wide mix of organizations and service areas that often overlap with little to no coordination between each other. Like other regions, these entities are constrained by mostly advisory powers, and are limited in their effectiveness because they maintain their own operating boundaries which frequently repeat at the regional scale the fragmentary structure existing at the local level (McDowell, 1996). The observer of this effort quickly discovers a veritable menagerie of intermediate level organizations—those between the state and town levels—mostly dependent on state government funding due to inability to raise significant operating revenue on their own. This leads to the potential for disjointed results and project duplication, ending with questionable results in policy implementation or success. There are also service delivery areas for a number of state functions, which creates another layer of government that is regional in nature and provides services to the benefit of, and in partnership with, local governments as well as private and nonprofit organizations. The end result is a political and functional fragmentation at multiple levels, which results in a complex organization of small, medium, and large provision units that are linked by common production units and resources (Parks and Oakerson, 2000).

Connecticut and the Metropolitan Hartford Region have a foundation from which to coordinate and deliver services regionally. There exists a framework by which the relationships between multiple jurisdictions can be adapted to allow for regional governance while still recognizing local preferences (Parks and Oakerson, 2000). There are 96 entities in Connecticut that exist to address issues of regional concern (OLR Report, 2010). Due to the large number of entities we will focus on some examples of regional collaboration that have worked to date, and which provide expanded potential for increased regional cooperation and/or service delivery. The best positioned, yet perhaps most unfamiliar to the general public, is the region's Regional Planning Organization (RPO), the Capitol Region Council of Governments (CRCOG).

CRCOG is the largest of the eight state COGs with 30 member communities (OLR Report, 2010). CRCOG, like many regional planning organizations, is financed by a variety of means including state and federal funds, grants from a number of sources, and membership fees. More important to this discussion is the issue that they neither have the ability to raise tax revenue, nor the authority to expand their work or engage in the delivery of local services. They do function as the Metropolitan Planning Organization for coordinating federal transportation funds, coordinating some public safety and homeland security programs, initiating limited land use planning under state law, and assisting municipalities with joint purchasing, regional GIS, solid waste planning, and online permitting.

Table 12.1.   Duplication of Service Delivery at the State Level

Economic Development Districts	8
Dept. of Emergency Management and Homeland Security Regions	5
State Tourism Districts	5
Transit Providers	15
Dept. of Environmental Protection Districts	2
Conservation Districts	5
State Police Regions	11
Judicial Districts	13
Judicial Branch Areas	22
Regional Education Service Centers	6
Regional Planning Organizations	14
Workforce Development Boards	5
Community Actions Agencies (includes federal dollars)	12

Source: Compiled by the authors.

CRCOG has the potential to advance a regional agenda, because it has existed within the established political framework of a state and region emphasizing local control and voluntary participation since 1966. These facts provide the organization with some functional, institutional, and historical credibility. CRCOG's legacy could assuage politicians and citizens alike that strengthening its role would not necessarily entail the end of localism and the rise of some sort of absolute metropolitan government. An important point to make still is the overwhelming contention that a primary outcome of bolstering Hartford's COG would be to build consensus among elected officials about what problems could be addressed at the metropolitan level (Wikstrom, 1977). It would be interesting to see the outcomes of a similar survey done today.

Another existing regional system that offers potential is the metropolitan area's Regional Education Support Center (RESC). RESCs provide services to individual school districts as well as the general public. The services include professional development training for teachers; school construction services, operations and facilities services; cooperative purchasing and other business services; certain special education services; and preschool and care programs for infants as well as adult education and job training programs. The Capitol Region Education Council (CREC) is the RESC that services Hartford and 36 surrounding communities, including 14 communities that are outside CRCOG's operational boundaries (OLR Report, 2010).

CREC has become an increasingly powerful agency because of its role in helping implement initiatives to desegregate Hartford's public schools. The effort to desegregate has been going on for over 20 years and came as a result of a 1996 state Supreme Court decision regarding the 1989 *Sheff v. O'Neill* lawsuit that called for an end to the racial, ethnic, and economic isolation of Hartford's minority students. One of the solutions has been the creation of magnet schools throughout the metropolitan region whose school population would consist of suburban students and students from Hartford. CREC has become an operator of 15 of these magnet schools, which are spread throughout the region, with many of these schools having opened within the last 10 years.

The entire plan to end segregation has been described as fragmented because the court decision left the responsibility of planning and implementing development activities to the state, which in turn has either lacked internal initiative to increase the amount of Open Choice seats (seats allowing city students to attend schools in select suburban communities), or which has faced external resistance from particular communities for placement of city students due to a lack of financial incentives (Frank, 2007). The court case has long been a source of anxiety for wealthier suburban districts, whose residents feel that home rule protections would be violated if they were forced to accept Hartford children into their schools or vice versa (Frahm, 1992).

Education in Connecticut is delivered primarily on a town-by-town basis. This results in the duplication of administrative costs, as well as the delivery of substandard education for less affluent and less white districts. There are 17 Regional School Districts, generally no larger than two or three towns, which provide an opportunity for smaller municipalities in Connecticut to collaborate and provide more cost-effective education for their communities (OLR Report, 2010). Regional school districts have faced their own challenges, usually related to funding. There have been instances in which tensions have arisen between member towns of a regional district over the level of funding that each member should have to contribute to its operation. However, such regional districts offer viable alternatives to the system of singularly municipality based districts that dominates Connecticut.

The structure of governance for CREC and that of other RESCs consists of a body of representatives from their member Boards of Education, which, similar to CRCOG and other COGs, results in the inclusion of elected representatives from individual municipalities on a body that provide services on a regional basis. CREC is perhaps one of the best examples of how a regional approach can be taken to address service delivery, but which nevertheless adds another layer of educational bureaucracy that simultaneously dilutes the financial resources available for funding public education, while also making long-term planning difficult and disparate.

The Metropolitan District Commission (MDC) is one of the oldest regional organizations in the Hartford region, having been established in 1929. The MDC is currently made up of eight member communities including Hartford, and is responsible for providing potable water and sewer services in the region (OLR, 2010). Its original charge allowed water and sewer services but also empowered the commission to provide services for inter-town highways, refuse disposal, flood control, and more important regional planning, although the last service was never fully acknowledged and was subsequently passed onto another agency. There has long been resistance to an expansion of the MDC into something larger than the regional entity that it is. That resistance has come from within the agency itself and from member communities who have feared giving up control to Hartford (Conant, 1964).

The MDC has been a consistent provider of quality services for its member communities, and its governing structure offers the same benefits as CRCOG and CREC in that every community has decision making authority. The board is governed by 29 commissioners from the eight communities, which is large when compared to that of the CRCOG governing body (which represents 30 communities). Unlike CRCOG and CREC, the MDC Board is made up of non-elected members who are appointed by the governor (8), local legislative bodies (17) and the majority/minority leaders of House and Senate (4 appointments/1 each) (OLR Report, 2008). The number of commissioners from each town apparently differs according to population (Hartford-9, East Hartford/West Hartford-4 each, Newington/Wethersfield/Windsor-2 each, Bloomfield/Rocky Hill-1 each), although the exact logic is not clearly spelled out in the MDC's charter (MDC Charter Section 2–3). There are provisions within the MDC Charter that allow for a narrow window of time in which the election of commissioners can take place through a petition process. Given the resources and infrastructure currently in place—both human and organizational—how do we move a regional agenda forward that would allow metropolitan Hartford to see itself as a region that has strong functional interdependencies that results in better coordinated planning and service delivery?

THE WAY FORWARD

Where do we go from here as the metropolitan Hartford region? More specifically what needs to be done to leverage existing strengths so that we as a region can take advantage of current and future opportunities to collaborate and better mitigate any number of important challenges that we face? A full answer to this question is beyond the scope of this chapter, but it is important to sketch out some of the key ingredients for a path forward that can build on prior and current work in the region.

Fortunately the metropolitan Hartford region is not alone in mounting a response to shared regional challenges. Many regions across the country have effectively responded to either crisis or ambition and forged a regional vision. Such visions, if augmented by capacity building, allow for significant policy change and, perhaps more important, implementation. For purposes of developing a sketch of a way forward for the metropolitan Hartford region, these elements will be considered under the headings of vision, leadership, and capacity.

A Common Vision for the Metropolitan Area

Developing a common metropolitan vision either for a specific issue, such as transportation or the environment, or for one more broadly conceived, has been a frequent way for metropolitan regions and states to attempt to build common ground for joint action on metropolitan challenges and opportunities. There are models for the region to use as a starting point including Chicago 2040, Envision Utah, Minnesota Milestones, Oregon and Multnomah Benchmarks—just to name a few. Such regional ventures often bring together diverse stakeholders over time to engage in an intensive process to examine their situation and opportunities as a region. A vision built in this way can serve as a common ground for future regional action. Efforts at articulating a regional vision have been made for metropolitan Hartford in the past, but have largely been ignored or not implemented because of a perceived lack of transparency in outcomes or because of a lack of political investment at the local level.

Metropolitan Regional Leadership

The metropolitan Hartford region and the state of Connecticut have in the past developed broad vision frameworks for moving a regional agenda, but have not in most cases built broad support for implementation. Given the lack of a general government, county government, or government at the regional scale it is important that we consider responses to the challenge of a fragmented metropolitan region.

What kind of metropolitan regional leadership is needed to conceptualize a vision for a way forward in a state that faces unique and entrenched obstacles? Prior efforts at urban revitalization in Hartford were often driven by senior members of the business community at a time when the leaders of the region's major corporations, known as "Hartford's Bishops," lived here and had a vested interest in the success of Hartford and its metropolitan area (see McKee and Bacon, this volume). While these corporations still have a vested interest in the sense that they continue to have a major presence in the city, their executives have less of an incentive to provide civic leadership because the global economic system that they operate in draws investment, both financial and human, away from Hartford and to other areas of the country (Julien, 1995).

Decades of Study and Recommendations for a Way Forward

For a number of decades, Connecticut has passed legislation and undertaken a number of initiatives that were supposed to mitigate the fragmentation that exists today. The Metropolitan District Commission was established in the 1920s. The Connecticut Development Commission, established in the 1930s, advocated for regional planning in the 1950s, recognizing that economic development and planning were not activities that should be done on a town-by-town basis (CDC Report, 1959). During the 1960s the state created the Connecticut Commission, which was tasked with studying the need and feasibility of metropolitan government (Public Research and Management, 1975).

The state, in the 1970s, produced a report, entitled "Sub-state Regionalism in Connecticut: Findings and Recommendations," the goal of which was to address problems associated with the vast number of local and regional entities that existed in an effort to design better systems for the delivery of state services. The Greater Hartford Process Incorporated was formed in 1971 as a major initiative undertaken by the business community that sought to create a vision for the future of the region out of concern for many of the same challenges the region continues to face today (crime, housing, transportation, job creation). They acknowledged then as is done today that the manner in which the region functioned was too fragmented and that change was necessary (Greater Hartford Process, 1972). Beyond the practical prescriptions of the plan, the strong underlying intent of the effort was to create regional leadership so that regional problems could be addressed on a regional basis (Condon, 2011).

During the 1990s, The Metro-Hartford Millennium Project, led again largely by senior business leaders, produced a number of recommendations that sought to improve the region's economic competitiveness, and listed as a long-term recommendation the passing of legislation that would provide real authority and resources to organizations that could move a regional agenda. Most recently, the Archdiocese of Hartford commissioned the 2003 report, *Connecticut Metro-patterns: A Regional Agenda for Community and Prosperity in Connecticut*. In 2005 Metro Hartford Alliance, the city's Chamber of Commerce, and the region's growth council undertook a regional assessment in an effort to produce, for the first time, the Comprehensive Economic Development Strategy.

All of these initiatives taken together provide a basis from which to launch a necessary effort to address a metropolitan regional vision for the future. A number of sources of leadership could be drawn together for a truly regional response to produce the needed strategic vision. In the Minneapolis–St. Paul region more than 40 community leaders, including corporate and civic leaders such as the Governor and Mayors of Minneapolis and St. Paul, along with regional academic leaders, were convened by the McKnight Foundation to undertake the Itasca Project, the aim of which was to address concerns about the region's economic competitiveness and quality of life. The 30 towns in the region and their elected officials in the Council of Governments could be invited to join with corporate, business, and civic leaders such as Leadership Greater Hartford, the Metro Hartford Alliance, the Hartford Foundation for Public Giving, and our colleges and universities to address a broad or more narrowly focused issue or set of issues for the region's future. To build a metropolitan regional vision, a credible, diverse, and effective leadership group is a necessary element to build and implement a metropolitan vision.

Nationally noted regionalist William Dodge has spoken of the mismatch between how we govern ourselves and from where challenges are emerging. He said that we have national, state, and local governments but that key challenges are emerging at the international, metropolitan, regional, and neighborhood levels. While Dodge applied this comment to the challenge of the metropolitan regions across the country, the metropolitan Hartford region faces a number of challenges that compound this overall national regional challenge. Devising a way forward depends in part on a clear-eyed situation assessment of where the region is. Some of the situational assessment elements suggest a steep climb for the region to mount metropolitan scale responses to critical challenges in transportation, housing, education, and economic development.

The Metropolitan Hartford region has a number of elements that make it distinct from many others:

- A high overall regional average per capita income;
- A major disparity in income and education from the core to some other parts of the region;
- A core city that makes up a small fraction of the overall region's population with 30 municipalities making up 800,000 in population;
- No general-purpose government between the state and 30 cities with a very large array of state-dictated regional structures with little or no taxing authority;
- Heavy reliance on property taxes as the preponderant source of revenues for municipalities;
- A strong state government with diverse powers and revenues with restricted local access to additional revenue streams.

When considered together, these factors provide a situational assessment that must be addressed by fashioning functional metropolitan regional structures. The importance of a supportive state posture from the governor and general assembly, of strong leadership from local elected officials, and from the business community and other sectors will be needed to rise to respond to the systems currently in place.

Metropolitan Regional Capacities

It is all very well to have a common metropolitan vision for the region brought about by a credible and diverse leadership. The administrative and organizational capacity to implement, measure, and oversee that vision, while maintaining the viability of individual towns and cities in the region, is also equally important. Some of the potentially important areas of capacity include: (1) shared services to get public services in the region to a more cost effective scale where appropriate; (2) tax reform to soften the heavy reliance on property taxation at the town level; and (3) regional quality-of-life metrics.

Connecticut, and more specifically the Greater Hartford Region, is positioned to adopt the fundamental changes necessary to ensure that social, political, and economic progress can take place despite the real obstacles it faces. A process should also be chosen in a way such that it respects the historically significant emphasis that is placed on local government and local control. Localism and regionalism do not have to be mutually exclusive goals because they complement and depend on each other for their effectiveness (Parks and Oakerson, 2000).

CRCOG can serve as the starting point for any real discussion or initiative aimed at creating a regional framework for improving governance, efficient service delivery, and planning. We must thoroughly evaluate CRCOG's current capacity. Its boundaries should also be examined in order to determine to what extent the responsibilities of the various existing regional entities can be folded into its current operations, so that we can undertake a strategic positioning analysis for the state, existing regional entities, and local governments.

The Council is made up of locally elected officials who will either work to take an agenda like this further, or act as the biggest obstacles to moving it. This is so, because on the one hand, they are the front-liners of the unsustainable dependence on property tax in the face of an aging constituency; and on the other hand, they can argue that the people they represent (primarily suburban taxpayers) have little desire to cede local control to or finance the costs of services for communities that have social and policy challenges associated with poverty, crime, low performing schools or other things considered urban (Wikstrom, 1977). It should be noted that it is quite possible that Hartford residents and officials might express the same reservations about losing control of their city and how services and programs are delivered and financed.

So while we already have some regionally minded elected officials, we must enhance and demand advocacy for understanding how we already comprise a region and that there are benefits to operating like one. Entities like Councils of Governments can become leaders in helping inform and develop regionally engaged citizens. Politically speaking, there is little incentive for locally elected officials to promote a regional agenda or approach given the perceived steadiness of taxpayers' commitment to the local. As a state and as communities, we have been shaped to believe that there is no other way to govern beyond the local and state levels. There has been no leadership that even attempts to provide the information needed to show that there are alternatives to local service delivery and governance. A movement, with the assistance of organizations like Leadership Greater Hartford, the Metro Hartford Alliance, and the Citizens Network of the Capital Region, can provide the political push as well as the political coverage to begin an honest dialogue about who we are as a region and how we will either prosper or decline together (Parks and Oakerson 2000: 175). This can result in the empowerment of citizens and building of a consensus.

Once we build some capacity around the regionally engaged officials and residents, we can bring them together to help develop Regional Quality of Life Indicators similar to the visioning and quality-of-life projects that have been developed by a number of states over the past two decades. The basic rationale of these exercises is to mobilize public awareness on issues; get a sense of values and priorities of states, regions, and local governments; focus on common aspirations for their futures and forge goals; track key indicators of progress; and gather support to improve results once published. A majority of states and many sub-state units of government across the country have gone down this path.

Property tax reform and decreasing local dependence on them is a perennial issue for both local and state office holders. Yet there has been little progress in this direction. Connecticut is often described as being one of the most property-tax-dependent states for funding education and other local services. The property tax, on average, accounts for 69.8 percent of revenue to which Connecticut towns and cities have access. In 2011, the state took initial steps to diversify local revenues by approving new revenue streams for local governments. It is likely that these modest steps will be overwhelmed by the current trajectory of costs at the local level and exacerbated by long-term pension and benefits costs for public employees, increasing energy costs, duplication of effort at the local level, and the absence of a regional economic development agenda. On a positive note, the state did reinvest in the Regional Performance Incentive Program that in 2007 attracted participation from 129 towns who competed for $8.6 million in grants to fund regional efforts (PRI, 2007). The state appropriation of $14.6 million in 2011 to the RPIP is dwarfed by the $192.3 million appropriation in direct revenue to municipalities that was intended to serve as property tax relief, but does nothing more than support the current outdated system of service delivery. Given the realities of Connecticut and its aversion to metropolitan government, this was a missed opportunity to expand regional capacity and service delivery.

CONCLUSION

The metropolitan Hartford region faces significant public policy challenges that could be met more effectively by strong collaboration among the region's cities and towns. In a region and state that has been significantly challenged on an economically competitive basis, Greater Hartford has significant institutions and assets with which it can advance a regional agenda that will promote economic and social growth. As Hartford has continued to evolve through its economic stages (see Walsh, this volume) and developed into a region with strengths in aerospace, precision manufacturing, financial services, and healthcare, its inability to match policy improvements in education, workforce development, and development of affordable housing to meet the demands of those industries has allowed competitor regions to disrupt investment and industry growth in metropolitan Hartford. The slow but steady movement of resources (human and financial) from Hartford to surrounding communities has had the effect of creating an interdependent region, separated by political and psychological boundaries, that prevents coordinated planning and decision making conducive to regional economic prosperity (Frug, 1999). Despite the shortcomings that exist in metropolitan Hartford, the region can reinvent itself to continue competing nationally and globally.

In the context of Levine's (2001) model for regional economic development, metropolitan Hartford can build upon its prominence as a center for the FIRE sector as well as the value added industries in manufacturing and increasingly research in life sciences that are engines for economic growth. The region also benefits from quality-of-life factors that include abundant recreational opportunities, quality education at both the primary and post-secondary levels, quality (albeit costly) housing, and proximity to a waterfront, and a seasonal climate with such variation that it can meet the varied demands of the people who live here. Yet metropolitan Hartford's future success is limited by an inability of policy makers, local and state, to adequately articulate governance and planning capacity that allows for regional problem solving and prosperity.

Advancing a regional agenda in metropolitan Hartford will require executive leadership at the local level supported by executive leadership at the state level. At the local level, chief elected officials have to provide leadership that will allow for a clearer articulation of the financial pressures and limitations facing municipalities, so that taxpayers can be better educated about the fact that property taxes they pay are used to finance local government and service delivery. Executive leadership is also needed at the state level because the state is complicit in perpetuating the status quo system primarily through education and general government aid provided to towns and cities.

State aid must be used as both the carrot and the stick to encourage more significant regional collaboration and planning. The recession that began in 2008 has dramatically altered public finance in Connecticut. Towns and cities face significant pressures as stimulus dollars dry up, as the state's economic recovery continues to lag, and as our general economic competitiveness is challenged by lower costs of living and of doing business in other regions. Connecticut is limited in its ability to control high land costs, higher energy costs, and higher standards and costs of living. It does, however, have significant potential capacity for controlling the cost of government and working to ensure that policy outcomes and service delivery are done in a more efficient manner. There are options, derived locally and nationally, that can be acted upon to advance the region's collective interests while respecting and preserving a system of local government important to the character of individual towns, to the state's rich history, and to the political reality of a state steady in its habits.

NOTE

1. The Connecticut Institute for the 21st Century, a nonprofit organization committed to expanding opportunities to discuss regional opportunities and issues, in collaboration with Blum Shapiro, an accounting, tax and business consulting firm, has produced a report titled *Examining the Effective and Efficient Delivery of Public Services in Connecticut* in February 2012, which has shed a more detailed light on the issue.

REFERENCES

Amento, Carl, William Cibes, Rick Dunne, Martin Mador, Matthew Nemerson and Lyle Wray. 2010. "Regions as Partners: Reducing Budget Gaps, Planning More Appropriately and Delivering Serviced More Efficiently-Recommendations to Governor-Elect Malloy."

AngelouEconomics. 2005. "Metro Hartford Regional Assessment." Retrieved from: http://otc.uconn.edu/wp-content/uploads/2009/01/regional_assessment_hartford-20051.pdf.

The Brookings Institution Center on Urban and Metropolitan Policy. 2003. "Is Home Rule the Answer? Clarifying the Influence of Dillon's Rule on Growth Management."

Capitol Regional Council of Governments. 2001. "Capitol Region Transit Strategy." Hartford, CT.

Capitol Regional Council of Governments. 2011. "Bus Rapid Transit from Hartford to New Britain: Fact Sheet—August 2011." 6. http://www.crcog.org/publications/Transportation-Docs/NBHBusway/CRCOG-BuswayFactSheet2011-08.pdf.

Center for Transit-Oriented Development. 2005. "Transit and Regional Economic Development."

Center for Transportation Excellence. 2011. "2010 Transportation Ballot Measures." 3 Nov. 2010. Web. 27 December 2011.

Collier, Christopher. 1992. "Sleeping with Ghosts: Myth and Public Policy in Connecticut, 1634–1991. *The New England Quarterly* 65(2): 179–207.

Conant, Ralph Wendell. 1964. "Politics of regional planning in Greater Hartford." Hartford, CT: Greater Hartford Chamber of Commerce.

Condon, Tom. 2011. "Visionary '70s Plan Re-imagined Region." *Hartford Courant.* 21 July.

Connecticut Advisory Commission on Intergovernmental Relations (CACIR). 1987. "Home Rule in Connecticut: Its History, Status, and Recommendations for Change. Hartford, CT. Connecticut Advisory Commission on Intergovernmental Relations."

Connecticut Center for Economic Analysis. 2001. "The Impact of the Regional Transit Strategy on The Capitol Region of Connecticut: A Dynamic Impact Analysis."

Connecticut Department of Transportation. 2011. "Busway Fact Sheet." *New Britain-Hartford Busway.*

Connecticut Development Commission (CDC). 1959. "Progress Toward Regional Planning in Connecticut."

Connecticut Economic Resource Center (CERC). 2007. "Communities, Connecting to Compete." http://www.cerc.com/Content/Communities_Connecting_to_Compete.asp.

Connecticut General Assembly Legislative Program Review and Investigations Committee. 2007. "Connecticut's Regional Planning Organizations."

Connecticut General Assembly Office of Legislative Research. Regional Government Organizations. Ryan F. O'Neil, Mary M. Janicki. 2010-R-0072. Hartford, CT: Office of Legislative Research.

Filchak, John. 2013. "A State Divided II." Northeastern Connecticut Council of Governments, Dayville, CT.

Frahm, Robert. 1992. "Spotty Segregation will be hard to end, officials say." *Hartford Courant*. 2 Dec.

Frank, Rachel Magdalene Perez. 2007. "Spotty Sheff Enforcement: Testimony Portrays Fragmented Response to Desegregation Effort. *Hartford Courant*. 9 Nov.

Frug, Gerald E., and David J. Barron. 2008. *City bound: how states stifle urban innovation*. Ithaca: Cornell University Press.

The Greater Hartford Process, Inc. 1972. "The Greater Hartford Process." Maryland: The American City Corporation.

Greenlee, Gina. 2004. "Two Cities Better Than One." *Hartford Courant*. 27 July.

Grumm, John G., and Russell D. Murphy. 1974. "Dillon's Rule Reconsidered." *Annals of the American Academy of Political and Social Science* 416. 120–132.

Hershberg, Theodore. 1996. "Regional Cooperation Strategies and Incentives for Global Competitiveness and Urban Reform." *National Civic Review* 85(2): 25–30.

Horton, Wesley W. 1993. *The Connecticut State Constitution: A Reference Guide*. Westport, CT: Greenwood Press.

Judd, Dennis R., and Todd Swanstrom. 2008. *City Politics: The Political Economy of Urban America*. New York: Pearson Longman.

Julien, Andrew. 1995. Fading ghosts city, business searching for a new partnership in post bishops era. *Hartford Courant*. April 10.

Kane, Brad. 2011. "Airport hotels suffering as Bradley airport regroups." *Hartford Business Journal*. 14 Nov.

Lancaster, Lane W. 1930. "Hartford Adopts a Metropolitan Charter." *The American Political Science Review* 24(3): 693–698

Levenson, Rosaline. 1966. *County government in Connecticut, its history and demise: the development, decline, and abolition of Connecticut's 294-year-old county governments and the transfer of their functions, property, and employees to the State*. Storrs, CT: Institute of Public Service, Continuing Education Services, University of Connecticut.

Levine, Joyce. 2001. "The Role of Economic Theory in Regional Advocacy." *Journal of Planning Literature* 16 (183): 183–201.

Mazey, Mary Ellen. 1997. "Creating Regionalism Amid Fragmentation." *The Regionalist* 2(2): 49–56.

Megan, Kathleen. 2010. "In College, But Not Quite Prepared: Majority of Students Need Extra Instruction; States Smaller Schools." *Hartford Courant*. 28 Oct.

McCarthy, Kevin E. "Metropolitan District Commission Governance." 2008-R-0035. Hartford, CT: Office of Legislative Research.

McDowell, Bruce D. 1996. "Regionalism: What is it, where we are, and where it may be headed." *The Regionalist* 1(4): 1–6.

Orfield, M., & Luce, T. 2003. *Connecticut Metropatterns: A Regional Agenda for Community and Prosperity in Connecticut*. Minneapolis: Ameregis.

Palmer, Jamie L., and Greg Lindsey. 2001. "Classifying State Approaches to Annexation." *State & Local Government Review* 33(1): 60–73.

Parks, Roger B., and Ronald J. Oakerson. 2000. "Regionalism, Localism, and Metropolitan Governance: Suggestions from the Research Program on Local Public Economies." *State & Local Government Review* 32(3): 169–179.

Rusk, David. 2000. *Cities without Suburbs: A Census 2000 Update.* Washington, D.C., U.S.A.: Woodrow Wilson Center Press.

The Sloan Center on Aging and Work at Boston College. 2008. "Connecticut Indicators: Aging & Work."

Spencer, Mark. 2011. "Asians, Hispanics Lead Population Growth in State." *Hartford Courant.* Hartford Courant. 10 Mar.

Spiegel, Saul. 1992. "From Home Rule to Regionalism." 1992–R-1101. Hartford, CT: Office of Legislative Research.

Stacom, Don. 2011. "Economic Advice: Plan Now For 2016 Commuter Train Service." *Hartford Courant.* Hartford Courant. 25 Oct.

Substate Regionalism in Connecticut Findings and Recommendations. 1975. Prepared for the State of Connecticut Department of Finance and Control: Planning and Budgeting Division by Washington/Atlanta: Public Research and Management, Inc.

Tondro, Terry J. 1999. "Fragments of regionalism: State and regional planning in Connecticut at century's end." *St. John's Law Review* 73(4): 1123–1158.

Walker, David B. 1995. "Regionalism in Connecticut and Country: Dormant or Resurgent?" *The Regionalist* 1(3): 61–68.

Wallis, Allan. 1995. "Regional Governance and the Post-Industrial Economy." *The Regionalist* 1(3):1–11.

Wikstrom, Nelson. 1977. *Councils of Governments: A Study of Political Incrementalism.* Chicago: Nelson-Hall.

Wong, M., with T. McNamara, S. Shulkin, C. Lettieri, and V. Careiro. 2008. "State Profile Series. Connecticut Indicators: Aging & Work." The Center on Aging and Work at Boston College.

13

A Sobering Era with New Possibilities

Tom Condon

HARTFORD IN TIME

New York has McSorley's Old Ale House, Key West has Sloppy Joe's, and, in the early 1970s, Hartford had the White Swan. The Swan was a bar on Park Street, the main stem in Hartford's burgeoning Latino neighborhood. The bar (owned by a genial Portuguese American named Tony Luis) and the street welcomed all, and, like Rick's in *Casablanca*, everyone went there. There were politicians such as Lt. Gov. T. Clark Hull, journalists such as myself, neighborhood residents, Hartford cops, musicians, activists, students, Capitol staffers, tourists, the occasional bookie—it was Noah's Ark with a liquor license.

The Swan had funky music, round tables, peanut shells on the floor and . . . hope. Promise. A city with such a cool place must have great potential, must be going places. Everything seemed, almost euphorically, to point that way. People were moving to Hartford from the small towns in the region, as they had for more than a century. I'd come from New London, a small city on the Connecticut coast that had been eviscerated by the great oxymoron, urban renewal, and over the years I'd meet other expats from New London, including an acting city manager, a police captain, a judge, and others. The *Hartford Courant*, where I'd landed a job, was shedding its image as "the gray lady of Broad Street," and becoming a feisty and dominant state newspaper.

Hartford had a bright young city council that was remaking downtown, bringing new people and ideas into government and building a Civic Center and arena that would take Hartford into the big leagues. Some of the council's decisions would turn out to be questionable, such as locating the new police station in the North Meadows, almost out of town, but then it was part of the good momentum. The city was moving, doing things.

There was a buzz then about Atlanta becoming a hip, "regional city," and many thought Hartford could become Southern New England's regional city. And for a time, it seemed to be happening. The Hartford Civic Center opened in 1975 with a performance by Glen Campbell. A team from the World Hockey League, the New England Whalers, was induced to come to Hartford from Boston and renamed the Hartford Whalers. When the team was absorbed by the National Hockey League in 1979, Hartford was, at least as defined by the sports world, a big-league town.

Brash and inventive young artists, many of whom lived in lofts in the Colt Complex in the South Meadows, created a burst of street theater in the mid-1970s that defined the city for a few years. The "Sidewalk" and "Thursday is a Work of Art" events were memorable, everything from skywriters, mimes, concerts in downtown alleys, and sculptures with chairs, to the "Samba Truck," a sound truck that would park at a street corner and expel a man in a tuxedo and a lady in a ball gown, who would begin dancing the samba.

A young hip crowd began frequenting Mad Murphy's, a bar across the street from Union Station on colorful Union Place. An organization called Peace Train started a hugely popular New England Fiddle Contest. The Knox Foundation and its architect/activist director, Jack Dollard, restored an antique carousel for Bushnell Park. Real Art Ways became an alternative arts center in downtown, and later in the Parkville neighborhood. The city elected the first African American mayor in New England, Thirman L. Milner.

It was all good, or so it seemed. In the early 1980s, the tallest office building in the state, 38-story CityPlace, was under construction, and another half-dozen major office towers were in the works or on the drawing board.

But as the 1980s wore on, the momentum, if that's what it was, stalled. The construction downtown was, in the words of former city councilman George Levine, "phony growth," office buildings built to take advantage of federal tax credits, not to respond to a local demand for space. As evidence thereof, the city council allowed three major swaths of downtown to be cleared of historic buildings and active, useful businesses, for office towers that were never built. Two decades later a residential tower was built on one of the sites; the other two remain empty.

When the national economy slowed in the beginning of the 1990s, Hartford suffered. Nearly a dozen banks in Greater Hartford failed in 1991 and 1992, including landmark Connecticut Bank & Trust, an icon of Hartford history.

In the go-go 1980s, several thousand residents, including many prominent folk, invested with a real estate firm called Colonial Realty. It was forced into bankruptcy in 1990, and revealed as a con, a fraud, a giant Ponzi scheme that was using investors' money from one partnership to pay off investors from another. Two of its three founders went to jail and the third committed suicide, but the collapse of the company was another blow to the local economy.

One by one, local institutions fell by the wayside. The last of the city's great department stores, G. Fox & Co., closed, as did the White Swan and Mad Murphy's. The manufacturing jobs that had been integral to the city's economy fell away, from 25,000 jobs after World War II to an anecdotal number, a few here and there. Postwar suburbanization, ushered in by cheap cars, cheap gas, new highways, and government housing loans, drew many middle-class residents, first whites and then African Americans, to the fast-growing suburbs. Jews and Irish left the North End, a process sped along by the urban riots of the late 1960s; many Italians went south to Wethersfield and Rocky Hill; French Canadians left Frog Hollow, etc. They were replaced by African Americans from the South, West Indians, and Hispanics—mostly rural Puerto Ricans. These folks got jobs in factories and in tobacco fields north of the city, but then most of those jobs disappeared.

Crime increased. The loss of entry-level factory jobs helped foster an illegal economy. Drugs and gangs got into the city, particularly in the huge, early World War II-era housing projects. The projects—Charter Oak Terrace, Stowe Village, Bellevue Square, and others—had worked wonderfully well in their first years, when they were transitional homes to working families. But as the unskilled job market dried up, the projects became a permanent home to the very poor, and became decrepit and dangerous. In the mid-1980s, Hartford police were making more than 20,000 arrests each year, the majority of them drug-related.

The downward spiral accelerated. As the city became poorer, it had greater social services and law enforcement needs. But with fewer companies and residents, and only the property tax available to city government to raise revenue, taxes increased. The once-stellar Hartford Public School system began to fail.

As many middle-class people viewed it, staying in Hartford meant paying higher taxes for fewer services, poor schools, and a higher threat of crime. Some also factored in the costs of private schools. By sad coincidence, the parochial school option shrank as the city's only Roman Catholic high school closed, as had five, and soon six, of eight Catholic elementary schools. So, many people who could afford to move did so. A typical pattern was for children raised in the city to move to the suburbs, and then come back to move the parents, or more usually one parent, to a suburban location. As a columnist wandering the city I heard people say "We got my mother out" more often than I would have liked.

In September 1987, I too reluctantly moved out of Hartford. I lived in Asylum Hill, I was getting married and needed a bigger place, and West Hartford at the time was less expensive than the West End. The West End still held its value then, both because of its grand, century-old homes and because it is was, and to some degree still is, an activist neighborhood that certain people seek to live in.

I was also ready to go. My neighborhood had worn me down. It had been a cool, comeback area when I bought a gorgeous "perfect six" condo there in the late 1970s. I could walk to work, jog through Elizabeth Park, and be downtown in minutes. But as elsewhere, the momentum slowed. I endured three burglaries. I came home once to see a man urinating on the side of the building. A neighbor was mugged. What really wore me down was the noise: car horns, revving motorcycles, and loud music at all hours. If you can't sleep in a neighborhood, the social contract is broken.

The damage caused by loss of the middle class cannot be understated. As Harvard scholar Robert D. Putnam points out in *Bowling Alone* (2000), it is middle-class people who serve on boards and commissions, volunteer for community tasks, and lead clubs and other organization. This civic engagement or "social capital" is essential to healthy communities. Putnam's thoughts were brought home to me dramatically when I wrote about a Little League field in the North End in the 1990s and learned that it was run by a man from Manchester.

The city seemed to come unglued in the late 1980s and early 1990s, in the last years of the administration of Mayor Carrie Saxon Perry, whose pro-social-service, anti-business stance had Aetna and Travelers thinking about leaving town. Large banks and corporations run by the "Bishops," Hartford's name for its homegrown business chiefs that had heavily influenced the city for a century, were acquired by larger banks and corporations, lessening their local connections as they went global (Chen and Shemo; McKee and Bacon, this volume). Hartford began to show up on "Ten Poorest Cities" lists. The kidnap and murder of a female bank executive from a downtown parking garage in 1989 seemed a nail in the coffin for downtown.

The election of engaging and witty ex-firefighter Mike Peters in 1992 signaled a fresh start. He oversaw the replacement of most of the big housing projects with less institutional, less dense, and more attractive housing. The state took over the failing Hartford school system, which had all but flatlined, on his watch. The system very slowly began to improve, aided by a State Supreme Court decision, *Sheff v. O'Neill*, that ordered the desegregation of the city's schools (Dougherty, this volume). While the decision has resulted in some good new magnet and charter schools, three-fourths of the city's children still attend racially segregated schools (and that is a significant improvement). The decade also saw the beginning of the "Six Pillars of Progress" projects initiated by Gov. John Rowland, which included downtown and neighborhood housing, a convention center, and other projects.

In 2002, Peters was replaced by Eddie Perez, who became a "strong mayor" under a charter change that went into effect in 2004. Perez can be credited with hiring a school superintendent, Steven Adamowski, who made dramatic improvements to the city's struggling school system. His emphasis on schools of choice, in tandem with magnet schools built under the *Sheff v. O'Neill* decision, has given hope to many city residents that their children can get a decent education.

But Perez succumbed to the temptations of power and was convicted on corruption charges in 2010. Former council president Pedro Segarra replaced him, and was poised to be elected to a full term in the fall of 2011. An openly gay lawyer, cautious and careful by nature, Mr. Segarra has focused on quality-of-life issues such as clean parks and removal or improvement of blighted buildings, and stressed honesty and transparency in government. Though he has separated himself from his predecessor, he has not yet articulated a comprehensive vision for the city.

While other cities are growing and erasing the differences between city and suburb, Hartford still seems stuck in time and in its small historic boundary lines. It is still plagued by poverty, crime, and unemployment. It relies on its old businesses, and is thankful to have them, but does not have much in the way of vital new businesses.

The city is not dead by any stretch. It retains much of its government, medical, and insurance sectors, and has even added a little to its higher education presence. Despite some losses, it retains a fine arts community. City churches continue their missions, often with suburban parishioners who volunteer in soup kitchens and shelters.

But such contacts between city dwellers and suburbanites are all too rare. Downtown is what postwar planners made it, an office park that suburban dwellers drive into in the morning and retreat from at night, in a balkanized region that doesn't work together very well (Rojas and Wray, this volume). Greater Hartford remains a nice place to live for most of the region's 1.2 million people. Yet, a city or a region is about making connections, about chance meetings that lead to business ventures or cultural start-ups. The isolation of commuters in multiple small towns in Greater Hartford works against this dynamic, largely to the detriment of city residents. As Nick Bacon says, Hartford is the smallest central city of any of the country's 50 largest metropolitan regions (Bacon and Chen, introduction, this volume).

Yale professor Douglas Rae observed in his marvelous book about New Haven—*City: Urbanism and Its End* (2004)—that when business leaders lived in the same city as working people, they would make contact, in churches, fraternal lodges, or civic organizations, and this was a good thing, a chance for informal mentoring, job contacts, information. When only the poor are left in cities, and business leaders are involved in their suburban communities, the contact is largely lost. Hartford and Greater Hartford are what some call the "Two Connecticuts" (see, e.g., Horan, 2002).

While some suburbs prosper, the city itself remains so poor that when compared with New Haven, Bridgeport, Springfield, Worcester, and Providence, Hartford has the highest poverty rate for individuals (in some cases 60 percent or 70 percent higher), lowest median household income, smallest percentage of married couple households, highest percentage of female-headed families with no husband present, and the highest percent of adults 25 and older who have not completed high school (also see Table 1.1). This was written by the city's own planning staff in 2010 for the draft of a planning document titled "One City, One Plan."

WHAT WENT WRONG

Hartford was a vital city for a long time (Walsh, this volume), but in the postwar period it was a victim of suburban sprawl; the postwar, auto-driven, government-incentivized movement out of the cities and into newly minted subdivisions in surrounding suburbs. This was a triumph for the housing industry and the auto-industrial complex; the petroleum, car, steel, rubber, and road construction industries that worked together to change the face of the country and enrich themselves in the process. They equated moving to the suburbs with progress, the American

Dream, a lifestyle celebrated by such television shows as *Leave It to Beaver* and *Ozzie and Harriet.*

But as the poet Ogden Nash observed, "Progress was fine for a time, then it went on too long." As the decades passed, the country belatedly realized that there was a serious downside to sprawl. There was waste of energy, additional pollution, and loss of open space and farmland. But the expanding conurbation also eviscerated older urban centers such as Hartford and left the poor behind in them. In discussing the effects of sprawl in *Suburban Nation* (2001), Andres Duany et al. write, "Far more troubling, though, is the concentrated poverty that remains in our inner cities." Hartford's variation on this thesis was particularly acute, for a number of reasons, including:

Size

Though Hartford was a wealthy and innovative city in the 19th century, there was one governmental innovation it missed. It was never granted the power to annex its suburbs. Indeed, in 1854 West Hartford broke off from Hartford to become a separate town. This may be connected to an ancient sense of localism, or something no one thought necessary. For whatever reason, Hartford emerged as an 18-square-mile city, a tiny core of what became a much larger region. Size matters. A city that contains its own suburbs has access to resources, notably middle-class people, to help it thrive. A city that is walled off from its suburbs does not.

The problem was well described by David Rusk, a former mayor of Albuquerque, New Mexico, in his 1993 book, *Cities Without Suburbs.* Rusk looked at Hartford and several other cities, such as Detroit, Philadelphia, Camden, Newark, and Bridgeport, with "inelastic" boundaries, boundaries that have been fixed for decades or centuries. He then contrasted these with another group of "elastic" cities that have been able, by annexation, city-county merger or other means, to expand and become regional or "metro" cities. This group includes such cities as Indianapolis, Nashville, Portland (Oregon), and Austin. Looking at Hartford and the other inelastic cities, Rusk found they had lost population and gotten poorer, with neighborhoods that were "increasingly catch basins for poor blacks and Hispanics." Poverty was more concentrated. "The income gap between city residents and suburbanites steadily widens. City government is squeezed between rising service needs and eroding incomes. Unable to tap the areas of economic growth [its suburbs], the city becomes increasingly reliant on state and federal aid. . . . The suburbs are typically fragmented into multiple towns. . . . This fragmentation reinforces racial and economic segregation. Rivalry among jurisdictions often inhibits the whole area's ability to respond to economic challenges," he wrote (see Bacon, this volume). With the high concentration of poor residents, services are expensive and taxes go up. Poverty makes education difficult, so schools become less able to turn out trained workers. Crime goes up. Businesses leave or fold. Cities in such straits "are no longer places to invest or create jobs." Rusk opined that Hartford was at a "point of no return." It's actually returned a bit since then, but is not thriving, by any stretch.

The small size also ensures that Hartford will keep appearing on the "10 Poorest Cities" lists. By just measuring the urban core, and not the region, Hartford will invariably lose to a city that includes its suburbs. After the 2000 census, I compared Hartford to Jacksonville, Florida. Both had about 1.1 million people living in their metro areas. But while 120,000 people lived in the 18-square-mile city of Hartford, 800,000 people lived in the 841–square-mile city of Jacksonville. According to census data, Hartford had 35,741 people living below the poverty line, 30.6 percent of the population. Jacksonville had more than twice that many poor folks, 87,691. But since there were so many more people within the city limits, the percentage of people in poverty was only 12.2.

Hartford had just been named the second-poorest city in the country in its population group, behind Brownsville, Texas, based on percentage of residents living below the poverty line. But cities such as Jacksonville, which had merged with surrounding Duval County, had many more poor people. If someone measured core city to core city, Hartford would be about even. But no one does that. In 2010, Hartford was No. 3 on a list of "America's 10 Dead Cities." Same problem.

Highways

Hartford was a lovely city, as countless visitors and residents such as Mark Twain observed. Aggressively retrofitting it for cars and building highways through the center of it did tremendous damage. Andres Duany cites Hartford in *Suburban Nation* (2001) as one of America's cities badly hurt by kowtowing to cars. Starting in the 1950s, Hartford began taking down buildings for surface parking lots. Obviously some accommodation had to be made for cars, but the city might have survived in better shape, had it not been for the highways (see Figure 13.1).

In 1956, President Dwight D. Eisenhower signed the Federal-Aid Highway Act of 1956, the law that created today's interstate highway system. The Dwight D. Eisenhower National System of Interstate and Defense Highways, as the 41,700-mile asphalt ribbon is now called, was the greatest public works project in history. It has provided a theretofore unimaginable level of mobility, convenience, and economic opportunity. At the same time, it has made us dangerously dependent on foreign oil, all but killed trains and trolleys, and—thanks to the indefensible decision to run the highways through cities, a decision Eisenhower later disowned—eviscerated hundreds of America's finest and most handsome municipalities. While many cities were split by one highway, Hartford took a double whammy.

First, I-91, the north-south interstate, cut the city off from the Connecticut River, the historical reason for its being. Two generations of Hartford children grew up not knowing the river was there. Then I-84, the east-west highway, wreaked even more havoc. The highway, particularly the three-quarter-mile elevated portion or viaduct that runs from Sisson Avenue to the edge of downtown, created a barricade that separates the North End and Asylum Hill—largely minority communities—from the Capitol area and downtown.

Figure 13.1.   Highway Construction in Downtown, Hartford. (Hartford Public Library)

The concrete swath through the core of the city took out some world-class, ir-replaceable architecture, such as the former Hartford Public High School building and many elegant homes. It constricted the growth of downtown and rendered a lot of land unusable—it is known as "no man's land." The presence of the highway meant once-elegant streets had to be widened, and more buildings torn down for more parking. Parts of the city near the highway ended up looking like an archeo-logical site. Indeed, a once-handsome and functional commercial building that held a department store stood forlorn and isolated north of I-84 for years, decaying to the point where it became known as the "Butt-Ugly Building." It was finally demolished in the fall of 2010. Another eyesore adjacent to I-84, the Capital West building, was scheduled to come down in 2012.

Most successful downtowns have housing within walking distance, which cre-ates part of the worker and customer base for downtown. In Hartford, much of the area within walking distance is paved over, for roadways or parking lots. Longtime political writer Don Noel observed in a 2010 interview with this writer that the hub-and-spoke highway system made it exceptionally easy for residents to move out of Hartford in any direction. Putting the highway engineers in charge of city planning almost sacrificed the place for the means to get there. This was true in many cities, but more so in Hartford. Not for nothing is there a "Welcome to Downtown Hartford" sign in front of a surface parking lot, in a prime location across from Bushnell Park where a hotel once stood.

Form of Government

At the end of World War II, Hartford was run by a confusing mishmash of boards and commissions, including a 20-member board of aldermen. It was what someone called a "hydra-headed government." But at the beginning of the *Pax Americana*, the city had one of the strongest Chambers of Commerce in the country, and the chamber determined to create a more modern and coherent form of government. The chamber created an entity called the Governmental Research Institute, a citizen-watchdog group that would both keep tabs on government and help it when feasible. To head the agency, the chamber brought in Leslie M. Gravlin, whose impressive background included a three-year stint as Minnesota's commissioner of administration under legendary Gov. Harold E. Stassen. Gravlin and his agency helped draft a new charter that, when adopted in 1947, gave the city a standard, modern council manager form of government. For two decades, it worked reasonably well. The city council elected one of its members the mayor; the manager was the chief operating officer.

But in 1967, they fiddled with it. In the charter revision of that year, some wanted a strong mayor, others wanted to keep the council/manager form. They reached a compromise. The mayor would be directly elected, getting more visibility, but would no longer be a voting member of the council. "It was a terrible compromise. It was a mistake," said George E. Hill, director of the University of Connecticut Institute of Public Service and a member of the 1967 charter commission, in an interview with *The Hartford Courant* in 1997 (Condon, 1997). Hill, who had been the mayor of Mansfield and head of the Connecticut Conference of Municipalities, said direct election of the mayor gave the aura of authority, when in fact the office had become ceremonial and has no statutory authority.

What resulted was a confusing and unstable form of government, in which the deputy mayor, a member of the nine-member council, usually had more power than the mayor. "Whoever had five votes had the power," said former Deputy Mayor Nicholas Carbone in conversation with this writer. Mr. Carbone may have been the most powerful deputy mayor in the country in the 1970s. Because five-vote alliances could change from morning to afternoon, it was hard to get any long-term policy enacted. People coming to the city to do business were invariably confused, as well. City employees were not sure who to report to, so council members gained more influence than they otherwise might, and often usurped the role of the city manager. It was not unheard of for a council member to be sitting in on a police promotion interview. The system drove Mayor Mike Peters to distraction; he cited it as a reason he left office.

After several years of trying, residents passed a charter change that made the mayor the chief operating officer of the city. The change went into effect in 2004, and Eddie Perez was the first "strong mayor." Perez's school improvements gave a tantalizing glimpse of how a good strong mayor system might work; sadly he failed in other areas rather badly, and was convicted on corruption charges (see McKee and Bacon, this volume). In the first years of the new system, much time has been spent working out the balance—what the lines of authority and responsibility are between the council and the mayor. Though the system appears to be more stable under current Mayor Pedro Segarra, it remains a work in progress.

FIXES FAILED

As we've seen, there have been major efforts to revitalize Hartford in the postwar era, one Sisyphean effort after another, from Constitution Plaza to the recent "Six Pillars" projects that include the science and convention centers, G. Fox Building renovation, and housing and riverfront improvements. While these have all helped in some ways, they haven't turned Hartford into a vibrant, prosperous city. It might be instructive to see why not.

In the early 1950s Connecticut General Life Insurance Co. (now CIGNA) announced it was moving out of downtown Hartford to a new, modern campus it would build on former farmland in Bloomfield. This was an alarm to city and business leaders, who were determined to revitalize downtown. They had a target, an 11–acre area on the city's East Side, a largely Italian neighborhood known as Front Street. It was, depending on point of view, a colorful ethnic enclave like Boston's North End, or a slum. Fighting over the question stopped investment in the area, actualizing the slum argument. The "relocation load" was 108 "marginal" businesses employing more than 1,000 workers (businesses the city would kill to have back), 187 families and 31 individuals. The project, glass-and-steel office buildings, retail, and a hotel built over a 1,875-space parking garage, was built from 1958 to 1964. It won all sorts of accolades and design awards when it opened. But today it is largely considered a failure, for a couple of reasons. Key parts of it were never built, most notably the housing component. With no residential base—the folks who used to live there all moved to the South End, Wethersfield, or elsewhere—the stores had to rely on lunch hour, essentially, to survive. One by one, they closed. Also, a proposed pedestrian bridge to Main Street was never built, and a connection to the riverfront was not completed for another 30 years. This, in addition to widening Market Street between the central business district and the plaza, made sure there would be little contact between the plaza and the downtown it was supposed to revitalize. It, like much of what the city's hub-and-spoke highway system produced, was for suburbanites to drive to, park, and then drive home without setting foot in the city. The plaza did keep companies such as Phoenix and Travelers in the city. And after the long-vacant hotel was recently purchased by investors who plan to turn it into apartments, people may finally live there.

But the project didn't revitalize the city because it failed to discern the real problem. Hartford and other cities were losing demand for building space and retail sales because companies and office workers were moving to the suburbs. Slum clearance was not going to change that, says Yale professor and former New York City planner Alexander Garvin, who analyzed the plaza in his well-regarded 1996 book *American Cities: What Works and What Doesn't*. As he saw it, Constitution Plaza didn't.

Of course, it's hard to know what would have worked. With the benefit of hindsight, Hartford would have been better off fixing up Front Street—it did have flooding problems—in the hope that it would catch on as a cool place, like Boston's North End. But that might have sent the big insurance companies to the suburbs. Harvard economist Edward Glaeser (2011) views projects such as Constitution Plaza and others across the country as an "edifice error," the mistaken thought that cities could build their way out of decline.

Greater Hartford Process didn't make the same mistakes as were made in the Constitution Plaza project. Sadly, it made some other mistakes. To the extent it is remembered today, it is for the failed effort to build a new community in suburban Coventry. It was more than that. In the early 1970s, business leaders formed an entity called the Greater Hartford Corporation, to develop a vision of the region. It hired a subsidiary of the Rouse Co., then best known for having built the new city of Columbia, Maryland, and created a nonprofit called the Greater Hartford Process Inc., along with a separate development company, to design and implement a plan.

The people behind the effort understood that urban blight and suburban sprawl were two sides of the same coin, a regional problem that could only be addressed on a regional basis. They knew the area's fragmented governmental structure wasn't up to the task. They hoped Process would bring the region together. They understood that plans had to be acted on, or they would sit on the shelf (McKee and Bacon, this volume).

The business community put up millions of dollars. Process had a staff of more than 40 people, twice the current size of the Capital Region Council of Governments' staff, the largest council of governments in the state. Hartford Process released a 150-page planning document in 1972 that was prescient in many areas, calling for changes that were either decades away or are still on the drawing board, everything from community-oriented policing to healthcare for all to individualized learning in schools. It made an impassioned plea to preserve open space and sensitive ecological areas such as ridge lines, understanding that poorly planned, low-density sprawl was damaging the environment.

Process got some work done in Hartford, notably the 264-unit SAND housing development in the North End. But the whole effort got hung up on the Coventry project. They hoped to build a 20,000 person "new town" inside the Eastern Connecticut community, which then had only 8,500 people. Some of them didn't want to expand that much that quickly. The secrecy of the project spawned all kinds of rumors. Just before it was to go to the local planning and zoning commission, in 1975, Process pulled the plug. The national economy was reeling from the Arab oil embargo and a recession, and such projects were shut down all across the country. Almost simultaneously, Process ran afoul of Latino leaders in Hartford, who had been largely if inadvertently left out of the planning (see Simmons, this volume). Process limped on for a few more years, with some neighborhood planning projects, and then folded.

There've been more than a dozen other studies and efforts to revive Hartford since the demise of Process; the most significant of which began in the mid-1990s. There were actually three separate initiatives that to some degree intertwined. The first was Adriaen's Landing. A West Hartford architect, William Mead, and Bloomfield engineer Josiah Kirby brought an idea to Phoenix president Robert Fiondella in 1995 to develop a 33-acre parcel on parking lots and brownfields, much of which the company owned, along the Connecticut River. Mead called the project "Adriaen's Landing" after Adriaen Block, the Dutch explorer who stopped in Hartford in 1614. Also, Mead's wife was Dutch, and he thought the name might be an entrée to Dutch investment. (The name was a spelling challenge, and Fiondella was often urged to change it. But Mead passed away in 2000 during the project's development, and out of loyalty, Fiondella insisted on keeping the name.)

Two years later, as planning went on in secret in Mead's office, Gov. John G. Rowland decided to make a major investment in Hartford. "This is Hartford's time," he announced, and appointed a committee headed by Lt. Gov. M. Jodi Rell to recommend some development projects. In March of 1998, based on the committee's report, Rowland announced the "Six Pillars of Progress" plan, which included a new convention center, 1,000 new housing units, development on the riverfront, a downtown attraction, renovation of the Hartford Civic Center and restoration of the former G. Fox Building into Capital Community College. The cost was then estimated at $300 million; over time it would more than double.

Two months later, on May 13, Fiondella presented the plan for Adriaen's Landing. The 33-acre site would feature a domed 40,000-seat stadium and a convention center straddling the Whitehead Highway, as well as a science museum including a replica of the historic ship USS Hartford above I-91. The densely packed site would also include restaurants, shops, and apartments. It was an extravagant plan, but just a plan. Later in that hectic year, Rowland began holding secret meetings with the owner of the New England Patriots professional football team, Robert Kraft, who was having trouble securing public money for a new stadium in Massachusetts. On Nov. 19, Rowland and Kraft announce a deal in principle to move the Patriots to Hartford. "Touchdown!" read *The Hartford Courant* headline (Puleo, 1998). Making a long story short, the play was called back. The headline perhaps should have read "Fumble!" The following April, as the project hit some delays—for one, it became unclear whether or not it would fit on the 33-acre site—Kraft bowed out. It's an open question how serious he was in the first place, but in any event, the Patriots got a new stadium in Foxboro, and there they remain.

Rowland and the legislature saved and restructured the original project the next year by approving $455 million for a convention center, an attraction (which would become the Science Center of Connecticut) and the other pillars. The legislature also found $100 million for a University of Connecticut stadium in East Hartford, where United Technologies had donated 75 acres of land (see Bacon, this volume). Also in the mid-1990s, a planning effort called the MetroHartford Millennium Project hired well-regarded Toronto planner Ken Greenberg to do a downtown plan. The plan, made public in 1998, was simple and straightforward; it called for development, transit and pedestrian amenities to be focused on a "circuit line" around downtown, to make downtown more walkable and livable, and less car-dependent. Though not all his ideas were adopted, they provided a framework of where to put some of the "Pillars" projects (and for the free downtown circular bus service).

Over the next several years, the G. Fox Building was beautifully converted to Capital Community College. The Connecticut Convention Center and the Science Center of Connecticut were built on the Adriaen's Landing site, as was some retail space. A half-dozen downtown housing developments were built and opened, some neighborhood housing was completed, and riverfront improvements continued. The Civic Center, now the XL Center, was renovated.

Has this three-quarter-billion-dollar investment renewed Hartford? Partly, at best. There are more middle-class people living downtown. The 2010 census counted 1,852 people in downtown Hartford—56 percent white, 15 percent African American, 15 percent Latino, and 12 percent Asian—an increase of 65.7 percent in the decade. Though it still doesn't feel like a 24-hour city, residents are coalescing into a downtown community.

Still, the community college, convention center, and science center are mostly places, like Constitution Plaza, that people drive to, and then drive from. They add more to the traffic than the street life (though the convention center does seem to have filled a need for more meeting space). As Harvard's Glaeser (2011) says, without demand, building is largely "folly."

It hasn't been all doom and gloom since the days of the White Swan; there've been notable successes. The nonprofit Riverfront Recapture, over nearly three decades, has reconnected the city with the Connecticut River, and built regional parks and trails on both banks. The Riverfront model is one to emulate; it was steady progress over a long period of time, not a "big bang" one-time dream. Putting the Civic Center downtown—some wanted it in the South Meadows for easier highway access—added life to downtown, at least on the nights of hockey or basketball games. Getting rid of the old public housing projects, radically changing the schools, and refocusing on the parks, as Mayor Segarra has done, are all positive steps. A new plan called the iQuilt (see Chen and Bacon, Conclusion, this volume), which will connect the downtown arts and cultural institutions around Bushnell Park with walkways, signage, and other amenities, shows promise. But more is needed.

WHAT NOW?

A study of the efforts to restore Hartford after World War II should leave anyone wishing to try it again with a profound sense of humility. Very smart, very committed people have tried mightily and failed. Yet these efforts, and those in similar cities across the country, offer some guidelines and points to consider. These include:

Leadership

A study of 25 mid-size, postindustrial cities including Hartford by the Federal Reserve of Boston (Kodryzcki, et al., 2009) found that the cities which made the strongest comebacks were those with strong leadership and collaboration over long periods of time. It didn't seem to matter who the leader was—it ranged from energetic mayors or business organizations to nonprofit foundations and developers—but someone stepped up, got the major players behind a plan, and then executed it. In New Haven, for example, a partnership between city hall and Yale University since the early 1990s has changed the face of the city. Yale has helped restore the downtown retail district, put up money to lure biotechnology companies to the Science Park incubator, and offered incentives to its employees to buy homes in the city. Hartford needs a way to get those kinds of results.

Metro or Retro?

Perhaps the most serious question facing Hartford is whether it can thrive, or even survive, as the "hole in the doughnut," the region's poorhouse, the tiny, impoverished core of a larger and wealthier region. This year, as in every year of property revaluation, there's a battle over how the commercial and residential taxpayers will share the property tax burden. The real problem is that with relatively little property and high costs, there's no good way to divvy it up. With the state's largest unemployment rate and downtown office vacancy now approaching 35 percent, Hartford is not on a path to prosperity. As the smallest city in its metro area among the nation's 50 largest metropolitan regions, Hartford should at least initiate discussions of much more regional shared services (see Rojas and Wray, this volume), even of merging into a larger city. Such a thought is heretical in the land of small towns and steady habits, and probably a non-starter. But if it were studied and found to be beneficial to all involved, perhaps Yankee frugality would push it along.

Consider. If the eight members of the Metropolitan District Commission, the regional water and sewer authority—Bloomfield, East Hartford, Hartford, Newington, Rocky Hill, West Hartford, Wethersfield, and Windsor—consolidated into one municipality, the result would be a city of nearly 400,000 people, larger than St. Louis, Pittsburgh, Tampa, and Cincinnati, about the same size as Miami and just smaller than Minneapolis. It might be politically prohibitive, but it is at least worth thinking about. As the various attempted fixes prove, the current balkanized polities probably cannot create a regional city. The state could. With the economy slow to recover, this may be the time to at least convene a meeting.

Cars

A key factor in the demise of the city was the too-aggressive retrofitting for cars. For instance, between 1960 and 2000, the number of downtown parking spaces tripled from 18,000 to 46,000, with parking lots then constituting about a quarter of the city's total land area (McCahill, 2010). Some of this damage must be undone. Of actual plans in play in the city, the most exciting is the Hub of Hartford, a plan to remove the three-quarter-mile elevated section of I-84 that runs from Sisson Avenue to the edge of downtown and replace it with an urban boulevard. This bridge-like behemoth virtually walls the city in half, creating a barricade that separates the North End and Asylum Hill from the Capitol area and downtown. The highway also renders a lot of land unusable—it is known as "no man's land"—increases tailpipe pollution and adds griminess to what was a lovely downtown.

The highway was built in 1965 with a 40-year life expectancy, which came due in 2005. State Department of Transportation officials were just going to keep it going, for $100 million or so, when a group of citizens rose up and said, in effect, "No." The message struck a chord. The original group of neighborhood, business and planning people, now called "The Hub of Hartford Steering Committee," attracted the support of city officials, the Capital Region Council of Governments (CRCOG) and, eventually, even the Department of Transportation (DOT). Money was found for a study of alternatives and Goody Clancy, a well-regarded Boston urban design firm, performed it. The firm weighed possible alternatives for the viaduct—everything from another viaduct to a tunnel to a surface boulevard. The group and the consultant had a breakthrough moment when they realized they could make a surface boulevard work by relocating the railroad tracks to an area north of the highway. Everyone likes the idea. The city will get to reclaim 15–20 acres of prime land close to Union Station, including developable land along the western edge of Bushnell Park, where the report (2010) recommends a new street be built. There is the chance to reconnect streets severed by the highway and connect Asylum Hill to downtown with a bike/pedestrian path.

Amtrak likes the idea because it won't have to replace and maintain the century-old Asylum Avenue rail overpass, and the DOT likes the idea because it won't have to maintain an elevated highway, which is considerably more expensive than keeping up a surface road. Indeed, according to a preliminary cost analysis, the surface road is the least expensive option to build and maintain, compared with a new viaduct or, especially, a tunnel (the cost of a tunnel, along with some complications from the underground Park River, make it an unlikely option). Additionally, with the road at grade, it becomes relatively easy to finish the downtown platforms, getting a full downtown surface for the first time in many decades and allowing downtown to grow to a size appropriate for a region of 1.2 million people. Though there is much still to do and the project is years away, the Hub of Hartford is the first major effort to reverse the damage done to the city by its overly aggressive retrofitting for cars.

Revive the Economy

Hartford has the highest unemployment rate in the state, and lack of jobs is at the root of many of the city's social ills. The traditional methods of job training and economic development mostly aren't working; for the past decade demolishing historic buildings for strip-mall chain pharmacies is what passes for economic growth. There needs to be a radical new approach.

In the 1970s, a corporate executive named Dan MacKinnon started an entity called the Maverick Corp., a nonprofit that created small industries all over the city. He employed only convicted felons, who had no high school degree and no job training. He put them to work building and rehabbing houses, recapping tires, building office furniture, assembling industrial furnaces, reupholstering movie seats, and building outdoor concrete furniture, such as benches and trash cans. They had to be on time, in uniform, ready to work, no excuses. After a year, they had to move to private-sector jobs. His workforce reached a high of 450, and at least a third ended up in permanent manufacturing jobs. Though the enterprise folded after MacKinnon left to join state government, the model may be one to revisit. One of the understated successes of the Adriaen's Landing project was something called the Jobs Funnel, which trained and employed hundreds of city residents in the construction trades. The city needs something like that on an ongoing basis. Indeed, a permanent nonprofit development entity would be a way to keep moving forward on infill projects that the city always needs.

Tax Reform

The city needs to keep its heritage companies healthy and also foment the creation of small businesses. To do that it must be fiscally competitive, and not have the highest business taxes in the state. A major underlying problem for cities such as Hartford is that they are very expensive to run. Without regional, state, or federal help, too much of the burden falls on businesses and the remaining middle-class taxpayers, who can avoid the trouble by moving to the suburbs. Reforms that made cities less reliant on property taxes would be a huge boon to cities such as Hartford, which have vast social costs and relatively little property.

As with many cities damaged by postwar industrialization and suburbanization, bringing Hartford back is a major, ongoing challenge, more apparent now than in the days of the White Swan. It must be viewed as a process, not, as so often in the past, a big-bang project. Yet with increasing climate and energy issues, the time is right for the resurgence of cities, because they are energy efficient and the cradle of commerce. Making it happen is the domestic challenge of the age.

With its aerospace and insurance industries, Hartford is tied to the global economy. Whether it can broaden and strengthen that tie, become the regional city that was the dream in the early 1970s, remains to be seen. The Brookings Institution has argued persuasively for several years that metropolitan regions are the real drivers of the national and global economy. Metros congregate smart people who develop new patents, new businesses, and new jobs. They build transit systems and create exciting places to live. Can Hartford get past its ancient localism, act like a metro, and compete with Hamburg and Florence instead of Bloomfield and Windsor? I would argue that it has to.

REFERENCES

24/7 Wall St. 2010. "America's Ten Dead Cities: From Detroit to New Orleans."

American City Corporation. 1972. *The Greater Hartford Process.* Columbia, MD.

City of Hartford. "One City, One Plan." Accessed at: http://planning.hartford.gov/oneplan/pocd.aspx.

Clancy, Goody. 2010. *I-84 Viaduct Study: Options for Replacing the I-84 Viaduct in Downtown, Hartford.* Accessed at: http://falcon.txcc.commnet.edu/blogs/secourses/files/2007/08/2010 1001DraftReport.pdf

Condon, Tom. 1997. "Hartford Mayor Should Be Given More Power." *Hartford Courant,* August 12: A3.

Duany, Andres, et al. 2001. *Suburban Nation: The Rise of Sprawl and the Decline of the America.* New York: North Point Press.

Garvin, Alexander. 1996. *American Cities: What Works and What Doesn't.* New York: McGraw Hill.

Glaeser, Edward. 2011. *Triumph of the City: How Our Greatest Invention Makes Us Richer, Smarter, Greener, Healthier, and Happier.* New York: Penguin.

Greenberg, Ken. 1998. "The Downtown Hartford Economic and Urban Design Action Strategy." Accessed at http://www.hartfordinfo.org/Issues/wsd/EconomicDevelopment/default.asp.

Horan, Jim. 2002. "A Tale of Two Connecticuts." Connecticut Association for Human Services. Accessed at: http://www.cahs.org/publications/Essay.pdf.

Kodryzcki, Yolanda, et al. 2009. "Reinvigorating Springfield's Economy: Lessons from Resurgent Cities." Boston: Federal Reserve Bank of Boston. Accessed at: http://www.bos.frb.org/commdev/pcadp/2009/pcadp0903.pdf.

McCahill, Christopher. 2010. "Losing Hartford: Transportation policy and the decline of an American city. Congress for New Urbanism." Accessed at: http://www.cnu.org/sites/www.cnu.org/files/mccahillc_cnu18.pdf.

Puleo, Tom. 1998. "Touchdown! Deal Gives Hartford Home Field Advantage; Rowland, Kraft Plan Kickoff Here in 2001." *Hartford Courant,* Nov 19: A1.

Putnam, Robert D. 2000. *Bowling Alone: The Collapse and Revival of American Community.* New York: Simon & Schuster.

Rae, Douglas. 2004. *City: Urbanism and its End.* New Haven: Yale University Press.

Rusk, David. 2000. *Cities without suburbs: A Census 2000 Update.* Washington, D.C.: Woodrow Wilson Center Press.

14

Conclusion: Inheritance, Inertia, and Inspirations

The Potential Remaking of Hartford

Xiangming Chen and Nick Bacon

This book has sought to fill a void in comparative global and urban scholarship: the substantial lack of research on Hartford, Connecticut, and other small New England cities. To help meet our goal of advancing an urban discourse on these cities from a small hodgepodge of largely ignored fragmentary studies to a more coherent body of work, the following section draws from all 14 contributions to highlight a few theoretical themes and implications for further research. In addition, we briefly present four episodes of municipal redevelopment, community renewal, and neighborhood organizing that represents varied bottom-up responses to entrenched negative urban legacies and inspire broader actions for possibly remaking Hartford for the better.

SPATIAL INHERITANCE: LESSONS FROM HARTFORD

Hartford is one of America's oldest cities, and its contemporary form and structure cannot be understood without reference to its long history. First settled in the 1630s alongside Wethersfield and Windsor, Hartford rapidly expanded development within and beyond its boundaries. By the 18th century, Hartford was densely built up with farms, villages, roads, and turnpikes. In the mid-19th century Hartford began to industrialize rapidly, and developed in a distinctly polycentric fashion around several production centers from Bristol to Mansfield, all linked together by rivers, roads, and rail. Hartford became the center of the region largely because of its role as the state capital, its burgeoning insurance sector, and its own increasingly powerful role in industrial manufacturing, particularly in industries like machine tools, arms, and transportation (Chen and Shemo, this volume).

Hartford, having become a center of defense and aerospace, quickly grew into a vast auto-centric sprawl-driven region during the various wars of the mid-20th century, especially World War II and the Cold War. During the 1970s, generalized economic crisis in conjunction with a declining demand for key Hartford products like military equipment, hit the city hard, devaluing the industries and urban spaces which had heretofore defined the region and assured its affluence. While a variety of private and public entities took drastic measures to make Hartford a competitive city in these trying times, each urban strategy failed (McKee and Bacon, this volume). The Hartford of the 21st century has inherited an urban structure and industrial tradition which are increasingly incompatible with the new challenges of a globalizing world. The urban legacy of Hartford's glorious past and subsequent decline weighs heavily on its contemporary state of stagnation.

HARTFORD'S CONTEMPORARY TRANSFORMATION AND INERTIA

A contemporary portrait of Hartford must decipher its dual processes of transformation and inertia. On the one hand, we must identify how spatial resilience and ongoing economic, social, and political changes interact to exert their influence today. On the other hand, we must clarify how formerly dominant spaces and processes have been negated or superseded by new forces. In this section we look at the regional and local impacts for how an auto-centric city designed for middle-class families earning their living in a few key industries and living in a cornucopia of small independently governed communities is changing in the wake of protracted deindustrialization and accelerated globalization.

While we assert that Hartford can only be understood at the scale of its entire urban region and that both research and policy (Bacon and Chen; McKee and Bacon; Rojas and Wray; Condon, this volume) have wrestled with the problematic spatial definitions of the city based solely upon archaic legal boundaries, we nevertheless note the negative influence of Greater Hartford's excessive jurisdictional fragmentation on the region's social and spatial structure. Hartford has some of the nation's most socially and economically diverse suburbs, largely due to its extremely balkanized system of governance. Since the 18th century and especially since the last quarter of the 20th century, urban governance has increasingly become the fiscal and strategic responsibility of municipalities. The first consequence of this phenomenon is spatial chaos, as the metropolitan region has been planned and structured by 57 distinct municipalities. The second is intensified spatial segregation, characterized by polarized enclaves of affluence and poverty. One particularly clear window into these processes is the case of public education (Dougherty, this volume). Connecticut relies more than any other state on local property tax revenue for education. For this reason, some of the country's best public schools are located in the region's municipalities. On the other hand, because these towns tend to zone out low-income housing, Connecticut has the nation's highest educational achievement gap. The region's poor are confined to municipalities with some of the country's worst public education systems. Hartford has the most extreme and concentrated levels of poverty and related indicators (Simmons, this volume).

A related dynamic that is profoundly impacting Hartford is the intensified localization of urban planning. On the one hand, more wealthy towns have had the power to resist unwanted projects and galvanize desired developments. On the other hand, inner cities, some working-class suburbs, and certain rural towns, have had to compete for declining jobs and property taxes by attracting new commercial development, even when the specific projects are undesirable to local residents. This is particularly important because Hartford is no longer the region's only municipality with high levels of stress or even the epicenter of the region's economic and socioeconomic decline. While it has always been common for certain towns to occasionally have pockets of disinvestment, some of Hartford's municipalities have seen such extreme levels that the towns themselves have become devalued; i.e., they have undergone "podunkification" (Bacon, this volume). Unlike wealthier municipalities or growing exurbs, the urban strategies of "urban podunks" usually materialize as massive mega-projects with little or no (or even negative) local use values, and are either constructed as necessary evils to attract revenue, or even forced upon municipalities by the state. In certain cases, however, such as in Lawrence, Massachusetts (Barber, this volume), localities can be appropriated by new residential groups, such as poorer immigrants with transnational ties. In a way, the earlier and continued stratification of suburbs (inertia) has become more visible and intensive as a result of the more recent and transformative forces of globalization and transnational migration.

In this sense, Hartford's trend of extreme social and economic differentiation has also helped generate authentic urban communities. In spite of—or perhaps because of—its economic decline, central Hartford is unusually transnational for a city of its size and location, as demonstrated by its large concentrations of certain immigrant and core refugee groups (Bauer, this volume). Although, unlike Portland (Moser, this volume), Hartford does not have a centralized refugee population, it has nevertheless developed substantial immigrant communities. Notably, the municipality of Hartford is extremely Caribbean, especially for the Northeast of the United States. What is more interesting, however, is that this Caribbean population is extremely differentiated socio-spatially. Hartford is essentially split in half, with a significant population of West Indians, primarily Jamaicans, in the North End, and with Puerto Ricans dominating the South End. From a comparative standpoint, both populations are striking. Most New England cities (with the exceptions of Boston, Bridgeport, and New Haven) have very small black populations. Yet, Hartford not only has a substantial black population, it is significantly differentiated both socially and spatially, with noticeable divides between African Americans and West Indians. Unlike blacks, Hispanics are more common to small New England cities. However, with the exception of cities in Connecticut and western Massachusetts, such as Springfield (Sacks, this volume), Dominicans, rather than Puerto Ricans, dominate (e.g., Lawrence, Massachusetts; see Barber; this volume). Recently, minorities have significantly increased their presence in other municipalities in Greater Hartford. West Indians have moved just north into Windsor and Bloomfield; Puerto Ricans have extended just west into West Hartford and New Britain (Sacks, this volume); and both groups have settled in mixed communities east of the Connecticut River, such as East Hartford and Manchester.

In summary, the contemporary state of Hartford and its region is a product of the opposing forces of inertia and new transformations. Old structures of municipal governance have survived from the 17th and 18th centuries to the present day. Similarly, but from a moment closer to our own, the region's intensive mid-20th-century suburbanization, with its dual appropriation of central Hartford into an enclave of minorities and the poor, has become foundational to the city's urban structure. Still, new transformations have significantly altered Hartford, even while certain aspects of the city have stayed the same. For instance, while Hartford is still the most concentrated center of minorities and the impoverished, both populations have exploded outward throughout the region's landscape, both in new clusters in older urban areas (e.g., manufacturing towns and inner-ring suburbs), and in somewhat shapeless dispersions throughout the region. Meanwhile, the economic bread and butter on which Hartford has subsisted for generations, such as insurance and advanced manufacturing such as aerospace, has been dwindling (or in the latter case, disappearing) (Chen and Shemo, this volume). To respond to its economic decline, new styles of urban development have been channeled through preexisting municipal governments. The dual forces of transformation and inertia have shaped, and continue to reshape, Greater Hartford.

MAIN IMPLICATIONS AND CAVEATS

Partly due to lack of space, and partly because we still lack an adequate literature to draw from, the preceding representation of Hartford is undoubtedly incomplete. Despite the sizeable number of contributions assembled in this book, it should not be taken as a comprehensive explanation of Hartford's trajectory of change and continuity. Rather, we see this effort as establishing a foundation from which others can go further in studying such under-researched places as Hartford and other small New England cities. In lieu of a comprehensive historical or contemporary portrait of Hartford, we hereby identify a few of this book's most important theoretical and practical implications.

a. *The region has become the city (or never left it).* Hartford can no longer be conceptualized as a small and impoverished city surrounded by large and wealthy rings of suburbs. While this representation of Greater Hartford was true enough throughout much of the 20th century, it has outlived its previous validity and utility (Bacon and Chen; Walsh; Bacon; Condon, this volume). While the city of Hartford has the region's largest concentration of poverty and minorities, it no longer holds the majority of either population. As inter-municipal migration continues, more and more municipalities can become burdened with the same challenges that used to haunt only Hartford, and spatialized gaps between the region's rich and poor widen further (Simmons; Dougherty; Sacks, this volume), the practice of segmenting Greater Hartford into a myriad of archaic legal entities is becoming more illogical and capricious. To understand and adequately address even the most basic urban and economic problems facing Hartford, we need to re-envision and reconstruct the city's political and analytical boundaries.

b. *Urban communities are experiencing more global-local complications.* Another key implication of this book is that urban communities, regardless of their scale, are becoming simultaneously more globalized and locally differentiated. Populations commonly considered homogenous are sometimes intensely differentiated internally (Bauer, this volume), while urban communities commonly seen as abandoned are sometimes actually meaningfully appropriated, in both social and economic terms by new, often "disadvantaged," groups (Barber, this volume). Even in areas of cities where particular racial or ethnic groups are relatively dispersed or are the minority of the local population, important social spaces are created and re-created, often in a global network of linkages. In fact, these linkages can become so strong that many immigrants are intimately and persistently connected to multiple spaces across the globe than with individual areas of their own cities and regions. This is increasingly the case at the more aggregate level of intercity connections, with two cities so disparate and different in scale and every other indicators—Hartford vs. Shanghai—now tied together through the global thread of Pratt & Whitney's manufacturing-service supply chains (Chen and Shemo, this volume).

c. *Comparable cities are far from identical.* Though cities like Hartford are often lumped together with other seemingly similar cities such as the three included in this book, they are often more distinctive and different from one another at deeper or alternative analytical levels. While Hartford has certainly withstood severe economic blows in recent years, the global economic crisis has exerted far less harsh an impact here than in its peer cities. This is because Hartford's economy is less historically dependent on manufacturing than those of cities like Springfield, Lawrence, and Portland. Largely due to its still-heavy concentration of insurance, Greater Hartford has higher rates of productivity and sizable concentrations of affluent and middle-class residents than other cities throughout the region. On the other hand, Hartford has not had the same success as other New England cities in areas like urban redevelopment. Cities like Portland, Maine (Moser, this volume) and Providence, Rhode Island, which was unfortunately left out of this book, have claimed that urban renewal strategies focusing largely on culture, arts and higher-end consumption have helped them achieve "urban renaissances" (albeit without benefit to poorer minority residents). Hartford, on the other hand, has not seen a return on its own variation of these urban regeneration strategies, although this process can benefit from diverse cultural and community-based initiatives and actions (see below).

d. *Urban strategies must be realistic and location-specific.* Greater Hartford has fewer options than it once did, and it has to scale its strategies to what is actually possible (Condon, this volume). Strategic urban responses in Greater Hartford have failed time and again when they have attempted to do too much (McKee and Bacon, this volume), while many realized tactics have arguably done more harm than good (Bacon, this volume). One way to create better urban strategies is to draw upon the city's strengths rather than pave over its weaknesses. Hartford may not have the same potential as its peer cities, for instance, to transform its downtown into a vibrant center, and yet its metropolitan region is ripe with a polycentric ring of booming town centers (such as Blue Back Square in West Hartford). Taken collectively, they compete nicely with the downtowns of cities like Portland, and work well locally in a metropolitan region where suburban sprawl makes up far more of its total urban space than other New England cities. Instead of using all of its resources on a downtown which has largely been obliterated by urban renewal, and which could never again be large enough to serve as the center of its gargantuan metro-region anymore, Greater Hartford might have better luck focusing on other regional nodes with more concrete potential. Of course, none of this is possible without responding to our first point; the only way to adequately address Hartford's urban problems is to expand its boundaries: to align Hartford's political boundaries with its actual urban boundaries and linked economic borders.

As we stress the value of these implications for future research, we are also mindful of the caveats and limitations of our effort in terms of what was not addressed that is critical to understanding the distinctive complexity of Hartford. First of all, we were not able to include a study that would drill down to the DNA of neighborhood dynamics, although we do provide a flavoring of it below. As a teaser, Hartford has turned out to be an outlier in a comparative study of 10 American cities, as only about one-quarter of its residents responding to a survey identified with any of the names of seven designated neighborhoods (Coulton, Chan, and Mikelbank, 2011). Second, we were unable to feature an investigation into the environmental and sustainable development issues regarding Hartford and the region. It is an unfortunate miss given the city's reputation of having Bushnell Park as the nation's first publicly financed public park, a project which involved the design ideas of the locally born pioneering landscape architect Frederick Law Olmsted (best known for Central Park in New York City) and, later on, the direct touch of his son, Frederick Law Olmsted, Jr. Third, this book is also silent on the role of arts in urban life and revival, which must be addressed in light of Hartford's rich artistic treasures in the Wadsworth Athenaeum and the Mark Twain House, among others (see below for a glimpse of its importance). While there may be other missed topics, this short list identifies the main caveats on the broad contributions of this book.

HARTFORD IN CONTEXT AGAIN

As we bring the book to a close, we return briefly to the broad theme of *urban legacy* and its inseparable twin—*global impact*—by placing the transformation of Hartford and other New England cities onto the future path and possibility of remaking these cities. This prospect will be shaped by the continued rescaling of urban decision-making from the geographically bounded unit of the city to the multilevel context of the globalizing city-region in both developed and developing countries. At the same time, urban decision-making has become and will continue to be more decentralized and democratic and attuned to the rights of the ordinary city resident (UN-Habitat, 2009). Daunting as they are, these challenges can also be new opportunities for rebuilding the future city. The opportunities, according to the same United Nations report, converge on the central positive role of improved urban planning that will involve recognizing the emergence of new and innovative activity, linking spatial and land use plans to infrastructure and transport planning to facilitate more compact development, and setting up better monitoring and evaluation of the planning process and outcomes.

While we recognize the powerful interventionist role of planning in shaping the future city, we need a sociological approach to bringing out the essential qualities of cities as malleable and remake-able places that lodge deeply in our collective senses of community, identity, and security (Chen, Orum, and Paulsen, 2012). These are enduring attributes of our working, living, and playing places that make up the city of today and tomorrow. They motivate us to be involved in participatory or bottom-up planning that can work well with governmental and professional approaches. Most important, when we sense the threat of economically eroded and environmentally unsustainable cities to the fundamental values we attach to place, we are more likely to be motivated to remake these cities so we can enjoy better places in the future. Here we give a short account of four diverse organizations or organized efforts, old and new, in Hartford that represent a broad-based bottom-up effort to improve Hartford.

SINA: Partnering for Community Development

In all American cities, but especially an economically depressed one like Hartford, community development organizations (CDOs) are critical grassroots players that make a big collective difference to the well-being of urban neighborhoods. However, shrinking government funding and foundation support, reinforced by tough economic times like the recent financial crisis, has imposed severe resource constraints on CDOs, making many of them more difficult to operate and forcing others to go bankrupt. In Hartford, one such CDO has stood the test of time and continues to be vibrant. A partnership between three major city and regional institutions, Connecticut Children's Medical Center, Hartford Hospital, and Trinity College, Southside Institutions Neighborhood Alliance (SINA) has for over three decades worked cooperatively with the community to develop leadership and improve the economic, physical, and social characteristics of Hartford's Frog Hollow, Barry Square, and South Green neighborhoods. As its vision, SINA serves as a catalyst to foster a vibrant urban community where residents, employees, and businesses, can enjoy a high quality of life and opportunities for success. SINA has pursued this vision through a comprehensive model and synergistic strategy of building community, integrating critical components of community life and education, housing, economic development, and public safety.[1]

Recognizing that community success depends on a strong infrastructure and that homeownership and safe affordable rental housing are cornerstones for achieving a sustainable neighborhood stability strategy, SINA provides such opportunities to neighborhood residents and those families and individuals that choose to reside in the Southside of Hartford. Having leveraged federal, state, and municipal grants and loans, SINA has built low-cost new housing on old lots around Trinity College and the two hospitals that has attracted homeowners, some of whom are first-time buyers, and helped stabilize a deteriorating neighborhood. With one of the lowest homeownership rates (at 25 percent among cities of 100,000 or more people), Hartford benefits from SINA's effective approach to building safe and affordable housing.

LGH: Building Communities by Building Leaders

As SINA has been building strong communities in the neighborhoods around its three anchor institutions, Leadership Greater Hartford (LGH) has been building communities across the Hartford region for over 35 years. With a vision to "create a region where the barriers of age, race, economics, and education are lowered and where all citizens come to believe that they live in a just and caring community," LGH builds strong and vibrant communities throughout Greater Hartford by developing, connecting, and inspiring diverse leaders.[2] It does so through a variety of programs designed to provide experiential learning through workshops, tours, and hands-on team projects. Participants in these programs obtain new skills while exploring key issues impacting Greater Hartford and thus become better and more connected leaders.

The flagship program of LGH for 35 years, *Quest* brings together emerging and established leaders from all sectors—corporate, government, small business, academia, and nonprofit—through workshops, community tours, and collaborative task-force projects that address pressing community needs. Participants learn leadership skills to inspire and direct change in a collaborative, dynamic, and diverse arena. They learn about themselves, recognizing and drawing on their assets and capabilities in their work and community. They also learn about the community, its challenges, assets, and potential. Whether they are from Hartford or other cities, participants study and discover the city's history and demographics through tours and lectures to better understand their communities' place in this diverse and complex city-region. Participants are organized into and engaged with task-force projects embedded in the communities so they can practice and apply their leadership skills and capacities to effect real change.[3]

NRZ: Grassroots Organizing by and for Local Residents

Besides the formal CDOs like SINA and LGH, Hartford features another neighborhood-based organization with a distinctive informal orientation and purpose. Established by the Connecticut State Legislature through Public Act #95-340, NRZs (Neighborhood Revitalization Zones) have existed since the mid-1990s to revitalize neighborhoods where there is a significant number of deteriorated property and property that has been foreclosed, abandoned, or blighted, or which poses a hazard to public safety. An NRZ functions as a collaborative planning process involving neighborhood stakeholders (e.g., residents, businesses, institutions) and federal, state, and local governments. An NRZ is expected to create a strategic plan which allows the neighborhood to request waivers of burdensome state and local regulations in order to streamline revitalization (City of Hartford, 2002). Reporting or linked to the City Clerk of Hartford, the NRZs are quasi-public neighborhood organizations that are governed by a committee consisting of local residents on which the City also appoints an official with a vote.

The cornerstone of an NRZ, its strategic plan must include assignment of responsibility for implementing each aspect of the plan, and be adopted by the planning committee and the city council by ordinance. For example, the Plan of Revitalization for the Frog Hollow NRZ, which includes the area where Trinity College is located, represents a plan for implementation for the decade starting in 2009. It consists of 54 strategic projects that range from the NRZ Committee's primary responsibilities to bold visions for the transformation of the NRZ. The first project on the list is to improve traffic circulation on and around a major avenue by reducing parking violations through targeted enforcement of parking restrictions. With more of a community organizing thrust relative to the Frog Hollow NRZ, the Maple Avenue NRZ, also near Trinity, holds a monthly meeting for all residents to voice and discuss various issues and problems facing the neighborhoods and looking for solutions. A dynamic community organizer with direct and strong political influence at the city level and beyond, the Chair of this NRZ has brought the Hartford mayor and his municipal officials, CT state legislators, and even CT Senator Richard Blumenthal to these meetings to listen to the concerns of local residents.[4] Despite being very grassroots, the NRZs in Hartford exert upward planning and political influence through their statutory status and organized activities, and thus help improve both the spatial and social fabrics of local neighborhoods.

iQuilt: Creative Place-making Through a Cultural Corridor

To tackle the major challenges accumulated through such a long legacy of urban decay in Hartford, community development and organizing often reaches its limits. It must be enhanced and scaled up by larger, citywide planning and renewal initiatives. One recent such initiative is the iQuilt Plan, which was triggered by a comprehensive study of Hartford's built environment conducted by the Urban Land Institute (ULI) in 2007. Having recognized that downtown Hartford is an unusually compact historic district packed with more than 45 cultural assets and destinations within a 15-minute walk—museums, performance spaces, historic landmarks, modern architecture, and public art—two of Hartford's key cultural leaders—The Bushnell and the Greater Hartford Arts Council—proposed to develop the iQuilt Plan to link those assets with a vibrant and innovative pedestrian network. Its centerpiece is the GreenWalk, a one-mile chain of parks and plazas connecting the gold-domed Capitol in Bushnell Park to the waterfront of the Connecticut River.[5] Following a 12–month planning process during 2011, the iQuilt Plan staged the three-day celebration of Hartford's cultural assets called *Hartfest* in September 2012, which emphasized Walking, Culture, and Innovation as three key themes.

While the longer-term prospect of iQuilt is unclear, it represents a bold effort to do creative place making, which refers to partners from public, private, nonprofit, and community sectors strategically shaping the physical and social character of a neighborhood, town, city, or region around arts and cultural activities. "Creative place-making animates public and private spaces, rejuvenates structures and streetscapes, improves local business viability and public safety, and brings diverse people together to celebrate, inspire and be inspired" (Markusen and Gadwa, 2010: 3). To what extent is iQuilt Hartford following the footsteps of a dozen American cities that have used arts and culture to achieve some success in urban renewal? In Providence, Rhode Island, which is often compared to Hartford as an economically depressed postindustrial city, city leaders have championed arts and culture initiatives—festivals, tax-incentive-fueled arts districts, and loans and technical assistance for arts facilities. In the early 1990s, the city uncovered its downtown rivers that had been paved over for decades. In 1994, artist Barnaby Evans installed a series of ceremonial bonfires on downtown rivers. The distinctive arts and cultural activities have stanched Providence' population decline and avoided greater distress, helping it shake off its image as the "armpit of New England" and taking on self-proclaimed "creative capital" (Markusen and Gadwa, 2010). Cities like Providence offer concrete and inspiring lessons for Hartford to leverage its rich cultural assets through and beyond an initiative like iQuilt.

INSPIRED TO REMAKE HARTFORD

As the urban future looms larger over all cities, Hartford and other New England cities confront some of the most serious challenges in the United States because they carry the longest and heaviest urban legacies of deep deindustrialization, poverty, inequality, and balkanized governance. Yet the above four examples of community development and urban regeneration inspire us to appreciate the resilience of community organizations like SINA, LGH, and the NRZs, as well as the creativity of iQuilt. Individually, they seem confined to specific locales and sectors, but collectively they amount to a greater positive force that is capable of remaking Hartford. In addition, they inspire us to see more clearly the timely significance of this book.

With Hartford, the once prosperous city, long faded into a distant memory, the contributors in this book have brought it back into a fresh analytical light. We see this book as a counter to the disproportionate focus of recent urban research on a small number of global and extraordinary cities such as New York and Shanghai. The book represents our hope that the emergent and systematic research on understudied small cities like Hartford, or what Jennifer Robinson (2006) termed "ordinary cities," will begin to impact urban scholarship more generally. But the knowledge obtained from urban studies must be put to action. The discipline must not be taken merely as an abstract social science by which to accumulate "urban facts." The study of the urban world is the study of the world where we live our everyday lives. The real tragedy of the dearth of scholarship on cities like Hartford is not so much that our research attention is finite and library incomplete, but that struggling cities lack the critical attention needed to develop strategies to face the complex obstacles and challenges which inevitably lies ahead. What we should be striving for beyond studying Hartford and the other cities in this book is to work cooperatively to remake them into better places.

NOTES

1. Extracted from SINA's website at http://www.sinainc.org/mission-vision/, January 31, 2013.

2. Extracted from LGH's website at https://www.leadershipgh.org/impact/For-35-Years/Mission-Vision.html, January 31, 2013.

3. Ibid.

4. Based on the first author's observations during his attendance at some Maple Ave NRZ meetings over the last four years.

5. Drawn from the iQuilt Plan's website: http://theiquiltplan.org/home/, January 31, 2013.

REFERENCES

Chen, Xiangming, Anthony M. Orum, and Krista Paulsen. 2012. *Introduction to Cities: How Place and Space Shape Human Experience.* Oxford: Wiley-Blackwell.

City of Hartford. 2002. *Neighborhood Revitalization Zone Information Packet.* City Manager's NRZ Representative Orientation Packet, Department of Planning, October 4.

Coulton, Claudia, Tsui Chan, and Kristen Mikelbank. 2011. "Finding Place in Community Change Initiatives: Using GIS to Uncover Resident Perceptions of their Neighborhoods." *Journal of Community Practice* 19 (1): 10–28.

Markusen, Ann, and Anne Gadwa. 2010. *Creative Placemaking.* A White Paper for The Mayors' Institute on City Design, a leadership initiative of the National Endowment for the Arts in partnership with the United States Conference of Mayors and American Architectural Foundation.

Robinson, Jennifer. 2006. *Ordinary Cities: Between Modernity and Development.* London and New York: Routledge.

UN-Habitat. 2009. *Planning Sustainable Cities: Global Report on Human Settlement 2009.* Sterling, VA: Earthscan.

Index

Index

About the Editors and Contributors

Xiangming Chen is founding dean and director of the Center for Urban and Global Studies and Paul E. Raether Distinguished Professor of Global Urban Studies and Sociology at Trinity College in Hartford, Connecticut, as well as distinguished guest professor in the School of Social Development and Public Policy at Fudan University in Shanghai, China. He co-authored *The World of Cities: Places in Comparative and Historical Perspective* (2003; Chinese edition, 2005), published *As Borders Bend: Transnational Spaces on the Pacific Rim* (2005), edited and contributed to *Shanghai Rising: State Power and Local Transformations in a Global Megacity* (2009; Chinese edition, 2009), co-edited *Rethinking Global Urbanism: Comparative Insights from Secondary Cities* (2012), co-authored *Introduction to Cities: How Place and Space Shape Human Experience* (2012; Chinese edition 2013), and is co-editing *Global Cities, Local Streets* (forthcoming). His articles have appeared in a large number of urban studies and social science journals.

Nick Bacon graduated from Trinity College in 2010 with a degree in Public Policy & Law and a concentration in Urban Planning. His thesis, a critical examination of the transformation of the Hartford city-region over the last four centuries, was awarded the first-place senior research prize sponsored by the Steven D. Levy '72 Urban Curricular Fund. Bacon is currently the Research Associate in Urban Studies at the Center for Urban and Global Studies, a Ph.D. Candidate in Cultural Anthropology at the CUNY Graduate Center, and a Graduate Teaching Fellow at Lehman College, where he teaches courses in anthropology and urban studies.

CONTRIBUTORS

Janet Bauer is associate professor of international studies at Trinity College and a member of Hartford's Immigrant Advisory Group. After completing a Ph.D. in Anthropology (Stanford University) and postdoctoral work in demography (Carolina Population Center), she focused her research and teaching on comparative immigrant and refugee issues. Her ongoing research explores the role of women in the transformation of urban public and political space in comparative Muslim diasporas (Hartford, Canada, Europe, and the Caribbean). Some of this work can be found in journals like *Cultural Dynamics*; *Comparative Studies of South Asia, Africa, and the Middle East*; *Feminist Studies*; *Anthropological Quarterly*; and in edited collections such as *Women in the Cities of Asia*. Her translation, and commentary on *"I am Raziye," the Life Story of an Iranian Woman Activist*, is forthcoming.

Llana Barber is an assistant professor in the American Studies department at SUNY College at Old Westbury, where she teaches courses in immigration and urban history. She completed her Ph.D. in History at Boston College in 2010, and is currently revising her dissertation into a book on the transition of Lawrence, Massachusetts, to a Latino-majority city (tentatively titled *Latino City: Urban Crisis, Ethnic Succession, and Suburban Politics in Greater Lawrence, Massachusetts, 1945–2000*).

Tom Condon is a deputy editorial page editor, columnist, and editor of "Place," a Sunday Commentary section of *The Hartford Courant,* which focuses on architecture, planning, transportation, and other aspects of the built and natural environment. Tom is a graduate of the University of Notre Dame and the University of Connecticut School of Law, and is a member of the Connecticut Bar. Since joining *The Courant* in 1971, Condon has won more than 30 journalism and community awards, including the New England Society of Newspaper Editors Master Reporter Award and most recently the 2007 American Planning Association Journalism Award and 2008 Allan B. Rogers Editorial Award from the New England Newspaper Association. Tom is also the co-author of *School Rights*, a book about parent activism in schools. He and his wife, Anne, are the authors of *Legal Lunacy*, a book of funny laws. Tom's work has appeared in many magazines and journals.

Jack Dougherty, an associate professor of educational studies, explores the history and policy of schooling and housing in metropolitan America through the Cities, Suburbs, and Schools Project at Trinity College in Hartford, Connecticut. Jack's prize-winning first book, *More Than One Struggle: The Evolution of Black School Reform in Milwaukee* (2004), examined how three generations of civil rights activism changed from the 1930s to the present in the urban Midwest. His edited volume, *Writing History in the Digital Age* (with Kristen Nawrotzki), is forthcoming. Jack's next book, *On the Line: How Schooling, Housing, and Civil Rights Shaped Hartford* *and Its Suburbs*, has been supported by a digital fellowship from the National Endowment for the Humanities.

James R. Gomes is the director of the Mosakowski Institute for Public Enterprise at Clark University in Worcester, Massachusetts. He began his career as a lawyer at the Boston firm of Hale and Dorr and as a Massachusetts assistant attorney general. He then became chief of staff to Lieutenant Governor John Kerry and executive assistant to Senator Kerry. Jim served as Massachusetts' undersecretary of environmental affairs during the administration of Governor Michael Dukakis. He later became president of the Environmental League of Massachusetts, a statewide policy and advocacy organization. In 2007, Governor Deval Patrick appointed him chairman of the Massachusetts Environmental Trust. Jim has taught or lectured at Brandeis, Clark, Harvard, Trinity, Tufts, Wellesley, and Williams. He holds a B.A. in Political Science from Trinity, an M.P.P. from Harvard's Kennedy School, and a J.D. from Harvard Law School. He lives with his wife and their two children in Arlington, Massachusetts.

Clyde McKee was professor of political science at Trinity College. Before he passed away in May 2011, he had studied, taught, and published articles, newspaper editorials, chapters, and books about Hartford and Connecticut for close to half a century. His most recent articles advocated the need for the state legislature to adopt Same Day Voter Registration laws and for voters on the presidential ballot for this year's presidential election to vote in favor of a state constitutional convention as outlined in the current state constitution. His comprehensive analysis of Connecticut's political system was published by the CQ Press Encyclopedia of the U.S. States and Regions in 2008.

Ezra Moser graduated from Trinity College in 2010 with degrees in American Studies and Urban Studies and was awarded the second-place senior research prize sponsored by the Steven D. Levy '72 Urban Curricular Fund for his thesis on Portland, Maine. In 2011, he received an MSc in City Design and Social Science from the London School of Economics. He has since worked for the United Nations in Kenya, as an urban researcher for the Center for an Urban Future, and as a planner for the New York City Department of City Planning. He is currently a planning and zoning specialist for a leading land-use law firm in New York City.

Jason Rojas is director of community relations at Trinity College and works to help maintain and further develop Trinity's long standing relationship with community institutions in the City of Hartford and surrounding region. He earned a B.A. in History from the University of Connecticut and a Master's Degree in Public Policy from Trinity College. Jason has done extensive work in the area of community relations through his work in local and state government in the Hartford Region and throughout the state. He is especially interested in promoting regional cooperation among municipal governments in the Greater Hartford region.

Michael Paul Sacks received a Ph.D. in Sociology from The University of Michigan in 1974 and is currently Professor of Sociology Emeritus at Trinity College. His books include *Women's Work in Soviet Russia: Continuity in the Midst of Change* (1976), *Work and Equality in Soviet Society: The Division of Labor by Age, Gender and Nationality* (1982) and a co-edited volume, *Understanding Soviet Society* (1988). Since 2000 he has sharply changed geographic focus and now is studying how smaller metropolitan areas of New England are being transformed in recent decades by the shifting ethnic group composition of the U.S. population, the aging of the baby boom generation, and the economic transformation of cities and suburbs. He has presented this current research in papers at conferences of the American Sociological Association, the Puerto Rican Studies Association, and the International Union for the Study of Population.

John Shemo is currently vice president and director of economic development at the MetroHartford Alliance. John has spent more than thirty years in municipal and regional planning and economic development in Connecticut. He served as town planner for East Hartford and as economic development director for South Windsor. He was the first executive director of the Corporation for Regional Economic Development serving southeastern Connecticut. Mr. Shemo earned his B.A. in Urban Studies from the University of Connecticut and his Master's degree in Public Administration from the University of Hartford. He is a past president of the Connecticut Economic Development Association as well as the Northeastern Economic Developers Association. In 2006 Mr. Shemo received the NEDA Member of the Year Award and in 2010 the CEDAS Member of the Year Award. His community work includes serving as president of the East Hartford Rotary Club and a director of Capital Workforce Partners.

Louise Simmons is professor of social work and the Urban Semester Program director at the University of Connecticut. She received her Ph.D. in Urban and Regional Studies from the Massachusetts Institute of Technology. Her academic interests include urban social movements, community organizing, community-labor coalitions, welfare reform and urban policy issues. She is the author of *Organizing in Hard Times: Labor and Neighborhoods in Hartford* (1994), editor of *Welfare, the Working Poor and Labor* (2004) and co-editor with Scott Harding of *Economic Justice, Labor and Community Practice* (2010). Simmons is a past editor of the *Journal of Community Practice* and served on the Governing Board of the Urban Affairs Association from 2006 to 2012, chairing it from 2011 to 2012. She was elected to the Hartford City Council from 1991 to 1993, and has been active in civil rights, labor, and community struggles in Hartford since the 1970s.

Andrew Walsh is managing editor of *Religion in the News*, associate director of the Greenberg Center for the Study of Religion in Public Life, and visiting assistant professor of history and religion at Trinity College. He holds degrees from Trinity College, Yale Divinity School, and Harvard University, where he earned a Ph.D. in the History of American Civilization in 1996. His academic interests focus on American religious, cultural, and political history during the late 19th and 20th centuries. Walsh also worked for *The Hartford Courant* for six years, serving as a reporter, bureau chief, and religion writer. His doctoral dissertation is entitled: "For Our City's Welfare: Building a Protestant Establishment in Late Nineteenth Century Hartford."

Lyle Wray served as executive director of the Capitol Region Council of Governments since 2004. He heads the regional planning organization for Hartford, Connecticut and the 29 surrounding towns in transportation, community development, public safety and homeland security. He served previously as director of Ventura County Civic Alliance at the Ventura County Community Foundation to engage citizens in identifying and addressing significant regional issues and producing a state of the region indicators report. He served as executive director of the Citizens League, a nonpartisan citizen based regional public policy organization, in the Twin Cities for 11 years. He served as both County Administrator and Human Services Director for Dakota County, Minnesota. He holds a B.A., M.A., and Ph.D. from the University of Manitoba, Winnipeg, Canada. He completed the Kennedy School of Government State and Local Government executive program at Harvard University. He co-authored "Results That Matter" on performance measurement.